To the memory of my mother

Contents

Preface   vii

Acknowledgements   ix

Part One: Introduction   1

   1. Spotlight on the office function and secretarial work   3

Part Two: Ownership, management, and organization   11

   2. Types of employer   13
   3. Departmental and staff organization   20
   4. Standard documents   25
   5. The office environment   32

Part Three: Office services and the secretary   45

   6. Office supplies   47
   7. Dealing with the mail   56
   8. Filing and indexing   67
   9. Reprography   86
  10. The accounts department   95
  11. Computers and the electronic office   106
  12. Personnel   118

Part Four: External organizations and the secretary   131

  13. Telecommunications   133
  14. Financial services   157
  15. Taxes and social security   169

Part Five: Secretarial skills   177

  16. Dealing with dictation   179
  17. Typewriting and word processing   191
  18. Composing and compiling   201
  19. Finding facts   211
  20. Displaying information   221
  21. Travel arrangements   231

Part Six: The secretary and office diplomacy   **241**

   22. Meetings and conferences   243
   23. Planning and priorities, reception, and reminders   263
   24. The human factor   271

Appendix I: Summary of the principal Post Office services   280

Appendix II: Summary of legislation affecting the office:
                Consumer protection
                Sale of Goods Act 1979   285
                Trade Descriptions Act 1968   286
                Unsolicited Goods and Services Act 1971   286
                Fair Trading Act 1973   286
                Consumer Credit Act 1974   287
                Unfair Contract Terms Act 1977   288
                Employment legislation
                Employers' Liability (Compulsory Insurance) Act 1969   288
                Equal Pay Act 1970   288
                Employment Agencies Act 1973   289
                Rehabilitation of Offenders Act 1974   289
                Trade Union and Labour Relations Acts 1974 and 1976 (as amended
                   by the Employment Acts 1980 and 1982 and the Trade Union
                   Act 1984)   289
                Sex Discrimination Act 1975   292
                Race Relations Act 1976   293

Appendix III: Glossary of computing and information processing terms   294

Index   299

Preface

Aim

The aim in this third edition remains the same as for earlier editions, namely, to present a text useful for any intermediate or advanced secretarial course. Besides covering the syllabus for the London Chamber of Commerce and Industry Private Secretary's Certificate Office Organization and Secretarial Procedures paper, it supplies information necessary for the Royal Society of Arts Secretarial Duties Stage II examination, the Business and Technician Education Council Secretarial Services module, and the Pitman Examinations Institute Intermediate Secretarial Practice examinations. The LCCI Secretarial Studies Certificate Office Procedures syllabus is also covered. Students working for the LCCI Private and Executive Secretary's Diploma, the RSA Personal Assistant's Diploma and the PEI Advanced Secretarial Practice examination will find many sections directly relevant to their courses.

Features of the book

The chapters have been written to give the teacher maximum flexibility of approach. Apart from the main text, each chapter has:

In a nutshell   Factual summaries for quick reference and revision.

Did you know?   Miscellaneous items to stimulate thought and enquiry on the part of the individual student.

Illustrations   A wide variety of line drawings and photographs with informative captions intended to clarify or enlarge on the information given in the text.

Activities   The level of activities is intentionally wide, so that tutors can make their own selection to suit their students' standard. Questions range from factual ones directing attention to the text, to those demanding more constructive thought or imaginative presentation. It is hoped that the more difficult ones will stimulate students to further research on their own account with their tutor's guidance. Group activities are provided on topics more suitable for joint enterprise. A large number of public examination questions are included.

Changes from second edition

The book has been thoroughly revised and updated to include current developments in office technology that affect each chapter. The chapters on computers and the electronic office and on telecommunications are almost entirely new material.

To keep the book to a manageable length, most of the 'In the office' sections have been omitted. The same applies to 'Typical documents and books of record' and to 'Typical reference books'.

Appendix I now covers Post Office services only (British Telecom services being incorporated into the main text at Chapter 13). A 'Glossary of Computing and Information Processing Terms' now forms Appendix III (the section on VAT having been absorbed into Chapter 4).

Acknowledgements

The author wishes to thank the many individuals and organizations who have helped her by supplying or checking information or by providing material for illustrations. They include:

Aircall plc; Anson Division of Gardner Mawdsley Ltd; ASI (Addressing Systems International Ltd); Bank Education Service; Banking Information Service; Bell and Howell Ltd, Business Equipment Division; C. P. Bourg Ltd; British Insurance Association; British Olivetti Ltd; British Rail; British Telecom; British Telecom International; Building Societies Association; Burroughs Protectograph; Business Equipment Digest; Business Equipment Trade Association; Business Systems and Equipment; Cable and Wireless; Canon (UK) Ltd; Cescom Electronics Ltd; Civil Service Commission; Co-operative Bank plc; Co-operative Union; A. B. Dick Ltd; Dictaphone Co. Ltd; Eltons Business Machines, Woking; Envoy Public Relations; Mr Adrian Fisher (partner in Pegasus Office Systems); Ferranti Computer Systems Ltd; IBM United Kingdom Ltd; ICL Ltd; Information Technology Ltd; Inland Revenue; Institute of Administrative Management; Institute of Qualified Private Secretaries Ltd; Haslertime Division of IVO Industries Ltd; Mr Philip Holden; Mr Tony Holland; HM Customs and Excise; HM Stationery Office; Kardex Systems (UK) Ltd; Kodak Ltd; Lion Office Equipment Ltd; Mrs Judy McCusker; MBS Data Efficiency Ltd; Mercury Communications Ltd; Merlin, British Telecom Business Systems; Moore Paragon UK Ltd; Ms Caroline Moss, Business Services Team, Surrey County Library; Mr David Mundy; Mr Graham Newton; Northern Telecom Ltd; National Girobank; OBM; Office Equipment News; Philips Electronics; The Post Office; Price Waterhouse; Project Office Equipment Ltd; Rank Xerox Ltd; Mr Keith Rennie; Roneo Alcatel Ltd; The Sharp Corporation; Mr Neil Stamper; STC Telecommunications Ltd; Sterotek Systems (Haslemere) Ltd; Telelift (UK) Ltd; Thorn Ericsson Telecommunications Ltd; 3M United Kingdom plc; TSB England and Wales; U-Bix (UK) Ltd; Unity Designs (UK) Limited, High Wycombe; Wiltshier Contract Furnishing.

Thanks are also due to the London Chamber of Commerce and Industry, the Royal Society of Arts and the Pitman Examinations Institute for permission to quote from past examination papers.

The author is also most grateful to her brother and sister-in-law, Charles and Selina Trotman, Miss Elisabeth Cowl, Mrs Jean King, and John Watson for help and support in a variety of ways.

Discrimination between the sexes
In a book on the subject of secretarial procedures using the current practice and terminology of the business world, it has not been possible to eliminate the use of gender and retain a fluent text. A deliberate distinction between the sexes is not implied.

PART ONE
Introduction

1

Spotlight on the office function and secretarial work

You are training to be a secretary—or you may already be one and wish to improve your knowledge and skills—but what does a secretary actually do? This book aims to answer this in detail, as you will see by a glance at the contents page. By the time you have completed it, you should have a clear picture of the duties a secretary may be expected to perform within the framework of her organization.

1.1 The clerical function

No matter what type of business a company conducts there will be a great deal of paperwork to handle. The company may basically be a manufacturing one making, say, thousands of washing machines a week, but there will still be an office. Steel needs to be ordered, contacts need to be made and deals concluded with suppliers of motors, letters have to be written to overseas agents and contacts made with purchasers at home. In a retailing company, there will be no manufacturing but the leases of stores need to be drawn up, estate agents contacted for new sites, merchandise purchased, etc. In both types of company there will be an accounts department checking on customers' credit, sending out and following up invoices and paying the company's own debts.

Office workers perform the important clerical function. Correspondence arrives daily and must be handled efficiently and correctly. Letters are opened by mail clerks, sorted and passed to the necessary person. The manager acts on the information and directs other office workers to reply to it, copy it, circulate it and file it. More information may be needed and may have to be found in reference books or in databanks. Accountants and cashiers deal with financial information. Therefore the purpose of any company's office is summarized as dealing with information. The secretary's role is vital, as written

and verbal information and requests often come to him or her first and also leave the company via the secretary's desk. The secretary may be the only contact many people have with the company.

1.2 Office services

Whether the office services in your own organization are departmental, centralized or a combination of both, whether they are largely automated or partly manual, you as a secretary will draw upon them and at the same time help to provide them.

(a) Centralized and departmental

In a small organization the whole of the office work may be performed in one room or area. In larger ones it may be done in a variety of places, with groups of workers providing specialist services for the whole organization. Examples of such services include: the control of office supplies (Chapter 6), filing and indexing (Chapter 8), reprography (Chapter 9), typing, word processing, and secretarial services (Chapters 16 and 17), reception (Chapter 23), finance (Chapter 10), and personnel (Chapter 12).

When a particular service is provided from one place, usually situated centrally within a firm, and has one manager overseeing the operation of the service, this is said to be centralized. For instance, there may be a central word processing department that provides copy for the purchasing department, production department, finance department, etc. Centralization offers many advantages—e.g., economic use of equipment (which is more likely to be wide-ranging and up to date than in departmental systems), optimum use of space, expertise of specialist staff, effective control and standardization of procedures, and a location known to all.

When a service is provided to suit people's individual needs within a department this is said to be departmental. For example the finance department could have its own word processing equipment and operator who works solely for it. But there may be times when the equipment lies idle or the operator may become overburdened with work.

In practice, a combination of centralized and departmental office services often exists, as for example in information processing systems (Chapter 11).

(b)   Manual and automated

An enormous contribution to the services performed by the office is now made by machines. Descriptions of these, together with their functions and purposes, are given in appropriate chapters throughout the book. Computers (Chapter 11) are the machines *par excellence*: in many modern offices a major part of the clerical function is carried out by computerized installations.

Using a machine to do a job does not necessarily bring about efficiency. It will do so only if the system is thought out methodically and the machine's place in it is logically planned.

1.3   Grades of secretarial work

Secretarial work is difficult to grade, as the titles of jobs are not standardized throughout industry and commerce. It is therefore important to find out before you accept a post exactly what duties are involved in it. Increasing automation is affecting the scope and content of secretarial posts, particularly in large organizations.

(a)   Typist, shorthand- or audio-typist, word processor operator

These posts may involve working directly for one or more executives, or in a typing centre or word processor centre (Chapter 17) under a supervisor. Typists must be skilled operators able to display work accurately and attractively—aided increasingly by word processors. In many organizations typists are called upon to type correspondence from machine dictation (audiotyping, Chapter 16). Shorthand-typists have the additional skill of being able to transcribe from shorthand notes. For all these posts a good knowledge of English—vocabulary, punctuation, and spelling—is essential (see also **17.9**(*f*)).

(b)   Secretary

As you will realize when using this book, a secretary's duties, while including those in (*a*) above, are wider, more diverse, and involve more responsibility. A secretary may work for one executive only, although (especially in organizations where there is a typing or word processing centre for the routine work) he or she may provide secretarial services for more than one.

(c)   Personal assistant (PA)

Some companies have a grade above that of secretary, called Personal Assistant. A true PA holds a very responsible post, undertaking a great deal of administrative and organizing work delegated by the boss, and may in turn delegate routine duties to a junior or assistant secretary. In some ways PAs' work resembles that of junior executives, but whereas the latter can make decisions affecting the company in their own right, PAs generally have authority only through their bosses.

1.4   Chain of responsibility

Teamwork needs to be well organized if it is to be efficient, for the consequences of any one member's actions affect the other members, too. Thus, all secretarial workers are responsible to and supervised by others in the office team: juniors are responsible to the senior person in the area in which they work; junior secretaries to the senior secretaries whom they assist; typing centre members to the supervisor; a supervisor to the Office Manager (or person in charge of office services); secretaries or PAs to the executives for whom they work. The same principle operates throughout entire organizations: no one works in isolation from the rest.

1.5 Methods of training for secretarial work

(a) Full-time courses

These achieve the best results in the least time (varying from six months to two years, according to the scope and intensity of the course). They are available at technical colleges or colleges of further education, private commercial colleges, comprehensive schools, and sixth form colleges. YTS and adult training schemes (see **1.6**) are also available.

(b) Day-release courses

Employees are released by their employers to attend part-time courses of further education and training, involving attendance for one day or two half-days each week, plus possibly a number of evening classes. Some employers prefer staff to attend block-release courses, entailing full-time college attendance for several weeks and then a complete return to duties within the firm. Sandwich courses alternate full-time tuition with work at the company (but these are not common in secretarial training).

(c) Evening classes

These are held at institutes of further education or private colleges. Training often has to be spread over a long period, and powers of determination, concentration and perseverance must be cultivated if satisfactory results are to be achieved while at the same time meeting the demands of full-time employment.

(d) On-the-job training

Some companies offer preliminary or in-service training and refresher courses to employees, geared especially to the needs of the company and the demands of the particular job (see also **12.4**).

(e) Short courses

These may be offered at technical, further education and other institutions, e.g., to teach skills required as a result of the introduction of new office technology.

1.6 Manpower Services Commission

The Manpower Services Commission is an independent body set up by the government as a result of the Employment and Training Act 1973 to be responsible for employment and training services in the UK. It offers two types of scheme:

(a) Youth Training Scheme (YTS)

Courses are open to all 16- and 17-year-old school leavers—two-year courses for entrants at 16 and one-year for entrants at 17. Trainees receive most of their training from the employers with whom they are placed, but each course must include a specified amount of off-the-job training, e.g., at colleges of further education and other colleges. The object of the scheme is to provide a broad base of training in skills useful for working life. On completion trainees may move on to employment or further training, e.g., in secretarial work. Unemployed trainees receive an allowance; employed trainees (to whom the scheme is also open) are paid in the normal way by their employers.

(b) Adult training schemes

The Manpower Services Commission is restructuring adult training provision into two main programmes.

(i) A job-training programme directed at known employment needs to provide training support for the creation and growth of business; or

(ii) A Wider Opportunities Scheme (WOPS) to help unemployed people to improve their foundation skills, retain their employability and cope with the changing content of jobs.

Courses are held at colleges of further education, private colleges or Skillcentres run by the Department of Employment. No cost falls on the individual for training received. Skills in which trainees are trained are mainly those needed for the new technology and for changing patterns of work, and cross occupational boundaries.

1.7 Openings for secretaries

Although there are duties common to all secretaries, no two secretaries' work is exactly the same. The type of organization concerned (limited company, partnership, local authority, etc.) makes a difference, and so do the size of the organization and the aptitudes and temperament of each secretary. The biggest differences, however, are caused by the types of work handled by various organizations.

Do you want to work for a commercial or industrial business? Remember that the objective of any organization is to make a profit in the face of sometimes cut-throat competition. This means that each employee's time should be at a premium, prosperous companies demanding especially quick, accurate, efficient work from their secretaries. To promote efficiency, such organizations provide the best and most up-to-date machines and equipment and you are therefore very likely to be concerned with sophisticated systems and methods. Staff welfare and social needs, too, are generally well looked after. However, in some posts the work itself tends to be restricted and humdrum. You might have to balance very good working conditions against less interest and satisfaction from your work in such organizations.

Perhaps you would prefer to work for a firm that sells services to the public, such as a group of architects, engineers, accountants, surveyors, doctors, dentists, solicitors. Again, these firms must make a profit to exist. Your work might involve a good deal of personal contact with members of the public wanting the services in question. Conditions vary according to the degree of prosperity of the firm and the outlook of its staff: some are brisk and businesslike, while others are less progressive.

You might be interested in becoming a secretary in the Civil Service or local government, which provide services to the public financed by taxes and rates.

You may find really interesting and worthwhile work with charities. They must make the best possible use of their income but the emphasis is on helping people in need. Equipment may be less up to date but this does not mean that methods need be inefficient.

With these general considerations in mind, decide where your own interests lie. Would you like to work with doctors and hospitals; for animals, with the RSPCA or veterinary surgeons; at schools, colleges or universities; at hotels or clubs; for newspapers, magazines, libraries, book publishers or booksellers; for Members of Parliament; for artists, musicians, authors; at research establishments; for insurance companies or banks; for shipping companies, airlines or travel agencies? The list is almost endless. If you are able to work for an organization with whose activities you can identify your own interests, being a secretary is not merely pleasant, but absorbing.

1.8   In a nutshell: General qualifications useful in secretarial posts

- Shorthand speeds: 80 wpm onwards (beginners); 100—140 wpm (senior posts).
- Typewriting speeds: 35 wpm onwards (beginners); 50—80 wpm onwards (senior posts).
- Transcription speeds: 15—20 wpm (beginners); 25 wpm onwards (senior posts).
- Practical experience of word processing and understanding of general principles.
- Ability to communicate readily and intelligibly in clear, accurate and concise written and spoken English.
- Knowledge of secretarial duties and office organization and procedures.
- Background knowledge of structure of business, commerce, commercial law, accounts, statistics, economics, etc.
- For some posts a fluent knowledge—rather than a smattering—of a foreign language.
- For senior posts, an outline knowledge of the general principles of management in order to understand the boss's problems and be able to assist when appropriate.
- General knowledge, including an awareness of topical national and international events.

Examination certificates

(a)   Single subject certificates

A variety of single-subject certificates at elementary, intermediate, and advanced stages are offered in business subjects by examining bodies such as the London Chamber of Commerce and Industry, the

Royal Society of Arts, the Regional Examining Unions, and the Pitman Examinations Institute. Some relevant subjects are also offered by the GCE,[1] CSE[1] and similar examining boards. There are specialist examinations for medical and legal secretaries as well as reception skills. Computer literacy, word processing and information technology examinations can also be taken.

(b) Group certificates

- Business and Technician Education Council (BTEC) diplomas and certificates in Business Studies at Higher, National and General[2] level, including clerical and secretarial modules where appropriate.

- London Chamber of Commerce and Industry (LCCI):
  Secretarial Studies Certificate (for a first or junior secretarial post)
  Private Secretary's Certificate (for secretaries to middle management)
  Private and Executive Secretary's Diploma (for secretaries to senior management)

- Royal Society of Arts (RSA):
  Diploma in Office Studies (Stage I)
  Diploma in General Reception (Stage I)
  Diploma in Business Studies (Stage II)
  Diploma in Secretarial Studies (Stage II)
  Diploma for Personal Assistants (advanced level)

- Scottish Business Education Council (SCOTBEC):
  Junior Secretarial Certificate (Stage I)
  Secretarial Certificate (Stage II)
  Advanced Secretarial Certificate (Stage III)
  Scottish Higher National Diploma in Secretarial Studies (Stage III)

(c) Foreign languages secretarial certificates include:

- London Chamber of Commerce and Industry (LCCI):
  Secretarial Language Certificate
  Advanced Secretarial Language Certificate
  Foreign Languages for Industry and Commerce (oral)

- Royal Society of Arts (RSA):
  Languages for the Office (general language skills)
  Certificate for Secretarial Linguists (intermediate)
  Diploma for Bi-lingual Secretaries (advanced)

1.9 The prospect

You will realize that, as a well-qualified and efficient secretary, you should be able to contribute much to your company. However, the limits of your job may be ill-defined and dependent to a high degree on the energy and effort you put into it and the amount of responsibility you are prepared to take.

They depend also on how much scope your boss is willing to let you have. He or she should obviously be prepared to give you more, if you show yourself to be a well-qualified person with a serious attitude towards your work. This means being able not only to perform your own duties efficiently, but to see them in the context of your company and, in turn, to see your company in the wider framework of the business world.

In the next few years you will encounter still greater advances in office technology, particularly in larger companies. This will reduce routine work still

1. GCE O level and CSE examinations to be replaced by GCSE from 1988.
2. To be replaced by CPVE award from 1985.

further and should free you to do more demanding tasks, provided you have ambition and ability (see also **11.14**). Above all, flexibility and adaptability should be your watchwords. Keep up to date, and be ready to take advantage of any opportunities for your own training and development.

Preparing for advanced secretarial examinations provides a spur to improving your skills and keeping up to date with the latest developments. The Private and Executive Secretary's Diploma (London Chamber of Commerce and Industry) and the Diploma for Personal Assistants (Royal Society of Arts) provide ample opportunities for secretaries wishing to prepare for really responsible posts.

Note
The Institute of Qualified Private Secretaries Limited aims to establish the status of the qualified private secretary within the professions, commerce, industry, and all other fields in which he or she may be employed; to offer advice and guidance to those wishing to make a career in private secretarial work; to provide members with information on appropriate professional matters; and to promote a free exchange of ideas, opinions, and experience among members. Meetings (open to all members and guests) are organized by 12 regional branches throughout the UK.

Holders of the LCCI Private and Executive Secretary's Diploma are eligible to become full members. Holders of the RSA Diploma for Personal Assistants are eligible for associate membership and have the option to transfer to full membership after two years if they are still working as secretaries. In addition, student membership is offered to candidates for both the LCCI Private and Executive Secretary's Diploma and Private Secretary's Certificate.

1.10 Checklist of personal qualities desirable in a secretary

Tick those you think you have; underline those you think you need to cultivate.

Are you . . . ?

Accurate	Alert	Calm	Careful
Cheerful	Clear-headed	Conscientious	Consistent
Cost-conscious	Courteous	Discreet	Honest
Logical	Loyal	Methodical	Neat
Punctual	Reliable	Resourceful	Tactful

Can you . . . ?

Concentrate	Keep your temper	Pay attention to detail	Take responsibility

Have you . . . ?

Common sense	Initiative	Poise	Restraint

PS None of us is perfect!

1.11 Did you know?

The Institute of Administrative Management have analysed office work into eight grades (A through to H) to help organizations to evaluate jobs and evolve suitable salary structures. Typing (including copy-typing, audiotyping, and shorthand-typing) is graded according to speeds achieved and the complexity of the work. Secretarial work is graded from C (junior secretary), through D (secretary to departmental manager) and E (senior secretarial work for senior executives and regular committee minuting work), to F (executive secretary).[1]

Activities

1. Your boy-friend works in a factory, and tends to regard office staff as unproductive and useless. Put forward the arguments you would use to convince him that the office plays a vital part in the work of the firm.

2. Which office services could be centralized? Give the advantages and disadvantages of centralizing one of these services. (LCCI, PSC)

3. Write or type answers to the following questions: (a) Why do you want to be a secretary? (b) What do you think a secretary's work comprises? (c) What personal qualities do you think an efficient secretary should have? (You may like to tackle these questions again at the end of your course and to compare the two sets of answers.)

4. Your brother, aged 26, has just decided to open his own estate agency office in the local High Street. He wishes to employ a secretary/receptionist and asks your advice as to the standards of education and training that he should demand and qualities he should look for in the ideal applicant. Set out all the points that he should consider. (LCCI, SSC)

5. Your young cousin will be leaving school in a couple of years and is interested in training for office work. Explain the options available to your cousin, setting out the information clearly on a sheet to enclose with your letter to her.

6. Imagine that you are working for one of the types of organization mentioned in **1.7**. One of your duties is to look out for any occurrences and developments in that field reported by the press, on television or on radio. Start a folder now for relevant notes or cuttings, aiming to produce an informative file for reference.

7. What would be the personal qualities and qualifications you would hope to find in a Secretary to two Managers in the Public Relations Department of a well-known firm? The job involves working in an office with four other Secretaries and helping out with general office duties, such as opening the post and operating a small switchboard. (LCCI, SSC)

8. How are the duties performed by secretaries, particularly in large organizations, being affected by increasing computerization? Do you see a future for secretaries in the age of the 'electronic office'? (LCCI, PSC)

---

1. Grading here is affected by the amount of thinking and decision-making involved and of supervision of other staff.

PART TWO

Ownership, management, and organization

2
Types of employer

There are many types of business organization and their legal frameworks will affect the way they are run.

2.1 Sole trader

A common type of business organization is that of the sole trader: one person owns and runs the business. The owner provides all the money needed—or, if it is borrowed, pays interest to the persons lending it—and supplies all necessary premises and equipment. The owner takes all the profits and meets all the losses and, being responsible only to himself (or herself) does not need to consult others but can take snap decisions to the advantage of the business. By their nature, sole trading concerns are usually small businesses such as the local butcher's or chemist's for, as they expand, it becomes necessary for them to change their organization to that of either partnerships, where the burden of providing capital and meeting running expenses is shared, or limited companies.

2.2 Partnership

A partnership is an association in which a number of individuals combine their resources—whether capital, expertise or working time—for the purpose of a business venture. They own the business jointly and share in its management. There must be a minimum of 2 partners but not more than 20, though there is no upper limit in the case of solicitors, accountants and members of a recognized stock exchange. Partnerships are usually formed and run according to individual agreements, which may or may not be written. Generally speaking, this is the practice followed:

(a) Capital
Partners contribute capital to the business according to the agreement.

(b) Profits and losses
The share of the profits each partner receives or of the losses he or she may have to meet is determined by agreement; it may be related to the proportion of the capital contributed.

(c) Liability
Every partner is fully liable for any partnership losses, even to the extent of selling his or her own private goods and resources.

(d) Management
Generally, all partners take part in the management of the business, major issues being settled by unanimous agreement and minor differences by majority vote.

2.3 Limited partnership

A limited partner contributes a capital sum and usually receives a proportionate share of the profits.

In the case of loss, however, a limited partner's liability is restricted to the capital he or she has contributed. There must be at least one general partner in a limited partnership—i.e., with unlimited liability for meeting losses.

2.4   Limited company

As a business grows the simple structure of sole trader or partnership is usually unable to provide necessary capital. The business needs to become a limited company.

Companies registered under the Companies Acts are limited companies. Each is regarded by the law as one person, existing separately from its members; it continues to exist (as long as it is solvent) no matter what changes occur in the number or nature of its shareholders. Shareholders' liability is limited to their investment in the company. Companies fall into two groups:

(a)   Private limited company

A company may have a minimum of two shareholders but there is no maximum limit. The transfer of shares is restricted and the public is unable to buy shares or debentures. The company's name must end with the word 'limited', e.g., SavaCentre Ltd. Annual accounts and auditors' reports must be submitted each year.

(b)   Public limited company

A public company must have at least two shareholders but there is no upper limit. There is a minimum issued share capital (£50 000 in 1985) and the shares must be offered to the general public. The letters plc or PLC must appear at the end of the company's name, e.g., Marks and Spencer plc. The company must submit annual accounts and auditors' reports.

2.5   Company ownership and management

(a)   The shareholders

They own the company, since they provide the capital. The number of shares each possesses may determine the number of votes he or she has when voting on important issues. What they say or do as individuals does not bind the company because they are not its agents. The shareholders elect a board of directors to run the company.

(b)   The board of directors

The directors administer the company and formulate policy so that it can prosper and make a profit. Some of the (*non-executive*) directors will be people of standing in the business world, with knowledge and experience useful to the company. They may spend little time on the premises, but this is no reflection of their concern for the company. Other (*executive*) directors will be full-time employees of the company, probably in charge of a section of the company such as finance or marketing or production. The board delegates authority to senior managers and their subordinates to carry out the agreed policies.

(c)   The managing director

He or she is the senior director with a comprehensive knowledge of the company, who co-ordinates the board's policies and puts them into effect.

(d)   The chairman

Appointed by his or her fellow directors, the chairman takes the chair at board meetings and general meetings of shareholders. He acts as the company's chief spokesman and represents it at many outside functions like exhibitions, dinners, Chamber of Commerce and trade association meetings.

(e)   The company secretary

He or she is responsible for organizing the work of the board. He calls board meetings; collates and presents information in such a way that the members can reach prompt decisions, which he records in the minutes; and acts as their professional adviser in legal, accounting, and taxation matters. It is also the company secretary's duty to communicate with the shareholders. He or she keeps shareholders' records, sees that dividends and debenture interest are paid, and organizes shareholders' meetings. In smaller companies there may also be administrative duties—perhaps being responsible for office services, accounts, legal matters, and public relations—but in larger concerns these may be handled by other members of staff.

2.6 Company terms

As a secretary—especially if you are employed by a limited company—you will find it helpful to understand some of the terms commonly used when company matters are referred to. Here are some of them:

(a) Incorporation

Any new company must be formed in accordance with the Companies Acts 1948, 1967, 1976, 1980, and 1981, and must be registered with the *Registrar of Companies*, who issues it with a *Certificate of Incorporation*. After receiving this certificate, a private company is able to commence business. A public company, however, must next issue a *prospectus*, giving a brief description of the company so that prospective shareholders can assess its prospects and the investment value of its shares. A copy must be sent to the Registrar of Companies, who will not issue a *trading certificate*, permitting the company to commence business, until the amount of capital named in the prospectus has been raised.

(b) Memorandum and Articles of Association

At its formation a company's Memorandum and Articles of Association must be submitted to the Registrar of Companies for registration.

The *Memorandum of Association* sets out the objects for which a company is formed. These objects are usually worded in wide terms to cover any foreseeable relevant activity. If it is essential to change them later, this can be done, so long as three-quarters of the company's members present at a general meeting vote in favour. The *Articles of Association* contain the rules for the administration of the company, covering such matters as the appointment of directors, voting, shares, dividends, etc. These rules must not conflict with the provisions of the Companies Acts.

A company's Memorandum and Articles of Association can be inspected by any member of the public at the *Companies Registry*—where records are kept on microfilm—on payment of a small fee. It is often important for anyone doing business with a company to know exactly what its legal activities are, for if a contract is made involving that company in performing activities not shown in its Memorandum the contract cannot legally be enforced (though under a provision of the European Communities Act 1972, innocent third parties are generally protected).

(c) Company seal

This is an embossed mark, pressed onto documents requiring a company's official authorization. It must bear the name of the company. To prevent irresponsible use the seal is kept under lock and key and is accessible only to the company secretary and directors.

(d) Annual return

This contains information about the company's capital and details of the current board of directors and company secretary. It has to be sent to the Registrar of Companies within 42 days of each Annual General Meeting. A copy of the Annual Report and Accounts and Auditors' Report must also be filed (see **22.1** *(a)* (i)).

(e) Stocks and shares

Anyone investing money in a company receives certificates impressed with the company's seal, stating the number of shares held. Any shareholder can be required by the company to disclose whether he holds the shares for himself or on behalf of someone else. Shares may or may not carry voting rights.

Any person who acquires voting shares amounting to more than a specified percentage (at present five per cent) of the total issued share capital of any company whose shares are quoted on the Stock Exchange, is obliged to notify that company within five days.

(f) Dividends

These are sums paid to shareholders from profits made by a company. It is the directors who recommend the rate of *final dividends* (to be declared by the members at the Annual General Meeting); they are not obliged to recommend that one be paid at all if they consider the profits would be better ploughed back into reserves.

Dividends are paid first to *preference shareholders*, who receive a fixed dividend, and next to *ordinary shareholders*, who therefore stand either to gain or lose over preference shareholders, according to the amount of profit left for distribution when their turn comes. If a person lends money to a company, he is called a *debenture holder*, and he must be paid an agreed rate of interest on his loan before any shareholder receives a share of the profits. The company is bound also to repay the loan itself at a specified or unspecified date.

The types of business we have looked at so far have all existed to make a profit for their owners. However, there are other commercial enterprises, not driven by the profit motive.

2.7   Co-operative movement

(a)   Retail co-operative societies

Co-operative ownership is quite distinct from company ownership, in that each member of a society has just one vote, irrespective of the number of shares held by that member, so that control is not weighted towards those with larger investments.

There are approximately 100 retail co-operative societies in all parts of the country, with 8 600 000 members (1985). In each co-operative society the members elect a board of directors which controls the society's affairs through managers it appoints. The board elects one of its number as president. A chief executive is appointed by the board or by members on the recommendation of the board. The board must report at regular meetings to the members for its conduct of the society's affairs.

The co-operative movement differs from limited companies in several other ways, including the following:

(i) *Profit distribution* Each retail society buys goods at wholesale prices for sale to its customers at retail prices. The profit thus made is returned to members in a number of ways, the most important of which has been the *dividend* which is allocated in proportion to the amount the member has spent in the shop. These dividends need not be withdrawn in cash but may be accumulated as savings. In most societies co-operative dividend stamps have replaced the conventional dividend payment but some societies are now operating 'community dividends'

(for social and cultural purposes) or member benefit schemes (discounts and special offers for members only). Part of the profit is set aside for facilities for members, including education.

(ii) *Capital* Moderate interest only is given on share capital because the motive for owning shares is to belong to the co-operative.

(b)   The Co-operative Union

Co-operative societies are organized nationally into the Co-operative Union, which provides legal, educational, industrial relations, statistical and other services for the retail societies. The Union is democratically controlled by the annual Co-operative Congress.

(c)   Co-operative Wholesale Society (CWS)

The CWS provides goods which the retail societies sell, acting in some cases as importer, manufacturer, and banker. It is owned and controlled by the retail societies. The retail societies subscribe capital to the CWS in proportion to the number of their members. They elect the board of directors and appoint delegates to general meetings of the shareholding societies. Dividends are calculated in proportion to the volume of business transacted with the CWS.

(d)   Worker co-operatives

In Britain, co-operation developed mainly through the retail societies. However, there have been a number of worker–producer co-operatives. In this type of organization, the workers own and control the concern in which they work.

2.8   Public corporation

Public corporations are business organizations set up by Act of Parliament. They are operated by the government for the benefit of the nation. Each is managed by a board appointed by a Minister answerable to Parliament. The board controls day-to-day operations, but the government is responsible for general policy. Capital is provided in the form of securities guaranteed by the government and by government loans. The government takes the profits for the public revenue and meets the losses. Like other types of company, a public corporation is regarded by the law as one person, existing separately from its members. Each board controls the pay and working conditions of its staff, who are not civil servants. Examples of public corporations are: the Port of London Authority, British Rail, the National Coal Board, and the Post Office.

2.9 Public authority—local government

The management of a local authority is undertaken by the elected councillors, responsible to the electorate throughout their term of office. As well as attending full Council meetings, councillors serve on one or more committees specializing in specific aspects such as finance, planning, etc. Each committee is usually responsible to the whole Council and must report to it periodically; in many cases, approval is needed from the whole Council before action recommended by a committee can be taken. The Chairman (or Mayor in boroughs) is elected by the councillors to undertake various civic functions as well as taking the chair at full Council meetings.

A Council is an incorporated body, with an existence separate from its councillors.

District councils are responsible for local matters, e.g., housing and environmental health; and county councils for wider strategic concerns, e.g., education and social services. Both types work autonomously.

Local authorities' powers derive from Act of Parliament. They receive advice and sometimes instructions from central government. They are also controlled by the grants from central government necessary to supplement income from rates, rents, fees, etc.

The elected councillors receive information and advice from the local government officers, i.e., the permanent officials who carry out council decisions and maintain the services provided for the community.

2.10 Public authority—central government

The work of central government is carried out (as in local government) by two groups of people: those put in power by the electorate for a limited period, and the permanent officials—i.e., the civil servants. The first group includes:

(a) Secretaries of State and Ministers

The work of government is divided among departments or ministries, each being responsible for a certain field. Each of these Departments of State is headed by a responsible Minister, who may be, in the case of more important departments, a Secretary of State. All sit in Parliament and are responsible to Parliament for their departments.

Within any Department of State, it is the Minister who must make decisions on major matters, not the civil servants; therefore it is the Minister and not the staff who may have to resign if a grave error of judgement is made. To supplement the intimate knowledge gained of the broad workings and major problems of the department, the Minister is able to draw on the wide range of information provided by the staff. He or she is in some respects in a similar position to a local government committee chairman, who also holds temporary office and is guided by the expert knowledge of the officers. However, the responsibility for a decision taken is the Minister's alone, whereas responsibility is shared by all the members of the local government committee and sometimes by the entire council.

(b) The Cabinet

Members of the Cabinet are usually chosen from the Secretaries of State and Ministers although occasionally a Minister without Portfolio may be selected. Under the chairmanship of the Prime Minister, the Cabinet establishes government policy and tries to resolve conflict between departments. Decisions are taken by the Cabinet as a body, and responsibility is borne collectively by members, not individually. From time to time, a Prime Minister may 'reshuffle' his or her Cabinet, giving members an opportunity to widen their experience and so make Cabinet decisions more effective.

2.11   In a nutshell

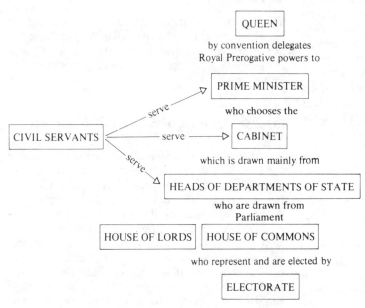

Figure 2.1   Salient features of central government.

2.12   Did you know?

1. Companies limited by guarantee must be private companies. They can now be formed only if they have no share capital, and are usually non-profit-making organizations. Each member agrees to contribute a stated (usually nominal) sum to meet liabilities when the company is wound up.

2. Under the Companies Act 1980 penalties are imposed for *insider dealings*, e.g., on directors who buy or sell shares because of inside knowledge or who pass on such knowledge to others.

3. The Companies Act 1981 abolished the registration of business names, making it the responsibility of companies to protect their own names. If an established company finds by consulting the Companies Register that a newly incorporated organization has adopted a name too similar to its own it can ask the Secretary of State to direct the other company to change its name within 12 months of incorporation.

4. Some of the provisions in the Companies Acts 1980 and 1981 have been introduced as a result of directives from the European Economic Community.

Activities

1. State the chief differences between: (a) limited companies and partnerships (b) public limited companies and private limited companies.

2. Find out (a) what type of local authority area you live in (b) who your local councillor is (c) where education policy for your area is decided and administered.

3. Compile a brief report on how your college or school is managed and administered, including the part played by any boards or committees representative of staff, students, local industry and commerce, or other outside bodies.

4. Summarized versions of company prospectuses and company reports are to be found in

financial and some daily newspapers. Cut out and file copies of these for study.

5. **Group activity** Several types of organization are described in this chapter. Discuss how their differences in structure might affect the duties of secretaries working within them. If possible, do some research in advance by talking to friends already working in different spheres and by studying any careers literature available.

3
Departmental and staff organization

3.1 The secretary's place

Secretaries, clerks and other supporting staff are employed in all departments of an organization. Your duties as a secretary will be concerned with the particular side of the work handled by the department to which you are assigned. A knowledge of the organization's departmental structure is therefore essential if you are to perform your duties efficiently within its framework.

3.2 A Large business

(a) Departmental organization

The titles and work of departments may vary according to the type and size of the organization. An example of a possible set-up is given in Figure 3.1. A summary of departmental functions follows here. You will find more detailed information in appropriate chapters.

(i) *Production* Companies produce goods to be sold. The production staff provide an important

function by operating the necessary machinery to make them, check the quality and control, timing, progress, economics, appearance, and finally distribute them.

(ii) *Marketing* The public need to know about a new product as soon as it is made. Therefore the marketing people are required to research the market, draw up marketing plans and estimate the cost, advertise, visit prospective customers, follow up the customers, provide an after-sales service and present a good company image.

(iii) *Purchasing* No goods could be made without the purchase of raw materials and goods for manufacture. This must be done at the right time, in the right quantities and the right quality. Purchasing of internal items, e.g., stationery or machines for the company, is also the purchasing department's responsibility.

(iv) *Accounts* The company must know where it stands financially and therefore the accounts department records all financial transactions, customers' payments and organization costs. They pay wages/

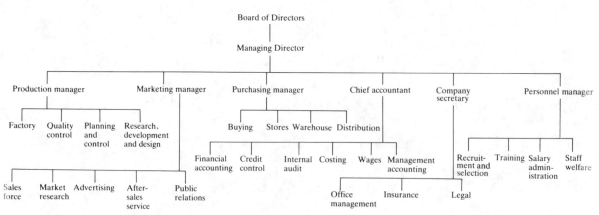

Figure 3.1 An example of an organization chart.

salaries, budget for the forthcoming years and compare forecasts against actuals.

(v) *Company secretary* The company secretary's staff may be responsible for the legal aspects of the company's business, for keeping records of the shareholders and preparing board papers. In smaller organizations the finance director may act as company secretary.

(vi) *Personnel* The work of the department may include recruiting and selecting staff for positions throughout the organization, arranging training and induction, salary administration, staff welfare, staff retirement, pensions and redundancies.

(b) Management and supervision

Money, time and effort must be utilized fully within any organization and it is very important that managers at all levels plan, control, organize and co-ordinate their staff efficiently to gain advantage of their best abilities. The board of directors delegates the authority to senior managers to take charge of complete areas, e.g., production, marketing, accounts, etc. These senior managers may then delegate to middle management who are responsible for specialized areas; they may pass instructions to departmental heads and so the process goes on. All along this chain the managers oversee (supervise) all the work that is being carried out.

(c) Organization charts

Just as secretaries or clerks are responsible to their superiors, so are all managers, executives, and supervisors responsible to theirs, and all should know the limits of their particular spheres of responsibility. Ultimately, everyone in the company is responsible to the board of directors, and they, in their turn, are responsible to the shareholders for the successful running of the business. Equally, the board are responsible *for* the work of all the staff, and all managers below them are responsible for the work of the staff over whom they have been put in authority, even though they may have delegated some of that authority to others. It is as well to note that the actual titles of managers and executives differ according to the size and type of company, and the extent of their authority may vary also.

The areas of employees' authority and responsibility may be set out in organization charts. These

charts clarify the position and can be an aid to good management. However, they may encourage inflexibility, both in overall planning and in the performance and scope of individual duties, unless provision is made to update them as required. They illustrate the way in which a company is organized—i.e., according to departments and the levels of authority and spheres of staff responsibility. Figure 3.1 illustrates departmental structure, and also *line* relationships, as shown, for example, in the direct responsibility and authority the marketing manager has over the sections of the staff dealing with advertising, market research, etc. Figure 3.2 illustrates in addition a *staff* relationship, one which is independent of the direct lines of authority; in this case, the secretary works with the office manager only, and has no authority in his or her own right. A *lateral* relationship would exist between the staff in charge of filing, reprographics, typing services, and communications, as they are all on the same level of authority, with the same degree of responsibility to the office manager. The office manager also has a *functional* relationship (not illustrated) with other managers throughout the company (i.e., by virtue of what he or she does for them all—providing office services) and this is unconnected with the place of the office manager in the hierarchy.

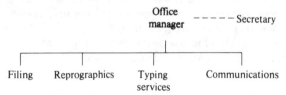

Figure 3.2 Extract from an organization chart.

3.3 A small business

In a small organization, the division of duties may be much less distinct. Functions that would be quite separate in a large one may be merged and performed by one group of people or even one person. For instance, in a small partnership, duties could be divided as follows: policy-making and management—the partners; provision and sale of professional services—the partners; financial accounting—an accountant (possible part-time) assisted by a clerk or secretary in routine matters; office management—a clerk or secretary or one of the partners; personnel work—the partners assisted by a clerk or secretary; purchasing—the partners assisted by a clerk or secretary. Members of the business team must therefore be flexible in outlook, and prepared to do a variety of jobs. However, the limits of their authority and their responsibility to other members of the team must still be defined.

3.4   Local authority

Staff of a local authority are divided into departments—each concerned with a special aspect of the work—and often further subdivided into sections. Management is in the hands of senior officers, chief of whom are the chief executive and the treasurer (or accountant), together with the technical officer, the town planning officer, the director of social services, and the environmental health officer.

(a)   Chief executive

This is the chief official—often a barrister, solicitor or accountant—chosen for managerial ability. He or she forms links between the councillors and the staff, on the one hand, and the councillors and the general public on the other. Having a specialized knowledge of local government law and procedure, he or she is able to guide and advise the council, committees and chairmen, although not making policy decisions personally. The chief executive co-ordinates the work of the council's employees and they are responsible to him or her.

(b)   Treasurer

The treasurer is also a key figure, being responsible for advising the council on financial affairs. He or she sees that accurate accounts are kept and produces estimates and budgets of expenditure. A wide knowledge of council administration is needed for this position, as the work involves co-operation with other departments.

(c)   Staff grades

Staff may be divided into the following categories:

(i) *Administrative*   Those concerned with implementing the council's decisions and the efficient organization of staff resources.

(ii) *Professional* and (iii) *Technical*   Those doing work requiring specialist professional and technical qualifications, e.g., lawyers, accountants, architects, engineers, and surveyors.
(iv) *Clerical*   Supervisors, secretarial, and clerical workers.
(v) *Miscellaneous*   Those who do not fit into any other category.
(vi) *Manual*   Labourers, refuse collectors, outdoor staff, etc.

3.5   Central government

(a)   Departments

The departmental stucture of a government department or Ministry is very complex and depends entirely on the work that is being handled by the staff.

(b)   Staff grades

The grading structure enables staff to be deployed in a flexible manner with opportunities for promotion commensurate with their abilities. For example, the Administration Group structure admits staff at different entry points according to academic qualifications (see Figure 3.3). Opportunities for promotion are accelerated for administration trainees, provided they prove their ability. An open structure exists for the higher levels (see Figure 3.4): posts are filled by the most suitable staff, without regard to their academic background or to whether their previous

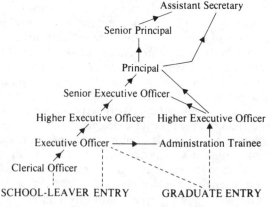

Figure 3.3   Civil Service administration group.

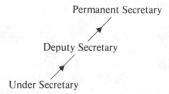

Permanent Secretary

Deputy Secretary

Under Secretary

Figure 3.4 Higher Civil Service grades.

Civil Service experience has been of a general or more specialized nature.

The kind of work done by any civil servant varies according to the type and seniority of the post. Some senior staff advise the Secretaries of State and Ministers in reaching decisions. Other interpret policy decisions and apply them to particular cases. Others are supervisors. Some gather and summarize information for their superiors or deal with the public in person or by telephone or letter. Yet others do secretarial and clerical work. In other words, their work may be managerial, executive, supervisory, secretarial, or clerical, as in any other organization.

3.6   In a nutshell: Comparison of working conditions in large and small organizations

- LARGE: As there are many employees, duties tend to be specialized.

- SMALL: Since fewer employees exist to do the work, the duties of each are likely to be more varied, wider in scope, and more flexible.

- LARGE: The employee's work, as part of the whole concern, appears insignificant, and less satisfaction with the job may result.

- SMALL: The employee has an easily recognizable place in the concern, and the results of the work can generally be seen. Managerial policy can be seen being put into effect.

- LARGE: There is likely to be more automation and standardized procedures.

- SMALL: Although some machines must be employed, others would not be used enough to justify installation.

- LARGE: Because there are more jobs and more departments, promotion and transfer chances are good.

- SMALL: Often there is little chance of promotion within the firm.

- LARGE: There is likely to be a known salary scale, probably kept under frequent review.

- SMALL: There is often no set salary scale, and salaries may be above or below those in large firms. The timing and amount of increases may be uncertain.

- LARGE: Social and welfare facilities are usually provided, and educational opportunities (where appropriate).

- SMALL: Only limited welfare facilities may exist, if any at all.

- LARGE: Luncheon and refreshment facilities are often available, sometimes at subsidized rates.

- SMALL: Employees may have to make their own luncheon arrangements. Luncheon vouchers may be provided.

3.7   Did you know?

1. Under a credit sale, a customer owns the goods immediately he has paid his deposit or his first instalment. If he defaults, the seller can sue him for debt, but cannot reclaim the article.

2. Under a hire-purchase agreement, the seller can take back the article if the hirer defaults, as the seller owns it until the hirer has completed payment. However, where the hire-purchase price is £5000 or less, and the hirer has already paid one-third of this, only a court order can enable the seller to claim back the article.

Activities

1. You work for a manufacturing company and are responsible for the sorting of incoming mail each morning. In this morning's mail you find the following items:

(i) A letter from a lady who has just moved into the area and is looking for work in the Wages or the Costing Offices.
(ii) A credit note for £25 for returnable containers.
(iii) Advertising material and a new price list from a firm of Office Equipment Suppliers.
(iv) A letter from a prospective customer asking for a Representative to call on him as soon as possible.
  (a) State to which Departments you should send the items.
  (b) Indicate what action you would expect the Departments to take (LCCI, SSC)

2. It is the policy of your company to allow new secretaries to spend a short time in each department to familiarize them with company procedures. You have just completed this initial training. Write a short description of the functions of ONE of the departments in which you have worked during your training. (LCCI, PSC)

3. Type a leaflet to be handed to new students arriving at your college, enabling them to become acquainted with the main college departments and personnel.

4. Find out as much as you can about the work of secretaries in different departments of (a) business concerns, (b) local or central government. Reading newspapers and magazines may help, and talking to friends or former students now working. Collect a folder on the type of organization that interests you most.

5. Civil Servants work in a wide variety of spheres. Consult the Government offices section of *Whitaker's Almanack* for illustrations of this statement, and compare the departmental organization in the following: the Home Office, the Department of Education and Science, the Department of the Environment, the Departments of Trade and Industry.

6. What is an organization chart? Give four advantages and four disadvantages of such a chart. Draw a simple organization chart for the following people in the same firm: Sales Manager   Managing Director   Works Manager   Board of Directors   Chief Accountant   Company Secretary. (PEI, Sec. Prac. Adv.)

7. The following advertisement appeared in a national daily newspaper of 4 June 1984:

WORLDWIDE COSMETICS PLC has a number of secretarial posts available in both the UK and abroad. Good secretarial skills are essential and a knowledge of office routine and word processing is desirable.

The successful candidates must have initiative, enthusiasm and ambition and be prepared to travel. Knowledge of foreign languages would be an advantage. An excellent salary is offered and will vary according to age and experience.

Please apply in writing giving full details of education and experience to Mrs Jenny Adamson, Recruitment Manager, Worldwide Cosmetics PLC, 56–66 Waterloo Road, London W1 by 15 June 1984.

(a) It is evident that Worldwide Cosmetics PLC is a large company. What do you consider to be the main advantages of working in a large company as opposed to a small firm?
(b) Assume you are interested in one of the secretarial posts mentioned in the advertisement. Write an appropriate letter of application. (LCCI, SSC)

8. Describe briefly the work of a Public Relations department in an organization, and suggest how secretaries throughout the organization might play a supportive role. (LCCI, PSC)

9. **Group activity**   Either by personal contacts or by arrangements made through your tutor, investigate the organization of duties within two or three small firms in your locality. Divide into small groups for this purpose and then report your findings, incorporating an organization chart in your report if possible.

4
Standard documents

4.1 The secretary's part

Standard documents are designed to transmit information in the simplest, quickest, and most convenient way, and thereby to communicate with outside organizations and internal departments. As a secretary, you yourself may not have to handle some of the documents described in this chapter, but you should know their purpose. Others may concern you more closely, depending on the department in which you work.

4.2 External communication via documents

Standard documents may play a large part in external communication. In some spheres (such as publishing, insurance, banks, hospitals, airlines, trade associations, public utilities and—to a certain extent—local and central government) some of the documents used are appropriate only to those organizations, and cannot be dealt with here. However, the following (in alphabetical order) are some commonly used in many types of business, whether produced by conventional methods or by computerized systems.

(i) *Bill of exchange* (as defined in the Bills of Exchange Act 1882) An unconditional order in writing addressed by one person to another, signed by the person giving it, requiring the person to whom it is addressed to pay on demand or at a fixed determinable future time, a certain sum in money to or to the order of a specified person or bearer. Usually used in export trade.

(ii) *Bill of lading* Specifies the details of goods, and the terms under which they are carried, shipped on behalf of an exporting company. A copy must be produced by the importing company before they can claim the goods. Copies are also held by the shipping agency and the ship's master.

(iii) *Catalogue* Sent to prospective customers, listing and briefly describing the company's products. Each item has a reference number which should be quoted in any subsequent order placed. Often used as an advertising tool.

(iv) *Certificate of origin* A document stating the country in which the goods in question have been manufactured. Designed to ensure that the correct tariffs demanded by the importing country are levied.

(v) *Consignment note* Accompanies goods transported by outside agencies, and contains instructions for delivery.

(vi) *Credit note* Usually printed and/or typed in red, it notifies the customer of an allowance being made to him reducing his indebtedness—e.g., in respect of an overcharge made on the original invoice, or faulty goods or chargeable packing cases returned by the customer.

(vii) *Customs declaration* A list compiled by an exporter of goods dispatched abroad and their value, so that the correct customs duty can be levied on the purchaser by the customs authorities in the receiving country.

(viii) *Debit note* Notifies the customer of an additional amount due from him—e.g., in respect of an undercharge or omission on the original invoice.

(ix) *Estimate* Similar to a quotation (see (xvi) below), but prices given are less exact and intended as a guide only. Used often for services rather than goods supplied.

(x) *Inquiry* A request, made by a customer or a company's purchasing department, for details of goods offered for sale.

(xi) *Invoice*   (See Figure 4.1—invoices printed out via computer programs may differ in the extent to which calculations are shown.) Records a particular sale to a particular customer and includes details of goods, prices, carriage charges, discounts, VAT, etc.

(xii) *Letter of credit*   Documents made out by an importer transferring funds to a bank abroad to enable accounts with the exporter to be settled by the bank on the importer's behalf.

(xiii) *Price list*   A price list (or *prices current*, when prices fluctuate rapidly) may be issued separately from the catalogue.

(xiv) *Pro forma invoice*   This can be a demand for payment sent, for example, in advance of goods to a customer with a poor payment record. It may also be sent with goods on approval, to be used by the customer if he decides to buy them. However, it is not accepted by the VAT authorities (see **4.4**) who regard it only as an advice of what the goods will cost.

(xv) *Purchase order*   Sets out details of goods which the purchasing department wishes to buy.

(xvi) *Quotation*   A detailed answer to an inquiry, describing goods available, their prices, terms of sale, means of delivery, etc.

(xvii) *Receipt*   Acknowledges receipt of a remittance and shows the name of the sender and date of

VAT Regn No 765984312							Invoice No 84719		
LMN WHOLESALE SUPPLIES LIMITED 100 GATE STREET BIRMINGHAM 1									

To: City Retail Stores
    123 High Road
    Manchester 2
    Transaction: SALE
				Invoice date 9.4.19--
				
				Delivery note No. 7742
				Delivery date 9.4.19--					

Quantity	Ref. No.	Type	Description	Unit price	Total cost £	p	VAT Rate	VAT £	p
4 doz	92174	V2	Ice cream	·30	14	40			
10 lbs	92068	M3	Ice cream powder	.98	9	80			
					24	20	15%	3	63
12	91634	C4	Sponge cakes	·25	3	00			
20	91618	C6	Fruit cakes	1·05	21	00			
					24	00	zero	-	-
			TOTAL GOODS		48	20			
			VAT *less* Allowance for cash discount					3	63
									18
			TOTAL VAT		3	45†			
				£	51	65			
E & OE		TERMS: 5% 30 days on goods only							

Figure 4.1   Sales invoice incorporating VAT (reproduced by kind permission of Price Waterhouse). Where discount for prompt payment is offered, the value for VAT purposes is reduced by the amount of the discount, whether the payment is made in the prescribed period or not.

receipt. The original statement of account is sometimes used, by stamping it with the date and an acknowledgement and returning it to the customer.

(xviii) *Remittance advice note* Accompanies a remittance and explains why it is sent.

(xix) *Sales order* An order for goods placed by a customer and submitted either on his own organization's preprinted form or on that of the supplier. Sales representatives may carry serially numbered order forms in order books for their customers' convenience. An order to be met overseas is known as an *indent*.

(xx) *Service agreement* Sets out the terms of a contract under which the supplier agrees to maintain equipment for a stated period, after sale or throughout a period of hire.

(xxi) *Statement* Summarizes a customer's transactions with the selling company over a given month. It is sent by the accounts department as a request for payment, and therefore states the total sum due after deductions such as discount.

4.3 Value added tax

Value added tax (VAT) is an indirect tax levied by the government on goods and services. It is important for companies to show the rate of VAT on their invoices because organizations registered for VAT can claim the money back.

At the time of writing there are two rates of VAT. On most goods and services 15 per cent is charged. For instance, 15 per cent VAT is added to the bill for restaurant, or even take-away, meals. Some goods and services are *zero-rated*, e.g., food (as opposed to meals). This book does not carry any VAT. Some items are *exempt* from tax, e.g., bank charges. A business which is VAT-exempted cannot claim back any tax it pays.

The *General Guide* (updated periodically) gives comprehensive information about VAT and how it should be applied and collected. *VAT News* gives details of changes and amendments as they are introduced. Local VAT offices, whose addresses can be found in the phone book, provide comprehensive information on all matters relating to VAT.

4.4 Tax invoices

The amount of VAT being charged must be shown as a separate item on invoices for transactions between registered traders. These are known as 'tax invoices' and must be available to support claims for deduction of input tax. Tax invoices (see Figure 4.1) must bear the following details:

Seller's full name and registered address

Seller's VAT registration number (as evidence that the seller is entitled to charge VAT)

Customer's name and address

Invoice number

Invoice date

Type of transaction—e.g., sale, lease, hire-purchase, sale or return, exchange

Tax point, i.e., date of sale, which is the time at which the tax becomes chargeable; this determines in which quarter the seller pays and the buyer reclaims the tax in question

Description of goods or services

Quantity supplied

Unit price per item or group of items of same general description (excluding VAT)

Total amount payable (excluding VAT)

VAT chargeable at each rate, plus rate of tax applied

Total VAT being charged

Rate of any cash or trade discounts being offered

4.5 In a nutshell: VAT and common business documents and records

- *Quotation:* Should bear general statement explaining whether or not VAT is included in prices given.
- *Catalogue:* Should bear general statement explaining whether or not VAT is included in prices given.
- *Confirmation of order:* Should bear general statement explaining whether or not VAT is included in prices given.

- *Tax invoice:* See section **4.4.** Need not be provided for unregistered persons, but registered persons must have one to support claims for input tax deduction.
- *Credit note:* Should normally show all the details required on a tax invoice and include credit for the VAT paid (unless agreed otherwise between the registered traders involved in the transaction) as unregistered and exempt persons cannot claim back VAT from Customs and Excise.
- *Debit note:* Should show all the details required on a tax invoice.
- *Less-detailed tax invoice:* May be used by retailers when a tax invoice is asked for. For amounts of (in 1986) £50 gross or less, tax details are omitted, except rate of VAT and the amount payable including VAT, provided the goods or services supplied are all chargeable at the same rate of VAT.
- *Statement of account:* Often not detailed enough to mention VAT, since it usually includes only the totals of invoices submitted and of credit notes received.
- *Petty cash book:* See **10.1**.
- *Petty cash vouchers:* May show analysis of value of purchase and VAT paid. (Vouchers cannot be used to support claims for reimbursement of input VAT: a supplier's tax invoice showing VAT total separately (or less-detailed tax invoice if under £50) is necessary.)
- *Receipt:* Should show VAT element separately.
- *Discounts:* Where cash or trade discounts are allowed, VAT is calculated on the *net* value of the goods or services, after deduction of the discounts.

4.6   Internal documents

Although the standard documents mentioned in Section **4.2** are intended in the first place for external communication, sets (see **6.3**) of some of them are prepared so that copies can be circulated to internal departments. Figures 4.2 and 4.3 illustrate this point.

Some documents are used *solely* for departmental liaison, like the goods received note in Figure 4.4. For example:

(i) *Warehouse order*   An internal form prepared from customer's order by the sales order section and sent to the warehouse to dispatch goods from stock.

(ii) *Requisition*   An official request for goods to be released from stock, usually countersigned and approved by persons in authority.

(iii) *Stores issue note*   Records and accompanies goods released from stock, and from it stock records can be adjusted.

(iv) *Goods received note*   Lists goods received.

Others are used *primarily* for departmental liaison. For example:

(v) *Works order*   When goods must be specially manufactured to meet a customer's requirements,

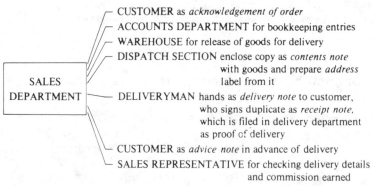

CUSTOMER as *acknowledgement of order*
ACCOUNTS DEPARTMENT for bookkeeping entries
WAREHOUSE for release of goods for delivery
DISPATCH SECTION enclose copy as *contents note* with goods and prepare *address* label from it
SALES DEPARTMENT
DELIVERYMAN hands as *delivery note* to customer, who signs duplicate as *receipt note*, which is filed in delivery department as proof of delivery
CUSTOMER as *advice note* in advance of delivery
SALES REPRESENTATIVE for checking delivery details and commission earned

Figure 4.2   Communicating by means of an invoice set.

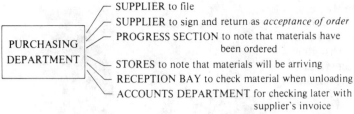

Figure 4.3 Communicating by means of a purchase order set.

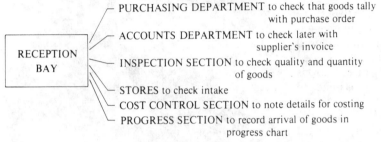

Figure 4.4 Communicating by means of a goods received note set.

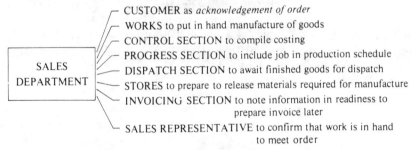

Figure 4.5 Communicating by means of a works order set.

the Sales Department prepare a works order. See Figure 4.5 concerning a works order set.

4.7 Document transport systems

Documents can be sent to persons or departments within a firm by a variety of methods:

(a) Visual display unit

Documents stored in a company's computer can be called up and displayed on the screen of a visual display unit (VDU). The document can then be completed as necessary and then either re-stored in the computer or displayed on the VDU of whoever may next need to take action. (See Electronic Mail, **13.9**.)

(b) Airtubes

Papers or other small articles are inserted into special containers or carriers, put into a system of tubes, and propelled by forced air from a fan or blower to their destinations. Some systems connect only two points; others present a choice of destination from a central dispatch point, the sender dialling or keying-in the outlet required for automatic delivery. Where documents in a tube can travel in one direction only, a second channel is often provided for those needing to be sent in the opposite direction. Some, however, are designed to travel in either direction, electronic controls preventing collision. If a ring-main system is used, outlets can easily be added when extra receiving or dispatch points become necessary. Airtube systems may cover great distances, linking departments in different buildings.

(c) Open conveyors

These are used for transmission within the same building. In a typical electronic system, where there is a choice of destination, documents in lightweight cases travel along conveyor belts or troughs until diverted at the appropriate delivery point, indicated in advance by the operator depressing push-buttons on the case or conveyor. Where one point is linked to one other only, no electronic addressing is necessary and documents can therefore travel without containers. Transporter systems use self-propelled trolleys, generating their own current from miniature horizontal or vertical railway tracks.

(d) Elevators

Documents are put in carriers and taken by elevator to the floor required, where they are collected and distributed. Some elevators are continuously in motion and automatically accept and unload containers at the required points.

Figure 4.6 Telelift automatic internal distribution system for documents and light goods. (Courtesy of Telelift (UK) Ltd)

4.8 Did you know?

1. Cash discount is a stated percentage which a customer can deduct from the sum he owes a supplier if he settles his account within a given time.

2. Trade discount is the discount allowed by a wholesaler to a retailer on goods for resale.

3. FOB (free on board) means that the charge stated includes delivery to and loading on the ship.

4. CIF (cost, insurance, and freight) means that the charge stated includes delivery to the ship, loading onto it, carriage to the port of delivery, and insurance.

5. E & OE (errors and omissions excepted) means that if errors are discovered later, the seller is entitled to adjust the details quoted on the invoice.

Activities

1. (a) What is the purpose of an invoice?
   (b) What references to Value Added Tax might it contain?
   (c) To whom might copies of the invoice be distributed in addition to the customer? (LCCI, PSC)

2. (a) Explain the purpose of a Statement of Account.
   (b) In what ways does it differ from an invoice? (LCCI, SSC)

3. The following documents are all used when processing a Purchase. You are required to place them in the order in which they would be likely to be used and to describe the purpose of each document.

(a) Statement of Account
(b) Advice Note
(c) Purchase Requisition
(d) Quotation
(e) Cheque
(f) Order
(g) Enquiry
(h) Goods Received Note
(i) Credit Note
(j) Invoice   (LCCI, SSC)

4. You work in the Sales Department of a small company. Briefly explain how you would deal with the following situations:

(a) You receive an order, from a new customer, for goods in stock worth £200, which has come to you direct rather than through a salesman.
(b) Orders are often made during a telephone call and there is no system for ensuring that information given is complete. Delays are often experienced because of this procedure.
(c) A customer telephones to inform you that an assignment of goods delivered by your company has arrived in a damaged condition. (LCCI, PSC)

5. As a secretary in a sales office, your duties involve co-operating with sales representatives employed to follow up enquiries from customers. Describe briefly the types of documents you would expect to use or be familiar with in the course of your work. (LCCI, PSC)

6. Copies of some documents raised in the course of buying and selling are used also as a means of informing internal departments of the progress of transactions with customers and of action to be taken. Mention 3 such documents, and describe and explain the typical routeing of copies. (LCCI, PSC)

7. As a student, you are asked at various times to complete standard documents concerned with your college or school or local education authority administration. Compile a list of these, stating the groups of people, departments or outside bodies which they link.

8. **Group activity** Compile folders, with explanatory notes, of examples of the documents mentioned in this chapter. Each member of the group could concentrate on either a specific document or a particular type of business organization as a source of material. Circulate the folders when completed.

5
The office environment

5.1 The secretary's part

Like any other member of staff, you, the secretary, benefit from good office design, well-chosen, suitable furniture, adequate lighting, heating and ventilation, and as a result achieve a higher level of efficiency than you would under poor working conditions. You may have an opportunity in a small organization to voice your opinion about these matters if rearrangement or new furniture is contemplated. If your office is open plan, such points will already have been taken care of. You will have been taken care of, too, in the departmental planning, and placed near your boss.

5.2 Cellular office design

In some organizations, offices are designed on the concept of separate rooms for individual workers or groups of workers (see Figure 5.1). The type of furniture to be found in each room depends upon the duties of its occupants: for example, drawing boards and desks for draughtsmen, tables for mail clerks, typewriting desks for typing centres, computer terminal workstations for all types of staff, etc. The size of a room must, of course, be suitable for the number of people working in it: cramped conditions are not conducive to a high standard of efficiency, but the allocation of too large a room to a solitary worker is not economic. To a certain extent, the size and standard of furnishing reflects the status of the occupant. An organization is prepared to spend more to furnish and equip a room that will be used by senior staff or seen by important visitors than one used by junior staff only.

5.3 Open-plan design

This is based on the concept of large areas of floor space with no dividing walls (see Figure 5.2). In landscaped offices the whole area is planned. Working space is calculated and allocated and members of departments grouped together. To be satisfactory, landscaping must suit a company's individual requirements: this involves taking into account its procedures, its equipment and the number and duties of its staff. Furnishings, furniture, decoration, lighting, heating and ventilation are all intrinsic parts of the design, which is usually handled by specialist firms. New buildings designed for the purpose are the most suitable, though older

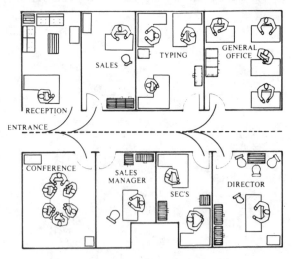

Figure 5.1 Cellular office plan. (Courtesy of *Office Equipment News*)

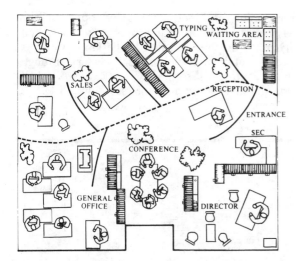

Figure 5.2 Open-plan office covering the same floor area as in Figure 5.1. (Courtesy of *Office Equipment News*) Note that more staff are accommodated and expansion is easier.

premises can sometimes be adapted. When budgeting, the cost of maintenance and cleaning, repairs, floor space (rent and rates), and salaries must all be taken into account.

As there are no dividing walls, communication between departments is improved; a more informal atmosphere may prevail, paperwork from written internal communications may be reduced and networking (see Chapter 11) made easier. This is only the case, however, if the placing of staff is systematically worked out: there will be a great deal of unnecessary movement and distraction if staff needing to co-operate closely are not placed near one another and if the various departments cannot be easily reached without disturbing other workers. Any reorganization that may become necessary can be carried out without too much difficulty because of the flexibility of open-plan design.

Noise is greater than in cellular offices, but can be lessened by sound-absorbent ceilings and by screens with acoustic panels in conjunction with carpets and thick curtains. Noisy machines can be placed apart. Special acoustic covers are available for lessening noise from some machines without impeding their operation. Screens also provide a certain amount of privacy for staff engaged in confidential work. The loss of separate rooms does not necessarily mean the

end of distinction between various grades of staff. Senior executives may be allocated more space and have better quality furniture.

The adoption of landscaping may force a company to examine critically its ways of working and to streamline its methods. As a company examines its methods, so too will it look at the machinery it employs.

5.4 Office machines

(a) General considerations affecting choice of machine

If it is decided that a machine will be advantageous many factors will affect the choice—e.g., the supplies needed (cost, availability, etc.), the staff required to operate or supervise it (degree of skill and proportion of working day involved), the accommodation available (size, weight, portability, power supplies, ventilation, noise), maintenance arrangements (by supplier or company's staff, degree of attention likely to be needed), expected life (changing technology, possible early obsolescence), etc. The effects of breakdowns or powercuts must be considered, and what alternative arrangements could be made in an emergency.

(b) Purchasing, leasing and renting

Once a machine or system has been selected, a choice must be made about how to acquire it. *Purchasing* ties up capital which might have been used for other purposes, or if invested could have earned interest. If a maintenance contract is made with the manufacturers, this will cost an additional sum after the expiry of any guarantee period. The depreciation on machinery has also to be reckoned with. As the law stands at present, some relief against the cost of purchased equipment may be set against tax. *Leasing* usually proves more expensive than buying but some organizations find it convenient to reduce their short-term commitments in this way. The contract with the lessor lasts for an agreed number of years, and usually includes the cost of maintenance. *Renting* has similar advantages to leasing, but the customer can end the agreement at any time, provided that he gives the agreed notice. This allows the customer to keep pace with new technology.

(c)   Choosing a suitable supplier

There is a wide choice of business machines and equipment on the market, particularly in the field of microcomputer systems. It is advisable to choose a supplier who can provide reliable after-sales service and who is unlikely to go out of business.

(d)   Updating machines

It is also important to find out if the manufacturer can update the equipment, i.e., supply additional features as technology develops, without the user having to invest in an entirely new system.

(e)   Integrated office

Microcomputer technology now enables computing and communicating equipment to be brought together into systems, forming an integrated electronic office. Data comprising text, images, and speech can all be processed and communicated within the same system (Chapter 11). By means of networks (Chapter 11) machines in a system can intercommunicate and the users share resources. Obtaining a machine with a networking capability may be important.

(f)   Compatibility

With the emergence of the integrated office, it is vital to ensure that pieces of equipment hitherto used separately can be operated in a combined system. Standards are devised to enable machines with different functions to communicate with one another and to ensure the different manufacturers' machines can work together.

5.5   Office planning

(a)   Workstations

These are desk units designed to accommodate the electronic equipment used by many staff performing a wide variety of jobs. It is important that they are designed *ergonomically*, i.e., to enable the people working at them to work at maximum efficiency (see Figure 5.3). The actual writing surface needs only to be small and within easy reach of the user, but more space is needed for visual display units and keyboards, calculators, telephones, dictation or

transcribing machines, etc. VDU working surfaces may be split-level: lower for an inset keyboard and higher for the screen unit. If a desktop printer is used, a slot in the worktop is necessary through which continuous stationery stacked on a shelf beneath is fed to the machine (see Figure 5.4).

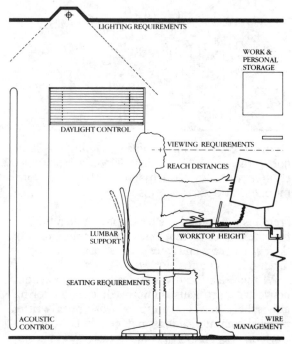

Figure 5.3   A diagram illustrating some of the key factors needing to be assessed in workstation design. (Courtesy of Business Equipment Trade Association, 8 Southampton Place, London WC1A 2EF, and taken from their publication *Introducing the Visual Display Unit to the Office*)

Reference books, trays, card indexes, disk storage boxes, etc., may be kept on shelving attached to screens which often partially enclose workstations, giving privacy to the users. Workstations may be linked to form groups if the work flow demands this. Segments inserted into the angles between desks enable the worktops to form a continuous run (see Figure 5.5).

Desk heights may be adjustable manually, electrically or by 'gas lift', i.e., by means of hydraulic pressure, to enable users to do keyboarding and

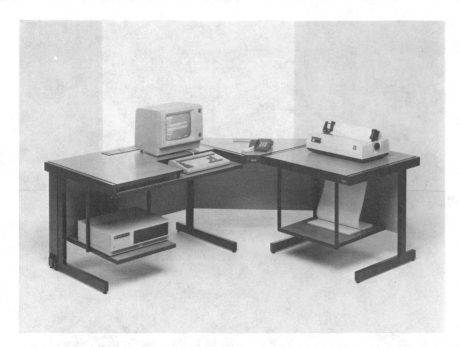

Figure 5.4 This microcomputer workstation includes a VDU/keyboard table with a movable plinth enabling the equipment to be set right- or left-handed to suit the operator. The split level places the keyboard at the correct working height. A 90° linking unit joins this table to a printer stand with a slotted surface to take paper feed from beneath, and provides additional clerical workspace. (Courtesy of Project Office Equipment Limited)

written or other work at the same workstation. The design of a VDU workstation and its surroundings needs care to enable the user to work efficiently and without undue fatigue. For example, the screen can be tilted to reduce glare and to suit the user's vision; the keyboard can be separate and placed in the most convenient place. Filters may be fitted over VDU screens to reduce glare and an antistatic liquid sprayed on them to reduce clinging dust.

(b) Cable management

Cables linked to a workstation for power, telecommunications, local area networks, etc., must be safely channelled to prevent hazards to the user. Cables from the machines may be fed through outlets in the work surface into channels running along the back and sides of desks (see Figure 5.5) and along the bottom or sides of screens. Power cables must be separated from the rest. Although hidden, cables must be accessible both for maintenance and for easy dismantling and moving of equipment during office reorganization. Access points are fitted with traps or covers to protect cables from misuse or spillage of liquids. Raised floors afford space underneath for cables and other services.

(c) Décor

The appearance of landscaped offices is extremely important, both for practical purposes and for the psychological effect on staff. Ceilings and floors provide focal points, and are used to supply colour and to reflect light. Patterns on carpets and curtains should harmonize or contrast with them and can be more striking than in small rooms. Carpets in any type of office are useful to absorb sound and to prevent loss of heat. A wide range of colours and styles is available, and the right choice can appear to lengthen, widen or lighten a room. Close-patterned carpets are the most effective, as treadings and stains are less obvious. Fitted carpets with few seams are

35

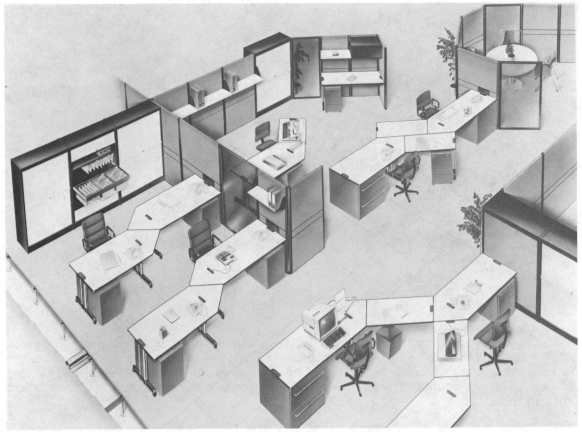

Figure 5.5 A small open-plan area. Note that the screens give privacy, especially in the conference area. They also act as space dividers and support shelving and other fitments. Desks interlock to provide continuous working surfaces and to save floor space. Cables from equipment are run through traps in the desk surfaces into channels along the sides and down into the raised floor. (Courtesy of Unity Designs (UK) Ltd, High Wycombe)

the most resistant to wear and tear. In landscaped offices especially, indoor shrubs, planted in movable containers, add to the general effect, besides freshening the air and acting as room dividers.

Furniture must be well made, durable, ergonomically suitable, and with non-reflecting surfaces that are easily cleaned and not quickly damaged. Much modern furniture is modular, i.e., manufactured in standard units which can be moved about or combined in a variety of ways to serve different purposes and to save space, e.g., units can be combined to form conference tables or reception seating, and taken apart when not required for that purpose.

(d) Chairs

Chairs should be of the right height and shape, easily adjustable or used in conjunction with adjustable footrests. Typists' chairs must be adjustable in several respects: the height of the seat from the floor, the tilt of the seat, the height of the backrest from the seat and the angle of the backrest to the upright. Some chairs for use at executives' desks have mechanisms enabling them to tilt or swivel. Chairs must be steady (see the '5-star base' illustrated in Figure 5.5). They should have no rough edges, no protruding parts or greasy fittings. Compare Figures 5.7 and 5.8 for chairs of ergonomic and nonergonomic design respectively.

Figure 5.6 (Courtesy of Tony Holland. First published in *Business Systems and Equipment*.)

(e) Miscellaneous furniture

Lockable cupboards and bookcases can be obtained with fixed or adjustable shelves, the latter being more useful. Some cupboards used for miscellaneous storage may be fitted with pigeonholes instead of shelves. Shelving is often manufactured in units that can be added to as required, and may be open or covered at the sides and back, fixed to walls or free-standing. Bookcases are often protected by glass fronts which may be hinged or sliding; hinged doors need more space in the room, but sliding doors make access to the whole shelf difficult and sometimes do not run smoothly. Cupboards for use as wardrobes are also supplied. Furniture can also act as screening and space dividers.

(f) Lighting

In many offices, natural daylight has to be supplemented by artificial light. The most common modern form is fluorescent lighting, as it gives an evenly spread light and produces more than double the light from each unit of electricity than the softer tungsten filament lighting. The degree of glare from fluorescent lighting depends upon its colour—a white light, for example, being much more intense than 'natural'—and on whether or not diffusers are used. These, in conjunction with reflectors, reduce glare and distribute the light. A softer effect can also be obtained if the fluorescent tubes are set above a false, translucent ceiling. Tubes can also be set into or hung from ceilings.

Because bright, harsh lighting tends to be reflected in VDU screens, ambient lighting of less intensity is used as general lighting. This may be achieved by uplighting, i.e., using fitments that direct light upwards and cause it to be reflected from the ceiling. Task lighting is then used, as required, for specific areas: this provides brighter light directed downwards to working surfaces. Luminaires (light fitments) may be free-standing or attached to screens or along workstation shelving.

(g) Heating, ventilation and air-conditioning

Light, and even electronic equipment, creates heat, and in some large buildings where lighting systems

37

Microprocessor-controlled energy management systems help to lower costs and reduce waste by co-ordinating energy consumption from lights, pumps, boilers, etc., with heat creation from such sources as machinery, lights, and even people.

Windows provide the cheapest and easiest form of ventilation, but sometimes other methods are necessary. A system of ducts can be used to circulate a central supply of fresh air through a building; the air reaches the rooms through grilles and diffusers blend it quickly with the warmer existing air, so that no cold draught is felt by the occupants. Fans help air to circulate within a room, and if fixed to windows in small rooms will expel stale air and draw in fresh air. In some areas, 'fresh' air needs to be cleaned on entering a room and filters can be fitted to fans for this purpose. Air-conditioning enables stale air to be cleaned by removing dust particles and recirculating it.

(h)   Planning techniques

When planning an office, a number of considerations have to be taken into account: the space into which staff, furniture and equipment have to fit; the placing of departments to facilitate the flow of work; safety and design factors controlled by legislation such as the Health and Safety at Work Act and the Offices, Shops and Railway Premises Act (see 5.7); general appearance; ease of communication between departments; degree of privacy; etc.

A plan can be drawn to scale, preferably on squared paper, showing the outline of the area, with doors and windows and any other fixed features marked in. Templates can be used, i.e., representations, often in cardboard, of furniture and fittings, cut out to scale from a stencil. Miniature drawings can also be made, or three-dimensional models are sometimes available from furniture manufacturers. For an approximate impression of a finished design, easily movable symbols can be placed on a magnetic planning board. Samples of carpeting and curtain materials mounted on boards help to give a good idea of the completed office.

Computer-aided design techniques save much time and effort. A plan of an office area is assembled on the VDU screen and stored for recall and/or amendment as required. Plans can be constructed quickly and always to a high standard. Representations of constantly used elements, e.g., furniture,

Figure 5.7   This chair is claimed to encourage a natural posture with freedom of movement, proper distribution of weight in order to align the spine to a good sitting position, less pressure on the lumbar region and better circulation. (Courtesy of Wiltshier Contract Furnishing)

are planned as part of the whole design, the heat thus generated is channelled into use in heating the premises. Otherwise, the types of heating found in private homes are adapted for office use.

Some forms of heating make the atmosphere too dry for efficient working. Humidifiers can relieve the problem. They contain water which is evaporated by heat and expelled as moist air. Also this will reduce the static electricity generated by synthetic materials, particularly carpets.

Solar film applied to windows reduces heat in summer, and so do blinds fitted to windows with a sunny aspect. Heat output can be increased by fitting reflective panels behind radiators.

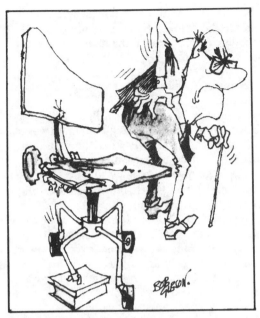

Specially designed to maximize stress

Specially designed to maximize stress and provide long-term physical hazard to all kinds of clerical and desk workers, an entirely traditional type of office chair is available under the slightly gimmicky tradename of 'GraunchHaunch'. Although of only moderately excessive cost, this type of seating is claimed to offer astonishingly poor value for money.

Its design is, say the manufacturers, fully anthropoperilous, and has a lifetime guarantee which specifically includes cramp, backache and a high probability of spinal injury. The chair is claimed to be suitable for all types of staff from Caliban to Quasimodo and may be adjustable if anyone can shift the knobs.

A four-arm base offering inadequate stability is fitted as standard, and omission of one castor enables the chair to tip easily to the right. Leaning to the left is facilitated by the canted backrest. Upholstery is in a choice of green Clamiskin, which is impervious to moisture and thus retains sweat to assure conservation of precious body fluids.

Another significant design feature is the seat cushioning: the edge of the upholstery is left open so that paper or old rags can be inserted to adjust the seat profile to the individual bottom. Additionally, the seat platform itself is completely flat, forming an ideal base for the stack of telephone directories usually required.

The GraunchHaunch may be seen and tested in thousands—in fact the majority—of offices throughout the UK. Anatomically correct seating, by contrast, is available from only a limited number of outlets, and its cost is marginally higher. Further information on the comparison between GraunchHaunch and Giroflex anatomically correct seating is available upon request.

Figure 5.8   Press releases are not usually written in a humorous vein. This one issued by Giroflex was published by *Office Equipment News* whose cartoonist Bob Gibson drew the accompanying cartoon.

screens, etc., may be stored to save redrawing. The computer system can produce lists of materials needed, to facilitate costings. Plans can be produced in layers by means of overlays for different aspects then combined to represent the whole concept.

5.6   Safety and health in the office

(a)   Safety

As a secretary, you have, in common with other employees, a general duty to co-operate over your company's safety policy and to avoid behaving in a way likely to endanger your own or others' safety. This means, for example, seeing that devices provided for the protection of staff are used and that potential hazards are reported to people in authority.

Necessary fire preventive measures should be taken by the company, e.g., checking that all fire extinguishers and other appliances are in working order, that fire doors are kept closed, that fire exits are unobstructed, that emergency routines have been devised and tested in fire drills, and that new staff have been informed of these. No-smoking regulations should be observed where necessary, e.g., in departments with particular fire risks such as inflammable or explosive materials. Remember that individual members of staff may be held responsible and can be prosecuted under the Health and Safety at Work Act if proved to be negligent. There must be continuous provision for office safety, a point to remember when arranging cover for duties normally performed by someone temporarily absent.

(b) Health

The possible health risks from working with VDUs have been under discussion and several white-collar unions are actively researching the matter. It is said that there is no significant risk to health. Some people may suffer eye strain but evidence appears to indicate at present that no permanent damage results to eyesight. Radiation risks are said to be minimal.

The atmosphere contains *ions*, i.e., particles of air that may be either positively or negatively charged depending on climatic and other conditions. Heat and static electricity generated by machines is said to diminish the number of negative ions, causing feelings of lethargy and malaise among office staff. It is claimed that these can be counteracted by installing devices called ionizers.

5.7 Health and safety legislation

(a) Offices, Shops and Railway Premises Act 1963

The Act applies to offices anywhere, even when they are on premises used for other purposes, such as factories or hospitals. However, it does not cover premises used as offices for very short temporary periods, nor those used for less than 21 hours each week. Neither does it apply in cases where the only workers are the employer's near relatives.

The following are some of the main provisions of the Act:

(i)   Premises, furniture and fittings must be kept clean.

(ii)   Rooms must be properly ventilated and lit, and have a reasonable working temperature—i.e., at least 16° C (60.8° F) after the first hour.

(iii) The total space available must be sufficient for an average space to be allowed for each worker of at least 3.7 m^2 (40 ft^2) or, where the ceiling is lower than 10 ft, 11 m^3 (400 ft^3).

(iv)   No worker should be expected to lift or carry loads heavy enough to cause injury.

(v)   Lavatories must be suitable, properly maintained and easily accessible.

(vi)   Washing facilities, with hot and cold or warm water, soap and towels, must be provided.

(vii) Drinking water must be available.

(viii) There must be suitable facilities for keeping clothing not worn at work.

(ix)   Sedentary workers must be provided with seating suitably designed and constructed for their work. All workers must have access to seating.

(x)   Floors, passages and stairs must be safe and free from obstructions and slippery substances.

(xi)   If no special first-aid room is provided, a first-aid box or boxes must be kept and maintained by a responsible person, who must record all cases treated. The contents are specified in Booklet No. 48 in the Health and Safety at Work series, available from Her Majesty's Stationery Office. Each box must also contain Leaflet SHW 1, which gives advice on treatment and is also available from HMSO. The arrangements for first-aid and accidents procedures must be definite and continuing and made known to all employees.

(xii) Machinery must have dangerous parts protected or be placed so that there is no risk of injury to employees.

(xiii) If an employee is disabled for more than three days, or dies as a result of an accident on the premises, a written report must be sent to the inspecting authority.

(b) Fire Precautions Act 1971 and associated legislation

The Fire Precautions Act 1971 restricts the use of certain classes of premises unless there is in force a fire certificate. Section 78 of the Health and Safety at Work Act 1974 extended the Fire Precautions Act to cover factories and other premises including those subject to the Offices, Shops and Railway Premises Act 1963. In addition, the Fire Precautions (Non-Certificated Factory, Office, Shop and Railway Premises) Regulations 1976 provide for fire precautions to be taken in the smaller premises which are not required to have a fire certificate under the Fire Precautions Act.

On 1 January 1977 the fire sections of the Factories Act and Offices, Shops and Railway Premises Act were repealed and replaced by Orders giving fire authorities (or, in the case of the Crown, the Home departments) the prime responsibility for general fire precautions in premises subject to these two Acts. However, in particular premises where prescribed quantities of defined explosive or highly inflammable substances are made, processed, used, or stored, the Fire Certificates (Special Premises) Regulations will apply and the Health and Safety Executive will be responsible for the issue of fire certificates.

(c) Health and Safety at Work Act 1974

The purpose of the Act is to promote, stimulate, encourage and, where necessary, enforce high standards of health and safety at work. It is an enabling Act, and lays down general principles and imposes general duties of care, while giving powers to the Secretary of State for Employment for the making of detailed regulations. It has been superimposed over already existing health and safety legislation, e.g., the Factories Acts, and Offices, Shops and Railway Premises Act (see above). The chief provisions of these remain in force until repealed and replaced under the Act by new regulations or approved codes of practice.

The Act applies to all people at work—employers, the self-employed, and employees (except domestic servants in private households). One of its main objects is to involve both management and workers, so that all are aware of the importance of achieving high standards of health and safety. It also imposes duties on designers, manufacturers, importers, and suppliers of articles and substances for use at work.

The aim of the Act is: *(a)* to secure the health, safety, and welfare of persons at work; *(b)* to protect the health and safety of the general public who may be affected by work activities; *(c)* to control the keeping and use of explosive or highly flammable or otherwise dangerous substances, and to prevent the unlawful acquisition, possession and use of these substances; *(d)* to control the emission into the atmosphere of noxious or offensive substances from work premises.

Duties of employers Employers must ensure that their employees work in conditions and surroundings that are as safe and free from health risks as is reasonably practicable. These requirements apply to work systems and plant (machinery, equipment, and appliances); materials and articles used; the place of work and entrances to and exits from it; the working environment and welfare arrangements and facilities. It is not enough for the employer to provide and maintain suitable surroundings and equipment: he must also provide information, instruction, training, and supervision, so that employees use them without danger to health and safety.

Written statement Every employer with five or more employees must prepare a written statement of his general policy with respect to the health and safety at work of his employees and the organization and arrangements in force for carrying out that policy. He must revise the statement when necessary and bring it to the attention of all employees.

Duties of manufacturers and suppliers of articles and substances for use at work Articles (i.e., plant, machinery, equipment, appliances, or components) for use at work must be of safe design and construction and have been properly tested and examined. Information about their proper use and the conditions necessary must be made available. Similar requirements apply to the provision of substances for use at work (i.e., any natural or artificial substance in the form of solid, liquid, gas, or vapour). Designers and manufacturers have a duty to carry out research to eliminate or minimize any risks to health and safety engendered by the design, article, or substance.

Duties of employees   Every employee (including members of management where appropriate) must take reasonable care for the health and safety of himself and others affected by his behaviour, and co-operate with his employer so that the employer can perform his statutory duties under the Act. He must not intentionally or recklessly interfere with or misuse anything provided by law in the interests of health, safety, and welfare.

Safety representatives and committees   In order that employers and employees can co-operate in promoting health and safety at work, regulations have been implemented to allow for the appointment of safety representatives and committees. Under the regulations, safety representatives with prescribed functions may be appointed by a recognized independent trade union from among the employees in a workplace. Safety committees may also be formed, if any two safety representatives submit a written request to the employer to do so. Where employees are not members of recognized independent trade unions, a guidance note gives advice to employers on the setting up of safety committees.

Company reports   The Health and Safety at Work Act requires prescribed companies to include in their directors' reports information about the arrangements in force for that year for securing the employees' health, safety, and welfare at work, and for protecting other people affected against risks to health and safety.

Health and Safety Commission   This is appointed by the Secretary of State for Employment and consists of members representing organizations of employers, employees, and local authorities. It is res-ponsible for developing policies in the health and safety field. It appoints the three-man *Health and Safety Executive*. This works in accordance with directions and guidance given by the Commission. It supervises the enforcement of legal requirements and the provision of an advisory service.

Enforcement and penalties   Inspection is carried out by the Executive's inspectors or by local authority inspectors working with the Commission's guidance. Where an inspector discovers a contravention of the Act he may:

(i) Issue a **Prohibition Notice** stopping the harmful activity until the remedial action specified has been taken. The notice can be served on the person undertaking the activity or a person in control of it.

(ii) Issue an **Improvement Notice** to remedy the fault within a specified time. The Notice can be served on any person responsible, e.g., employer, employee, manufacturer, or supplier.

(iii) Prosecute (in addition to or instead of a Notice).

(iv) Seize, render harmless, or destroy any substances or articles he considers to be a cause of immediate danger and serious personal injury.

Penalties   Failure to comply with a Notice may lead to prosecution, either summarily or on indictment, and/or imprisonment in the case of a Prohibition Notice. Any appeal against a Notice must be made to an industrial tribunal. Prosecution may result in fines on summary conviction and imprisonment and/or unlimited fines on indictment.

5.8   In a nutshell: Checklist on office safety

Are any of these a hazard in your place of work?

- Trailing flexes
- Worn wiring
- Overloaded power points
- Electrically-driven machines not switched off after use
- Flexes left plugged into electrical sockets at the end of the day
- Unguarded radiant electric fires
- Radiators draped with clothing, preventing a free flow of hot air and thus building up heat
- Cigarette ends in wastepaper bins

- Inflammable liquids or other substances exposed to heat
- Obstructions in corridors and gangways
- Worn or raised edges on carpets
- Use of furniture as substitutes for stepladders
- Inadequate lighting
- Filing cabinets with bottom drawers left open, or with too many upper drawers extended at the same time (causing toppling)
- Unacceptable level of noise, causing irritation and lack of concentration

5.9 Did you know?

1. Anthropometrics is the study of human measurements and movements necessary for fitting furniture to the maximum number of users.

2. The British Standards Institution prepare and promulgate national standards compiled for various products, e.g., building, textile, chemical, and engineering. Its technical committees consult with representatives of industry, the professions, government departments, consumer interests, etc. Standards are adopted voluntarily by users; except where safety or health are at stake, they are not enforced by legislation. They include recommendations about processes of manufacture and testing, dimensions, standards of performance and quality, safety, and terms and symbols used. They are reviewed after five years, or sooner if appropriate.

3. The Kitemark on a product indicates that the article has been made to a British Standard specification, and that it has been proved by independent testing to reach that standard.

4. The BEAB mark on domestic electrical appliances serves a similar purpose. Such products have been certified by the British Electrical Approvals Board, which collaborates with the British Standards Institution in formulating the standards concerned.

5. Some offices install ducts above ceilings which generate a low, background sound (white noise) masking conversations and noise from machines.

Activities

1. Open-plan design is now commonplace. Suggest reasons why many companies prefer this to cellular office design. Why may the introduction of the new technology have accelerated the adoption of open-plan design?

2. A workstation for an electronic office consists of considerably more than a desk. Seating, lighting, wiring, acoustics, storage capacity must also be given consideration to enable the operator to work efficiently. Briefly describe a modern workstation, designed to safeguard the operator's health and comfort. (LCCI, PSC, IP)

3. A secretary/receptionist's room is to be planned and furnished. The room is square, fairly small, and has one window. There is one door leading from the outside corridor and another giving access to the boss's room. The secretary will be expected to type, deal with the telephone, and do some filing, as well as receive visitors, who may have to wait in her office. Design a suitable layout and suggest appropriate furniture and furnishings.

4. You have been employed for a month as a temporary shorthand-typist with a small firm which finds it extremely difficult to recruit and keep staff. You believe that the poor working conditions are to blame. On leaving the firm, you write a tactful letter to the employer, Mr Pincher, setting out your chief complaints and reminding him of his obligations under current legislation.

5. You have just been appointed Safety Representative for your office which is situated on the fifth floor of a modern office block. You are concerned that there has not been a fire drill during the past year and that there are no instructions to employees in the event of a fire.

(a) Give reasons why fire drills are necessary.

(b) Draft a notice which can be placed on the office notice-board outlining the action to be taken when:

(i) a fire is discovered by an employee and
(ii) the fire alarm is heard. (LCCI, SSC)

6. A junior in your department comes to you badly shaken by an electric shock. Your employer is out on business for the day. (a) On learning of the accident, what steps would you take immediately? (b) Who will need to be notified of the accident, now or later? (c) Draft instructions for your employer to circulate within the department on the safe handling and operation of electric equipment. (LCCI, PSC)

7. What basic information should be given to a new employee in relation to safety in the office? (LCCI, PSC)

8. As Secretary to the Office Services Manager you have just been elected Safety Representative for your Department. The Department is situated on the eighth floor of a modern office block and employs sixty people who work in the following sections:

(a) General Administration Office
(b) Printing Department
(c) Stationery Stores
(d) Maintenance Room
(e) Filing Room

Explain the sort of safety problems which you might expect to encounter within the Department and any precautions that you feel would be necessary in order to ensure a safe place of work. (LCCI, SSC)

9. Your Manager has asked you to inspect the new branch office and to report on possible hazards to health and safety. List the points for which you would look when preparing your report. (LCCI, PSC)

10. A mail-order business has found it necessary through business expansion to move its office premises to a larger building in the vicinity of the old premises. The decision has been made to change from cellular (closed) to open-plan office layout for most of the personnel other than senior management: it is considered that this is suited to the structure of the building and affords certain advantages in terms of work flow.

(a) In what specific ways might the new form of layout and its effects compare with the old?
(b) Identify THREE safety factors which might need to be taken into account.
(c) Suggest, with reasons, FOUR activities/office units that might better remain housed in individual offices.
(d) How might the new layout affect the relationship between supervisors and (i) their own staff (ii) the staff in other departments? (RSA, DPA)

Group activities

11. Study Figures 5.1 and 5.2 and discuss the advantages and/or disadvantages resulting from the adoption of the open-plan office.

12. Using paper or cardboard templates to represent the rough outline of the following items of furniture and equipment, plan on an A4 sheet a typing centre for eight typists and a supervisor.

8 typists' desks	1 collating table
8 typists' tables	1 electric ink duplicator
1 supervisor's desk	2 filing cabinets
10 chairs	1 stationery cupboard
1 telephone table	1 bookshelf for reference books
	1 wardrobe/cupboard for coats

The plan devised could be a joint one. If individual plans are made, compare and contrast the different layouts adopted. Would the typist be working in a reasonably convenient and safe environment in every case?

PART THREE

Office services and the secretary

6
Office supplies

As a secretary you may be required to look after stationery and other office supplies. You should be able to do this in the most efficient way.

6.1 In a nutshell: Hints on control and ordering of office supplies

- Keep stocks clean, and stack in an orderly and logical fashion.
- Label exact contents of packets.
- Arrange small items so that all are easily visible.
- Label shelves.
- Ensure that no unauthorized person has access to supplies.
- Distribute supplies on stipulated days only.
- Accept written and signed requisitions only (stating the item and amount wanted, for whom required, and countersigned by a responsible person).
- Keep accurate records of stock held, e.g., record cards or sheets (see Figure 6.1).

STOCK RECORD CARD					
Item .... Min. level .... Max. level					
Suppliers .... Ref. no.					
.... Shelf no.					
Date	Order no.	Quantity received	Quantity issued	To whom issued	Balance

Figure 6.1 Example of a stock record card.

6.1   In a nutshell (*continued*)

- Adjust records, both when distributing and taking in supplies.
- Check all stock at least once a year.
- Set aside regular days for stock ordering.
- Decide minimum levels below which stock must not fall before reordering and maximum levels to be held at any one time.
- Refer to records to decide how much to reorder at a time.
- Remember that ordering too little means stocks run out quickly and fresh orders must be made.
- Remember that ordering too much may lead to waste, deterioration and pressure on space.
- (Small organization) Type order forms or write to outside suppliers.
- (Small organization) Sign the orders yourself and get your boss's countersignature, if necessary.
- (Small organization) Keep a carbon copy to check stock when it arrives.
- (Large organization) Send in a regular requisition on the required day to the central supplies section.
- (Large organization) Sign the requisition yourself and get your boss's countersignature if necessary.
- (Large organization) Keep a carbon copy to check stock when it arrives.

6.2   Stocktaking

Keeping accurate records reduces the need for the physical checking of stock. However, stocktaking is usually necessary at least once a year, to provide not only a check on the record-keeping but also a valuation of the stock held, for inclusion in the company's accounts. Twice-yearly or quarterly stocktaking at specified times may be preferred; spot checks on random items to discourage pilfering and detect inefficient methods may also be carried out.

Continuous stocktaking throughout the year may be adopted. With computerized systems, stock records are automatically adjusted after each buying or selling transaction, to provide up-to-date balances. When required, the stock balances for all items held can be printed out to supply an inventory or statement of stock in hand, which can be quickly valued and become part of the company's assets.

6.3   Stationery

(a)   Paper

(i) *Paper for correspondence*   Different weights and qualities are obtainable. Thinner paper is desirable when a large number of carbon copies is required or when it is important to cut down the weight of postal packets, e.g., when sending airmail letters. *Bond* paper is used for top copies, printed letterheads and continuation sheets. *Bank* paper is thinner but tough and suitable for file copies. Many different colours are available.

(ii) *International paper sizes*   The most common sizes are as follows:

	mm			mm
A0	841 × 1189		A4	210 × 297
A1	594 × 841		A5	148 × 210
A2	420 × 594		A6	105 × 148
A3	297 × 420		A7	74 × 105

(See Figure 6.2)

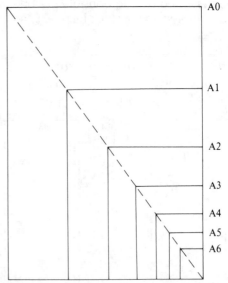

Figure 6.2   Every sheet within the international system is the same rectangular shape: whatever its size it remains in proportion to all the other sizes (see also **9.2**: reduction facilities in copiers).

(b) Envelopes

(i) *Types available* *Banker* envelopes have the flap on the longer side and *pocket* envelopes have the flap on the shorter side. The flap end measurement is quoted last. *Window* envelopes have a cut-out panel covered with transparent material through which the address on the document inside can be read. *Aperture* envelopes are similar to window envelopes, but the panels are not covered. They are not included in the POP range (see below). Care should be taken to fold the contents of both window and aperture envelopes so that they exactly fit. This prevents the contents shifting and the address being obscured. *Printed paper* envelopes are not sealed and have flaps which tuck in or are fastened by metal clips. *Polythene envelopes* are tougher and lighter than paper envelopes. They may be transparent or overprinted, with an opaque area for the address and stamp. *Internal envelopes* are reusable envelopes designed for sending mail within an organization. They are usually ungummed, with flaps tucked in or fastened with string and washer. Some are perforated to allow the contents to be detected. Often, space is provided in up to 20 or 30 'boxes' across the face for the names of sender and recipient, these being crossed through when the transaction is completed.

(ii) *Post Office Preferred (POP) range* The Post Office sorting machines are designed to take envelopes within a certain range of sizes only, those outside it being subject to delay, as they must be sorted manually. The maximum size is 120 mm × 235 mm and the minimum 90 mm × 140 mm. The longer side must measure at least 1.4 times the shorter side. The *POP* range should be used for flat letters but it does not apply to heavier or bulkier letters and packets.

(iii) *International envelope sizes* The following

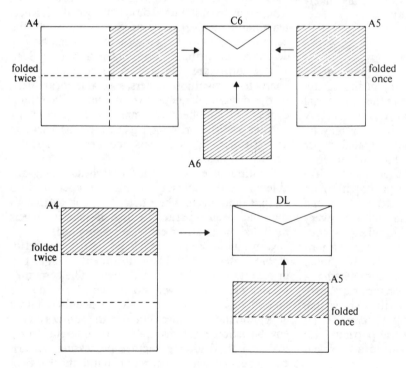

6.3 Examples of compatibility of International Organization for Standardization (ISO) envelope and paper sizes.

international envelope sizes for official, commercial, and professional use are recommended in BS 4264 (1976) to replace ultimately the existing wide variety of envelopes of only slightly different sizes.

	mm	
*DL	110 × 220	
*C6	114 × 162	} bankers
C5	162 × 229	

	mm	
*C6	162 × 114	
*DL	220 × 110	
C5	229 × 162	} pocket
B5	250 × 176	
C4	324 × 229	

*Within the POP range.

(iv) *Traditional envelope sizes*   As well as international sizes, envelopes of many and varied traditional dimensions are still available and likely to remain so if demand continues.

(c)   Stationery sets

Where sets of forms are required these can be prepared in one typing or printing using ready-packed sets. Each form in a set bears the same serial number but may be in a different colour for easy distinction. Thin 'one-time' carbon paper may be already interleaved, or chemically treated paper needing no carbon may be used which, when typed on, yields an impression on the sheet below. (Take care not to confuse this carbonless paper with plain paper when making handwritten entries!) Although the details typed will be the same in each case, every form in a set need not be identical in other respects, but may be preprinted with different explanations and instructions to suit its purpose. Additional columns may appear on some, to be completed at a later stage; or a column, for example, for prices, may be blocked out so that these details will not be visible when the sheet is reproduced. 'Spot' carbon is an alternative: by this method only the portions of a document that need to be reproduced are backed with a carbon coating.

Sets may be produced in a continuous form, with perforations between the sets, thus saving constant insertion, interleaving and ejection of documents by the typist. When typing is complete, the set is torn off at a perforation and the next set brought into position. On some, individual parts can be removed, if desired, without breaking the set. A special frame on the machine is needed to support continuous stationery, which may be supplied either in rolls or folded concertina-fashion. Attachments enable the sets to be fed in and aligned automatically to the desired typing line.

(d)   Stationery for computer and word processing systems

Stationery for computer printout is in continuous form, edged by sprocket holes to hold it on the printer tractor mechanism. Listing paper is available plain or ruled in numbered staves to facilitate reference to the data when printed. Widths usually range from 215 to 450 mm. It may be supplied in multi-part sets.

Continuous sets of preprinted forms are available. These may be of standard design or specially formatted to suit the particular program controlling the computer printout. Preset form layouts can also be designed for printout onto microfilm (see **8.9**). Where forms are intended to be read by optical character recognition readers, special fonts are used in the design. Magnetic ink character recognition codes and numbers are applied to documents needing security printing, e.g., continuous warrants and cheques. Special logos and designs can also be incorporated.

Continuous envelopes and letterheads are available for word processing systems, with perforations so fine that sheets when detached look as though they had been separately cut. Self-adhesive labels mounted on a carrier can also be supplied.

Continuous, sealed envelopes can be provided, already inserted with blank documents such as pay or remittance advices or statements. The computer printer prints selectively on the envelope and the insertions at one pass, i.e., all the details required appear on the enclosures but only the address on the envelope. Some systems enable additional enclosures to be inserted after computer processing. Return envelopes can also be incorporated into the design of the outgoing envelope, e.g., in sales promotion mailings.

6.4 Checklist: A miscellany of useful items to keep in stock

Adhesive labels (plain or printed with return address; separate or continuous)
Adhesive tape and dispensers
Blotting paper
Brown paper
Bubble film (for protective packing)
Carbon film (different weights/sizes for single copies and manifolding)
Cardboard
Clipboards (working papers clipped to writing surface)
Clips (paper and bulldog)
Compliment slips (printed with sender's status and address, to accompany enclosures in place of letter)
Correcting fluids/strips
Correcting tapes
Drawing pins
Dust covers
Elastic bands
Envelopes (all sizes)
Erasers
Fasteners (with long stems)
File folders
File reinforcers
Glue
Index cards
Memorandum pads (different sizes, some NCR)
Padded bags (to post books, etc.).
Paper (different sizes and quality)
Pencils
Pencil sharpeners
Pens (assorted colours)
Pins
Postcards (plain, headed with/without standard message)
Rubber stamps (with separate/integrated inkpads)
Rulers
Scissors
Shorthand notebooks
Staples
String
Telephone message pads
Telex message pads
Telex paper rolls
Typewriter cleaning materials
Typewriter ribbons
Word processor printer ribbons

6.5 Typewriter and word processing supplies

(a) Cleaning materials

(i) *For typewriters* These include *long-handled brushes*, used for cleaning the inner parts, and a number of devices for cleaning typefaces of typebar machines, e.g., *stiff-bristled brushes*, pieces of *plastic typecleaner* which can be rolled across the typefaces, *impregnated sheets* which release cleaning fluid on the typeface when typed on, *brushes* moistened by cleaning fluid released from a container attached.

(ii) *For word processor printers and single-element typewriters* Kits are available containing tubes of fluid for cleaning print-heads and elements, pads impregnated with fluid for cleaning the platen (to prevent the paper slipping), and buffing cloths.

(iii) *For floppy disks* Disposable cleaning disks, impregnated with cleaning fluid, may be inserted into the disk drive; as it is set in motion the disk rotates, cleaning the recording head.

(iv) *For word processor screens* Soft cotton cloths or pads are suitable for cleaning screens, provided they are free of lint.

(b) Print-heads

These may be cylinder heads, daisy wheels or thimbles (see also **11.9**) made of plastic or metal and bearing a suitable range of characters in a variety of styles, pitches and spacing. They may be stored in vinyl binders for protection.

(c) Typewriter correcting materials

Erasers may be *round* or *octagonal*, with a hard, gritty layer sandwiched between softer ones: they must be held so that the middle layer is in contact with the error. In *pencil-shaped* erasers, rubber forms the 'lead', and must be trimmed regularly. *Eraser shields* are like small stencils, made of metal, plastic or cellulose. Words or single characters can be erased through the cut-out sections without disturbing surrounding areas of the page. *Obliterating strips* are backed with a chalky substance to cover up errors. Different kinds are available for top and carbon copies and for airmail paper. *Correcting fluid* can be brushed over an error and the correct character substituted when the fluid has dried. Fluid can be applied from applicators resembling marker or ball-point pens. Various shades are available to match tinted paper.

For correcting ribbons see *(d)* below.

(d)   Ribbons

Typewriter ribbons may be made of *fabric* (silk, nylon or cotton): they are durable but the imprint becomes fainter as the ribbon wears. Ribbons made of *carbon* or *plastic film* give a very clear imprint especially suitable for quality correspondence. Some of these are *single-strike* (non-reversible). *Multi-strike* ribbons are reversible and can therefore be used again.

Ribbons may be supplied in one colour (*mono-chrome*), e.g., black, brown, blue, red, etc., or in two colours (*bi-chrome*).

Correctable ribbons may have an adhesive coating which lifts the incorrect character from the page, or they may deposit a chalky substance over the error.

Special-purpose ribbons include *OCR* ribbons used to produce text which is to be read directly by computer (see **11.10**, and *thermal* (heat-sensitive) ribbons, used with thermal transfer process printers.

Ribbons in *cartridges* are used on printers and on many typewriters. They are easier to load than those typewriter ribbons supplied on a *spool* and needing to be threaded by the typist for fastening to a second spool already on the machine.

When buying a ribbon, note the number of strikes quoted, as this indicates the ribbon's capacity better than the length. It is also important to ensure that the ribbon will be compatible with the typewriter or printer concerned. The machine manufacturer's own brand is certain to be suitable though perhaps relatively expensive. Alternatives to these may be found in a *Ribbon Grouping Guide* published by the Office Machines and Equipment Federation in conjunction with the Carbon and Ribbon Manufacturers' Association.

6.6   Stationery handling equipment

(a)   For general use

(i) *Binding machines*   Documents can be bound together to form booklets by means of manual or electric machines. The papers and the covers are perforated with holes set close together and up to about two dozen in number, and joined with spiral plastic binding. Other machines bind the edges of documents with reinforcing self-adhesive cloth, or plastic or paper tape.

(ii) *Crimpers*   Crimpers are devices which fasten papers together by pleating and folding them at one corner. The sheets can be pulled apart quite easily, but not accidentally. No staples are required, and so a stack of sheets will lie quite flat, not raised at the corners as when stapled.

(iii) *Guillotines*   These are devices for cutting or trimming paper. Some models will cut only one or a very few sheets at a time, while electric versions can deal with thicknesses of several centimetres. Some clamp and cut the paper in one operation. It is usual for adjustments to be possible to ensure that paper is cut accurately to the size required. A safety guard should be fitted round the knife.

(iv) *Laminators*   These protect valuable or frequently handled documents from becoming torn or dirty by applying a transparent film to both sides of the sheets (see also **9.2** *(d)*: thermal copiers).

(v) *Perforators*   Hand-punches are available that will punch a single hole and others that will punch double holes at adjustable intervals in the margins of sheets of paper. Electric models can handle greater thicknesses of paper than manual ones. *Paper drills* can drill up to four holes at a time at adjustable intervals in paper up to 2.5 cm thick. *Reinforcing punches* can strengthen holes as they are punched with paper, cloth or plastic rings, and *eyeletters* with more durable metal reinforcers called 'eyelets'.

(vi) *Shredders*   These reduce documents to paper shavings, often a more convenient method of destruction than burning, and safer where confidential papers are concerned than disposal in wastepaper baskets (see also **24.4** (a) (iv)).

(vii) *Staplers*   These can be used to fasten together sheets of paper. The fastening is secure, but can be undone by using the blade of a knife or scissors, or a *staple remover*, which is sometimes built into the stapler. Desk models are mounted on a base, and smaller versions are held like pliers, facilitating access to files and narrow openings. Staplers vary greatly in the thicknesses of paper they can handle (some heavy-duty ones taking up to 200 sheets at a time). They can be operated by hand, or electrically for long runs of work to be done at high speed.

(viii) *Tape and label printers* These emboss characters on rolls of self-adhesive PVC tape, contained in cassettes. The tape is cut off into strips by pressing a button, and can then be pulled off its backing strip.

(b) For continuous stationery

(i) *Bursters* These machines will separate and stack continuous forms or envelopes completed by computer. Some bursters will separate continuous forms printed side by side, detach them, and stack them in sequence. *Imprinter-bursters* will also print out on each form a signature, address or message prepared on a printing plate attached to the machine.

(ii) *Decollators* These machines will separate sets of forms and run off the interleaving carbon onto a spool for later disposal.

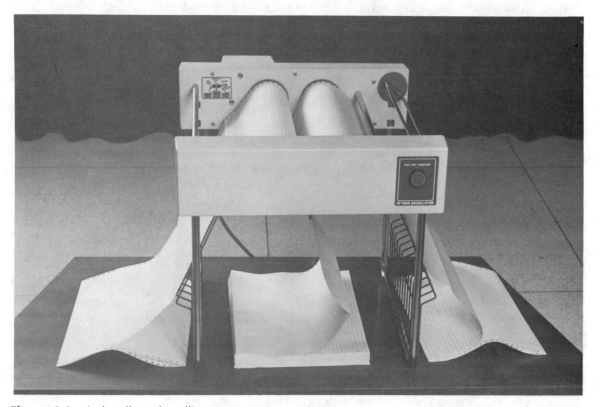

Figure 6.4 A decollator handling a two-part set of carbonless sheets. (Courtesy of Moore Paragon UK Ltd)

6.7 Did you know?

1. When quoting paper sizes, you should give the width first.

2. The purpose of the International Organization for Standardization (ISO), of which the British Standards Institution is a member, is to reach international agreement on standards in commerce and industry.

3. Metric measurements proceed in tens, and thus lend themselves to the use of decimals in arithmetic.

4. The following are prefixes used in the SI system.

mega	=	1 million times		deci	=	one-tenth of
kilo	=	1 thousand times		centi	=	one-hundredth of
hecto	=	1 hundred times		milli	=	one-thousandth of
deca	=	10 times		micro	=	one-millionth of

5. The following are some *approximate equivalents:*

½ litre is about 1 pint   2½ centimetres are about 1 inch
30 grams are about 1 ounce   1 kilometre is about 1000 yards

6. It is possible to buy typewriter ribbon economically in bulk. By means of an electric or manual dispenser, ribbon can be wound onto an empty spool, pierced and eyeletted.

7. BS 5729 *Guide to Stock Control* sets out guidelines for efficient stock control systems.

8. Message sheets are available with an adhesive strip which holds to the desk surface.

Activities

1. Draft and type (a) a stationery requisition form (b) a stationery stock card, suitable for use within a small firm using a central stock issuing system.

2. Your departmental manager requires an inventory of all the furniture, fittings, and equipment in the department. Draft and type a suitable form which staff can use to fill in details and from which the inventory can be compiled.

3. You are responsible for ordering, monitoring and storing the company's stationery. Describe fully how you would go about such tasks. (LCCI, PSC)

4. As secretary in a small firm you are responsible for ordering and handing out stationery. All records have previously been kept in your head, but after a short illness and time away from the office, you find that, after two weeks, you are running out of some stock. This has meant several urgent trips to a local stationer to buy essential items. Your employer is extremely annoyed as this proves costly and time-wasting. He has asked you to ensure that this does not happen in the future. What would you do to avoid a recurrence of this situation? (PEI, Sec. Prac. Inter.)

5. You are about to carry out the annual stock-taking of the stationery and office supplies held in your department's stockroom. (a) Describe how you would organize this task. (b) Compile the memo you would send to the secretaries in each section, notifying them of those arrangements which will affect them.

6. MEMORANDUM

To: Supervisor, Reprographics
From: Office Services Manager
Subject: Equipment (ref: Your requisition No 5)
          Date: 3 June 1983

We have been advised that the following items will be delivered during next week:

1	electric binding machine
1	crimper
1	electric shredder
1	50 mm guillotine
1	laminator
1	20 page collator
1	burster
1	electric perforator
100	reams A4 bond paper
100	reams A4 bank paper

Write a short paragraph on each of the above items to show how each might be used. (LCCI, SSC)

7. Your company is setting up a secretarial services centre, using mainly word processors and

electronic typewriters, but also some electric typewriters. Prepare a list of the supplies that will be needed.

8. As an office supervisor subject to budget constraints suggest FIVE means by which you might achieve an effective and efficient control of stationery within your unit. (RSA, DPA)

9. **Group activity** Divide into small groups to discuss possible systems for the ordering and control of supplies in your typing room. Each group should submit a report to the class tutor on the particular system it advocates.

7
Dealing with the mail

As a secretary within an organization you are required to deal with the mail on a day-to-day basis. It is very important that this is done correctly and quickly.

7.1 In a nutshell: Handling incoming mail in a small organization

- Sort the unopened mail into batches—sealed, unsealed (if any), and postcards, packets, and parcels.
- Follow security routine in case of suspicious-looking packets (see **24.4**).
- Place items marked 'Private', 'Personal' or 'Confidential' unopened in executives' sorting trays.
- Face up sealed envelopes, and slit tops with paper knife.
- Remove and unfold contents.
- Keep all envelopes for a day or two in case of queries.
- Pin enclosures to accompanying letters.
- Date-stamp each letter clearly.
- Check to see enclosures indicated are present and attach note of any omissions.
- Check that money enclosures are for correct sums and that cheques and postal orders, etc., are properly made out.
- Enter details in remittances book, e.g., date, amount, type of remittance, name of sender.
- Sign remittances book and obtain countersignature.
- Do not separate remittances from covering letters.
- Enter details of registered mail—e.g., date, name of sender and label number—in registered mail book.
- Keep a record of telemessages and overseas telegrams received.
- Date-stamp postcards and any unsealed mail.
- Sort and distribute all correspondence to persons concerned placing most urgent documents on top of the appropriate pile. If the letters are linked with files of the previous correspondence, present the files in order of priority.
- Where a letter concerns more than one person, take copies so that each has one, or attach to the original letter a circulation slip (or route slip) bearing their names in order of priority, and send it to each in turn.
- Pin any torn or RPP (Returned Postal Packet) envelopes to their letters, for investigation or comment. If referred to the post office they may wish to see the condition in which the packet arrived.
- Undo postal packets and parcels, keeping wrappings clear of other documents.
- Check off against orders items received in parcels, or list for future checking.

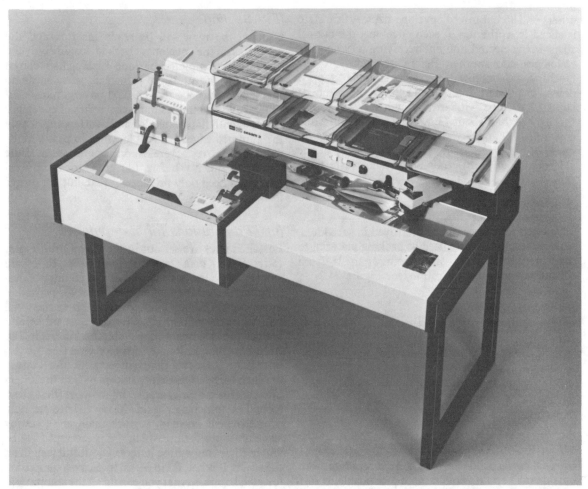

Figure 7.1 Incoming mail handling system. The feed hopper on the left holds the unsorted envelopes. These are then automatically transported one at a time to cutters which slit them on one long and one short side. The envelope then moves to suction cups which pull the front and back apart, enabling the operator to remove the contents easily. The inside of the envelope is illuminated, reducing the risk of leaving anything inside. A combined electric stapler and dater may then be used. The trays for the sorted mail are within easy reach of the operator. (Courtesy of C. P. Bourg Ltd)

7.2 Incoming mail in a large organization

The mail may arrive in bags delivered by Post Office van. Parcels and packets will probably be placed on trolleys in the mailroom and wheeled to a special table, where they are dealt with separately. The mail needs to be sorted, opened and distributed in a large organization on similar principles to those in a small one but as the volume is much greater more staff have to be employed and machines may be brought in to help them.

(a) Letter opening machines
These may be manually, electrically, or battery-operated and work much faster than manual methods. For some machines, presorting into batches according to size and shape is necessary, but

57

others will accept mixed envelope sizes. A thin strip is sliced from the top of each envelope, the cut-off strips being ejected into one receiving tray and the envelopes into another. Before insertion into the machine, the contents of envelopes should be tapped down, to prevent damage. Machines can often be adjusted to cope with extra tough envelopes, but those more than about 13 mm thick or of abnormal size must be opened by hand. Other types of machine merely cut a slit very close to the top of one side of the envelope, and there is no waste from these.

(b)   Shredders

Unwanted envelopes can be destroyed in shredders, and the resulting waste used as packing material to prevent the contents of outgoing parcels from shifting about. For illustration, see Figure 24.2.

(c)   Sorting devices

Sorters with hinged, labelled flaps may be used to hold letters ready for distribution. Sorting frames with pigeonholes labelled for the various executives or departments are useful in larger companies. Sorting trolleys enable mail to be dropped into labelled divisions and wheeled to the various departments for distribution.

(d)   Internal correspondence

Internal correspondence may be kept separate from outside mail and it is often more practicable to sort and distribute this a little later, when the main rush is over.

7.3   Outgoing mail in small organizations

(a)   Collection from departments

In a small organization the mailing clerk will probably fetch the mail from the executives' out-trays, or their secretaries may bring it. It is wise to stipulate convenient collection times from mid-morning onwards. By fixing a firm deadline near the end of the afternoon, it is possible to get executives to sign their letters in good time and so avoid a last-minute rush both in the office and at the post office.

(b)   Sealing

Usually, the mail will be ready inserted and the addresses on the envelopes checked, leaving only the sealing and stamping to be done. Licking flaps can be unpleasant and unhealthy. Instead, you can damp the flaps by passing them quickly over a moistened roller. A fast method is to place a series of envelopes in a row, with flaps extended and overlapping; if only the gummed edges are visible, you can pass a moistened brush over several in one operation. Seal the envelopes quickly before the gum dries. Self-seal envelopes need only pressure to seal, but are dearer to buy.

(c)   Preparations for stamping

Postal charges are set out in the *Royal Mail Postal Rates Inland and Overseas Compendia*. Rates are calculated on the basis of weight and country of destination. If mail is overstamped, money is wasted: if under-stamped even a letter marked first class will be treated as second class by the post office and double the deficiency is payable by the recipient. Accurate letter scales are therefore vital (see **7.4** (b)) but after a little experience it becomes unnecessary to weigh each letter. Before stamping, sort the letters into categories: for example, inland post (first class, second class, larger and heavier letters, etc.), overseas mail (airmail, surface mail, etc.), setting aside air letter forms, which are prestamped. Then you need put only those letters of doubtful weight on the scales. It is helpful to pencil in the postage needed for such letters, so that you can do all the stamping at one operation without breaking off to weigh letters or look up postage rates. Typists can help, too, by typing a prearranged symbol on the corners of envelopes going to unusual destinations or needing special treatment—e.g., urgent dispatch. Sometimes a stamp is needed for an envelope enclosed in a letter, and a procedure must be devised by which the mailing clerk's attention is drawn to this, perhaps by the envelope in question being clipped to the flap of the outer one.

(d)   Stamping

(i) *By hand*   Adhesive stamps may be affixed manually by tearing off a strip and moistening the whole length on a damping pad. Then press the stamp firmly on the envelope.

(ii) *Stamp dispensers* Stamp dispensers are helpful. As this hand device is operated, stamps are broken off in turn from a roll of stamps inside it. Each is moistened by being passed over a damp pad and then ejected. It can be used to stamp documents as well as envelopes.

(e) Buying stamps

Take care to buy sufficient stamps of each denomination. When in doubt, buy stamps of lower denominations, as these can always be combined to stamp the more expensive items. Keep some cash in your stamp box to pay for unforeseen items like parcels or registered envelopes. Stamps should be kept in a safe place so that none are lost or torn.

(f) Postage book

A postage book records the exact amount spent on postage of all items (inland and overseas letters, aerogrammes, parcels and registered mail) and the total, plus cash in hand, must balance with the money withdrawn from the petty cash for the purpose. It is a very time-consuming record to keep and suitable only for very small firms. Keep a wary eye on staff members who buy stamps from you for their personal use; this is in order, provided they give you the exact money in exchange. A postage book also provides a check on whether or not a particular letter was dispatched on a certain day, as often the name and town of the recipient are recorded under the date of dispatch, as well as the postage. However, some items are entered as bulk totals only—e.g., 12 Finance Committee minutes @ Xp = XXp.

7.4 Outgoing mail in large organizations

(a) Collection from departments

Mail for dispatch may be collected from departments and taken to the mailroom by juniors or messengers at regular intervals throughout the day, or—if the volume is sufficient—collection boxes may be installed at convenient points throughout the premises into which staff can drop letters as completed.

(b) Machines and equipment

Some or all of the following may be used:

(i) *Scales* The dials of some letter scales are fitted with charts setting out the postage rates for the main categories of mail. The postage charges are then easily calculated as the pointer registers the weight of each item. Such charts must, of course, be changed if the rates alter. They have to be fitted by the manufacturers, as great precision is necessary.

Electronic scales (see Figure 7.2) show on a digital display the exact weight of items placed on them. The user keys in the postal service required. An audible signal confirms the machine has accepted the rate, and the display confirms the service selected. The machine then calculates the cost from the appropriate postal rate stored in memory, and displays the result. A new memory chip is supplied by the manufacturer when rates change. If the packet could be sent at a cheaper rate the operator is warned by signals from the keyboard and on the display.

(ii) *Sealers* These may be incorporated into postage meter machines (see (iii) below) or may be larger, electric machines which open the flaps of envelopes as they pass from the stack under a moistened brush, seal them, and stack them again.

(iii) *Franking and postage meter machines* These print on each envelope the denomination selected and an optional slogan or return address. Adhesive stamps are therefore not required. Labels are franked for bulky items that cannot pass through the machine. An ascending meter records the units of postage used and a descending meter the amount of credit in hand. At the end of the day the total spent can therefore be compared with the amount of credit in hand. A control card showing these readings must be sent to the post office weekly. More credit is obtained by paying in a further sum to the post office in cash or by cheque. With some systems, value cards may be bought in set denominations from the post office bearing details of the amount of credit paid for. The card is inserted into the machine and when that sum has been exhausted the card is taken to the post office and another one inserted recording the fresh payment. Some older machines have a detachable meter, which must be presented at the post office for resetting. In some areas, post office staff call on companies for the purpose. The machines can be locked to prevent unauthorized use, and the date changed at the end of the day; adhesive stamps must therefore be used on letters presented after this has been done.

A computerized remote meter resetting system enables users of specially adapted postage meters to obtain further credit by Datel link with the manufacturer's computer. Details of the account number, meter number and register readings are communicated to the computer, which then issues a unique setting code number. When keyed into the postage meter this operates a combination lock, releasing the meter to issue more credit. The post office is paid by the manufacturer, who issues statements of account to users for payment.

The meter readings on franking machines provide a financial record of postage used, making a postage book unnecessary. With some machines it is possible to print out on a tally roll the postage for each item; if a departmental code is included against each, postage charges can be analysed departmentally.

Microchip-controlled machines (see Figure 7.2) remind the user to change the date and emit a warning signal when credit is getting low or when a high postage rate has been entered. The amounts and the number of items passed through the machine are automatically logged. Batch totals, for example of one department's mailings, are stored and called up on a read-out display when needed.

Electronic franking machines may be linked with electronic scales so that the postage value recorded on the scales is automatically franked on the envelope. Automatic feeding-in of envelopes may be provided often from the bottom of the stack so that more can be easily added. Some machines have a flexible envelope platform which aligns to the shape of bulky envelopes to enable envelopes of most thicknesses to be franked. Sealing devices may be incorporated into the machine to allow the envelopes to be franked and sealed automatically.

Machines are bought or hired from private manufacturers, who must obtain authority from the post office for their use, and supply their customers with a slip giving full particulars of the machine; copies of this detail slip are sent to the post office in notification. Machines must be inspected and maintained by the manufacturers at least twice every six months.

Franked mail must be faced up, segregated into first and second class, and tied in bundles according to prescribed regulations. It must normally be taken · to a designated post office for posting, although late-posted individual items, if enclosed in special large envelopes available from manufacturers, can be posted in agreed post boxes. Franked mail does not have to be faced and cancelled at the post office and so may be sorted sooner than other mail.

(iv) *Sorting frames*   Sorting frames are helpful for classifying different groups of outgoing mail, prior to stamping or posting—e.g., first class, second class, London, country and abroad, airmail, packets and parcels.

(v) *Mailbag fitments*   Mailbag fitments may be in the form of hooks from which bags can be suspended, or frames on wheels that hold bags open ready for bundles of mail.

(c)   Mailroom organization

The layout of a mailroom should take into account the flow of work: equipment should be placed in the right sequence, and staff should not have to walk about excessively or get in one another's way. A well-planned mailroom is shown in Figure 7.3.

7.5   Dispatching circulars and bulk mailings in a small organization

(a)   Collating

Duplicated documents will be arranged in piles, one for each page, on a table. If possible, place them within comfortable arm's reach, as you can then sit to do the job. However, if you have a lot of material to collate you may find it necessary to stand and this can be very tiring.

If you wear a rubber finger, this will help to separate the top sheet from the rest of each pile. Assemble these sheets in order in front of you to form a complete set. After jogging the set until the edges are even, you can then staple it. As you must do this close to the edge so that the pages can easily be turned over, the top left-hand corner is a suitable place. To allow for stapling, the reverse sides of double-sided sheets are often typed with a right-hand margin wider than usual. Look out for blank sheets or spoiled copies that must be withdrawn from sets.

Collating can be greatly speeded up if you arrange the piles in a convenient number order, especially if you pick up the sheets with both hands simultaneously. If you place the piles upside down—i.e., with the top edges nearest you, the assembled sets are in the best position for stapling: you do not have to reach over to

Figure 7.2 Electronic postal scales and franking machine. The scales on the left are displaying the weight and postage rate of the packet placed on them. The groups of keys on the touch-sensitive keyboard are headed: INLAND, EUROPE (SURFACE and AIR), OUTSIDE EUROPE (SURFACE and AIR), PARCEL COMPENSATION. Below them are keys labelled with appropriate categories of mail available, e.g., INLAND—letters, 1st class; EUROPE, AIR—letters and SURFACE—small packets; OUTSIDE EUROPE, AIR—Zone B printed papers, and SURFACE—printed papers reduced rate. At the bottom right are SERVICES available, e.g., RATE 1 REGISTERED LETTERS, ADVICE OF DELIVERY, DATAPOST, COD (cash on delivery), RECORDED DELIVERY, SWIFTAIR. The packet will not go through the franking machine on the right so franking must be done on one of the adhesive labels shown in the container. (Courtesy of Roneo Alcatel Ltd)

the farther edges and you can use greater force on the stapler.

It is important not to break the rhythm of the work. Assembling and jogging are therefore best done first, laying sets at right-angles to each other, and then the stapling all at once. If someone else can help you, one of you can collate and the other staple.

(b) Folding and inserting

This is the next step and best done in limited batches.

(c) Preparing the envelopes

(i) *Chain feeding* If the number of sets or the frequency of dispatch does not warrant the use of an addressing system, you can type envelopes more

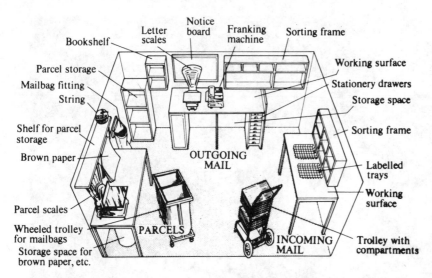

Figure 7.3   A mailing room. A well-planned layout is essential for efficiency—e.g., incoming and outgoing mail should be handled at different workstations, and parcels dealt with separately. (Courtesy of the Post Office)

quickly if you chain feed them. Before removing a typed envelope from the typewriter, drop the next in behind the platen. With one turn of the platen you can remove the typed envelope and also move the new one into the typing position.

(ii) *Continuous labels*   It is often quicker to type addresses on gummed labels in continuous form which can afterwards be torn off at the perforations provided and stuck on the envelopes. They can be passed through mechanical or manual dispensers for separating.

7.6   Dispatching circulars and bulk mailings in a large organization

In a larger company machines will be used. They may be capable of one of the following functions described, or of a combination of two or more of these, according to the money available and the amount of continuous work to be done.

(a)   Collators

These consist of divisions or stations which hold the piles of pages. Some have as many as 50 and others as few as 12. The size of papers to be collated and their thickness varies according to the dimensions of the stations. Some hold sheets to a depth of about 6 mm, while others take up to about 63 mm. In some electric machines, the top sheet from each station is ejected on a flat surface to form a ready-collated set; in others the top sheets are ejected or partially ejected for the operator to gather into sets; in manual machines the operator removes the top sheets from the convenient stations provided. In some models, the operator is warned by special devices if two pages have left the same station simultaneously or if none at all was ejected.

(b)   Joggers

These vibrate and thus jog papers placed on them into neat sets for stapling.

(c)   Perforators

These punch holes in the margins of sets for binding.

(d)   Folding machines

By adjusting these machines, different types of parallel fold can be obtained. The handling capacity varies from 500 to 1500 sheets an hour, of sizes from 5 cm to 33.5 cm in width and in length up to 107 cm. Some will fold stapled sheets, and others will perforate, score, and slit, as well as fold.

(e) Tying machines

These will tie packages and bundles of envelopes.

(f) Mailing systems

These combine a number of machines into one installation, with documents moving on from one to another in sequence. For example, collated sheets may be folded, then inserted into envelopes which are sealed and stacked. Some can insert a further sheet inside an already folded one as a second enclosure, and can skip papers not to be folded. Another type can collate material from stations incorporated in it and staple them. Envelopes are created on some machines, by folding and sealing. A system for computer-produced documents enables the correct choice of enclosures to be automatically inserted. All enclosures for one address bear special marks. A scanner recognizes them as part of the same batch and inserts them into the envelope together.

(g) Addressing machines and systems

Where mailings are sent frequently to the same persons or organizations, automatic addressing systems are helpful. They may be used not only for printing on envelopes but also on labels, postcards, invoices, statements, payslips and leaflets. Besides addressing, they are useful for printing any repetitive details.

(i) *Machines using master plates and cards* Masters are placed in a stack and pass automatically one at a time through the addressing machine's printing mechanism; here the address is printed on the envelopes as they move out from the feed tray. Masters may be marked so that the machine can pick them out for repetitive printing or skipping. *Embossed metal plates* last indefinitely; they can be embossed on the premises, using a special embossing machine, or sent to the manufacturers to do this. They print through an inked ribbon. *Foil* versions are cheaper and can be typed. A roller inked with duplicating ink is necessary to print through *stencil masters*, which give many impressions; these can be prepared on typewriters. Spirit is used to dampen *spirit masters*, typed or written with a backing of hectographic carbon and suitable for short-term use only. Typed masters may be prepared on perforated sheets and fitted into frames afterwards.

(ii) *Copying systems* Copiers can be used to print out from typed master lists on sheets or rolls of self-adhesive labels. With computerized systems, a computer can be programmed to print out in columns on continuous stationery, which is then separated into labels and applied to mail.

(iii) *Word processors* Word processors enable names and addresses stored on magnetic disk to be printed out on envelopes or incorporated into standard letters.

(iv) *Computerized address systems* These dedicated systems enable addresses to be keyed in and checked from a display, amended if necessary and stored on floppy disks. In some systems printout may be by dot matrix or daisy wheel printers on continuous adhesive labels or listed on a tally roll for reference purposes. Addresses may be indexed alphabetically and by numerical codes, allowing selective retrieval according to category required, such as by area, product, date of last order placed, etc.

Systems using thermal transfer non-impact printers print directly on envelopes through a heat-sensitive ribbon.

Figure 7.4 Computerized addressing system, using an integrated dot matrix printer and continuous labels. The display is above and to the left of the keyboard, with the disk drive to the right. (Courtesy of ASI (Addressing System International Ltd))

7.7   Reducing envelope addressing

(a)   Window envelopes

The use of these reduces the amount of addressing necessary. Only the enclosure needs to be addressed, as this is folded in such a way that the inside name and address is visible through the transparent panel.

(b)   Reusable containers

These are suitable for conveying letters between a company's head office and its branches or representatives, or between two companies in regular correspondence. They can be used for transmission within the UK and, in some cases, to and from overseas countries. Containers are made of nylon and strong enough to be used about 1500 times. They are addressed by means of plastic-coated address cards, bearing the address of one of the two organizations on one side and of the other on the reverse side. The card is inserted into a pocket on the container, protected by a transparent panel, and merely reversed for the return journey. Stamps or franked labels are inserted into a special pocket. Containers are closed by means of zip fasteners and made fast by thumb pressure on specially provided seals. Embossed seals must be used for registered mail. Openers are provided: some break the seal only, others unzip at the same time. Different styles of labelling are provided for the different postal services, e.g., first class, second class, special delivery, recorded delivery, business reply, etc., and specially designed containers are available for microfilm, books, computer tapes, cassettes, etc. Fibreboard and metal special-purpose containers are also obtainable, but not all are suitable for transmission by post.

7.8   Letter service

The Post Office still has an almost total monopoly for the collection, carrying and delivery of letters. You will find full details of its letter services set out in the *Post Office Guide* and associated leaflets. (See also Appendix I: Summary of Post Office services.)

The ordinary letter post enables letters for overseas destinations to be dispatched either by airmail or, for a lower rate of postage, by surface mail.

7.9   Parcels services

To send a parcel, a choice of methods is available to you:

(a)   Post Office

The Post Office operates a parcels service, both inland and overseas, subject to limits of size and weight, as described in the *Post Office Guide*. Parcels over the normal weight limit may be accepted under special contract terms. Overseas parcels may be sent by surface mail or airmail, and must be accompanied by a customs declaration (as explained in **7.10**). Parcels may also be sent by Datapost.

(b)   British Rail

(i) *Red Star Parcels—station to station*   This service is available from over 600 offices right across the country. Parcels handed in at a parcels point are sent on nominated trains for collection same day or overnight according to service. Charges are raised per package on a single scale according to weight. Surcharges are raised on long and bulky articles.

(ii) *Night Star—overnight delivery to the door* This is a guaranteed overnight delivery service to any address on the UK mainland. Full postal address including postcode must be quoted.

Parcels arriving on scheduled services at destinations by 0700 hours are delivered by noon the same day; those arriving before noon are delivered by 1730 hours, or money is refunded in full. Saturday morning delivery can be arranged at no extra charge. Charges are raised per consignment on a single scale according to weight to anywhere on the UK mainland. The service also covers Northern Ireland where parcels are guaranteed to be delivered next day. Surcharges are raised for long and bulky articles.

(iii) *Red Star Plus—same day delivery to the door* This operates on certain routes. Parcels arriving at destinations up to 1600 hours will be delivered same day, usually within 90 minutes of train arrival. Later deliveries can be made by special arrangement. There are restrictions in weight and size.

(iv) *Red Star Europe*   This is an overnight parcels service to 14 stations in Belgium from over 100 points in Britain. Latest acceptance times vary from station to station depending on their proximity to London (Victoria).

Charges are raised per consignment according to weight. Maximum weight per consignment is 50 kg and maximum dimensions are 90 cm × 40 cm × 40 cm.

International services operate to many other European countries.

Note All goods are carried at a limit of liability of £10 000 per tonne but for higher value consignments separate insurance may be purchased.

Special arrangements may be available to heavy volume users according to requirements, including collection.

(c) Private carriers

A variety of these services exist and they use different forms of transport (car, van or motorcycle). Some offer door-to-door collection and delivery. In some cases arrangements are made to suit the particular customer and in others scheduled services are run. A minimum collection charge is sometimes made; otherwise rates are usually based on weight, cubic capacity, and distance. Some carriers operate radio-controlled vehicles and can respond quickly to telephone requests for service. The progress of items in transit is monitored by computer in some services.

(d) Shipping and forwarding agents

These will make all the necessary arrangements for dispatch by sea or air. By sea, parcels may be transported as separate units or in containers along with others for the same destination. The latter method reduces the handling involved and thereby the risk of loss or theft. Parcels are taken by air on scheduled passenger flights, which may be specified by the customer.

7.10 Customs requirements for overseas parcels and letter packets

If you are sending articles abroad in a postal packet or parcel you must state their nature and value on a customs declaration form obtainable from the post office. This is to meet customs requirements. These forms are printed as adhesive and tie-on labels. The kind to be used in the particular circumstances is set out in the *Post Office Guide*. The *Guide* also explains whether or not a separate dispatch note must be completed.

7.11 Did you know?

1. The Post Office will arrange to collect free from customers in towns: (a) a posting of letters where these number at least 1000 or the postage totals a stipulated minimum amount, (b) 100 or more ordinary parcels ready at any one time, (c) 20 or more ordinary parcels as a regular arrangement.

2. By statute the Post Office is not legally liable for loss, damage or delay in respect of things in the post except for items lost or damaged in the registered inland postal service. However, compensation up to a stipulated maximum may be paid if it can be shown that a letter or packet sent by the ordinary mail services was lost or damaged. For further details see *Code of Practice for Postal Services*.

3. The chances of recovering a valuable item after theft may be increased if the owner has marked his or her postcode on it in invisible ink.

7.12 Useful reference books

Code of Practice for Postal Services
London Post Offices and Streets
Post Office Guide and associated leaflets
Post Offices in the United Kingdom
Postal Addresses and Index to Postcode Directories
Telephone directories

Activities

1. As secretary to the owner of a small business, your first daily task is to open the incoming mail. (a) Describe the procedure you would employ to record and direct the mail. (b) What precautions would you take when dealing with cheques, postal orders, and other enclosures? (LCCI, PSC)

2. Part of your job is to deal with the incoming mail for the firm of three partners for whom you work. How will you deal with the following:

(a) Registered letters
(b) Letters from customers containing remittances
(c) Letters marked 'Private and Confidential' or 'Personal'
(d) Letters which will need to be seen by more than one of the partners
(e) Letters from which enclosures have been omitted. (LCCI, SSC)

3. Briefly discuss under the following headings what you consider to be the benefits and problems of using franking machines:

Type and volume of outgoing mail; efficiency of the operator; distance of organization from the nearest post office; features of machines available. (LCCI, PSC)

4. (a) List the equipment you think would be suitable for a mailing room assembling and sending out a large number of circulars.
   (b) Describe briefly FOUR Post Office postal services which could be used for the issue of circulars and for mail order work. (LCCI, PSC)

5. Describe a variety of methods and equipment which might be used to reduce to a minimum the time spent on addressing envelopes. (LCCI, PSC)

6. The following questions all relate to Post Office services. Identify the service and explain how it works:

(a) Enables a letter to be sent to a Post Office for collection by a person travelling round the country

(b) Enables compensation to be claimed for an expensive item lost in the letter post
(c) Provides a current account facility
(d) Provides proof that a letter or postal packet was received by the addressee
(e) Specially printed envelopes or cards enable a company to pay the postage of potential customers. (LCCI, SSC)

7. List and explain the Post Office services that enable same day or prompt delivery.

8. Consult Appendix I and/or the current edition of the *Post Office Guide* (and supplements) to find the answers to the following questions: (a) Give the transmission times of air letters from the UK to (i) Japan (ii) Nicaragua (iii) Canada (iv) Sweden. (b) How frequent is the service and where would you find details of the postage rates in each case? (c) Under what conditions can circulars be sent abroad at a reduced rate? Does this concession apply also to the inland post? (d) Some inland postal facilities are not available for both the first class and second class letter services. Which services are available (i) for the first class letter service (ii) for the second class letter service (iii) for both services?

9. Study Figure 7.2 and the caption, and make brief notes on the services mentioned, so that you would be able to make sensible use of the postal scales.

10. You work in the sales office of a small concern which is trying to promote interest in its catalogues. You have been asked to give details of how use could be made of the Business Reply and Freepost Services offered by the Post Office. In your memo to Mr Brooks, the Campaign Officer, make sure that the difference between the two services can clearly be seen. (PEI, Sec. Prac. Inter.)

11. **Group activity** First, allocate to each member one or more of the chief Post Office postal services, as set out in Appendix I or the *Post Office Guide*. Each member of the group then compiles and types on a card five or six questions on the service(s) allocated, together with a 'Solution' card for each. A quiz can then be organized, conducted either by the tutor or by group members acting in turn as question master.

8
Filing and indexing

As a secretary you will be expected to file and retrieve correspondence and you should have an efficient system to enable you to do this as quickly and easily as possible.

8.1   In a nutshell: Running a small departmental filing system

- File regularly—preferably daily—to avoid a backlog of work, waste of time in searching for documents, and wrong decisions caused by ignorance of latest developments.
- Sort into convenient batches for filing—e.g., under letters of alphabet, numerical divisions, subjects, or geographical locations. This saves unnecessary walking and opening and shutting of cabinet drawers.
- Remove bulky and inconvenient clips and pins.
- Staple related papers, if necessary.
- Where appropriate, perforate papers in batches if sheets are to be attached to files.
- Open one cabinet drawer at a time and shut it before opening the next, to avoid accidents.
- Avoid having several upper drawers open at the same time in case the cabinet topples over.
- Arrange each sorted batch of papers into strict alphabetical (or other) order.
- Locate wanted files behind their guide cards and remove each in turn, keeping the place with a marker.
- Insert fresh material into the file (fastening if desired), in date order, placing the latest document on top.
- Neaten the papers, return the file to the cabinet and remove the marker.
- Start new files for fresh correspondents.
- Divide the contents of bulky folders into two files.
- Renew folders when these become worn.
- Do not remove files by their tabs.
- Substitute 'Out' markers for files removed from the system, giving details of title of file, borrower's name, date of removal, and space for date of return.
- Insert cross-reference cards at points where a file might be alternatively sought, directing the searcher to the file itself.
- Make a note of necessary repairs or improvements to be carried out when time permits.
- Keep your system simple and easy to follow.
- Display brief instructions so that others can maintain the system during your absence.

8.2   General principles of filing and indexing

Labelling papers, putting them away and getting them out again when wanted sound rather dull activities, but they must be done efficiently if office staff are not to be submerged beneath a sea of papers. You can compare the situation with that at home if you do not keep control of your personal possessions.

(a)   Keep and file essential documents only

Imagine that you are looking for an important letter. This is difficult to find, as you have not sorted your belongings for some time and have not thrown away trivial and ephemeral items the usefulness of which has long since passed. If you had kept less, your search would be easier.

(b)   File documents tidily, suitably and safely

When reducing your possessions to order, you would then put away neatly in suitable containers those that you decide to keep. This makes your room look tidy and pleasant to be in and also ensures that these important items are not lost, but kept safely and in good condition. You may like to lock away some confidential ones, like old diaries.

(c)   File documents accessibly

Having housed your belongings, you would naturally place the containers where you can reach them when needed. You would not keep your current address book in a box on top of a cupboard.

(d)   Index documents clearly

However convenient the place of storage, it is little use if the item you want is not clearly marked. It is frustrating to have to peer closely at an envelope in order to read the word 'Invitations' scrawled on it.

(e)   Classify documents logically

If you do not have a system by which you sort and classify papers you will never be sure where to find them. Having located your 'Invitations' envelope, you may be surprised to come across the names of the guests who attended your parents' silver wedding anniversary celebrations among those of the friends you asked to your last party.

(f)   Keep your system simple and provide instructions for using it

You may know exactly where everything is, but it would be wise to provide some sort of guide to your system, if anyone else is likely to be asked to use it. Of course, the simpler it is, the easier it should be for other people to follow it.

8.3   Keeping and filing essential documents

(a)   Discarding before filing

In many cases, where the information in an incoming letter is used and recorded elsewhere, documents can be discarded straightaway. For example, an invitation to a business lunch will be noted in your boss's diary and in your own and, later, details of useful contacts made or discussions held will be dictated and transcribed for the file. The invitation itself can then be disposed of at once. Correspondence exchanged in the process of arranging a business trip is often of no value either, once the programme is completed.

(b)   Releasing for filing

It is important to know when a document has been dealt with and is ready to be put away. Executives often have labelled trays in which they place letters to be filed, and in many organizations filing clerks are not allowed to remove documents until these have been officially released, i.e., marked with a pre-arranged symbol.

(c)   Deciding where to file

The ability to decide where a document should be filed derives from knowledge and experience when systems like subject filing (see 8.7 (c)) are used. In some cases a secretary may be able to make this decision, consulting the boss only when in doubt but in many organizations executives are responsible for indicating which file they consider to be appropriate.

(d) Regular sifting

Many organizations find it necessary to sift the contents of current files periodically to prevent overloading the system. In a large company a general policy for retention or disposal of documents, with set retention periods for different types, may be laid down and carried out by executives in conjunction with filing clerks. In a small organization an experienced secretary, conversant with all the work, may be quite capable of taking the necessary decisions, but she should never embark on such a task without first getting her boss's permission.

(e) Transferring non-current documents

It may be that some documents need to be removed from current files, but kept for possible reference. These can be placed in transfer cases, suitably indexed, and stored where they can be consulted if necessary, before eventual destruction by incinerating or shredding (see **24.4**).

8.4 Filing documents tidily, suitably and safely

(a) Folders

Folders, appropriately labelled, are used to hold related groups of papers. They may be made of manila (flexible cardboard) or plastic. Transparent wallets are useful, e.g., for travelling executives, as the contents are easily identifiable. Some folders, e.g., pocket folders, are designed to hold loose papers or bulkier items. Others enable papers to be held securely by means of threaded cord laces or flexible metal strips, or by spring grips. Ring-binders have clasps which can be opened at any point in the file. Rigid-post binders also enable papers to be removed or inserted without disturbing the rest. They have four posts passing through holes punched in the margins of the papers: two are attached to the top cover and two to the bottom cover, enabling the papers to be parted and the top cover lifted off wherever required.

(b) Furniture and equipment

(i) *Cabinets* These hold drawers in which files are placed on their spines one behind another. The drawers are pulled out, and access to the files is from the front. It is not usually practicable to have more than four drawers, as the user has to lean over the files to extract them. Besides the floor space occupied by the cabinet itself, allowance must be made when planning the layout of an office for the extra space taken up by the drawers when extended. Files can be rested on open drawers when being consulted. By means of compressor plates (see (v) below) drawers can be divided into compartments for miscellaneous storage. Cabinets can be obtained which are approached from the side, and in which files may be arranged one behind another, side by side or a combination of both. These are claimed to hold 25 per cent more than ordinary cabinets.

Drawer-shaped *card indexes* follow similar principles on a smaller scale and hold cards of various sizes from a few square centimetres upwards.

Collapsible filing drawers are made of cardboard or other lightweight material and can be assembled when required, to hold non-confidential papers needing to be retained outside the current filing system.

(ii) *Cupboards* Filing cupboards contain shelves on which files are stood on their spines side by side or suspended from them. This is known as *lateral* filing. Access is from the front of the cupboard, and as files on quite high shelves can be easily extracted, the capacity of a large cupboard can be double that of a cabinet. Cupboards can be closed when desired by roller shutters or blinds, or by retractable or folding doors, which take up little additional space in the room. Some are equipped with pull-out ledges on which files can be rested when being used. Some systems incorporate shelving of various widths so that part of the cupboard can be used for storage of miscellaneous items, such as box files, ring-binders, stencils, stationery, etc.

(iii) *Circular or rotary filing and indexing units* Such filing units may consist of tiers of carousels or turntables of files hooked onto a central column. This is really a development of lateral filing, as the files are placed side by side, and saves even more space—in some cases occupying only one-seventh of the area of a filing cabinet. The system is especially suitable for wedge-shaped files, like lever-arch or ring-binders, as the space available on the circumference is much greater than at the centre. Units may be free-standing or kept in cupboards (see Figure 8.1).

On a similar but smaller scale are tiered, horizontal wheel-shaped systems for *index cards*, attached to

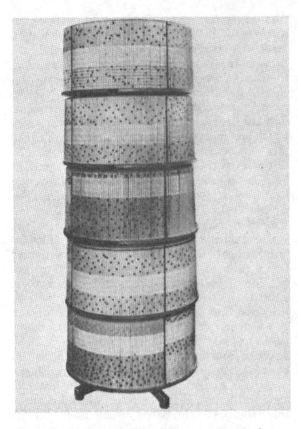

Figure 8.1 Rotary 'Vistafile' system. Note the signals on the spines. These give information about the files' contents. (Courtesy of Anson Systems, Anson Division of Gardner Mawdsley Ltd)

a spindle and rotated by the fingertips. Others form a vertical wheel, with the cards parting and falling back at the top to provide a writing surface. Some are small enough to stand on a desk, while others are freestanding or stored in cupboards.

(iv) *Box files* One type has a hinged lid which drops backwards when papers need to be removed or inserted; a smaller version exists for use as a card index. Another type has a spring clip to hold the contents in place. A lever-arch file is a ring-binder, inserted into a three-sided box, the spine of the binder forming the fourth side.

(v) *Fitments for freestanding systems* Metal supports, called compressor plates, can be slid along the floors of cabinets to the position required to keep free-standing files upright. Similar dividers are obtainable for cupboard shelves. Both types take up space.

(vi) *Fitments for suspended systems* With suspended systems wear on the spines is reduced and the files always remain upright. Suspension can be from rails at the sides of cabinets, or from rails at the front and back of cupboards or from a single central rail. Files can be suspended individually. They may also be inserted into suspended pockets, the pockets remaining in place when the files are removed. These fitments take up space, but more files can be accommodated if pockets are linked, an index strip and title holder being slid across the point of junction. When a file is removed, its absence is made obvious by the empty pocket. However, reorganization is more difficult. Much time can be wasted and irritation caused if linked pockets cannot easily be taken apart, reassembled, and retitled. Where pockets are used, any papers that fall out of files are still retained. Some pockets have extra wide gussets to accommodate bulky files or groups of folders.

(c) Protective equipment

Cabinets and cupboards can be purchased lined with special fireproof materials, which also afford protection from water, steam, and chemicals used in fire-fighting. Some are claimed to withstand the effects of falling masonry and of dropping through collapsing floors. If a room is fireproofed, ordinary equipment can be used, but this, of course, is not designed to stand up to violent impact.

For very important documents or for money, safes are obtainable with special combination locks. Otherwise, confidential papers may be locked away in ordinary cabinets and cupboards. It is possible to lock shutters and blinds. As some cabinets can be locked by a push with the thumb, it is important not to leave the vital key inside.

8.5 Filing documents accessibly

Quick access to documents is very important. Much waste can occur in central filing systems if retrieval is slow, as departments will take extra copies of documents before sending them to be filed. Generally speaking, if indexing is done well, access is quick, but some methods of housing documents are more effective than others:

(a) Filing cupboards

Cupboards give quicker access to files than cabinet drawers as once the cupboard is open there are no drawers to pull and the complete contents are immediately visible.

(b) Rotary filing

This is quicker still, as each tier can be rotated until the file or card wanted comes to hand, without the user having to move.

(c) Box files

Box files may hold an assortment or combination of sets of papers. They are therefore suitable as transfer cases to house papers removed from a current filing system but needing to be kept for reference, or for bulkier items like company reports, publicity brochures, and leaflets. They may be kept anywhere in an office, not necessarily as part of the main filing system.

(d) Tiered equipment

Several manufacturers provide lateral filing in tiers and angled banks that will fit into corners and into rooms of odd shapes.

(e) Movable equipment

Some movable sections are mounted on rails to provide quick access to other sections behind them. A complete system of lateral filing cupboards can be slid along on rail tracks; when access is not required, the cupboards are grouped close together, but can be opened up to form gangways when necessary. Smaller filing containers can be mounted on wheels or castors, and are especially useful where clerks need to write up records at their desks. Small filing systems housed in the pedestals of executives' or typists' desks or incorporated into low partitions in open-plan offices are readily accessible.

(f) Automated filing and retrieval systems

In some larger systems, filing and retrieval is aided by automated methods, including the following:

(i) A vertical conveyor belt made up of carriers supports free-standing or suspended files arranged vertically or laterally. Miscellaneous items may be also stored, e.g., large index cards in pull-out trays, magnetic tape reels and cassettes, components, stationery, etc. The operator presses a button on a small keyboard to identify the required file, the conveyor system rotates (either up or down, whichever is the shorter route) and the appropriate carrier is brought in front of the seated operator (see Figure 8.2). The rotation of the system is stopped immediately any obstruction is detected by an electronic scanner. The equipment saves the operator's time and physical energy and also saves floor space as the unit can extend right up to the ceiling. Units can be locked at night for security.

Figure 8.2 An automated filing system. The operator has just keyed in the appropriate file and carrier codes on a small keyboard recessed into the worktop at which she is seated. The Lektriever equipment then rotated automatically so that she is now able to extract the required file. (Courtesy of Kardex Systems (UK) Ltd)

Units may be linked to a computer. Information about the files is stored in the computer, enabling the operator, using a terminal, quickly to locate files and carriers required, to delete files from the directory (index), to enter new ones, to obtain lists of files that contain a particular type of information or that have been borrowed, and to monitor the capacity of the system. Carrier codes can be held in memory, enabling interrupted jobs to be resumed.

In systems where components are stored, information can be communicated from the operator's terminal to the mainframe computer about stock levels, to whom components were issued, etc., so that stock records held on the mainframe can be updated.

(ii) Another type of automated system consists of two banks of facing containers. When the operator keys in a code and presses a command button a conveyor stops at the required position between banks, draws onto it the container wanted and delivers it to the operator's workstation.

(iii) Another method links card or file retrieval units with closed circuit television: a located document is put into a transmitting unit and the image appears on a television screen elsewhere, within or near the building. A monitor screen enables the operator to check that the information is displayed correctly. Thus access is achieved without the enquirer physically touching the document—which is useful when a brief look is all that is required.

Figure 8.3   A computerized retrieval system. Each wallet stored on the trays is allocated a code, input to the system via the keyboard. For retrieval, the microcomputer matches the request keyed in by the operator with the appropriate stored code and causes the mechanism of the tray to pull forward the required wallet. Codes may be devised to allow a group of wallets with a common characteristic, e.g., date or subject matter, to be retrieved simultaneously. (Courtesy of A. B. Dick Ltd)

(iv) Figure 8.3 illustrates a system which enables cards to be retrieved automatically with computer assistance.

(v) Figure 8.4 shows a computerized system which takes original documents at the document entry station, scans them with a digital scanner and then stores the indexed images on high capacity optical disk in the optical storage and retrieval library. When required, images are retrieved onto the screen at the image workstation. Although optical disks are not erasable, the system enables the information they carry to be updated by keying in at the image

workstation annotations to the document images in the space left on disk after each recording. The user can retrieve a number of images simultaneously onto windows on the screen. Hard copy may be obtained from a laser printer.

8.6 Indexing documents clearly

(a) Visible systems

Visible systems combine the advantages of easy access and clear indexing or labelling. They display information in such a way that it can be seen at once

Image work-station

Optical storage and retrieval library

Laser printer

Document entry station

Scanner

Figure 8.4 A document image processing system (see **8.5** *(f)* (v) for description). Notice the 'windows' on the screen of the image workstation on the left of the picture. (Courtesy of British Olivetti Ltd)

with very little or no handling. In any visible system, cards can be removed or new ones inserted without disturbing the rest. Often it is the bottom edge of the card that is visible, but sometimes one vertical edge is exposed. On others, an oblique strip next to a cut-away corner bears the essential details and is extended down one side of the card; this edge—and if desired one or two columns next to it—is kept visible by each card being slotted onto guide rails fitted into the cabinet.

Visible index cards may be held flat in trays (see Figure 8.5), in loose-leaf binders, hung from walls or stood on desks. Figure 8.6 illustrates yet another method.

Strip indexes are stored in similar ways. They are composed not of complete cards but of strips fitted into a frame, each strip bearing concise details such as staff names, telephone extensions or room numbers. A whole sheet of strips is typed at a time and separated afterwards at the perforations. Different colours may be used for emphasis or classification. As strips can easily be removed, added or rearranged, listed information can easily be kept up to date. These indexes therefore have an advantage over lists typed on paper which need to be entirely retyped when changes occur. (However, lists held on disk in word processing or microcomputer systems can be updated even more easily: they may be called onto the screen and amended without the unchanged items having to be altered.)

Figure 8.6   Anson Vistafan visible card record system and cabinet. This gives the advantages of compact storage and easy visibility. Cards can be removed from or added to holders as required. (Courtesy of Anson Systems, Anson Division of Gardner Mawdsley Ltd)

(b)   Free-standing systems

This type of card index contains cards standing on edge one behind another. Equipment is cheaper than with a visible system, but the cards have to be thumbed through and parted to find the information wanted, and the edges, unless protected, become worn.

(c)   Feature cards

Whereas index cards enable a *particular* piece of information to be read or traced, feature cards reveal where *types* of information can be found. To yield the required information, these cards are sorted; e.g., by a metal rod (see Figure 8.7) or by a beam of light (see Figure 8.8). Some of these punched feature cards can be prepared as part of output from a computer and read by machines.

(i) *Edge-punched cards*   These are designed so that each section of the outer edges carries a particular piece of information, represented by a punched hole, slot or notch extending right to the edge. When a sorting rod is passed through a deck of cards those with holes at that place will be suspended from the rod while those with notches or slots will fall away (see Figure 8.7).

For instance, to sort out the cards of women employees from the rest, a rod would be passed

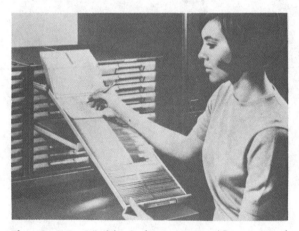

Figure 8.5   Visible index system. (Courtesy of Kardex Systems (UK) Ltd)

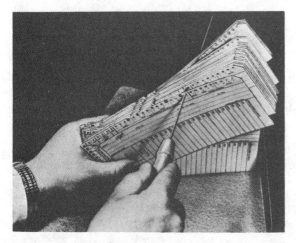

Figure 8.7 Edge-punched cards with needle sorter. The cards are supported on a squaring board to keep them in alignment. (Courtesy of Anson Systems, Anson Division of Gardner Mawdsley Ltd)

through all the cards at the section denoting sex—male or female. The cards with holes at that point would represent male employees and would remain on the rod, but the slotted cards for women would fall away from it. These dropped cards would then be locked by inserting another rod through them. Sorting into alphabetical, numerical or other order is also possible, by repeated sortings.

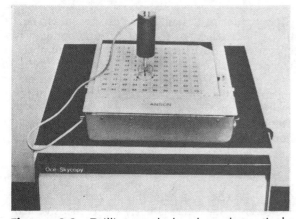

Figure 8.8 Drilling a hole through optical-coincidence feature cards over a light box. (Courtesy of Anson Systems, Anson Division of Gardner Mawdsley Ltd)

By inserting several rods simultaneously, cards having a number of features in common can be quickly extracted, e.g., male employees over 30 with a university degree. Special frames may be used for multiple manual or electric sorting, allowing cards to be rotated on a pivot so that the selected ones drop down.

Where cards are 'body punched' a slot is obtained by cutting away the area between two holes.

(ii) *Optical coincidence cards* Each document included in the system is allocated a reference number (starting at 1), and read to see on which topics it contains information. The coincidence feature cards for all of those topics are then assembled. These bear a grid pattern of numbered squares and a hole is drilled into them at that point of the grid representing the reference number of the document concerned (see Figure 8.8). Any one feature card will therefore show which documents have information on that topic. If several feature cards are aligned and placed on a light box, the light will pass straight through at those points where all the cards are perforated, revealing which documents deal with all those topics. In some very fast electronic systems, the operator selects on a visual display unit the features required, and the appropriate records are immediately produced.

(d) Labelling

To enable filed documents to be easily identified and retrieved, clear labelling is essential, for example, on guide cards and dividers separating groups of cards or files, or on folders and title strips. Box files may need lists of contents or index sheets for alphabetical divisions.

(e) Coding and signalling devices

The spines of files can be marked with letters, numbers or blocks of colour, so that a distinctive pattern is visible when all are in place. This is done in some tiered lateral and rotary systems, and draws attention to files wrongly replaced.

Certain facts can be indicated by attaching metal or plastic tabs, called signals, to the tops, spines or sides of folders and cards and to the visible edges in visible systems. The mere presence of a signal can signify that certain action should be taken—e.g., outstanding orders or subscriptions followed up. In other systems, the position in which a signal is

75

placed is important—e.g., the month of the year during which sales representatives' customers should be visited is indicated by the exact portion of the card edge to which the signal is fastened. Some signals are transparent or have holes punched in them to avoid obscuring any part of the card. One type is called 'telescopic', in that it can be pulled out through a slot in a card to extend across the distance required, thus forming an adjustable bar. This is useful in stock record cards, to denote when the level of stock declines to the reordering level.

(f)   Colour coding

Colour can be used to convey information and reduce chances of misfiling. Uses include coloured carbon copies for different departments, coloured folders for different divisions of a system, coloured guide folders and cards, coloured miscellaneous folders, coloured index tabs, coloured code marks on spines of folders and ring-binders, coloured signals to signify different information, and coloured index cards for different categories of customer or client.

8.7   Classifying documents logically

Indexing must be carried out in accordance with some logical system of classification.

(a)   Alphabetical

This is the method most widely used where filing under name of correspondent is needed.

(i) *Order*   Although it is easy to understand, clear rules must be given, as alternative methods exist. Many organizations adopt the following system.

The order is determined by the first letter of the surname or of the most important word in an organization's name, and then by subsequent letters.

Where surnames are identical, the accompanying initials or forenames are the deciding factors.

Organizations' names beginning with or composed entirely of initials precede those whose first significant words begin with the same initial letter.

Where surnames and initials are identical, alphabetical order of street or, where necessary, town is followed.

Alternative spellings Mc and M' are filed as Mac, and the order determined by the letter following the prefix.

Prefixes such as O', de, del, van, von are treated as though incorporated into the following surname.

St and S. are filed as Saint.

Unimportant items like 'and', 'the' and apostrophes are disregarded.

Titles are not taken into account when deciding filing order, but may be included in parentheses.

Hyphenated surnames are treated as one unit; where there is no hyphen, the second surname is treated as a forename.

(ii) *Space allocation*   A difficulty is that the number of new files made up under any one letter of the alphabet may exceed the space allocated to it in the filing system, necessitating time-consuming shifting of files and reorganization of cabinet or cupboard space.

(iii) *Miscellaneous papers*   It is possible to group odd papers not likely to develop sufficiently to justify making up separate files. 'Miscellaneous' folders, one for each letter of the alphabet, can be used which can double as guide cards or dividers. Such files often contain or bear an index of the papers they comprise.

(b)   Numerical

This is a simple, logical method, suitable for organizations dealing with large numbers of customers or clients, especially where the work is growing.

(i) *Expandability*   It allows for expansion, as a new file is placed next to the last existing one and is allocated the next number. The highest numbers, therefore, indicate the newest files, unless during 'weeding out' a new file is substituted for an old, superseded file rather than removing that number entirely from the system. An accession list of numbers should be kept showing to which file each number has been allocated.

(ii) *Alphabetical index*   Just as a telephone number is found by looking up the name of the subscriber, so a file number is obtained by consulting an alphabetical index. This lengthens the process of retrieval. However, if the index is fairly comprehensive and kept up to date, it can be very useful and may even make recourse to the file in question unnecessary. Typical information in a charity's index might be: full name, address, telephone number, date of application for membership, amount of subscription, when last paid. Also if the file number is used as a reference number on correspondence, the need to consult the index is reduced, and it is unnecessary even to read through the document in order to decide where to file it.

(iii) *Terminal digit*   Terminal digit filing is a variation on the conventional numerical system. The file code is broken down into pairs of digits read from right to left. The last two digits indicate the area of the system in which files with numbers ending in those digits are placed. The next pair might indicate the appropriate guide card division, and the final pair the folder number. For example, file 16 is placed behind guide card 86 on shelf 36, so its complete code is 16 86 36. This method makes the muddling of digits less likely when replacing files, and automatically indicates their location.

(iv) *Decimal*   Decimal systems use whole numbers for main divisions of files and decimal parts for subdivisions. A good example is the Dewey decimal system widely used in libraries (see **19.2**).

(c)   Subject

With this method, documents are filed according to their subject matter rather than under the names of the correspondents. It can be very suitable, especially where a number of jobs or projects are undertaken by, say, builders or architects, or where the type of product is more significant than to whom it is sold.

(i) *Need for knowledge of organization's affairs* Those responsible for subject filing must be conversant with the company's affairs if documents are to be placed on appropriate files. It is therefore most suitable for centralized systems or very small ones where one person is in charge.

(ii) *Need for carefully indexed headings*   Subject files may be indexed alphabetically—or in numerical order if an alphabetical index is provided. In any case, an index listing the subjects covered is desirable, but even with this it is possible for an inexperienced person to open a new file quite unnecessarily just because the particular wording of an existing subject heading did not occur to them. Subject headings must therefore be carefully worded, just as an index to a book must be thoughtfully done if readers are to locate the information they require.

(iii) *Cross-referencing*   If a document could be logically filed in more than one place, cross-reference sheets should be placed on the alternative files, directing the searcher to the file chosen; it is unwise merely to place without comment a copy of the document on all files, as this does not guarantee that copies of any reply are similarly distributed.

(d)   Geographical

(i) *Need for geographical knowledge*   Some knowledge of geography is necessary for this system, as files are grouped according to regions, usually alphabetically. Main divisions may be for continents, or countries, and subdivisions for states, provinces, and regions, with smaller divisions for towns. It is suitable for organizations with regional or overseas interests, branches or agents, and where sales or other activities need to be viewed and compared on a regional basis.

(ii) *Desirability of index*   An index is desirable to link names of organizations or people with the divisions in which their files are found.

(iii) *Need for some cross-referencing*   Cross-referencing may be necessary where areas overlap.

(e)   Combined systems

Besides the alphabetical or numerical indexing of subject and geographical filing systems, methods exist which combine alphabetical and numerical. For instance, in some alphabetical systems, each file opened is given a reference number (for use on correspondence) directly related to its position in the cabinet or cupboard. For example, BARNES has 2/1/8 as it is found under B (=2), first subdivision Ba–Be (=1) and is the eighth folder behind the guide card (=8). The reference number for the following file, BALL, is 2/1/9, since the order in subdivisions is usually chronological rather than strictly alphabetical. The names of these files and their numerical equivalents can be indexed on the guide card preceding them.

(f)   Chronological

Papers are normally placed in date order within files. Sometimes files or index cards may themselves be in chronological order, e.g., in follow-up systems (see **23.6**) or when orders or service requests and complaints are first received.

8.8   Computer databanks

(For computer storage media see **11.5** and **11.8**.) Information when processed may be organized by the computer system into files, temporarily or permanently, so that it can be located when required and reorganized again if necessary: e.g., a new file can be created by merging data, text or images from different existing files. The system acts according to commands from the user, following principles similar to those used in a manual system. For example: information may be *archived* (transferred from primary memory to backing store), *deleted* (discarded), *moved* (put into different file), *copied* (duplicates created), *printed*, *returned* (replaced into file after use), *located* (searched out by the system), *sent* (to locations specified either by the user at the time or by a stored distribution list), or *locked* (prevented from being amended or deleted).

Databanks and *databases* store many items of data for retrieval at terminals with access to the system. An item of data may be found by retrieving first the *file* and then the *record* in the file in which it occurs. Some systems like Prestel (see **19.8**) allow an item of data to be retrieved individually, using an indexing system which points the searcher on to other separate items which may be relevant (as in an encyclopaedia where the reader is led from one entry to another).

8.9   Microfilm

Documents are photographed at a reduced scale on roll film, which is then processed. When the photographed images need to be read they are viewed through a magnifying reader. See Figure 8.9 for the stages in a typical system.

(a)   Microforms

Microfilm is available in different forms to suit the uses to which it will be put (see Figure 8.10).

(i) *Roll film*   Documents are filmed first usually on 16 mm roll film (or 35 mm for large documents) which is retained as the master record. It is the cheapest microform and is most suitable for records referred to only infrequently, i.e., archival storage, as to retrieve a microfilmed document the film has to be run through until the appropriate point is reached. Roll film may be held reeled on one spool, but it needs to be threaded through onto a take-up spool if a simple low-cost film reader is used. When roll microfilm is used for active document files using computer-assisted techniques (see below) then roll microfilm is housed in cassettes or cartridges. Then self-threading microfilm readers are often used to speed up the retrieval of document images. A duplicate roll of film may be exposed at the same time as the first, or a second copy made on a diazo duplicator, in which case one is kept as the master copy and the other adapted to produce one of the following microforms more suitable for easy filing and retrieval.

(ii) *Fiche*   A fiche is a sheet of film bearing images in parallel rows. Where large batches of documents have to be circulated to a number of people, fiche is cheap to post. Micro-publishing employs fiche: e.g., catalogues and booklets may be reduced to as few as one or two fiches easily sent out to agents or customers. In some cases, microfiche cannot be updated. However, certain systems are now available which enable document images to be added or deleted after the first microfiche document images have been made and filed.

(iii) *Jacket* (see Figure 8.10)   Roll film can be cut into strips and stored in protective transparent wallets called jackets. A jacket may contain up to 70 A4 microfilmed documents usually relating to one person, organization or subject, and corresponds to a file of paper documents. The strips of film are fed by machine into channels in the jacket and once inserted cannot easily be removed. The file can be updated by feeding fresh pieces of microfilm into the vacant channels or starting a new jacket. Cheap copies can be made on to diazo film (see **9.2** *(c)*).

(iv) *Aperture cards*   These are cards into which is inset a frame of 35 mm microfilm, employed mainly for large documents, as used in drawing offices. For example, an engineering drawing may thus be reduced to convenient storage size. The card itself may be a punched card for use in a computer installation, bearing information about the drawing illustrated.

(b)   Production of film

Cameras can be of different kinds, according to the results required. A *planetary* or *flat-bed* camera enables documents of varying sizes to be filmed at different reduction ratios. Neither document nor

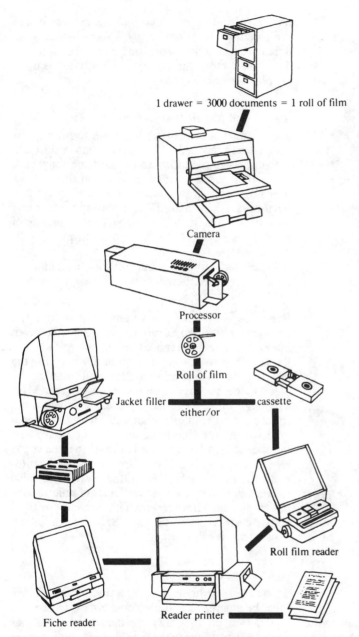

1 drawer = 3000 documents = 1 roll of film

Camera

Processor

Roll of film

Jacket filler —————— cassette
either/or

Roll film reader

Fiche reader

Reader printer

Figure 8.9 Flowchart of an office microfilm system. (Courtesy of the Imtec Group plc)

film move at the time of exposure. Duplicate 'shots' of a document or drawing may be easily made from one original. A flat-bed *step and repeat* camera is suitable for making microfiche, because the film moves on automatically after one exposure to the next image position. A *rotary* or *flow* camera is used to film continuously a series of documents of similar or the same size; the film and document move

necessary adjustments or repeat the process before the original is taken away. Manufacturers or bureaux undertake processing for firms without their own equipment, where confidentiality is not a factor to be considered.

(c)   Indexing and retrieval

Microfilmed documents, in whatever form, must be very clearly indexed or retrieval is made difficult. Documents on roll film and microfiche may have characters, codes or titles recorded on them at the time the roll was filmed and readable when magnified. Filed fiche, jackets and aperture cards may be located with the naked eye by means of printed or typed titles or typed strips of self-adhesive tape.

Particularly for fiche and roll film, a number of quick retrieval systems have been developed, including the following:

Image count systems use a number of techniques; with *target flash* small groups of frames at given intervals are left unexposed and show up as bright flashes when run through at speed. By indexing the exposed frames in relation to these and counting the flashes, the required frame can be located. With *scanning*, 'blips' recorded by a camera below the frames can be read by a photocell incorporated in a reader, the user entering on the keyboard the number of 'blips' to be sensed in order to retrieve the required document. The film then stops automatically at the right place. Other systems involve the recognition by the reading device of unique code patterns or code lines recorded in different positions before each batch of frames. (See also computer-assisted retrieval, below.)

Figure 8.10 Microforms. The left hand is supporting a 'no-rewind' cassette, and the right is holding roll film on a spool and microfilm jacket. (Courtesy of Bell and Howell Ltd, Business Equipment Division)

automatically. If a special attachment is added to the machine, documents can be fed in automatically as continuous stationery.

Film can be developed and dried within a separate processor, but sometimes both photographing and processing of exposed film takes place within the body of the camera unit. The operator can then inspect the result on the spot, and make any

(d)   Readers

To be read by the naked eye, a microfilmed image must be magnified and projected on the screen of a reader (see Figure 8.12). Readers need particular facilities depending on the type or types of microform for which they are designed. For example, roll, cassette, and cartridge readers need fast forward and rewind facilities; a frame grid is needed for fiche readers. Many readers enable the image to be rotated up to 90 degrees to enable users to read equally conveniently either horizontal or vertical frames.

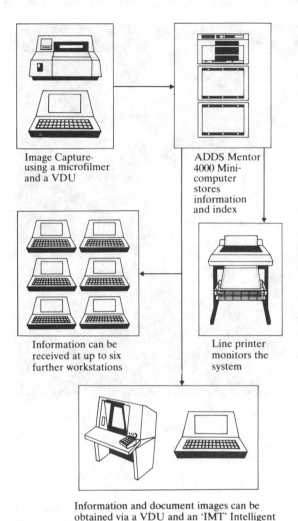

Image Capture-
using a microfilmer
and a VDU

ADDS Mentor
4000 Mini-
computer
stores
information
and index

Information can be
received at up to six
further workstations

Line printer
monitors the
system

Information and document images can be
obtained via a VDU and an 'IMT' Intelligent
Microimage Terminal

Figure 8.11 Sequence of operations in a computer-assisted microfilm system. Note that the line printer monitors the system by, for example, printing out an analysis of the documents accessed. It may also provide an index on paper of the documents stored, if not enough disk storage is available. (Courtesy of Kodak Ltd)

Desktop and portable models are available. *Reader-printers* can also produce enlarged prints, usually by the transfer electrostatic (plain paper) process (see **9.2** (*a*)).

(e) Computer-aided microfilm systems

(i) *COM (Computer output microfilm)* This may be produced by the computer sending alphanumeric characters to be printed in page format directly onto microfilm or microfiche via a computer output microfilmer, or as a separate off-line operation via a magnetic tape produced by computer. The latter has enabled bureaux to offer special COM printout services. COM is produced more quickly and cheaply than paper output obtained from line printers. Its reduced size makes it easier to file and distribute than paper printout.

(ii) *CAR (Computer assisted retrieval)* Microfilm cameras and readers may be interfaced with computers to speed the storage and retrieval of microfilmed documents. A microfilmer unit records a code number on each document it microfilms. This code number, together with information relating to the document, is input to the computer by an operator on a VDU keyboard, enabling an index of the microfilmed documents to be stored on disk. To retrieve information, the operator keys in details which will enable the computer to locate the document in the index, e.g., date, customer name, account number, etc. Appropriate information is then displayed on the VDU screen, e.g., the code number of the document and the location of the magazine or cassette in which it is stored. When the magazine is loaded by the operator into the reader, the document required is automatically displayed.

Figure 8.11 illustrates in diagrammatic form the sequence of operations in a computer-assisted microfilm system. Figure 8.12 shows input and output equipment that may be involved.

As documents can be readily located in whatever container they are housed, it is not necessary to sort them into order before they are microfilmed.

(f) Advantages of microfilm

Expensive filing space is saved (as shown by the following equivalents: microfilm jacket holds up to 70 documents, roll film holds from 3000 to 20 000 documents per 10 m, microfiche 15 cm × 10.5 cm holds from 98 to 500 images); a filing system becomes extremely compact, easy to handle, control, and protect from fire or theft; film containing thousands of documents can be mailed cheaply; originals are not handled and do not deteriorate or

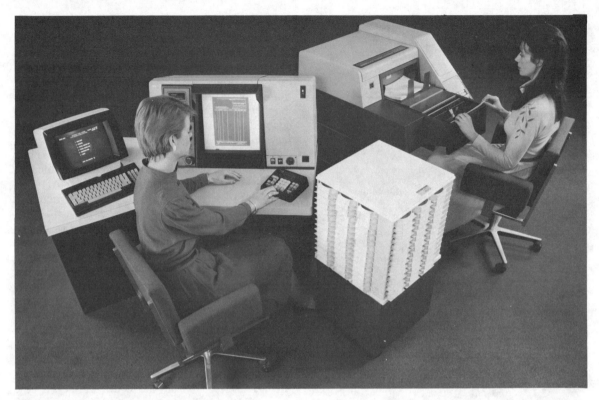

Figure 8.12   The Kodak IMT-250 Microimage terminal with the Reliant Intelligent Microfilmer 2000 are two of the units used in the Kodak KAR 4000 Information System (see Figure 8.11). On the right is the microfilmer unit. On the far left is the VDU, showing information that has been retrieved. An actual document is being displayed on the microimage terminal screen. A revolving carousel housing microfilm magazines is shown in the foreground. (Courtesy of Kodak Ltd)

become torn; duplicates can be made easily and cheaply (compared with the cost of photocopying individual paper documents); storage costs are much less than for paper files; individual documents cannot be lost when part of a continuous roll, reel, strip, or sheet.

8.10   Departmental and centralized filing systems

Filing can be done either departmentally or centrally, though many organizations compromise by maintaining a central system but filing within departments those papers that are confidential to the executives concerned or that are used exclusively by them. Electronic systems tend to be a mixture of the two. They may, for example, be departmentally

organized, with floppy disks being kept in containers close at hand to the stand-alone word processor or microcomputer which generates and retrieves the data. On the other hand, data may be stored centrally in a mainframe computer—yet by means of links to terminals throughout the organization it is readily accessible to all departments. Microfilm systems may be centrally based, storing mainly archive material, or may be organized departmentally especially where rapid electronic retrieval systems are used.

Centralized paper filing systems are more likely to be automated than departmental ones. They may make more effective use of floor space and equipment because the specialist staff are better able to analyse the demands made on the system. They need to devise efficient control procedures so that the whereabouts of every document is known, and to maintain satisfactory requisition systems with delivery to or collection by departments.

Departmental paper systems are usually smaller. They are easily accessible to the users but may for that very reason be mishandled unless strict control is kept. Improvements and innovations may be haphazard unless there is someone in charge who has enough interest in filing and enough time among other duties to bring them about. It is important to have a deputy, or at least clear instructions available on how to operate the system during staff holidays or sickness. There is liable to be some waste of space as equipment may not be fully taken up.

8.11 Special purpose filing system

(a) Computer disks, tapes and cards

These must be protected from dust, heat, and humidity to prevent contamination: therefore cabinets and cupboards in which they are kept are usually fireproof with insulated inner compartments. Reels may be placed in racks which may be stood in lockable enclosed units. Figure 8.13 illustrates a container for floppy disks. Such containers may be made of antistatic materials.

(b) Ledger cards

Stored in metal trays, these can be kept in filing-cabinet drawers. Some trays have one low side, enabling cards to open out into a visible system.

(c) Microforms

Microfilm jackets, microfiche and aperture cards can be filed in card index equipment. Special cabinets with roll-out shelves and retractable doors are available for cassettes, and roll and cartridge containers can be placed in pigeonholes arranged in tiers on a revolving base. If considered necessary, microfilm can be kept in fireproof storage equipment but some organizations prefer to have a duplicate microfilmed filing system kept in a different place from the main system as a safeguard. Figure 8.14 illustrates a rotary stand for microfiche.

(d) Plans

These can be suspended and held in adjustable clamps. They can easily be studied on the spot or withdrawn from the clip. Stands may be fixed to

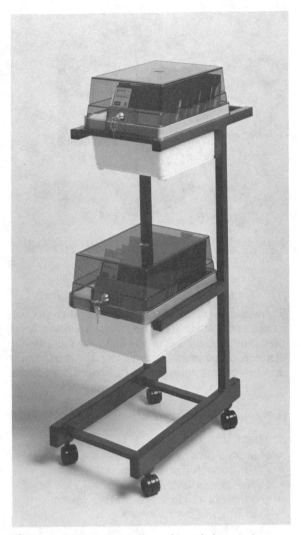

Figure 8.13 A trolley for diskette boxes. (Courtesy of MBS Data Efficiency Ltd)

walls, included in lateral filing cupboards, incorporated into trolleys or free-standing. Dust-covers are obtainable. Plans may also be kept flat, one on top of another in shallow drawers.

(e) Print-out

Folded computer print-out may be stored in clip binders, suspended from metal frames on stands (see Figure 8.15).

Figure 8.14 Rotary stand for microfiche. (Courtesy of Jetleys (Great Britain) Ltd)

(f) Transparencies and photographs

Transparencies can be placed in individual pockets in suspended wallets. As the wallets are transparent they can be held up to the light to identify the contents. Photographs may be stored flat in narrow drawers or kept rolled up in cardboard containers.

Figure 8.15 Computer printout holders. (Courtesy of MBS Data Efficiency Ltd)

8.12   Checklist for storing floppy disks

Make sure that you:
* Handle a disk as little as possible.
* Do not touch disk through slot in jacket.
* Label envelope when EMPTY with felt-tip or other pen.
* Do not pin or clip notes to envelope.
* Do not erase near the disk.
* Store disks upright.
* Store disks in suitable case, box or binder.
* Keep disks in relatively cool, dry conditions.
* Keep disks away from sunlight and heat.
Remember—Dust corrupts!

8.13   Did you know?

1. Company accounts must be kept for six years.

2. Generally speaking, documents relating to income tax should be kept for six years because the Inland Revenue can go back over that period in their investigations.

3. Bills are still payable until six years after the date on which they have been incurred. If the debtor acknowledges in any way that he owes payment the six-year period starts afresh from that acknowledgement. It is therefore advisable not to discard documents supporting any possible lawsuit for breach of contract relating to unpaid debts until after that period has elapsed.

4. A certificate of authenticity and intent is a statement given by a person in authority vouching that the microfilm is a true copy of the original documents. It may, for example, be issued by manufacturers or bureaux microfilming documents on behalf of clients. Such certificates are microfilmed at the beginning and end of the roll of microfilm, signed by both the microfilm operator and the supervisor, stating that the intervening documents have been microfilmed.

5. A person wishing to use microfilmed documents as secondary evidence in an English court of law may do so provided an affidavit (sworn statement) is made that they are authentic copies of the original. However, if the original document is one that attracts stamp-duty a microfilm copy may not be used.

Activities

1. What factors would you take into consideration when formalising a procedure for the regular removal of old material from active files and the disposal of dead files which were no longer required? (LCCI, PSC)

2. Discuss, with examples, how computerization is affecting filing and retrieval systems.

3. Describe the following filing classifications and then describe the most appropriate circumstances in which they might be used:

(a) numerical
(b) geographical
(c) alphabetical
(d) subject
(e) Dewey decimal. (LCCI, SSC)

4. Describe the system of classifying filing that you might expect to find in FOUR of the following organisations and explain why the system of your choice is more appropriate than any other:

(a) A Public Library
(b) A large firm of Solicitors
(c) A Health Centre with 40 000 patients
(d) A small firm manufacturing one product for sale overseas
(e) An Estate Agent. (LCCI, SSC)

5. You work for an organization which runs a Music Club comprising 3 divisions. In an effort to improve efficiency it has been recommended that the Classical, Popular and Jazz Music Clubs should share a computerised <u>Data Base</u> with supplementary filing being based upon <u>microfilm</u> system using <u>microfiche.</u> The present system of filing uses a <u>terminal digit classification</u> in the lateral files, plus a <u>visible card index</u>. Explain each of the 5 terms underlined. (LCCI, SSC)

6. (a) Explain the advantages of microfilm over paper storage systems.
   (b) Describe possible filing and indexing systems for the different types of microform. (LCCI, PSC)

7. The main disadvantage of printed output from computers is the large quantity of paper which is used. Paper is bulky, and becomes increasingly expensive. To overcome these disadvantages, COM has been developed. Describe what is meant by COM, and how it is used. (LCCI, PSC, IP)

8. List and discuss the essential steps necessary to devise and operate a successful departmental filing system. (LCCI, PSC)

9. As secretary to the Head of a Department, who sits on various committees outside of the company, you are asked for your ideas as to which files should not be placed into the new central filing system. List and explain your recommendations. On what basis could a method of centralised filing be chosen? (LCCI, PSC)

10. As a student, you should be able to find, without hesitation, lesson or lecture notes, class hand-outs, written work to be handed in for assessment, assignments that have been marked, etc. Write or type a brief explanation of your system, including the method by which you decide what to retain and what to destroy.

11. State FIVE key principles of a filing and retrieval system. (RSA, DPA)

12. **Group activity**   Discuss the rules followed by the Post Office when determining the alphabetical order for subscribers listed in their telephone directories. Then, following the rules set out in **8.7**(a), practise assembling in alphabetical order names selected by students in turn from a telephone or other directory.

9
Reprography

Reprography—the reproduction of documents—can be divided into two main divisions: **duplicating** *and* **copying**. **Duplicating** *processes are designed for running off at high speed (up to two prints per second) many copies made from a master that has first to be prepared. The more copies that are made, the lower the cost per copy because the cost of the master is shared over the whole run.* **Copying** *processes make facsimile copies of an original document. As no master has to be made and no checking is required, expensive staff time is saved. Multiple copies are made by repetitive copying so the cost per copy does not generally decrease throughout the run. Although copying speeds are slower than duplicating speeds some copiers have facilities that save time in other ways: e.g., integrated sorting and collating, and even stapling. The usefulness of some copiers is enhanced too by, for example, image enlargement, reduction, and double-sided copying without the intervention of the operator.*

Several factors may influence a choice between duplicating and copying: e.g., the durability of the copy, the suitability of its quality for the recipient (who may be a customer, a board member, another organization, a colleague, etc.). You should consider all these points when studying the following sections outlining the choice available.

9.1   Duplicating

(a)   Stencil process

A master can be prepared by typing on a stencil so that incisions are cut in the surface. The stencil is then attached to the cylinder of the duplicator and copies run off. Figure 9.1 illustrates the principle involved. Corrections are made by applying correcting fluid over the incisions, and retyping. Semi-absorbent copy paper is normally used, though if an interleaving device is attached to the machine it is possible to use other types. Several thousand copies can be produced of good quality. It is possible to obtain multicoloured copies, but a different stencil must be cut for the work in each colour, the ink drum changed, and the copies run through as many times as are necessary to take each colour consecutively. The latest duplicators enable stencils to be loaded semi-automatically and ejected automatically.

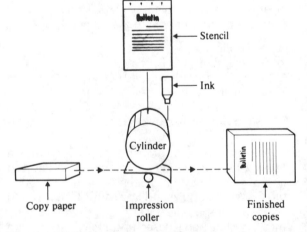

Figure 9.1   Stencil duplicating: pressure from the cylinder on the impression roller forces ink through the incisions on the stencil to the copy paper.

Word processor printers can print out on special stencils for subsequent running off on a duplicator; corrections can be made easily, using the word processor's editing facilities (see Chapter 17). Special stencils and stylus pens are used for written stencils.

A facsimile copy of an original document can be reproduced on a *thermal stencil* using a *thermal copier* (see **9.2** *(d)*) but better quality is obtainable from a stencil cut on an *electronic stencil scanner*. In Figure 9.2 the original can be seen on the left of the stencil. As the cylinder on which they are placed rotates, a photoelectric cell scans the original. When it senses a dark (image) area, a stylus on the machine cuts a corresponding pattern of minute holes into the stencil. Quality of reproduction is controlled by settings adjusting contrast and definition and eliminating unwanted background; these are automatic on the latest microchip models though manual controls are also provided to enable the user to make his own adjustments. Line drawings and photographs can be reproduced.

Stencils can be stored if further copies are likely to be needed. Excess ink is blotted off and the stencils are then hung from special metal frames to avoid creasing.

(b) Offset litho

Figures 9.3 and 9.4 illustrate this process. Masters are usually produced on platemakers, working on the direct electrostatic process (see **9.2** *(b)*). The image is formed on the plate, fused onto it and then

Figure 9.2 Electronic stencil cutter. (Courtesy of Roneo Alcatel Ltd)

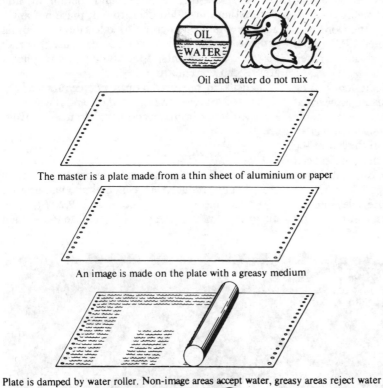

Oil and water do not mix

The master is a plate made from a thin sheet of aluminium or paper

An image is made on the plate with a greasy medium

Plate is damped by water roller. Non-image areas accept water, greasy areas reject water

Plate is inked up. Wet areas reject ink, greasy image areas accept ink

Figure 9.3   The basic principles of lithography. (Courtesy of Gestetner Ltd)

etched by applying a liquid containing a greasy element. When fusing is not done within the platemaker but on a separate machine, alterations can be made to the image, if required, before fusing takes place. Enlargement and reduction facilities are available on electronically controlled platemakers.

Plates produced on platemakers may be paper (yielding up to 2000 copies) or metal (up to 50 000). Paper plates are not usually stored, as new ones can be quickly and cheaply prepared. Metal ones may be kept if a protective coating is applied which must be removed before use.

Print quality is excellent. Where illustrations or exceptionally high quality is required, metal plates may be produced by photography.

When printing, the right balance of ink and 'water' (i.e., fount solution) must be obtained. Trained operators are necessary, especially for large, conventional machines. However, the latest microchip machines are programmed to perform many functions automatically, e.g., preparing the inking roller and paper feed, and cleaning and drying the blanket cylinder after each run.

Offset litho provides very effective colour

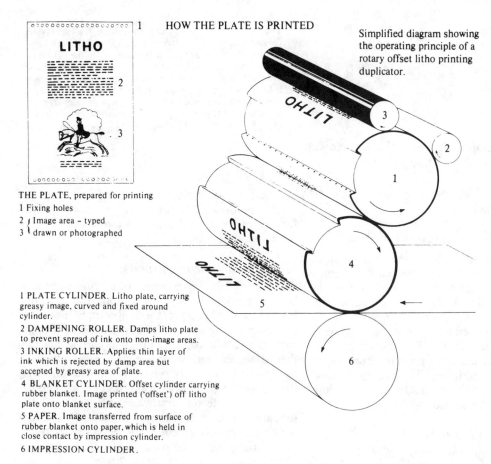

1   HOW THE PLATE IS PRINTED

Simplified diagram showing the operating principle of a rotary offset litho printing duplicator.

THE PLATE, prepared for printing

1 Fixing holes
2 ⎱ Image area – typed
3 ⎰ drawn or photographed

1 PLATE CYLINDER. Litho plate, carrying greasy image, curved and fixed around cylinder.

2 DAMPENING ROLLER. Damps litho plate to prevent spread of ink onto non-image areas.

3 INKING ROLLER. Applies thin layer of ink which is rejected by damp area but accepted by greasy area of plate.

4 BLANKET CYLINDER. Offset cylinder carrying rubber blanket. Image printed ('offset') off litho plate onto blanket surface.

5 PAPER. Image transferred from surface of rubber blanket onto paper, which is held in close contact by impression cylinder.

6 IMPRESSION CYLINDER.

Figure 9.4   How the plate is printed. (Courtesy of Gestetner Ltd)

printing, suitable for leaflets and brochures. A separate plate must be prepared for each colour required, and the ink rollers washed. Careful registration on the resulting copy is needed during each run. Any good quality copy paper may be used. Printing on A3 size sheets is possible on some machines.

9.2   Copying

(a) Transfer electrostatic process (plain paper copying)

Figure 9.5 illustrates this process in the version produced by one manufacturer. Different manufacturers use variations of it, e.g., drums coated with other light-sensitive media; fibre-optical systems (more compact than lenses). Some manufacturers use mono-component dry toner (ink powder) and some duo-component, while others use liquid toner—all these affecting the clarity, density and consistency of the image quality. Some fix the image by cold pressure bonding rather than heat fusing, affecting the permanence of the image and speed of delivery of copies. Plain paper copying is very widely used. It is quick and convenient and operators need little training. Good quality, clear images can be obtained from most originals. Two-sided copies can be produced. Copies can be made on most thicknesses of paper and also on film (providing overhead projector transparencies, printed overlays and masters for dyeline copiers—see **9.2** *(c)* below). Because

89

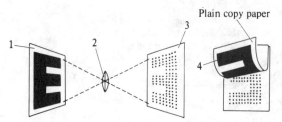

The original (1) is lit up and passed through a lens system (2) onto a positively-charged drum (3) coated with light-sensitive selenium. The charge, dispersed in the light non-image areas, is retained where the image appears (E) and attracts to it particles of negatively-charged duo-component toner powder dusted over the drum. Plain copy paper is then passed over the drum, receiving a positive charge and attracting toner powder particles to form a positive image (4). The toner is fused into the paper by heat and pressure.

Figure 9.5   Xerographic process. (Courtesy of Rank Xerox Ltd)

plain (non-coated) paper is used this method is superseding (b) below.

(b)   Direct electrostatic process

Copy paper coated with a light-sensitive medium, e.g., zinc oxide, receives a negative charge from a corona or charging unit. When the original is illuminated and reflected on the copy paper the charge is dissipated except on the image area, to which positively charged toner particles are attracted. Toner may be in liquid form and fused by heat, or in dry form and fused by pressure from metal rollers within the machine. This process is now much less widely used than plain paper copying because of the cost of coated paper.

(c)   Diazo or dyeline process

This process (see Figure 9.6) produces good quality, extremely clear copies, especially suitable for large-scale detailed work such as A2, A1 and A0 plans and drawings and for subsequent reproduction on microfilm. The specially coated copy paper needs careful handling, as it becomes ineffective if exposed to daylight. By passing opaque originals through other types of copier the necessary translucent masters can

be obtained. Multiple copies of large drawings are quickly produced. Machines used in drawing offices for copying plans and drawings are large but office versions are less bulky.

(d)   Direct thermal process

See Figure 9.7. Paper copies of originals are now seldom made by this process, but the principle involved is used in direct thermal computer or word processor printers (see **11.9**). By means of thermal copiers facsimile copies of originals can be made on thermal stencils for subsequent duplication. Originals need to be very clearly printed or drawn, otherwise the quality of the resulting thermal stencil is poor. Overhead projector transparencies can also be prepared on thermal copiers. *Laminators* (machines which enclose documents between layers of transparent film) are based on a similar principle. (See also transfer thermal printers, **7.6** *(g)*.)

(e)   Microchip facilities on conventional copiers

The mechanism of the latest copiers is controlled by microprocessor. A number of useful facilities result, including: a diagnostic panel notifying the operator

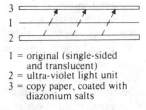

1 = original (single-sided and translucent)
2 = ultra-violet light unit
3 = copy paper, coated with diazonium salts

Exposure: Ultra-violet light is projected from 2 through 1 onto the coated surface of 3, neutralizing the salts on the areas not protected by the image.

Developing: 3 is passed through a processing unit where the image is developed and dyed by one of 3 possible methods: ammonia vapour, fluid or heat. (Heat-developed copies emerge dry, fluid-developed copies semi-dry. Fumes which occur with ammonia vapour can be absorbed if a special chemical unit is used.)

Figure 9.6   Diazo copying process (exposure).

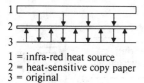

1 = infra-red heat source
2 = heat-sensitive copy paper
3 = original

2 is placed on top of 3 (face up) and fed with it into machine. Radiation from 1 passes through 2 onto 3, causing an accumulation of heat on image areas, turning adjacent heat-sensitive coating black in those places.

Figure 9.7 Direct thermal copying process.

by means of a code or speech synthesis of the nature of any fault; enlargement or reduction facilities in accordance with ratios preset by the manufacturer; zoom facilities, enabling the operator to choose the ratio necessary to fit the image on a standard size sheet; a display monitoring the stage reached in the process; a contrast adjuster, providing the exposure necessary to compensate for a faint image or a dark background; automatic control of the toner supply, ensuring consistent density of the image; interrupt facility, enabling the automatic resumption of a long run that has been interrupted to run off a few copies of another original.

Because of microchip technology, copiers now have fewer moving parts and are therefore more compact and less trouble to maintain.

(f) Copier management systems

Systems may be set up to monitor the use of copying machines throughout an organization. Some are intended to control or limit the volume of use, e.g., by locking the machines and issuing keys only to selected employees, or installing copiers that cannot be used until coins are inserted. Other systems may be geared to studying usage and analysing costs incurred between departments, e.g., log-books to be entered up by users. An effective method entails the user inserting a card that is bar-coded or electronically coded to identify him or her, and keying-in a personal identification number as a double check. The more sophisticated electronic cards have a reducing copy credit balance stored within the card (see also British Telecom phone cards, **13.2** (e)). Another system links a single copier or a group of copiers to a microcomputer; as each user keys in a unique identity code on the copier's keyboard, details of the copier used, the personal or departmental code, and the number and cost of copies obtained are stored centrally. Analyses and reports may be printed out as required.

(g) Digital copiers

The chief difference between a conventional and a digital copier is that the original image is converted into digital signals (see Figure 9.8) which can be rearranged by the image-processing unit in response to the operator's instructions—for example, to enlarge or reduce the image, expand it or compress it, change the position on the page of a portion of the text or image, or merge images from two pages onto one, e.g., a form outline and the variable details needed to complete it.

The technology involved in digital copiers (along with the necessary extra software) will eventually enable them, when linked to word processors, microcomputers, etc., to act as intelligent terminals in local and wide area networks (see **11.11**).

(h) Colour copying

It is possible to produce monochrome copies (in one of a range of colours) from black and white or coloured originals. The method is based on the transfer electrostatic process and employs interchangeable cartridges of different coloured toner. By printing in different colours consecutively, multicoloured copies can be obtained. A separate run, using a different cartridge, is needed for each colour. The operator can either use different originals for each of the colours, or use one original and mask out those portions not required to be copied in any one of the colours.

There are also copiers that make faithful, fullcolour reproductions of colour photographs or charts. The original is scanned through a series of filters, picking out in turn the three primary printing colours (yellow, cyan and magenta); the colours are then copied on the paper via separate developing units inside the machine. Only one pass is made through the machine as, in effect, three copies are made on the same sheet. Full-colour copying is expensive at the moment, and is used chiefly by

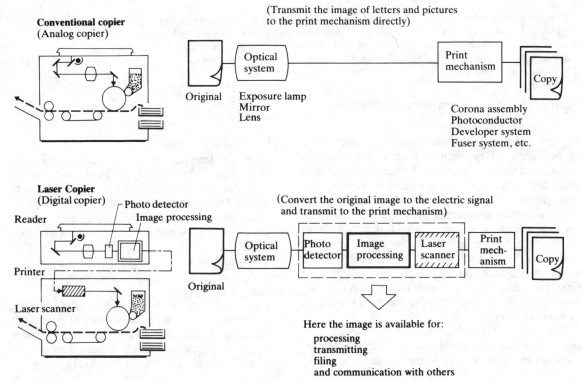

Figure 9.8   This diagram illustrates the difference between a conventional analogue copier and a laser digital copier. (Courtesy of Canon (UK) Limited)

copying bureaux offering a service to the public or by specialist organizations like designers to whom the use of colour in brochures, documents and displays is very important.

9.3   In a nutshell: Facts about copyright

- Under the Copyright Act 1956 anyone wishing to reproduce published material must first ask the permission of the holder of the copyright, indicated in the United Kingdom by the name following the symbol ©.
- Copyright may be infringed, even when only a line or two is copied, if the extract is a significant one.
- Librarians in non-profit-making libraries are allowed to make single copies of *extracts* from magazines or periodical articles for readers certifying that they intend to use the copy for research or *private* study.
- The copying of substantial parts, e.g., whole pages, may not even be done by librarians until at least 25 years after the date of first publication.
- The Copyright Licensing Agency Ltd is to operate a scheme whereby it issues licences to certain users, e.g. educational institutions, allowing them to copy extracts of most United Kingdom copyright holders' work without prior permission in return for an annual standard blanket fee, from which royalties are paid to authors and publishers.

... 'and this is our plain paper copier.'

Figure 9.9 (Courtesy of Tony Holland. First published in *Business Systems and Equipment.*)

- Even licensed users may copy no more than five per cent of a published work at any one time and no more than 30 copies may be taken (or a number sufficient for a class and their tutor).
- Permission must always be obtained before copying music, tables, charts, maps and examination papers, or significant extracts from newspapers.

9.4 Did you know?

1. Spirit duplicating is useful for producing coloured and multicoloured charts and diagrams, particularly as educational and training aids. Hectographic carbon (supplied in seven colours) is placed against the china-clay-coated reverse side of the master sheet, producing a mirror image when the master is typed or drawn on. The master is placed, image outwards, on the spirit duplicator drum. When rotated, this brings the copy paper into contact with rollers moistened with spirit, removing some of the deposit to form the image. Up to about 200 copies can be obtained. Masters can also be obtained by passing an original through a thermal copier. Although it is a cheap process, the image quality is poor and tends to fade. It has therefore been largely superseded in business by other reprographic methods.

2. Copiers with a *clamshell* design are hinged to allow the upper section to be lifted. This makes access easier, should copy paper become jammed in transit through the machine.

3. Each year, under the Public Lending Right Act 1979, payment is made from public funds to authors whose books were borrowed from public libraries during the previous year.

Activities

1. The students of your school/college are organizing a Christmas entertainment to which a party of elderly residents from a local old people's home are to be invited. Draft a suitable circular letter, including an attractive announcement of the main features of the entertainment, and then prepare a master for duplication. The medium used will depend on the machines available to you, but if you have a choice consider carefully which will be the most suitable in these circumstances.

2. As secretary in a large company which has premises on 2 sites, 10 km apart, you are asked to publish a company newsletter. Suggest items you would include and how you would organise the production and distribution of such a publication. (LCCI, PSC)

3. Compare and contrast any *two* methods of copying (not duplicating) with regard to process, materials, uses and limitations (if any). (LCCI, PSC)

4. Your employer asks you to recommend a suitable copier for a new branch office that is being set up. Originals of all kinds are likely to be generated. Longer runs may be required as well as one-off copies. No specialist operator will be available. Write a memo to your employer, explaining the type of copier that you would recommend and your reasons for suggesting it.

5. Your company is considering installing a centralised office copier. (At present there is a small copier in each of the main departments.) Prepare some notes for the Office Manager which can be included in a report to the Board of Directors, outlining advantages, disadvantages and any equipment or procedural changes which might be necessary. (LCCI, PSC)

6. Intelligent Copier Printers are playing an increasingly important part in the modern office. Say how ICPs are used, and outline some of their functions. (LCCI, PSC, IP)

Group activities

7. Discuss with your tutor an appropriate method of filing and indexing used duplicating masters prepared by your class during the course, and put this into operation.

8. Draw up brief instructions for using any copier or duplicator on which you have the opportunity to practise. This could be done in groups, each dealing with a different machine. The resulting instructions could be filed separately or combined into a handbook.

10
The accounts department

10.1 Keeping the petty cash (imprest system)

One of your jobs is to balance the petty cash account. You choose a time when you hope to remain undisturbed for a while, and unlock the cash box.

During the week, it is sometimes difficult to find time to enter up the petty cash book each time you make a payment, so whenever you have paid out any money you have contented yourself with placing a signed voucher in a special compartment of the box. Your company provides a pad of preprinted forms for this purpose. Each voucher provides space for the amount and description of the purchase, and the signatures of the persons making and authorizing it. If a supplier's official receipt is available, you attach this to a voucher.

Today, you sort your vouchers into date order and number them consecutively. Taking them in numerical order, you enter in the book the date and details of each: the amount of the payment you record in the 'Total' column and repeat it in an analysis column. These column headings—cleaning, repairs and renewals, travel, postage, etc.—correspond to the titles of accounts in the ledger. Where no particular column is appropriate, you use the one headed 'Sundries' (miscellaneous items). Where VAT has been paid, you enter this in the VAT column, and the price of the item concerned in the appropriate analysis column. Together they add up to the sum entered in the 'total' column. Then you insert the number of each voucher in the column provided, enabling the company's cashier to check later the evidence for each entry, and then file the vouchers neatly in numerical order in a folder.

When you have entered all the items, you cast the columns, to enable each total to be posted later as a debit entry to the appropriate ledger account. Then, you check that the subtotals of the analysis columns when added together equal the main 'total' column. (You have found occasionally that they do not, and then you have had to find the reason for the discrepancy. Usually carelessness in casting has caused it, a transposition in figures, or failure to note each payment in both the 'total' and an analysis column.) Next, you count up the money left in your cash box. This is your balance in hand, which when added to expenditure equals the total cash with which you started the period. (A discrepancy here could mean that some cash spent has not been accounted for. This is why you insist on receiving a voucher from anyone requiring cash, and why you never lend anyone money from the petty cash for private purposes.)

To close the account, you write in the balance in hand and insert the grand total. Level with this, on the receipts or debit side of the account you insert the corresponding total of cash in hand at the beginning of the period.

Now that you have closed the account, you cannot make any more payments until the cashier has checked your entries and vouchers and given you some more cash. As your company uses the imprest system, you know that he will reimburse the amount spent, to bring your cash float up to its original level. This method reduces the chance of grave error or fraud, because the total amount in your hands is known to be constant and you have to balance the account frequently to renew the float. Next, you reopen the account by writing on the receipts side first the cash balance in hand (brought down from the previous account), and then the amount of the cash reimbursement, with the word 'Cash' against it in the details column and the number (given you by

Receipts	Date	Details	Voucher	Total	VAT	Hos-pitality	Office sundries	Travelling	Postage
£				£	£	£	£	£	£
60·00	May 1	Cash	Fo CBS						
		Ballpoint pens	1	2·30	·30		2.00		
	" 2	String	2	1·15	·15		1·00		
	" 3	Bus fares	3	1·70				1.70	
	" 4	Stamps	4	14·00					14.00
		Coffee	5	4·14	·54	3·60			
	" 5	Typewriter ribbons	6	8·51	1·11		7·40		
				31·80	2·10	3·60	10·40	1·70	14·00
	" 5	Balance	c/d	28·20	L·81	L·23	L·79	L·28	L·26
60·00				60·00					
28·20	May 5	Balance	b/f						
31·80		Cash	Fo. CB6						

Figure 10.1   Extract from a petty cash book.

the cashier) of the folio or page on which the payment is recorded in the main cash book. You are now ready to make further payments as required.

Meanwhile, you carefully lock up your cash box once again. You are responsible for this money. Any loss will reflect on your efficiency at best, and at worst call forth suspicions about your own and others' honesty.

10.2   In a nutshell: Keeping the petty cash (imprest system)

- Obtain a voucher for every payment made.
- Each voucher should bear the amount, date, a description of the purchase, the signature of the purchaser, and the countersignature of an authorized person.
- If a supplier's official receipt is available, attach this to the voucher.
- Sort the vouchers into date order, and number them consecutively.
- In numerical order of voucher, enter details in the petty cash book.
- Enter each amount in the 'Total' column, and enter up the appropriate analysis column(s).
- Where no particular column is appropriate, use the one headed 'Sundries' or 'Miscellaneous'.
- Remember that VAT is *included* in, not extra to, an amount entered in the 'Total' column.
- Insert voucher numbers in the column provided.
- File vouchers in numerical order.
- Cast the columns, and check that the analysis columns' subtotals together equal the main 'Total' column.
- Look out especially for errors in casting, transposition of figures, and failure to record each item in both 'Total' and analysis columns.
- Check that total expenditure plus cash balance equal total cash in hand at the beginning of the period.
- Close and balance the account.
- Obtain reimbursement of the amount spent, to restore cash float to original level.
- Reopen the account in readiness for further payments.

10.3 Keeping accounts

(a) The purpose of financial accounting

Financial accounting (bookkeeping) is concerned with recording events as they happen or have happened.

In business, most goods and services are bought on credit—i.e., the purchaser receives the goods or services and is allowed to pay for them later. Buying on credit enables cash to be used to the best advantage; instead of parting with it straight away to settle debts as they occur, a person or organization can plan its use, to buy other goods or services or to lend to others (for example, the bank) and earn interest. However, there must be sufficient liquidity (cash available) for an organization to meet its commitments when required. It is therefore very important to keep a careful eye on cash flow. If an organization does not take care of its cash flow, it risks *bankruptcy* (insufficient funds to meet debts). A business may be making profits but still become insolvent if too much capital is tied up in long-term activities, leaving insufficient funds for current needs. It is therefore important to keep careful records of cash paid, received, and cash balances in hand (on the premises and at the bank).

Records of credit transactions must be equally accurate in order to show how much money the organization owes its *creditors* and how much it is owed by its *debtors*. The following terms are commonly used in the process.

(b) Financial accounting terms and records

(i) *Account* This is a record of transactions concerning the person, asset or activity named. The account may be *personal* (relating to a person—such as John Smith, a debtor, or Richard Brown, a creditor) or *impersonal*, i.e., *real* (relating to property like machinery or buildings) and *nominal* (relating to activities like *purchases and expenses*—wages, rent, purchases, postage—or *income*, such as rents received, sales and discounts).

(ii) *Debits and credits* In double-entry bookkeeping, each transaction is regarded as involving a giver and a receiver. This double aspect of giving (*credit*) and receiving (*debit*) is reflected in the various accounts. Thus, for every credit entry in a

ledger account (see below) there must be a corresponding debit entry in another ledger account. For example, cash paid out to Harry Jones is entered as a credit in the cash account and a debit in Harry Jones's account.

(iii) *Ledger* This is a collection of accounts. It was traditionally a book but nowadays is more likely to be a system of cards on which entries are made by machine (see **10.4** *(b)*) or a computer record.

(iv) *Ledger folios* By referring to the page number or reference number quoted alongside an entry, the other side of the transaction can be located.

(v) *Balancing an account* This involves comparing the total debit entries with the total credit entries to see which is the larger. The difference is then added to the lesser side, thereby equalizing the totals (see Balance c/d in Figure 10.1). Where the credit entries are the greater, the difference is known as a *credit balance*; where the debit entries are the greater, a *debit balance*. In modern machine systems, the balance is calculated and shown as each new item is recorded in the account, e.g., as in your account with the bank, a copy of which you receive as your bank statement.

(vi) *Trial balance* By means of a trial balance, a list is made of the balances on each account in the ledger. If the debit and credit balances agree, this shows—at any rate at first sight—that the double-entry system has been used accurately.

(vii) *Books of original entry* Theoretically, daily transactions are recorded first in the appropriate book of original entry and transferred (*posted*) later to the ledger accounts in batches. There are several books of original entry. The *cash book* records cash transactions as opposed to credit ones. It records cash and bank payments and receipts and is entered up from cheque stubs, paying-in slips, etc. Columns may be included for cash in hand and at the bank, and for cash discounts given and received. There may also be columns for VAT (for example, on cash sales). A *bank reconciliation statement* is drawn up to reconcile the difference between the balance as shown on the bank statement and that shown in the company's cash book. It summarizes, for instance, cheques received by the company but not yet presented for collection, cheques drawn by the company but not yet presented by the payees, bank charges deducted by the bank and not yet noted in the company's records, payments made directly into the company's account by credit transfer, etc. The *purchases book* lists in detail items bought on credit and is compiled from suppliers' invoices, with columns for VAT and cost of goods. For each of these items a credit entry is made in the supplier's ledger account. The second, corresponding entry is made on the debit side of the purchases account and VAT account, but this is not done at once: instead, it is incorporated in the figure for the total purchases made, which is entered at regular intervals, e.g., monthly or weekly. The *returns outwards book* lists purchases returned to the supplier because of, say, errors or defects. The *sales book* is similar in operation to the purchases book, but lists goods sold on credit. The *returns inwards book* lists goods sold that have had to be returned by customers. The *journal* lists items that are not appropriate to the books of original entry so far mentioned. It especially covers end-of-year adjustments, such as *depreciation* (the decrease in value of goods as a result of wear and tear, etc.).

(viii) *Subsidiary books*   In addition to books of original entry a business needs to keep further detailed records, e.g., a *wages book* (for the calculation and recording of wages). Other examples are the *postage book* (see **7.3** (*f*)), and the *petty cash book* (see also **10.1** and **10.2**), both being subsidiary books related to the cash book. The petty cash book is concerned with cash transactions too small and numerous to be conveniently entered in the cash book. A cash sum (*float*) is made available by the cashier to the petty cashier and recorded as a credit entry in the cash book. The corresponding debits to the appropriate ledger accounts are made later when the totals of the analysis columns are posted (see Figure 10.1). In a large organization, several departments may have petty cash floats, providing a ready source of small cash, and saving the time of the main cashier.

(ix) *Balance sheet*   This summarizes the financial state of a business as at a particular date. It sets out: *liabilities*, i.e., items owed to other individuals or organizations; *assets*, i.e., items of value to the business, including furniture, equipment, buildings, money owing, etc.; *capital* provided by the owners to run the business. (See example above.)

(x) *Trading and profit and loss account*   This summarizes the trading position for a period and gathers together the sales, purchases and expenses to show

Example of a balance sheet

WISDOM AND SOLOMON, PARTNERS

Balance Sheet as at 31 March 19

	£	£	£
Fixed assets			
Plant and machinery		21 600	
Furniture and fittings		7 640	
			29 240
Current assets			
Stock	3 600		
Sundry debtors	15 200		
Cash at bank	1 060		
Cash in hand	400		
		20 260	
Current liabilities			
Sundry creditors		12 500	
			7 760
			37 000
less Long-term loan			10 000
			27 000
Capital			
T. Wisdom			15 000
K. Solomon			12 000
			27 000

(a) the *gross profit* before expenses are deducted, and
(b) *the net profit* (or *loss*).

(xi) *Income and expenditure account*   This is a similar account but is used in non-profit-making or professional organizations.

(xii) *Turnover*   This refers to the volume of business or net sales, found by subtracting sales returns from total sales.

(c)   Management accounting

The managers of a business are also concerned with planning for the future. Having estimated what their sales, purchases, expenses, etc., will be for the coming period, they draw up a *budget*, which is checked from time to time against the actual position so that they can see if the business is going according to plan. Any variation from the budget is investigated and suitable action taken.

10.4 Machines and devices that aid accounting

(a) Calculators

Calculators add, subtract, multiply, divide and give percentages. Modern electronic machines produce answers in fractions of a second, displayed as green fluorescent figures on a display panel (LCD or liquid crystal display). Some machines print on tally rolls mechanically through inked ribbons or

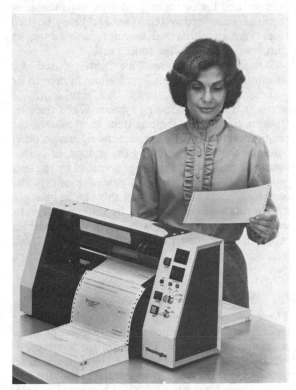

Figure 10.2 A continuous cheque-signer. (Courtesy of Burroughs Protectograph) This machine will take cheques in continuous form once they have come from the computer, will sign them, count them and stack them. A 'jog' button is used to ensure that the cheques are in correct alignment for signature. Security control of the machine is achieved by the use of two keys, one held by an executive and the other by the operator.
Note Blank cheques for demonstration purposes were used for this photograph.

via cassettes containing ink rollers, or thermally, a nearly noiseless non-impact method. Red print is used for credit or minus items, and all figures are printed with a function symbol (add, subtract, total, etc.) alongside. A non-add key enables items such as the date to be printed without being included in the calculations. On some models automatic printout of the number of entries made in a particular calculation can be obtained by depressing a specified key.

Keyboards are 10-key, i.e., with numeric characters from 0 to 9, plus the function keys controlling operations. Some include double or triple cipher keys, saving the need to depress the 0 key repeatedly for hundreds or thousands. Many include a raised spot on the figure 5 for easy identification in 'blind' or touch operation.

Calculations are performed on registers within the machines, enabling subtotals to be obtained. Machines with stores or memories can hold results, adding or subtracting them from a running total. Constant factors are held automatically for repetitive calculations, e.g., when multiplying or dividing by a repeated number.

Programmable calculators operate on instructions contained on magnetic cards, tape or cartridges (for the carrying out of a routine). New information is entered on the keyboard.

Sometimes the decimal point is automatically included without the operator keying it in, usually when the machine is being used for adding or subtracting. However, when it is on calculator mode the operator must select the number of decimal places required. Many calculators can be set by the operator to give answers to the degree of rounding up or down required. A floating decimal point gives the answer up to the capacity of the machine, i.e., as many places of decimals as there is room for.

Some calculators are portable, the display models being as small as pocket size. Some incorporate other devices, like digital clocks, stop-watches, and alarms. Calculators may operate from batteries and/or the mains, with or without an adaptor. Office calculators are usually desktop models with selectable print and/or display facilities (i.e., they will print only, display only, or do both).

Print-out reduces the chance of error, because the operator can check the accuracy of keyed-in items against the record on the tally roll; also, when figures displayed are simultaneously printed out the operator does not have to transfer them, so there is no risk of misreading or transposition. When a typing error is made, a CLEAR key will delete the last item; repeated depression of this key (or operation of a different one) will delete the whole calculation.

Other safeguards include the provision of devices like glowing lights, flickering figures on a screen or locking of the machine, which warn the operator that the capacity of the machine is being exceeded. (Flickering figures on a battery-operated machine may also signify that the battery power is weakening.) In such cases, most machines automatically dispense with numbers on the extreme right of the decimal point, as these are the least important ones. The letter E displayed after a total or F printed in red against the answer on the tally roll warn the operator that the total is incorrect or that, although the total may be correct, it has exceeded the capacity of the machine or store for further operation.

(b)   Accounting machines

Accounting machines with typewriter and numeric keyboards plus function keys may be used to produce accounts records. Some enable sets of documents to be typed simultaneously, e.g., purchase ledger card, purchases day book and remittance advice. Continuous stationery units may be fitted to support documents like invoice sets. Many have automatic feed devices ensuring correct alignment of documents. Dual feed devices enable records like ledger cards to be continually inserted and removed, while day books or journals which receive a succession of entries may be held in the machine for longer periods. Programs on magnetic cards, tapes or cassettes may be inserted which enable the steps in a particular accounting task to be controlled automatically, i.e., the machine will automatically carry out the calculations required and print them out in the right sequence at predetermined places. Programs may also be stored on integrated circuit chips; PROM (programmable read only memories) can be changed only by the manufacturer if updating is necessary. Some machines print out automatically from cards with magnetic stripes which store data such as customer's name and address, accumulated totals and current balances.

(c)   Microcomputer systems

Because accounting machines are designed for one purpose only, they are being rapidly superseded by microcomputers which may be used for any task for which suitable software is available. For example, details of new transactions may be keyed in on the computer keyboard so that purchase, sales and general ledgers may be updated, and the results displayed on the VDU screen. A printer may be used if hard copy of the information is needed. Disk storage may be used for accounting records, expandable as required. Password systems (see **11.7**) may be used to prevent unauthorized access to and editing of computer accounts files and records.

Spreadsheet programs are widely used for accounting and budgeting and allow figures to be processed and moved around in a similar way to words in a word processing system. When the user changes the figures for one item in a column the program automatically updates the figures in other columns that are affected by the change, i.e., other figures at positions on the page specified by the user program. For example, if a stated profit is the target, the sales costs affecting this can be changed by altering constituent costs by different degrees, until the required profit is reached. A spreadsheet program can therefore help management to test out hypotheses before deciding on a course of action. (See also **11.12** *(c)*.)

(d)   Manifold bill boards

These are used in small organizations where the amount of work does not justify the installation of accounting machinery. They promote accuracy, as much repetitive writing is avoided by their use. A set of documents is placed in appropriate positions on a posting board (see Figure 10.3). They may be of carbonless paper, or backed with spot carbon or interleaved with carbon paper. Fewer sheets have to be assembled if double-sided carbon paper is used: as well as imprinting a copy on the document below it, it yields one also on the underside of a translucent sheet above it. One writing completes three entries, e.g., statement, ledger card and journal; remittance advice note, ledger card and journal; stock control sheets and individual record cards; earnings card, payroll, and payslip. Similar systems enable dual entries to be made simultaneously, e.g., cheque and payment record, petty cash voucher and journal

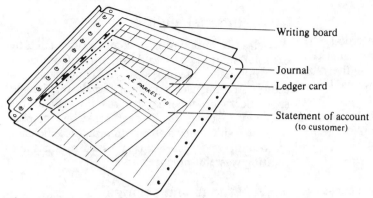

Writing board

Journal

Ledger card

Statement of account
(to customer)

Figure 10.3 Manifold bill board.

sheet (building up a record of all transactions, complete with analysis and VAT columns).

(e) Cheque writers and signers

These enable cheques to be automatically written and signed. They may be manually or electrically operated. Where large numbers of cheques are concerned, an automatic feed device may be used.

A signature may be etched on a plate which imprints on cheques through an indelible ribbon, preventing unauthorized alterations. The amount may be printed in two colours, one for pounds and the other for pence, and engraved into the fibre of the paper A prefix, i.e., 'the sum of' is automatically printed to fill any gap before the amount that could be illicitly filled in. Plates may be engraved with an amount limit, e.g. 'not over £200', for further security. Specially designed numerals also prevent amounts being superimposed.

The quantity of cheques passing through a machine is counted by a non-resettable meter. On electronic models, a signature register keeps a record of the number of signatures printed and of the amounts recorded on the cheques, printing out these details with totals on a tally roll.

Two keys, each held by a different person, may be needed to unlock machines for use. Sometimes a third key is necessary to enable the signed cheques to be removed from the locked box in which they are stacked. Similar precautions may be used with continuous form cheque signers and writers; these may also have an automatic cut-out at the end of a run. The paper feed may be adjusted to take cheques alone or cheques attached to payslips or remittance advices (see Figure 10.2).

(f) Coin and note counters

Coins may be counted automatically either continuously or in preset batches directly into wrapped tubes or plastic or large cloth bags. Any denomination of coin may be counted: a selector device enables the diameter and thickness of the coins that are to be counted to be preset, and the rest are rejected and collected in a hopper. Electronic models show the number of coins counted on an LCD display. Some machines can deal with only one denomination at a time while others enable all denominations to be counted, batched and bagged simultaneously. Coin counters are used to prepare wages packets, to count sales takings and to sort coins for banking.

Electronic note counters enable the required size of a batch of notes to be preprogrammed on the keyboard and shown on the LCD display. Batches may be totalled separately or accumulated, the cumulative figure being held in memory. The number of notes counted and the number of batches may be displayed. Slow motion counting may be selected if the notes need to be visually checked during counting. A diagnostic panel gives warning signals of faults, including those caused by jammed notes, and any incomplete batches. Batches of notes may also be weighed in order to check the approximate number of notes they contain.

10.5 Credit control

The accounts department must take precautions to prevent bad debts occurring as a result of credit extended to customers. Action taken may include:

101

(a) Credit references

When new customers place substantial orders, the department may check up on their financial reliability by obtaining references from the customers' banks through the company's own bank. If a customer belongs to a trade association this may also be approached, or a trader with whom the customer has done regular business. Information may also be obtained from credit reference agencies.

(b) Credit limit

As a result of these enquiries, the department sets a credit limit for each customer. The customer's payment record is then periodically monitored. Where a computerized system is used, checks are automatically kept so that accounts staff are alerted to defaulters.

(c) 'Stop' list

Customers with doubtful payment records may be placed on a 'stop' list if they seriously exceed their credit limit, i.e., delivery of goods on order is stopped until the existing debt is paid off.

(d) CWO/COD

If the department has reason to believe that a customer may default, an order may not be accepted unless accompanied by payment in advance (cash with order). Alternatively a pro forma invoice may be sent and payment collected at the same time as the goods are delivered (cash on delivery).

(e) Debt collection

Action may be taken by:

(i) *Overdue account letters* Typed or printed standard letters may be sent to customers who have not settled their accounts, the tone becoming more urgent and demanding the longer the customer delays. They are sometimes printed at the foot of statements of account marked '2nd demand', '3rd demand', etc. The first of such letters may be automatically generated by computer when the credit limit is exceeded by an amount specified in the program.

(ii) *Debt collection agency* The matter may be handed over to debt collection specialists. This in itself may spur a customer on to pay up, to avoid acquiring a reputation as a poor credit risk.

10.6 Internal audit

As well as the checking of the company's accounts by external auditors, as laid down in the Companies Acts, internal audit is carried on as a continuous procedure. Accounts department staff make regular and spot checks on financial records throughout the company in order to discover error and combat possible fraud. They also aim to promote efficiency by locating weaknesses in established routines and spotting wasteful practices.

10.7 Wages and salaries

Note PAYE procedures are dealt with in Chapter 15.

Many staff in the accounts department are engaged in the calculation, payment, and recording of wages and salaries. Documents and records used include the following:

(a) Earnings records

A record is prepared in respect of each employee, bearing details of gross pay and net pay after deductions, i.e., the statutory deductions of National Insurance contributions and income tax. Statutory sick pay payments are also shown (see **15.8**). Sometimes this record may be the deductions working sheet (P11) required by the Inland Revenue for PAYE income tax (see Chapter 15). In other cases the company may use its own substitute (if approved by the Inland Revenue), especially if many details have to be shown in order to arrive at the sum due. For instance, for some workers several hours may be paid at an overtime or shift rate, and holiday pay may be noted separately; non-statutory deductions may include several items like superannuation contributions, payments to a provident or benevolent fund, savings and union dues.

(b) Payroll

A payroll contains earnings details of all a company's employees and therefore groups together the details noted on all the individual earnings cards.

(c) Payslips

A payslip is given to each employee in explanation of how his wage or salary is arrived at. It bears details similar to those on the earnings card. Pay-slips may be prepared as a full sheet and torn off afterwards at perforations provided. Where wages are paid by credit transfer, i.e., credited direct to the employee's bank account (see **14.3** *(e)*), the employee receives the payslip only.

(d) Coin analysis

Each employee's wages are analysed into the denominations of notes and coins required to enable the exact amount to be paid. The analyses for all the employees are then totalled ready for the collection of the cash from the bank.

(e) Wages envelopes

Sometimes a wages envelope bearing the details of its contents is used instead of a payslip; or the payslip may be folded to show the employee's name and inserted in a window envelope. The enclosed notes and

coins may be displayed so that the employee can check the amount before opening it (see Figure 10.4).

(f) Time cards

These provide proof of times of arrival and departure as a basis for calculating payment for hours worked. They may be signed by a responsible person or stamped automatically by a time clock.

(g) Pension advice

This is a statement accompanying a pension payment to an ex-employee, setting out such details as the gross amount with tax or other deductions.

(h) Computerized systems

These operate on similar principles to manual systems but earnings and deductions documents may be in a format adapted to suit the system.

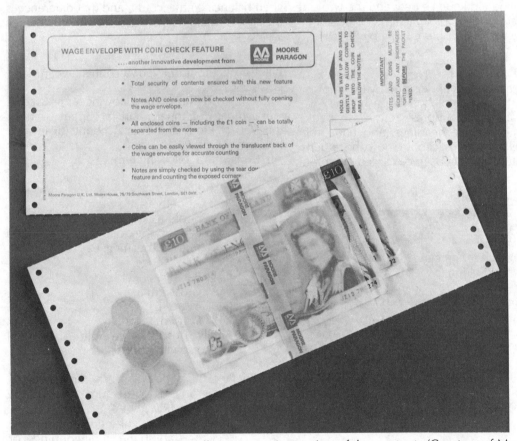

Figure 10.4 A wages envelope allowing easy inspection of the contents (Courtesy of Moore Paragon UK Ltd)

Permanent information such as employees' names works or reference numbers may be held on disk, along with current totals of gross pay and deductions to date. The new data, e.g., hours worked, normal rates and overtime rates, is input to the system: it may be keyed in, or source documents such as time and clock cards may be prepared in OCR style, readable directly by the computer system. The calculations are then printed out on payroll, wages slips and earnings deductions sheets (see Chapter 15). All records are automatically updated in readiness for the next wages operation. Cash analysis is also per-formed by the computer. In some computer systems, wages envelopes are already sealed, complete with contents folded in a prearranged way, when they pass through the printer unit; by means of appro-priate spot carbon backing, printed details appear only where required. Because the contents of envelopes are thus concealed when they emerge from the computer, this system is very suitable for payroll preparation. Another way of ensuring security is to print through a carbonless or carbon-backed envelope, the face of which is blocked out to obscure the information printed through it.

10.8   Did you know?

1. The nineteenth-century Truck Acts made it compulsory for wages to be paid in cash, but the Payment of Wages Act 1960 permitted payments by cheque or credit, provided the employee agreed.

2. If you find a difference between the two sides when balancing an account, and that difference is divisible exactly by 9, look for a transposition error in the figures, e.g., 784 instead of 748 (the difference being 36, which is divisible exactly by 9).

Activities

1. (a) What do you understand by the Imprest system of keeping Petty Cash?
   (b) Draw up an Imprest Petty Cash Book, with suitable headings, and enter the following transactions. Show the expen-diture and the balance carried down on 29 May 1981.

Opening balance £50

May	1	Bought postage stamps	£5.00
May	5	Taxi fare	£1.75
May	6	Postage for parcel	£0.60
May	7	Office Stationery	£5.75 (including VAT 75p)
May	8	First class package	£0.40
May	11	Bus fare	£0.25
May	13	Rail fare	£1.50
May	15	Flowers for Reception	£3.00 (including VAT 45p)
May	19	Office Stationery	£5.29 (including VAT 69p)
May	26	Postage stamps	£5.00

(LCCI, SSC)

2. Describe the main books of account that you might expect to find in an Accounts Department. (LCCI, SSC)

3. Explain THREE of the following terms used in your company's annual report: (a) current assets (b) turnover (c) Profit and Loss Account (d) interim dividend. (LCCI, PSC)

4. Explain the following terms:
   (a) cash card
   (b) cash flow
   (c) imprest petty cash system
   (d) cash book. (LCCI, PSC)

5. (a) Select **4** of the following terms and explain their meaning:
   (i) Sales Ledger
   (ii) Balance Sheet
   (iii) Gross Profit
   (iv) E & O E
   (v) *Proforma* invoice
   (b) Briefly describe the role of internal auditors, within a large company. (LCCI, PSC)

6. Briefly explain the petty cash imprest system and how it is linked to the remainder of the accounting system. (RSA, DPA)

7. (a) In what ways might a trading company seek to establish the creditworthiness of a prospective customer?

(b) What is meant by 'credit control' and how does it work?

(c) Complete the following Sales Figures table:

Sales figures for December 1983 to May 1984

Month	UK	Export	Total
	£	£	£
December	2,000	2,500	
January	3,500		6,250
February		2,750	7,500
March	4,250	1,750	
April		3,750	8,500
May	3,250		7,000
Totals			

(LCCI, SSC)

8. List, with a brief explanation, the chief documents and records used in a wages system.

9. State eight ways a firm's accounts help the management to control the organization. Indicate briefly how each use achieves this purpose. (PEI, Sec Prac Adv.)

10. Calculate the answers to the following, working out each one first in your head, then on paper, and finally using a ready reckoner or calculator (as available). Compare the answers you obtain by the various methods. (a) Subtract a discount of 20 per cent from £412.00. (b) Referring to page 27 calculate how much VAT is payable on goods costing £19.60. (c) Your caretaker worked six hours overtime this week at £3.05 an hour. How much gross is due to him?

11. **Group activity** Obtain as many illustrations or descriptions as you can of accounts department machinery, for collection into an annotated folder for reference by your group. Some members might visit office equipment showrooms; others might write to manufacturers for brochures; one or two might report on equipment available within your college or school.

11
Computers and the electronic office

11.1 Why use computers?

Almost every medium-sized or large company will use computers to help run the office. As a secretary you will probably have to work with a computer in your day-to-day duties, so you will need to know something about computers and the way they are used. A computer really does make office life easier because it can do all sorts of different jobs.

The same computer could be used, for example, as a word processor, for filing, printing invoices, working out statistics for the accounts department, and communicating with other offices. What it does depends on the *program*, the long list of instructions by which the programmer tells it what to do.

11.2 Systems analysis

When a company decides to install a computer (of any size), it usually gets a *systems analyst* to study the ways in which the machine might best be used. If the company is a large one, the systems analyst may be a full-time employee, looking after the continuous improvement and adaptation of the computer system. The systems analyst will recommend what kinds of program and computer equipment are required.

11.3 Computer programming

Programming is for experts. Computer programs are written in *languages* with names that are usually abbreviations or acronyms: Cobol (COmmon Business Oriented Language), RPG (Report Program Generator), Fortran (FORmula TRANslator), BASIC (Beginners' All-purpose Symbolic Instruction Code). This is of passing interest only, as

the user of the computer in an office will have no way of knowing what programming language was used.

Many companies buy ready-written programs 'off the shelf', or buy programs that can be tailored to specific needs but are mostly standard. This reduces the cost of the system, for programming is very expensive and time-consuming. Once it is installed and running, a well-designed computer system can take over much of the routine (and boring) work and at the same time provide accurate information about the business quickly and efficiently.

11.4 Types of computer

Computers in the office can be divided broadly into two categories:

(a) Mainframe and minicomputers
(b) Microcomputers

Computers are classified according to their size, power, and type of processing unit. The most powerful type of computer is the *mainframe computer*. Only large companies are likely to use a mainframe computer, as these machines are very expensive to buy and run.

A *minicomputer* is the next size down, a sort of 'small mainframe'. It is a slower, less powerful version of the same class of computer, and is designed for businesses who do not need (or cannot afford) the capacity and speed of the smallest mainframe.

The smallest type of computer is the *microcomputer*. The name derives not from the small size of the machine—although the largest microcomputer can fit comfortably on a desk—but from the fact that the main processing circuits are on a single silicon chip, known as a *microprocessor*.

From the office worker's point of view the main difference between the two categories is that of location: mainframe and minicomputers require their own special room, often air-conditioned, and trained computer staff to operate them, whereas microcomputers can be found dotted round the building, wherever there is a need for one.

11.5 All you need to know about the way computers work

Despite the differences in size, all computers work on the same principles, and all have the same kind of internal organization. At the heart of the computer is the *central processing unit* (CPU). The CPU is connected to the computer's *random access memory* (RAM). The RAM is an electronic system for storing information, either numbers or letters, and then subsequently retrieving it. To visualize the RAM, think of an enormous array of thousands of little boxes, each one with a numbered lid so the computer can find it. The computer can go to any of the boxes, and either place a number or letter inside or read the value of an existing number or letter.

Each memory location (each box) represents the smallest item of information the computer can handle, called a *byte*. The number of bytes available is a measure of the size of the RAM. The RAM is used to contain two separate kinds of information: the information that is being processed and the program.

The computer is no use at all if it cannot communicate with the outside world, so it is fitted with *input* and *output* devices. The most common input device is the familiar QWERTY *keyboard*, and the most common output devices are the even more familiar TV screen, known in computer circles as a *monitor* or *Visual Display Unit* (VDU), and the *printer*. Details of other input and output devices are given below, but one is worth a mention at this stage as it is a vital part of the system: the *backing store*. When the power is turned off, the RAM loses its memory. It is therefore essential to have some means of keeping a permanent electronic record. Although recording tape is sometimes used, the computer *disk* is the usual way. The disk varies in size, form and

cost, according to the type of machine, but it is basically a cross between a gramophone record and a tape. The surface is coated with magnetic oxide, like a recording tape, and a pick-up arm fitted with a magnetic head either records or plays back the disk. A disk can hold from 100 kilobytes to scores of megabytes, according to size and type. It is preferable to a tape, in the same way that a gramophone record is better than a tape—you can choose any track and play it, without having to wind through the whole thing. A disk drive as fitted to a microcomputer would have an *access time* (the time it takes to find any given item of information) of a few thousandths of a second. If that seems fast, getting information from the RAM would take less than a millionth of a second. (See also **11.8**.)

The program for the computer will be recorded on the disk, and before anything else can happen, the program (or parts of it) must be 'read in' to the RAM. Once it has its instructions, the computer can set about its task, which may also involve looking at (or accessing) the disk for data or for more program.

So to start up a computer, the sequence will always be roughly the same: turn it on; load the program into RAM from the disk or tape; start work.

11.6 Practical office systems: The microcomputer

In practice, the office computer system may appear to be more complicated. We can start by looking at a typical microcomputer, which might be used for word processing and filing.

The system is illustrated in Figure 11.1 and consists of the *computer*, fitted with two *disk drives*, a *monitor*, and a *printer*. Switch on. The computer, disk drive and printer may all have separate switches. Find the program disk. Microcomputers generally use 5¼- or 3½-inch disks, which are protected by a square plastic sleeve or pack. Make sure the disk goes in the right way. A couple of keys, or sometimes a simple typed instruction, will get the disk to load. From there on, the program takes over. In some cases, the computer may require two programs. The first of these is called the *operating system*. Operating systems have names like CP/M, Unix and MS–DOS. The operating system is really just a program that tells the computer how to control

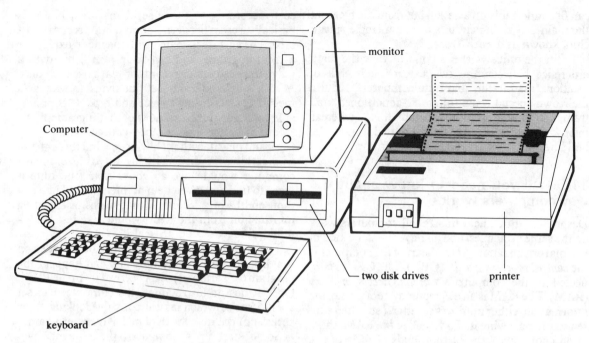

monitor

Computer

two disk drives

printer

keyboard

Figure 11.1   A typical simple, self-contained business microcomputer system.

the disk drive, printer, and whatever else is attached. After the operating system is loaded, the main program, which may be on a separate disk, can go in.

Once the program starts up, the screen will tell you what to do. Some programs are more obscure than others. One may say 'Put data disk in drive 2', another may say 'I/O D2?' which may require a look at the instruction manual for translation. Programs are getting better—more 'user-friendly' in this respect.

Word processing programs are generally easy to use, and the best way to get acquainted is to take an hour or two to find your way round it. It is impossible to harm the computer by pressing the wrong keys. Sometimes microcomputers are linked together in what is called a network. This is explained in more detail below (see **11.11**).

11.7   Practical office systems: The mainframe computer

If you are working for a big company then you will probably be using a mainframe computer. In

business, the mainframe computer will almost certainly be serving more than one *terminal*, and quite possibly several printers. The mainframe computer itself (take this whole section to refer to minicomputers, too) will live in its own room, probably air-conditioned to keep it at exactly the most favourable temperature. The room may well have a filtered air supply, to exclude dust as far as possible. The computer and its backing store will take up quite a lot of room. Most mainframe and minicomputers use hard disk storage, and each of these storage units takes up as much space as a small desk. Whereas the microcomputer uses a printer that is not too far removed from the office electronic typewriter, the mainframe computer may well drive a *line printer*, capable of printing thousands of lines of print per minute. Such printers are too large and noisy to go into the average office, and will probably be located in the computer room.

Unless you work in the computer department as a computer operator, you will never have to visit the computer room to use the machine.

Because it is so fast and powerful, the mainframe computer can cope with simultaneous input from many terminals. Each terminal will have a screen and a keyboard; a typical example is illustrated in Figure 11.2.

Using a terminal is not very different from using a microcomputer. Everything is controlled by the program (computer experts sometimes call programs 'software', as opposed to the machines which are called 'hardware'). What appears on the screens of the terminals depends on the type of business, the type of computer, and the application. Terminals can be used for entry of orders, inputting daily information about stocks and customers, accounts, almost anything. But instead of putting in your own program disk as you do when using the microcomputer, you simply select what you want from a range of options—known as a *menu*—presented to you on the screen. In most systems at least some of the options require the entry of a *password*. This prevents unauthorized people changing critical data such as salaries.

Sometimes a terminal will have its own printer, but often if you want something printed out you can ask for it with the terminal, but the actual printing is done by the line printer in the computer department.

Large laser printers are found in computer rooms. They are very fast and handle large volumes of work. Information from the computer—text, graphics, format and fonts required—is assembled by the printer into images, which are written by laser beam on to a light-sensitive drum (a similar process to the transfer electrostatic process described in **9.2** *(a)*). Printing is silent, a page at a time.

11.8 Computer peripherals: Backing stores

Already, you will have realized that there are lots of different input and output devices that can be connected to the computer. Such devices are known collectively as computer *peripherals*, and the following sections give a summary of some of the more important ones that you are likely to meet. The first range of devices to consider are backing stores.

(a) Disks
Disks come in a range of sizes. Three types are popular for microcomputers. The most common is the 5¼-inch floppy disk (or diskette, or flexible disk,

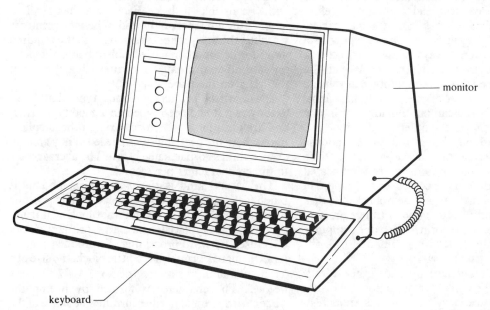

monitor

keyboard

Figure 11.2 A typical terminal for a mainframe or minicomputer. The switches next to the screen control communications with the computer.

or just 'floppy'). The disk is protected by a square plastic sleeve, which is not removed: there is a slot that lets the machine get at the disk's surface. Disks of all kinds are delicate. DON'T touch the surface of the disk, bend it, or smoke while using it. The 5¼-inch disk holds between 100 and 800 kilobytes.

Second in popularity is the 3½-inch disk, sometimes called a *microdisk*. This is built into a rigid plastic protective box with a cover that slides back when you put the disk into the machine. These disks have about the same capacity as the 5¼-inch versions.

Third is the *Winchester* disk. This is a very different kind of disk storage system. There is only one disk, permanently built into a special cabinet about the size of a video recorder. Although you can't replace the disk in a Winchester system, the disk has such a large capacity—several megabytes (millions of bytes)—that it is not really a problem. The Winchester disk has a very fast access time.

There is actually another type of floppy disk, the 8-inch disk, but these are becoming less common as the performance of the smaller types improves.

All disks, even the Winchester, are prone to failure from time to time. Floppy disks in particular will become worn, and the computer will suddenly decide that it can no longer read them. It is therefore wise to make copies of disks (known as *back-up* disks) at regular intervals when you are typing data into a microcomputer. Always be aware that a disk fault, or even a brief power failure, will lose all the work you have typed in, from the point when you last made a back-up. Almost all microcomputers have two disk drives, so you can put a blank disk in one slot and the full disk in the other to copy it.

It is worth mentioning briefly that you cannot use a new floppy disk straight out of the pack. It has to be *formatted*. Formatting is nothing more complicated than putting the disk in the computer and typing in the right instruction. The computer checks the disk is undamaged, and records various things on it so that it can be used. A disk formatted in one computer will not necessarily work with a computer of a different make.

The various forms of hard disks and other storage devices used in the computer department will not form part of the secretary's work. It is enough to know that they are very fast, hold enormous amounts of information, and are very expensive.

(b) Tapes

Some microcomputers use cassette tapes for storing programs and data. Tapes can hold a lot of information, but are much slower to use than disks. In the computer department they may have huge tapes on reels. These store very large amounts of data, but suffer from the usual tape problem of long access times if the information you want is at the other end.

The disk and the RAM share a characteristic in that they are both random access storage devices. The computer can go immediately to any of the recorded data. A tape, on the other hand, is a serial access device from which information can be retrieved only in the order in which it was recorded.

11.9   Computer peripherals: Printers

If you are using a microcomputer with a printer in the office, or have a printer attached to the terminal you are using, then it is probably one of two types, a daisy wheel printer or a matrix printer.

The *daisy wheel printer* uses a mechanism that is practically identical to that used by an ordinary electronic typewriter. The daisy wheel is a plastic wheel with 'petals' like a daisy. Each petal has a raised letter of the alphabet on the end. When the printer is working, the daisy wheel spins to bring the required letter to the top, then a mechanism bangs the petal forward on an ordinary typewriter ribbon, to print the letter on the paper.

Daisy wheel printers produce type that looks exactly as if it had been typed on a good typewriter, and are ideal for word processors or other applications where the best quality is needed. They are not, as such things go, particularly fast. The average is six to fifteen characters per second.

The second kind is the *matrix printer*. This is much faster than the daisy wheel, typically printing a line a second. The print does not look as if it has been done on a typewriter, so matrix printers are not often used for word processing. To produce characters, the matrix printer has a little block, the size of a letter, containing a matrix of 5×7 or 7×9 tiny needles. The character is formed by hitting the ribbon with selected needles forming the shape of the required letter. The letter is therefore made up of little dots, which are visible on a close look.

The matrix printer can also be used to do simple drawings, since the needles in the matrix can be operated individually by the computer; *computer graphics* such as pie charts, graphs and histograms can be printed out by suitable statistics programs.

Both the daisy wheel and matrix printer can be fitted with a normal typewriter-style *friction feed* for individual sheets of paper, a *tractor feed* for continuous lengths of computer paper (it has sprocket-holes down the edges), or a *sheet feed* for automatically feeding sheet after sheet of typing paper. *Continuous stationery*, as computer paper is called, is perforated so that it folds neatly and can be torn up into individual sheets. The sprocket holes are engaged by the tractor feed so that each 'sheet' is registered in exactly the right position in the printer.

There are many other types of printer, all much less common than these two. Perhaps the next most popular are *thermal printers*. These work in more or less the same way as matrix printers but have no ribbon. Instead, the needles of the matrix blacken special heat-sensitive paper by heating up. Thermal printers are fast and very quiet, but the paper is expensive. (See also **7.6** *(g)* (iv).)

Ink-jet printers use static electricity to direct tiny ink droplets onto the page. They are fast, silent, and produce good quality printing. On the debit side they are expensive and require more maintenance than the others.

As a secretary, you won't have to deal with the really fast printers in the computer room.

11.10 Computer peripherals: Input devices

(a) Keyboard

The computer keyboard is similar in layout to a typewriter keyboard, but may have extra keys. Just as with typewriters, the layout differs from make to make. The most usual extra keys are *function keys*. These are generally marked F1, F2, etc., and can be used for different purposes in different programs. The keyboard is generally connected to the computer by a flexible cable. Small computers may have all the electronics built into the keyboard casing.

(b) Joystick

A control stick is sometimes used to supplement the keyboard. It is used to move something, generally a cursor, about the screen. The cursor is a flashing square or arrow that is used to point to something on the screen of the monitor. For example, you might select an item from the menu by moving the cursor against it and pressing the 'fire' button on the joystick.

(c) Mouse

A mouse is an improvement on the joystick. Instead of a control stick, you have a small plastic box on the desk in front of you. To move the cursor, you just move the mouse in the appropriate direction, across the desk, and the cursor follows. This is a more natural action than using the joystick. The mouse has one or two 'fire' buttons on its back.

(d) Touch-screen

Some monitors are built with a system that can detect where a finger is placed on the screen. You can select menu items simply by touching the appropriate part of the screen.

(e) Bar-code reader

Anyone who shops in a modern supermarket will be familiar with bar-code readers. The reader is a pen-shaped device that is plugged into the computer. At the tip of the reader is an optical sensor that detects printed marks. Moving the bar-code reader smoothly across an appropriate bar code (there is one on the back cover of this book) reads a number directly into the computer. Bar codes are widely used in stock control and other applications where lots of items have to be checked.

In addition to those listed above there are many other specialized input devices. Computer input can be from *punched cards* (becoming obsolete), *magnetic strips* (like the one on a credit card), *magnetic ink* (look at the numbers along the bottom of a cheque), or even typewriting. A special machine can be used to read a page of type into the computer—the technique is called optical character recognition (OCR).

One final input device that the secretary may encounter is the *Microwriter*. This a small machine with a special keyboard designed to be operated by the fingers of one hand. Letters are produced by pressing different combinations of keys. The Microwriter has a display that shows one line of type, but can if necessary be connected to a monitor. It can of course be connected to a printer. It is self-contained, battery powered, and can store a few pages of text.

11.11   Networks

Computers and other machines can be linked together so that information can be passed from one to another. Such a link-up is called a *network*. There are two forms of network, the *local area network*, and the *wide area network*. The local area network is confined to an office, or at most to a building. Wide area networks can span the world.

Networking greatly increases the power and flexibility of computers and their peripherals. Just about the simplest form of local area network would be two microcomputers sharing a Winchester disk and a printer, illustrated in Figure 11.3. Each machine works separately until it needs to access the disk. Then it uses the network to write on or read from the disk (computer terminology uses 'write' and 'read' instead of 'record' and 'play', but it means the same). If both computers tried to use the disk simultaneously there would obviously be problems, so various systems are used to ensure that every machine on the network checks that the network is free, and if necessary waits. Because the rate at which data is transmitted through the network is very rapid, there is not usually a perceptible delay.

Other more subtle problems can arise. Suppose the first computer was in use updating an accounts file. Unknowingly, someone uses the second computer to print out the same file. The result could be wrong information on the printout, caused by the second computer working on a partially updated file. To solve this problem, a technique known as *file locking* is used. The computer carrying out the updating locks the file, so that no other machines can use it.

A more complicated network is shown in Figure 11.4. This shows a minicomputer, with a network of microcomputers, printers, and other machines, such as might be used in a modern office. Note that there is a dedicated word processor (basically a computer specially designed for word processing and unusable for other purposes), a telex machine and three types of printer. Each microcomputer or terminal that is linked to the network is referred to as a *work-station*.

As each microcomputer has access to the files held on the hard disk system of the minicomputer, information held there can be obtained by any of the microcomputers, subject to the right password. Thus the accounts manager can obtain historical data about sales, for example, and use his microcomputer to produce his statistics. In the illustration the accounts manager has a matrix printer; the general manager has a daisy wheel printer—why do you think this is?

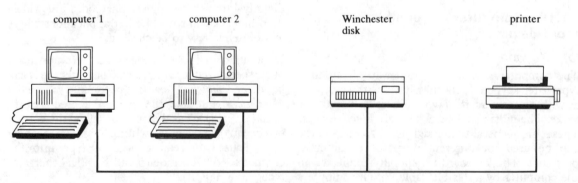

Figure 11.3   A very simple network. Not only can either computer use the Winchester disk or printer, but information can also be sent from one computer to the other.

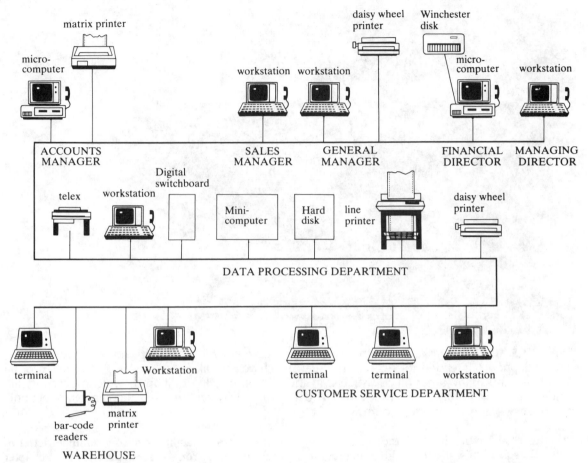

Figure 11.4   A local area network for a small company. Note that some of the workstations have telephones for an 'electronic mail' system.

Wide area networks link offices in different parts of the country—or even different parts of the world—by special communication lines. In the United Kingdom the lines are provided by British Telecom. Transatlantic and other long-distance links are usually made by satellite. Wide area networks link the same kinds of machine as local area networks, but you may well find a *facsimile machine* at each end of the long-distance link. The facsimile machine can scan any document or photograph and transmit a copy of it to the machine at the other end of the link (see also **13.12**).

It is possible to transmit information over the normal 'speech' telephone lines, using a device called a *modem*. The output of the computer is converted into an audible signal, and sent down the telephone lines. A modem at the other end translates the signal for the receiving computer. Because telephone lines are intended for speech, they are not ideal for data. The speed of transmission is only a fraction of what can be obtained using proper data lines, and the reliability is not as good. The one advantage is that of cheapness. The same network that handles data can also handle spoken information, although it is not yet possible for a computer to recognize speech. (See also **13.7** for modems.)

11.12   Types of software

The software designed for a business computer system is known as *applications software*, and may be

113

Figure 11.5   One Per Desk. This machine combines a powerful microcomputer, its own backing store, and a telephone. Intended for networking, such machines are likely to appear on the desks of all executives, and many other office workers, in the near future. In addition to word processing, file handling and graphics (a statistics program can be seen running), a synthesized voice can relay electronic mail or answer the telephone. (Courtesy of ICL)

written specially or purchased by the company ready to use. Because of this, all sorts of different programs are in use. Here are four typical classes of program, which will give you an idea of what to expect.

(a)   File handling systems

One of the most useful features of any computer is its ability to store large numbers of files, and to search for and find any file or files very quickly. For example, a list of customers would be a common type of file. Each record within a file would contain all the information about one customer, and typing in the customer's name (or number) would locate the right file and display it on the screen of the monitor. The information could then be updated (a password might be needed) and returned to storage.

A file handling system can do much more than this. It would be possible to locate and print out the names of all the customers who are in arrears with payments. These files could then be linked with a word processor facility to send a reminder letter to each customer. You will see at the end of this chapter how different jobs, once separate, can be linked together by computer systems.

(b)   Word processors

Although you can buy dedicated word processors, or word processors that link to existing electronic typewriters, the computer can carry out word processing very efficiently. Word processing programs are used in just the same way as dedicated word processors, but in a well designed networked system have the advantage that they can use information held in the files, and can store as much text as anyone could possibly write by using hard disk storage. Word processor programs vary a lot in 'user-friendliness'. A few can take days to get to grips with, but the better ones are so simple that you will be at home with them after a few hours. (See **17.9**.)

Figure 11.6 A portable microcomputer, intended for executives. It combines computer, printer, and a small monitor in a package small enough to fit into a briefcase. It can be linked to a network when in the office. (Courtesy of the Sharp Corporation)

(c) Spreadsheets

Spreadsheet programs are widely used in accounts departments, and for management accounting. The idea of a spreadsheet is very simple and rather clever. Imagine a very large sheet of paper (two or three metres each way) ruled up into little boxes. The screen of the monitor provides a 'window' that lets you look at part of the sheet; the window can be moved around the sheet as you wish. Imagine that someone has typed in a column of figures, and below that, a total. The computer has been instructed to calculate the total automatically.

Now if you change one of the figures in the column, by moving the cursor over it and typing the new number in, the total will change automatically. You can make totals of the totals if you want, or use complex mathematical formulae instead of just

addition. Spreadsheets take a lot of the hard work out of management accounting, and reduce the chances of mistakes (see also **10.4** *(c)*).

(d) Graphics programs

Computers can take numerical data and turn it into charts or graphs. The results can be printed out on a matrix printer, or if a high degree of accuracy is needed, on a *plotter*. A plotter is a specialized printer, designed to produce drawings under computer control. Graphics programs are often combined with statistics software that makes the required calculations before printing it out in graphical form (see also **20.5**).

11.13 Information processing

Information processing is the general term given to any computer processing of data within a business. At the lowest level, a self-contained word processor is carrying out information processing. More complex systems can deal with many activities within a company. The following paragraphs give an indication of the way a system might work.

An order received from a customer goes to the customer service clerk, who calls up the customer file on a terminal and enters the order. The computer checks the customer for creditworthiness, to ensure that the order should be cleared for dispatch. An invoice is printed out and sent to the customer. A dispatch note is printed out on a printer in the warehouse, along with a location code. Warehouse staff locate the items required, and use a bar-code reader to check off each item as it is packed. The item description appears on the warehouse terminal to confirm it is correct. The order is shipped.

The computer updates the stock levels of the items, and also updates the customer file with the date of shipment in case there are any queries.

If stock levels fall below a calculated minimum, which will vary according to the rate of sale and the time it takes to obtain new stock, the computer produces a stock order report for the inventory control manager. Sales statistics are produced regularly for the sales manager.

The managing director and financial director can use their passwords to obtain detailed financial and activity reports whenever they want them.

11.14   In a nutshell: Effects of electronic office systems on office organization

- Because information is so readily available to all types and grades of staff, it is a resource that needs careful management if it is not to become an embarrassment.
- Because managers can obtain their own information they do not have to rely on support staff getting it for them. Information systems do the sorting and monitoring that these members of staff have traditionally done.
- Traditional office functions are becoming merged, as a result of equipment which can handle all aspects of information processing.
- Because resources can be easily distributed, there is less centralization.
- Information is available to enable decisions to be made on the spot, creating possible problems with teamwork.
- Through changing patterns of work, departmental groups and roles are changing, e.g., there is less emphasis on the part traditionally played by the mailroom.
- Information processing is done by the majority of staff—unlike data processing in mainframe installations which needs to be handled by specialists.
- Because information is so readily available, systems must be evolved to ensure the *integrity* of information, i.e., its reliability and accuracy.

Bad news, I'm afraid—it's total amnesia!

Figure 11.7   (Courtesy of Tony Holland. First published in *Business Systems and Equipment*.)

Did you know?

1. 1 Kbyte (kilobyte) = 1024 bytes
   1 Mbyte (megabyte) = 1 024 000 bytes
   1 Gbyte (gigobyte) = 1 024 000 000 bytes

2. Some manufacturers supply plastic overlays for the top of a microcomputer keyboard reminding the user of the prompts and operating key functions for a particular program.

3. A turnkey system is a computer system that is ready to use because it comes complete with hardware and software from the supplier.

Activities

1. (a) Explain the main function of the following computer personnel:

   (i) Programmer (ii) Systems analyst

   (b) Explain TWO of the following computer terms:

   (i) Hardware/Software (ii) Computer peripherals (iii) Binary arithmetic (iv) Random Access/Serial Access (v) Timesharing (LCCI, PSC)

2. Explain 5 of the following terms, and give 1 example of each:

   (a) Glossary   (b) Graphics   (c) Merging (d) Peripheral equipment   (e) Real-time system (f) Continuous stationery (g) Source document (LCCI, PSC, IP)

3. Computers are often blamed for mistakes in customers' bills. Suggest points in the procedure at which such errors might occur and describe briefly the means of checking provided.

4. Describe how a Microwriter could be of great benefit to company personnel who spend some of their time away from the office (example: sales representatives), and say briefly how they are used. (taken from LCCI, PSC, IP)

5. (a) State briefly what is meant by the term 'information processing'.

   (b) In the office of the near future, it will be possible to originate, transmit and retrieve information in the form of words, numbers or graphics entirely by means of electronic information processing equipment. List 6 of the principal items of office equipment which the new technology comprises.

   (c) Developments are moving towards a total electronic communication system, where all the equipment is interconnected, or 'convergent'. What are the advantages to a firm of installing such an integrated system? (LCCI, PSC, IP)

6. (a) What advantages does a local area network bring to a company? (b) Describe 5 devices likely to be linked within a local area network.

7. How are the duties performed by secretaries, particularly in large organizations, being affected by increasing computerization? Do you see a future for secretaries in the age of the 'electronic office'? (LCCI, PSC)

8. **Group activity** By studying Figure 11.4 you should be able to gather a good deal about the work of the departments shown, the type of documents handled and the part played by the information-processing equipment. Discuss what you have deduced.

12
Personnel

Personnel is responsible for the recruitment, training and welfare of all staff within an organization. In a small company this is generally performed by one person and in a large company there is usually a whole department headed by a personnel manager or director.

12.1 Recruiting staff

As a secretary, you may be in the position to see both sides of staff recruitment. You will certainly need to apply for jobs yourself and in doing so to learn how to present your capabilities to the best advantage, while quickly assessing the probable opportunities a new post would offer you (see **12.13–12.17**). You may also assist in your company's recruitment of new staff. This is possible if you work in a small organization; as you gain experience and take on more responsibility you may even select junior staff yourself. In the personnel department of a large organization your work would bring you into close touch with the recruitment methods used.

(a) Job description
This is a guide to the duties involved in a job, its scope, the degree of responsibility assumed by the holder, and to whom he or she is answerable. Its contents are supplied by the head of the department or section concerned—preferably in consultation with the current job-holder—and, in the case of a large organization, with the personnel department. Job descriptions help to avoid the overlapping or non-coverage of duties within an organization and are invaluable when new staff have to be recruited and in assessing performance.

(b) Job specification
From the job description, the type of qualities and qualifications demanded for performing the job can be seen. The job specification can then be prepared—either as a separate document or as an extra section added to the job description—setting out the attributes to be looked out for when selecting the successful candidate.

(c) Press advertisements
These should include the salient features of the vacant post, taken from the job description and specification. Sometimes candidates may be invited to send for further details, or these may be made available at a subsequent interview.

(i) *Need for brevity* If the vacancy is to be advertised successfully it must be carefully drafted. It must be short and to the point, omitting unnecessary verbiage. It is not essential to use complete sentences. Concentrate attention on points most likely to interest potential applicants—e.g., location, type of work, salary, any unusual features.

(ii) *Classified advertisements* These are classified by editors—i.e., sorted into categories for the convenience of readers. The example on page 125 might appear under 'Situations Vacant' or more specifically 'Office Vacancies'. Newspapers generally

118

print advertisements in alphabetical order, according to the first word or words. It is therefore advisable to start with the key words—e.g., 'Assistant Secretary'—the ones that will attract the attention of likely applicants.

In this type of advertisement, the price charged by the newspaper is based on the number of words used; hence words are kept to a minimum and abbreviations used, as long as they are easily understood.

(iii) *Display advertisements* For more prominence you might display the details. They are drafted to occupy a definite amount of space: the depth is quoted in centimetres and the width according to the number of columns occupied across the page. Thus an advertisement might be said to occupy three column centimetres. The cost is calculated on the space used, irrespective of the number of lines or words contained in it.

(iv) *Choice of newspaper* Choose the kind of paper potential applicants are likely to see. Some daily papers devote many pages to advertisements, while others have comparatively few. It may be that local papers or specialized journals and magazines carry the type of readership most useful. You can consult *Willing's Press Guide*, for example, for lists of British and overseas newspapers and periodicals. Notice which publications bring in the most satisfactory replies; this is why it is a help if applicants mention how they learned of the vacancy.

(v) *Timing of publication* Work out carefully the best date for the insertion of the advertisement. Remember that time must be allowed for applicants to answer, for their applications to be sifted and a shortlist of the most likely ones compiled, for invitations to interviews to be sent out early enough to enable alternative dates and times to be fixed if necessary, and for the chosen candidate to accept the post and (if already working) to hand in the required notice to the present employer. Even then, the post cannot be taken up until the necessary period of notice has been worked. You will see that careful planning is needed if the work of the company is to be carried on with the minimum of dislocation.

(vi) *Box numbers* The use of a box number prevents the company being inconvenienced by applicants telephoning for appointments or further details when this is not wanted. It also enables an organization to remain anonymous—useful when knowledge of senior staff changes might be helpful to rival concerns. A box number can, however, lead to delays, as the newspaper must pass on the replies to the company. Also, many applicants prefer to know the name of the organization to which they are applying. Some may even withdraw upon learning it—especially if they have unwittingly applied for a job in their own company.

(d) Employment agencies

Your company may decide to enlist the help of an employment agency. These will supply permanent staff, usually in return for a percentage of the engaged person's salary, payable by the recruiting company. An agency obtains a specification of the job to be filled and notifies suitable persons on its register; these attend interviews at the employing organization which makes the final selection. Newspaper advertisements, designed to attract custom to the agency, may also include anonymous details of the post. Technical and managerial staff, as well as clerical and secretarial, can be recruited in this way. For temporary secretarial vacancies, the whole process of selection is usually left to the agency. (For legislation on the conduct of employment agencies, see summary of Employment Agencies Act 1973 in Appendix II). Permanent staff may also be recruited through Department of Employment Jobcentres established throughout the UK.

(e) Speculative job applications

Occasionally, people will write in on their own initiative to the company to ask if there are any vacancies. Keeping a file of these enquiries will sometimes lead to the successful filling of a post.

(f) Application forms

Enquirers may be sent application forms to complete and return with their letters of application. Business reply service envelopes are provided by some large organizations. These forms must be carefully drafted to elicit the exact information required in the most useful order. Details from them may later be used—in the case of successful applicants—to compile staff record cards.

You may find it helpful to ask applicants for junior posts to fill in forms on the premises; you can get some idea of their capabilities by noting how long

119

completion takes, whether instructions given on the form are noticed, and whether answers are neatly and concisely expressed.

(g) Shortlists

In a large company personnel department staff will sort through the replies received to advertisements and, in consultation with the manager of the department in which the vacancy has arisen, compile a shortlist of the most suitable applicants. They will then invite these people to an initial interview, sometimes inviting applicants to telephone to fix a date or to indicate in their replies when they would definitely not be available for interview. In a small company, the processing of applications will often be handled by the executive concerned. You, as the secretary, might well assist with the correspondence involved and, as you gain experience and take on more responsibility, you may be asked to draw up shortlists yourself for vacancies among the junior clerical and secretarial staff.

(h) Conducting recruitment interviews

Personnel department staff are skilled in the art of interviewing candidates for posts of all types. You also could well apply some of the following techniques if asked to interview junior secretarial candidates.

(i) *Planning your part*   It is important to give an impression of briskness and efficiency, so prepare a plan of campaign before the applicant arrives. Your task falls into two parts: one is to give an accurate description of the job, so that the applicant can decide if it is suitable; the other is to assess the applicant's suitability and competence. A good plan is to list brief headings to guide you, leaving space on the right for remarks you wish to jot down. Keep your writing to a minimum at the actual interview so that you can give your full attention to the applicant. Where there are several applicants, you may find it easier to compare their performance and spot their strong and weak points if you grade them (e.g. from A down to E) on each aspect.

You may well include a brief practical test of typing/shorthand/audio typewriting/word processing ability.

(ii) *Questions to ask*   Headings for questions might include: qualifications (including confirming de-

tails given on the application form and enquiring if further study or training is being undertaken); previous employment (including details of work, reason for leaving, evidence of ability to work without supervision); personality and temperament (including likes and dislikes, home background, hobbies); school or college (including courses taken, clubs joined, positions of responsibility held). If the candidate is nervous, encourage him or her to talk. It is no use *your* filling in the gaps in the conversation when it is the interviewee's reactions you want to assess. Phrase your questions so that 'yes' or 'no' is obviously not a sufficient answer. Look to see what the applicant's experience has been and ask about this; vaguely worded questions can be confusing and do not draw out the required information.

(iii) *Information to give*   Headings under this section might include: details of post to be filled (including duties, salary, hours, lunch arrangements, leave, sick leave provision, whether pension scheme operated, notice required, whether a probationary term required); desirable date of commencement; how result of application will be notified to candidate.

(iv) *Concluding an interview*   Keep your eye unobtrusively on the clock during the interview, and do not let a garrulous candidate overstay the allotted time. You will have other jobs to do and probably other applicants to see at appointed times. However, remember to leave enough time to invite applicants to raise any questions they may wish to ask. A convenient way to indicate that the interview is over might be to say: 'I mustn't keep you any longer now. Thank you so much for coming to see me.' Then go on to explain the arrangements for communicating the result. Make sure that you can obtain from the applicant the names and addresses of referees (see **12.16**) if it is the practice of your company to take up references. You may like to conclude by giving a practical test.

(v) *Travelling expenses*   If travelling expenses are to be met by your company make sure that the applicant has completed all the necessary details on a claim form. You yourself may be authorized to make the refunds on the spot or you may refer the applicant to the cashier. If only unsuccessful candidates are reimbursed you may have to keep the claim forms and send on the cheques later when an appointment has been made.

120

(i) Appointment procedure

A letter is usually sent to the successful applicant, offering him or her the job. Sometimes the offer may be made instead by telephone or at the conclusion of the interview, but it is the custom to confirm in writing. On receiving the applicant's acceptance, the company should notify the unsuccessful candidates.

Unless a written contract of employment is issued, the company must provide a statement in writing of the main terms of employment (see Checklist below and Appendix II: contracts of employment, statutory provisions, page 291).

12.2 Checklist: Items covered in a typical written statement of terms of employment

- Job title and main duties.
- Date of commencement; whether or not employment with previous employer counts as part of continuous period of employment.
- Job location.
- Pay: amount; scale; frequency; how and when paid; basic/overtime rates.
- Hours: numbers; lunch break; starting and finishing times/flexible working hours.
- Holidays: date of commencement of holiday year; holiday entitlement; when it may be taken; public holidays.
- Holiday pay: rate; pay in lieu of holidays not taken up at time of termination of employment.
- Sick leave: when medical certificate required; limits of paid sick leave; incapacity due to injury.
- Pension or superannuation scheme details.
- Notice required from employer and employee.
- Disciplinary rules.
- Grievance procedures.

12.3 Induction programmes

A settling-in period is inevitable before a new member of staff can make a full contribution to the company's work. Difficulties are minimized when successful induction schemes are run with the object of acquainting the newcomer with company aims and organization of staff and resources.

Appropriate departmental information is given— e.g., the layout and work of the department and how this fits into the pattern of the organization's work as a whole; introduction to immediate colleagues with an explanation of the scope of their duties; the work of associated departments or sections; procedures for requisitioning supplies; lunch and coffee breaks; explanation of flexible working hours (if appropriate); procedures for using equipment and centralized services; fire precautions and other safety procedures; methods of communication within the company. Details may also be provided about car parking and canteen facilities, how and when wages or salaries are paid, holiday arrangements, and sick leave and pension scheme regulations.

Induction procedures are usually arranged by personnel department staff (in a large organization) and carried out in conjunction with the head of the department concerned. They may be concentrated into a half-day or whole day (or longer) on arrival, and followed up over a period by the head of department by means of informal interviews to check on progress and resolve queries.

In a small company, induction arrangements may be less formal, although the aims are similar.

12.4 In-service training

In the case of school-leavers or others who would benefit from further training, arrangements may be made by a large organization for attendance at day-release, evening, or short courses at local further

121

education centres, leading to professional qualifications or increased skill. Some companies run their own courses for employees needing special skills—e.g., management and secretarial trainees, sales representatives, or service engineers. These courses range from a few days' to several months' duration.

12.5   Internal promotion and assessment

In a large company one means of motivating staff to maintain and improve work standards is a system of internal promotion. Vacancies are publicized in staff bulletins and memos or on notice boards, and suitable applicants called to interview. Much importance is attached to the candidate's record and progress to date within the organization. In addition to work performance, standards of health and attendance are considered, temperament, initiative shown, and general promotion potential.

In many companies regular assessments are made of staff by their superiors. Standard questionnaires may be used to make assessment as objective as possible and to enable valid comparisons to be made. After questionnaires are completed a meeting is usually arranged between the employee and the superior so that they can discuss progress, etc. Some companies may grade the assessment, e.g., A—excellent, E—poor.

12.6   Retirements, redundancies and resignations

The personnel department staff in a large company are responsible for implementing retirement and redundancy policies. They arrange presentations to retiring staff and see that superannuation payments due are sent on to them. In the case of redundancies, they must ensure that the company complies with current legislation (see Appendix II). They check to see that due notice has been given by staff resigning to take up other appointments. To recruit and train new staff is very costly. The personnel department may therefore interview staff resigning, to find out their true reasons for leaving. By doing this they hope to reveal and remove causes of dissatisfaction and so reduce staff turnover.

12.7   Staff welfare

This may come within the purview of the personnel department. They maintain contact with staff absent on sick leave, and ensure that the regulations concerning medical certificates are kept. They may arrange hospital visiting, and in cases of bereavement see that letters of condolence are sent. Confidential advice is often made available to staff in personal difficulties. Social and sports activities may also be organized.

12.8   Job evaluation

The personnel department may operate a job evaluation scheme, whereby all staff are graded according to the type of duties performed. This enables a pay structure to be established throughout an organization.

The introduction of new technology may not necessarily change the previous grading of jobs, unless large-scale reorganization is involved. The 'pioneers' working with this equipment may be given extra rewards for devising new procedures but once these have been established their jobs may be simpler and quicker to perform than before. However, upgrading may be justified—for example, when staff are able to do new tasks made possible by the ease with which information is retrieved using the new technology.

12.9   Legislation affecting personnel

Copies of relevant Acts of Parliament and associated codes of practice are available in the personnel department. If disputes between workers and management arise, the personnel manager may be approached in the first place for information about the rights of the parties, and may be involved in subsequent grievance procedures set in motion by trade union representatives.

12.10   Personnel records

Staff records may comprise a file for each employee, containing the original application form and correspondence and information concerning the employee's progress through the company.

Often, index cards are kept, summarizing the chief points. They may contain two basic types of information: *personal details* (name, address, telephone number, date of birth, nationality, education, previous experience, etc.) and *activities since joining* the *company* (e.g., title of first appointment, promotions, rises in salary, formal internal or external further training, health and attendance record, assessment gradings).

Information about individuals can be collated to yield statistics about staff in general. Sorting according to category of employee is made easier in small manual systems if edge-punched cards are used (see **8.6** *(c)* (i)); groups of people holding certain qualifications, for example, can be easily identified by this method.

Where staff records are held on computer, information can be easily collated and analysed under whatever headings are required. Security of information may be protected by password systems (see **11.7**), restricting access to staff files and allowing only authorized persons to edit or delete entries in them.

Because of the confidential nature of the work, discretion is an essential quality in personnel department staff.

12.11 Flexible working hours

Under this system, the working day is divided into *core time* (e.g., 1000 to 1600 hours) when all staff must be present, and *flexible time* (e.g., 0800 to 1000

"Good heavens! it can't be core time already!"

Figure 12.1 (Courtesy of Tony Holland. First published in *Business Systems and Equipment*)

hours and 1600 to 1800 hours), during which they can arrive and depart at different times—subject to the demands of the work being met. The middle of the day (e.g., 1200 to 1400 hours) is sometimes part of the flexible time, staff usually being required to take a lunch break of at least 30 minutes.

(a) Advantages

Working hours can be adjusted to suit the demands of the work and personal commitments and preferences; travel rush hours can be avoided; premises are open longer for customer contact; 'credit' or 'debit' hours up to a set maximum can be accumulated over the settlement or 'accounting' period adopted by the company (e.g., a month), and paid off in the next. Because staff are more in control of their hours of work, there is often an improvement in their morale and efficiency.

(b) Disadvantages

Staff may not be available when required; congestion may occur during core time in some areas of work (e.g., telephone switchboards); heating and lighting costs may rise because of the extended working day; cleaning of the premises may be more difficult to arrange.

(c) Recording systems

Reliable records must be kept of hours worked during flexible time, to avoid abuse of the system and to maintain staff confidence in wage/salary payments affected by hours worked. A number of systems are available, in addition to manual signing-in under supervision. One is similar to a clock card system: employees insert cards into a time recorder for punching or printing on entry and departure. Other systems use counters or meters linked to a master clock or control unit: the counters are set in operation by a key (see Figure 12.2) or identity card inserted by each employee on arrival, and switched off in a similar fashion when the employee leaves the premises. The counter automatically displays the total hours worked to date in the current accounting period, making manual calculation unnecessary. Electronic systems show totals in a panel display on the insertion of the employee's key, card or badge, a printout of all staff members' totals being automatically provided in a locked unit available to

123

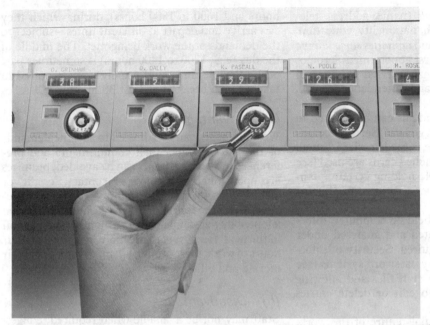

Figure 12.2   The Haslertime HT2001 meter system is key-operated. Each employee has a personal meter which records cumulative hours within the parameters of the defined programme, e.g., 0800 to 1800 hours. At the end of each period, meters are returned to zero using a special key. (Courtesy of Haslertime Division of IVO Industries Limited)

management. Accumulated debit or credit hours are automatically carried over as a balance to the next accounting period. Output from such systems may be in the form of magnetic tape or disk for use as input in computerized payroll systems. Additional non-standard information, e.g., about absences through sickness, holidays or business visits, may be input by personnel staff via a terminal. Departmental staffing levels and patterns of work may be revealed by the system, including part-time working and job-splitting (whereby the working week is divided equally between two employees) and home-working (whereby employees are based at home, and communicate electronically with their office). Management can study reports output by the system either on paper or retrieved from floppy disk.

(d)   Absence indicators

Some recording units will incidentally indicate which staff are absent or present at any time during flexible hours, as they light up when in operation. Lenses can be in different colours to denote other useful information—e.g., red for fire security officers, blue for cheque signatories, etc. Indicator panels linked to computers can be placed in central areas such as reception, personnel, etc. Printouts can be obtained on demand from computer-linked units, listing those absent and present, say, at the start or end of core time.

12.12   Trade Union membership

All employed persons may normally become members of a trade union. Some trade unions restrict their membership to particular industries or organizations or grades within those groupings. Others cover a wider range and there may sometimes be more than one union available to represent any one class of worker. In large concerns, particularly national companies or public bodies which have branches or units in different areas, there will usually be an organized branch of a union. In smaller or purely local firms this is less likely. Many concerns find the existence of the trade union helps them organizationally but in others the concept of trade union membership or organization may be resisted. Some organizations have house or company associations which are usually less effective and some professional organizations such as the BMA also embody some of the features of a trade union.

Benefits and facilities offered by trade unions vary in detail from one to another but may be as follows:

(a) Protection from unfair work practices or dismissal or other disciplinary matters.
(b) Negotiation of pay and conditions of employment.
(c) Legal services (usually at national level) in cases of industrial injury, etc.
(d) Some level of strike pay and other support in the event of industrial action properly taken.
(e) Benevolent funds and insurance schemes, in some cases.
(f) Those trade unions who have political funds may 'sponsor' members of parliament, i.e., contribute towards the day-to-day expenses of MPs who stand for election to a constituency in the ordinary way, or contribute to general party funds.

Branches elect their own officers and committee and usually delegates to county, regional or national committees or conferences, who in turn decide on major policies. Such conferences can resolve that their union affiliates to the TUC (which speaks with a national voice and can negotiate for all unions affiliated to it).

Similarly, unions can affiliate, subject to certain procedures specified by law, to a political party. By this means trade unions give in theory at least, the ordinary worker some say or influence at the higher level.

Trade union contributions in many organizations can be deducted from pay as an alternative to being collected by cash, etc.

Grievance procedure, i.e. the steps to be taken by an employee in the event of a grievance, is often mentioned in a contract of employment. If you are not satisfied with a working practice or conditions, go first to your supervisor; if you get no satisfaction then you may approach your trade union representative.

12.13 Applying for a post

You have been working for some time as a shorthand-typist and would now like to find a job with a little more scope. The following newspaper advertisement interests you:

ASST. SEC. reqd. for Office Man. large cosmetics mfg. company, Noford. Promotion prospects for competent sh/typ. Some exp. desirable. Salary by arrangement. Apply Box 69 this newspaper.

The work of the company appeals to you, its situation is convenient and there are promotion prospects. You apply that same day as follows:

(Your address)

(date)

Box 69,
The Daily . . . ,
High Street, Noford.
Dear Sirs,
In the Daily . . . dated . . . you advertised for an Assistant Secretary for the Office Manager. I wish to be considered for this vacancy.

At present I am working as a shorthand-typist for Messrs. . . . Having held this post since . . . I am now anxious to find a position offering more responsibility. My shorthand and typewriting speeds are . . . and . . . respectively.

My duties also include some audiotyping and word processing.

Before taking up my present post, I attended a secretarial course at . . . College, Notown, where I passed the following public examinations:

(You list these.)
In addition, while at school I obtained external certificates in the following academic subjects:

....

If you wish to pursue my application, I shall be pleased to let you have the names of referees.

Yours faithfully,
(Your signature)

Your application evidently interests the company for three days later you receive a letter inviting you to an interview with the personnel officer. Luckily, they have suggested a time which you can fit into an early lunch hour, so you confirm straightaway that you will be able to attend. You are glad that you are not yet compelled to reveal your intentions to your present boss: if you don't get the job, you can imagine the relationship becoming a little strained as your next attempt to leave is awaited! You write to the personnel officer as follows:

(Your address)

(Date)

The Personnel Officer,
PQR Co. Ltd,
Noford.
Dear M . . . ,
Thank you for your letter of . . . inviting me to an interview. I confirm that I shall be pleased to attend, as requested, at . . . on . . . .
Yours sincerely,
(Your signature)

Next, you find out as much as you can about the company and exactly where it is situated. Consulting a street map, you use the alphabetical index of streets to find the appropriate map number and section. Judging how long the journey will take is not so easy: delays may arise on public transport and you may become caught up in traffic congestion. Also, when you reach the actual building, you may have to spend time searching for the right entrance or the right floor. You don't want to feel flustered, so you make a generous estimate, preferring to arrive, if necessary, fifteen minutes early rather than one minute late.

Then you decide what to wear. You choose an outfit you have worn several times in the office. It is neat and smart and avoids the extremes of current fashion.

You then spend a little time marshalling personal facts, reviewing your present job so that you can describe the main duties without hesitation, and mentally going through the examinations you have passed, so that you can give a brief, logical summary. The interviewer may ask for this information to make you talk, even if the details are in your letter of application. If the company wish to see your examination certificates in the event of your getting the job, you decide you can offer to take them along for verification when you join the company. You also check up on how much notice you would need to give your present boss before being free to take up a new appointment.

The appointed day arrives and you reach the company's premises safely. The personnel officer is skilled at helping nervous applicants to feel at ease and the interview is much less of an ordeal than you feared. A second short interview ensues, this time with the office manager. You learn you must wait for a couple of days for the result of your application as there are other candidates still to be seen.

You like what you see of the company, so you are very pleased when a letter arrives, offering you the post. Now the time has come to break the news to your boss who is dismayed but accepts your resignation so that you can take up the post on the required date. You are therefore free to write (by return, as requested) the following letter:

(Your address)

(Date)

The Personnel Officer,
PQR Co. Ltd,
Noford.
Dear . . . ,
With reference to your letter of . . . , I am pleased to accept the post of Assistant Secretary to Mr. . . . , Office Manager.

I look forward very much to joining the company on . . . .
Yours sincerely,
(Your signature)

However, until that day arrives, you must not be lured from your present duties. Your boss will not remember you with pleasure if you leave affairs in confusion and make no preparation for your successor!

Figure 12.3 Which one would you choose for the job?

12.14 In a nutshell: Applying for a post

- If the advertisement invites telephone enquiries prepare carefully what you will say, in case you are already being assessed.
- When sending a letter of application do so as soon as possible after the advertisement has appeared in the newspaper. It is still customary—and helpful to the company—to handwrite your application.
- Refer to the source of the advertisement in your letter.
- Give your age and details of your education, training, and experience (if applicable). If details are lengthy, *type* them out and attach to the letter as a separate *curriculum vitae*, or statement of your qualifications and experience.
- If you have external examination certificates, state the actual subjects, where these are academic or commercial; some other subjects are of little value in the business world.
- If you are invited for interview, make the suggested day and time convenient, if at all possible, and confirm, preferably by letter, that you will attend.
- Find out exactly where the company is situated and how you will reach it.

- Allow extra travelling time for unexpected contingencies.
- Choose a neat and unostentatious outfit to wear, with accessories in good taste.
- Assemble personal facts in your mind, to avoid hesitation at the interview, and anticipate questions that may be asked.
- Decide what you want to find out about the company and the job—think of the questions you would like to ask at the interview.
- Be ready to give the earliest date on which you could take up the post.
  If you are offered the post and decide to accept it, do so in writing by return.

For an internal application

- Find out as much as possible about the new post and department before you attend any interview.
- Be ready to give reasons at the interview for wanting a transfer (apart from improved salary).
- Identify areas of work particularly enjoyed or disliked in present post.

12.15 Finding a vacancy

(a) Personal recommendation

You might be lucky enough to know someone of authority within an organization who is willing to recommend you for a post.

(b) Enquiry

By writing to the organization of your choice, you might qualify for a chance vacancy. At least, if you are considered suitable, your name might be noted for any appropriate post needing to be filled soon afterwards.

(c) Employment agency

See **12.1** (d).

(d) Newspaper advertisement

When answering an advertisement, make sure that you are the type of person the organization wants, otherwise you will be wasting their time and yours. For instance, if someone in a particular age group is wanted, do not apply if you are much younger or older. If the advertisement states that someone with special qualifications or experience is preferred, you will stand little chance without them unless you are exceptional in some other respect.

12.16 Providing references and testimonials

(a) Reference

This is a confidential assessment of your character and abilities. You do not see it, and it is not your property, as it belongs to the prospective employer to whom the referee sends it. In a first letter of application, it may be as well not to give the actual names of referees. This is because you may decide later that you do not want the job anyway, and they will not then have been troubled unnecessarily by the potential employer. In any case, many employers do not write to referees until they have interviewed secretarial candidates, especially when filling junior posts. Always ask permission before you quote anyone's name as a referee: a person may not feel he or she knows you well enough to be helpful, or may for some reason, such as travel or holidays, be unable to answer an inquiry quickly, prejudicing your chances.

(b) Testimonial

This is an open letter, i.e., not addressed to any particular person, but 'To whom it may concern'. It is your property. Although it testifies to your character, it is less valuable than a reference, as it obviously will not contain any derogatory remarks. If you are asked to provide testimonials, always send copies in case they get lost. You can take the originals with you to an interview in case anyone wishes to check them.

12.17 Attending an interview

(a) Putting across your personality

Try to keep calm at the interview, so that your true personality comes across. It is a mistake to undersell yourself, but even more important not to make boastful claims that you would be unable to substantiate if given the job. If your taut nerves lead you to chatter unnecessarily, keep a rein on your tongue, as no employer likes to be at an interview conducted by the candidate! If, on the other hand, you are almost speechless, you must make some effort to answer questions intelligently; the interviewer wants to know what you are like, and a laconic 'yes' or 'no' will not help. Above all, be yourself and not some artificial character you have assumed for the occasion. Give your own opinions, if asked, not the ones you think are expected; you may be wrong about these, or the employer may *want* someone with an independent mind. Remember that your personality is being assessed to see if you fit in with colleagues as yet unknown to you.

(b) Finding out what the job involves

Be sure to find out as exactly as possible what your job would involve—e.g., how much use you would make of your shorthand, audiotyping or word processing skills, how much responsibility you would

have, and whether there are prospects for advancement, both in salary and scope of duties.

(c) Explaining why the job attracts you

At some point, you will probably be asked what attracts you in the post. Try to give a reason less blatant than 'the high salary' or 'the long holidays', as you don't want to give the impression that you are interested only in what you get out of the post. If you are to work at first under a more experienced secretary, you can say you consider this a valuable way of gaining experience. The mention of promotion prospects can indicate your willingness to accept more responsibility in due course. You can suggest that you wish to work for a progressive organization or that you are impressed by the company's products, if these remarks are appropriate. Occasionally, you may find a link between an organization and one of your hobbies—e.g., art, music, wildlife, architecture, etc. The important thing is to find something positive to say.

12.18 Did you know?

An employer is not compelled by law to give a reference.

Activities

1. Staff agencies throughout the United Kingdom provide temporary workers to industry and commerce. (a) Under what circumstances might an employer use a staff agency for finding temporary staff? (b) How can the agency make a profit in its function of providing staff? (c) Why would an employer often prefer to employ temporary staff rather than full-time staff? (d) What advantages might there be for a young secretary just leaving College in registering with an agency for temporary work? (e) What are the main disadvantages of becoming a 'Temp' as opposed to having one full-time job? (LCCI, SSC)

2. Design an application form suitable for persons applying for secretarial posts within your firm and explain the use made of a completed form in the subsequent recruitment procedure. (LCCI, PSC)

3. Your company has inserted the following advertisement in a newspaper:

SENIOR SECRETARY required for busy sales office. The applicant should be over 25 with experience in a similar post. For further details telephone 01–111–1234, extension 84.

Describe the preparations that you consider should be made by the member of staff on extension 84. (LCCI, PSC)

4. You are secretary to the office manager, who is responsible for office systems and equipment throughout the company. You are soon to leave, and he wishes to recruit a junior to assist you and eventually to replace you. He asks you to compile from the many applications received a shortlist of likely candidates to call to interview. How would you decide whom to include? (LCCI, PSC)

5. You are secretary to the Office Manager who is expecting 8 people to attend for interview at

intervals throughout the day. What arrangements would you make to ensure that their reception goes as smoothly as possible? (LCCI, SSC)

6. A vacancy has arisen in your company for a secretary to the Sales Manager. A shortlist has been drawn up from the applications received, and the Personnel Department have sent out the necessary invitations to interview. (a) Explain what you consider to be the purposes of calling these interviews. (b) Describe briefly the arrangements that would need to be made to conduct the interviews efficiently. (LCCI, PSC)

7. Outline the points which, in your opinion, should be covered in a systematic course of induction training. (LCCI, PSC)

8. Your company endeavours to promote staff from within the organisation. State the advantages of this system. Suggest how the Personnel Department could select a member from among the Secretarial Services Unit Staff to be put forward for promotion to a secretarial position. (LCCI, PSC)

9. Your firm is considering introducing flexible working hours. Suggest (a) the resulting advantages to individual staff and to the firm AND (b) the possible effects on the organisation and administration of the firm. (LCCI, PSC)

10. Describe items you would expect to see covered in a typical contract of employment for an office worker. (LCCI, PSC)

11. A medium-sized but rapidly growing commercial company has appointed you to the newly established position of personal assistant to the Marketing Manager, on promotion from the post of secretary to the Chief Accountant. Two girls from outside the company with limited experience in secretarial work will shortly be taking up appointments as your secretarial assistants.

(a) Prepare an induction programme for your assistants.
(b) Suggest a programme of training for (i) yourself, and (ii) your assistants.

Make and state any assumptions that you consider to be necessary or appropriate. (RSA, DPA)

Group activities

12. With the help of your tutor discuss what points should be included in a job description for secretary to your head of department in your college. Each member of the group should then compile and type his or her own version, deciding on suitable subheadings and display. If desired, the resulting documents can be discussed by the group, judging them on their degree of helpfulness to the users.

13. Your tutor may like to stage some mock selection interviews for an imaginary secretarial post. When you are not playing the part of a candidate for a job, do not waste the time, but consider how you would answer the questions posed, noting debatable points that may arise from other students' efforts.

PART FOUR

External organizations and the secretary

13
Telecommunications

13.1 Secretarial telephone technique

(a) Receiving a call

(i) *Greeting* If you are a secretary answering the telephone in your own or your boss's room, you need only quote your office's extension number as a greeting, as the switchboard operator has already handled the call. You may hand the caller over immediately to your boss if this is appropriate, but other calls you may deal with yourself.

(ii) *If the boss is away* Keep a pad for rough notes near the telephone on which to write. If your boss is asked for but is not available, offer to take a message, or say you will ring back when your boss is free. In a case where you think your company is under no obligation to ring back, or where the caller cannot predict his movements, suggest a time when he might ring again. Sometimes, it may be appropriate to transfer the caller to another extension.

(iii) *When a caller is holding on* Telephone time is costly, so offer to ring back with information that might take some time to find, rather than expect the caller to wait. In any case, all the time your receiver is off the hook, no other caller can contact you.

(iv) *Taking a message* Have some system for taking telephone messages. Always find out the following details: caller's name and position in organization; caller's telephone and extension numbers; date and time of call; the actual message. Read back these points to the caller for confirmation before he rings off. Sign any message you take, and type out the details. Your company may use special preprinted forms for messages: these save time. The message is of no use if you do not pass it on, so place it where the person it concerns cannot fail to see it. Pads with 'telephone message' or other appropriate heading in bright, conspicuous colours are helpful. It is wise to check later that the message has, in fact, been seen and acted upon.

(v) *Business image* As you reflect the company's image to the caller you should always be as efficient, courteous and helpful as possible.

(vi) *Security* Before disclosing confidential information make sure that the person asking for it is entitled to receive it.

(b) Making a call

(i) *Planning* Use your telephone pad to jot down in advance the main points you wish to make, if your call promises to be lengthy or complicated. Have any necessary files to hand.

(ii) *Reference sources* Place telephone directories (Phone Books) in a convenient spot. As well as telephone numbers the Phone Books give useful information on telephone services, national and international dialling codes, action to take in cases of complaint or query, etc. Local information such as useful numbers and places of interest is included. International telephone directories are also available.

To avoid constant reference to directories, you will find it helpful to compile an index book or card index of useful numbers and extensions. You will also need to display a list of internal telephone extension numbers for making calls to other members of staff.

(iii) *If you are cut off* If you should be cut off during a call you have initiated, it is your place to ring again. This procedure ensures that both parties are not simultaneously ringing each other and finding the lines engaged.

133

(iv) Getting a number for your boss If your boss wants to speak to someone and asks you to ring the number, make sure before you start the call that your boss is ready to take over, so that you do not keep the other person waiting.

13.2 British Telecom public switched telephone network

(a) Digital exchanges

Electro-mechanical public telephone exchanges are being replaced by 'System X' digital exchanges which provide clearer speech and faster call connection. Voice signals are changed to digital signals and back without losing quality. Exchange areas are linked by optical fibre cable to form a national network. Computer-controlled exchanges enable outgoing calls to be logged. As a result itemized telephone bills are possible, listing all trunk and overseas calls made.

(b) Direct dialling

(i) National All UK subscribers can dial their own long-distance calls. Each exchange is allocated a unique area code number which the caller dials, followed by the subscriber's number and this brings about an automatic connection. This area code should be shown on headed notepaper alongside the exchange name.

(ii) Local codes When calling a neighbouring area a local code is used which is different from the area code. No codes at all are necessary when making a call within the same exchange area.

(iii) IDD Most overseas countries can be dialled direct (International Direct Dialling) by all UK subscribers. Numbers often consist of many digits so it is particularly important to dial carefully without long pauses between digits. The equipment may take up to one minute to connect. The telephone tones heard (ringing, engaged and number unobtainable) often differ from UK tones. Information on dialling codes and telephone tones is available from IDD leaflets for the countries concerned.

(iv) Code books Area, local and IDD codes are listed in dialling code instruction books issued to all subscribers and in Phone Books. Details of current charges are set out in a leaflet obtainable by dialling 191 and asking for the Enquiry Operator. The *International Telephone Guide,* published by BT International, lists IDD countries' international access codes, the country codes, area codes, a selection of charge bands and time differences, with hints on dialling overseas. Copies may be obtained free of charge by ringing Freefone BTI.

(c) Standard telephone services available

ADC (advice of duration and/or charge) on prior request BT operator will inform caller of cost and duration of operator-connected call.

Alarm call by arrangement BT operator rings specified number at agreed time.

Conference call by arrangement, BT operator can connect up to 18 parties in different locations for inland conference calls or up to 5 UK parties connected for international call to another number.

Customer controlled forwarding user specifies in advance up to 10 UK or direct-dialled overseas telephone numbers, to any one of which incoming calls can be automatically directed by BT exchange forwarding equipment when own telephone unmanned. Commands to activate service or to change current forwarding number are given from telephone handset.

Directory enquiries caller may ask BT directory enquiries operators for telephone number of any person whose name and address are known to him provided number is not ex-directory.

Fixed time call call (or series of calls on consecutive days) booked in advance, to be connected by BT operator at or about specified time.

Freefone caller dials BT operator, quotes a Freefone number or name and is then connected free of charge. Called organization pays for all the operator-connected calls as well as rental for Freefone name or number based on area over which calls received.

Personal call caller specifies to BT operator person or deputy required and telephone number where located. Call charge is made only when that person or deputy is brought to telephone. Personal fee payable as soon as operator makes initial attempt to obtain required person; one fee payable only, irrespective of number of attempts made.

Remote call forwarding   caller telephones local number at local call rates and is automatically connected by BT exchange forwarding equipment to company's office in distant area. Company pays for forwarded call. Enables company without office in area to establish presence there.

Telephone credit cards   holder (BT subscriber or agent) quotes card number to BT operator before making call so that charge can be deferred and included on normal telephone bill. Charge for each card held plus extra fee per call.

Temporary transfer of calls   calls for specified number intercepted (on request to BT operator) and automatically transferred to another given number.

Transferred charge call   at caller's request BT operator asks called person to accept charge for call (debited to telephone account).

GUIDELINES (recorded information services) include:

FT Cityline   Financial Times index and business news summary.

Leisureline   daily selection of main events and places of interest in and around London and (summer) Edinburgh.

Timeline   speaking clock (time is given every 10 seconds and is correct to within 15 milliseconds).

Travel-line   travel information on roads within 50 miles radius of each centre given.

Weatherline   Meteorological Office weather reports for selected areas.

(d) In a nutshell: 'Star' services

If you have a multi-frequency telephone (see **13.3** (a) (i)) and pay extra rental, you have access to the following advanced facilities from your telephone handset:

Code calling   up to 27 telephone numbers (comprising a maximum of 16 digits each) can be stored, and recalled by using a short code.

Repeat last call   by keying-in a short code the number last called is called again, saving having to redial an engaged number.

Charge advice   at the end of a call a recorded announcement gives its cost.

Reminder call   by keying-in a short code the telephone will ring at the chosen time.

Call diversion   incoming calls are automatically switched to any chosen alternative number (provided it can be dialled direct).

Three-way calling   a first call is held while another call is made, then both can be interconnected for a three-way conversation.

Call barring   incoming calls can be stopped and outgoing calls restricted.

Call waiting   a call in progress can be held while an incoming call is taken.

(e) Payphones

(i) *Public payphones* Telephone kiosks or booths are provided for public use in streets or other public places like railway stations or airports. Conventional pay-on-answer coinboxes are being replaced by microprocessor-controlled installations with press-button dialling and digital credit displays, showing the amount of credit remaining as the call proceeds.

One type is designed for coins: any wholly unused coins are refunded at the end of a call and a follow-on button enables further calls to be made using unexpired credit. With another type, the user inserts a holographic card (purchased at post offices or other retail outlets) which represents units of credit. The digital display indicates the credit remaining at the end of the call and returns the card.

Microprocessor-controlled payphones cut maintenance time and costs because they automatically generate signals at the exchange when out of order or when coinboxes are full.

(ii) *Rented payphones* These may be installed on private premises (at the request of the owners) to which the public has access, e.g., doctors' waiting rooms, hotels, shops, etc. The payphone may be wall-mounted, trolley-mounted or portable. The renter keeps the money collected in the payphone and meets the quarterly charge on his telephone bill. Some models can be used by the renter as an ordinary telephone when required. Microprocessor-controlled rented payphones similar to public payphones (see above) are being widely installed.

(iii) *Trainphones* Payphones are being installed on InterCity train services, enabling passengers to dial directly to any part of the UK and overseas. It is not possible to receive incoming calls. The equipment uses the cellular radio switching system to enable calls to be transmitted as the train moves from one radio cell to the next (see **13.4** *(b)*).

13.3 Telephone Equipment

Although at present only British Telecom and Mercury Communications Ltd (see **13.16**) are permitted to provide the public switched communications network, apparatus connected to it can be provided by other suppliers, if it has been approved by the British Approvals Board for Telecommunications. To gain approval, apparatus must comply with British Standards Institution telecommunications standards.

(a) Telephone instruments

Many different styles are available. They may be placed on tables, mounted on walls or raised on stands. Where necessary they may be weatherproof and fireproof. Some are one-piece instruments with the dial incorporated in the handset. As instruments are now plugged into phone sockets placed where required, they can easily be moved from one area to another. Modern instruments often provide extra facilities, such as volume control switch for incoming speech, automatic redialling of the last number called and storing frequently called numbers in memory.

(i) *Telephones with keypads* Dials are being superseded by keypads. It is easier to key in numbers

quickly on these, but connections are made no faster unless the push-button telephone is an MF (multi-frequency) instrument (see 'Star' services, above). This is distinguished from the conventional phone by 'star' and 'square' buttons (see Figure 13.11).

(ii) *Loudspeaking units* These enable conversa-

Figure 13.1 Hawk cordless telephone. This has a base unit powered from the mains electricity supply via a transformer, and a handset with integral batteries that are recharged automatically once the handset is replaced on the base unit. Calls are made and taken from the handset. This can be used up to 100 m away from the base unit from which the ringing tone is announced. If the special button on the base unit is pressed, the holder of the handset can be paged when wanted. The telephone can be programmed to redial automatically an engaged number and to store the next number to be dialled. It is best to site the base unit away from electrical appliances which could cause interference to the radio signals that link it to the handset. These signals can also be blocked by large obstructions in their path. The telephone is designed for use as an extension off an exchange line. Each instrument has a preset, permanent security code which protects it from unauthorized access by other cordless telephones. (Courtesy of British Telecom)

tions to take place without a handset. The user is free to move away from the telephone instrument and to handle papers more easily. With voice-switched models the parties to the call must speak in turn. The conversation can be listened to by others in the vicinity of the telephone but an optional handset may be available for confidential conversations. A mute button bars outgoing speech during confidential asides.

(iii) *Cordless telephones* See Figure 13.1.

(iv) *Advanced telephones* These combine telephone and data facilities. An example is illustrated in Figure 13.2.

(b) In-house call-connect systems

In organizations with several outside lines and many extensions from them it is necessary to have a system switching incoming and outgoing calls to and from extensions. These are of two basic types:

(i) *PMBX (private manual branch exchange)* All calls are handled by the switchboard operator, who gives personal service to extensions, including diverting or filtering calls on request. This type of equipment is suitable for smaller organizations.

(ii) *PABX (Private automatic branch exchange)* A PABX relieves switchboard operators of the need to handle outgoing calls because extension holders can normally contact one another and dial outgoing calls direct without the operator's assistance. The operator still deals manually with incoming calls (although direct dialling-in facilities exist enabling callers to go straight through to certain extensions).

The latest PABXs are microprocessor-controlled. They may be operated by means of buttons, keys or touch-sensitive panels. Light-emitting diodes indicate lines and extensions in use. Self-diagnostic panels display details of faults that may develop. One such system is illustrated in Figure 13.3. This type of equipment offers many aids to the efficiency of both switchboard operator and extension user, including:

For the extension user

Call diversion extension user instructs system to divert all calls to another extension if his own is engaged or does not answer.

Abbreviated dialling up to 20 numbers can be stored and retrieved in response to short code dialled by extension user.

Figure 13.2 The Displayphone is a convenient desktop telephone and data terminal. It is capable of transmitting voice and data simultaneously, enabling the user to access a database for information during the course of a telephone conversation. Prompts are displayed on the screen to guide the user in the routines involved. Personal reminders may be stored, to be recalled automatically at a preset time. Logging-in codes for connection to a central computer may also be stored. Facilities on the telephone include: storage of up to 81 numbers; holding calls automatically and manually; a muting facility enabling asides to colleagues without the caller hearing; displaying pre-programmed numbers before initiating automatic dialling; automatic timing of calls. To save space, the keyboard is retractable and slides under the machine when not in use as a data terminal. (Displayphone is a trade mark of Northern Telecom Ltd)

Last number recall automatic dialling of a previously engaged number.

Call back extension is automatically connected to a previously engaged or unanswered number when that number next completes a call.

Enquiry calls extension user can hold a call while consulting another extension or number and can alternate between the two numbers or return to the held call.

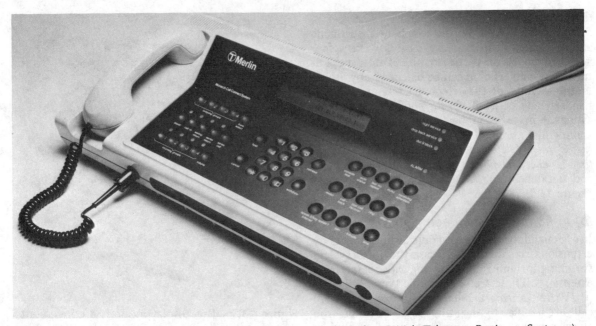

Figure 13.3 Monarch call-connect system. (Courtesy of Merlin, British Telecom Business Systems)

Call transfer to operator   if a transferred call fails the caller is not cut off as the call is automatically reconnected with the operator.

Extension group hunting   extensions are grouped according to type of work handled; equipment searches for a free extension in the group when a call comes in.

Conference calls   up to four parties can hold a conference, including one on an outside line.

Call barring   equipment can be instructed to prevent outgoing calls or some types of outgoing call to be made from some extensions or to prevent incoming calls.

Operator paging extensions   extension can be signalled to indicate that switchboard operator has a message.

Incoming call to engaged number   a special tone indicates to an extension that an incoming call is waiting.

Music-while-waiting   waiting caller is reassured by the sound of background music that he remains connected while the call is being attended to.

For the operator

Call queuing   if all positions are engaged a queue of calls is formed, each showing a different light signal according to waiting time. The calls are automatically connected in the order in which they came in when this becomes possible.

Waiting return   an incoming call unanswered by an extension is automatically returned to the operator after 30 seconds.

Hold and retrieve   operator can hold a call while dealing with another and then return to it. Nine calls can be held simultaneously.

Intrusion   operator can contact an engaged extension in an emergency. A warning tone indicates the operator's presence on the line.

Extension status   the operator can see at a glance whether an extension is free, engaged or unobtainable and whether any diversions are in effect.

Operator paging extension   extension can be signalled to indicate that switchboard operator has a message.

The equipment automatically records details of external calls made, i.e., sending extension, the number called and length of call.

Extension numbers and facilities to extensions may be changed from the console without expensive rewiring because it acts as a terminal to the computer, into which it can input new instructions.

(c) Key systems

These need no switchboard operator because all extensions can receive any incoming call on the external lines provided and can transfer calls to one another as required. Extensions can also communicate with one another. These systems are particularly suitable for a secretary needing to speak to her employer and to switch calls through when necessary. Outgoing calls can be made from any extension; a lamp display indicates the status of external lines (i.e., engaged or free). Engaged extensions may also be indicated. Facilities include holding a call while contacting another extension, diverting or transferring incoming calls to another extension, conference calls, last number redial, short-code dialling, etc. Extensions may have even more facilities where a key system is linked to a computerized PABX.

(d) Internal telephone systems

Because extensions can communicate with one another on a PABX, a separate internal system may relieve traffic congestion and reduce the chances of outside callers finding extensions engaged. Modern internal systems are microprocessor-controlled. Extension numbers can be changed electronically if required. Some systems use telephones with small display panels (see Figure 13.4): when not in use, this shows the user's extension number. When a call is being made the number keyed-in is displayed as a check and remains during the call. When leaving the office the user can key in the extension number on which he can be found or the date of his return, and this number will show on his display and any caller's display. The user can also input a short announcement lasting a few seconds which any caller will hear. An announcement can be broadcast to all or some extensions. Some equipment can be programmed from the keypad to store regularly used numbers for automatic calling when required; one

Figure 13.4 Ericom Direct, a digital internal communications system (Courtesy of Thorn Ericsson Telecommunications Ltd)

model has a voice recognition facility programming the equipment to recognize the voice of the user when he speaks the number or name of the person to be called. Paging calls to pocket pagers or to mobile radio systems can be made from some internal systems. Some systems are even linked to other, remote internal systems to widen the area of communication.

(e) Autodiallers (callmakers)

These may be linked to or incorporated into telephone instruments and enable frequently called telephone numbers to be stored electronically. Recall is achieved at the press of a button. *On-hook dialling* makes it unnecessary for the user to lift the handset until he hears through a loudspeaker monitor that the call is being answered.

(f) Call meters

These display the number of units used during a call or series of calls. Cumulative totals may be recorded.

Some meters are designed for use with switchboards and others for individual telephones. Cash equivalents of units used may be displayed if the user keys in relevant information (see Figure 13.5).

(g) Call loggers

These keep records of the use to which an organization's telephone service is put. The duration of a call, the time of day, the number dialled and the extension from which the call is made is recorded by the computerized equipment, analysed according to the program devised and printed out as required. Management are thus able to determine whether a better distribution of external lines and extensions is desirable, whether certain types of call should be barred from some extensions, etc.

(h) Telephone answering machines

These enable callers to hear a prerecorded announcement inviting them to leave a message which will be recorded for playback and attention later. On some models a set time is allowed for the caller's message, another call being necessary if the caller needs to say more. Most models shut off automatically when the caller stops speaking. A closing announcement is given when the tape is full. Recording time ranges from about 30 minutes to 3 hours. A succession of machines can be used when demand is heavy. An interrogator device enables recorded messages to be played back to a person on a distant telephone in response to his quoting a special code. By repeating the code at the end of the tape the messages are automatically erased.

Some machines merely answer calls with an announcement but have no recording facilities.

Figure 13.5 Sherwood Plus call-cost monitor. The equipment illustrated monitors the cost of telephone calls from an individual telephone or extension. The keypad on the right-hand side is used (a) to program the machine in advance with the appropriate call charge bands for commonly used dialling codes, and the amount of time allowed per unit; (b) to indicate which charge rate should be applied (peak, standard or cheap) to the particular call being made. The machine's microprocessor then calculates and displays the cost of the call as it proceeds. If required, the integral thermal printer will print out a record of the call (number dialled, date, time and cost of the call, duration in minutes and seconds). A security code must be entered before the machine can be reset to zero. The cost of the previous call can be called on the LCD, and also accumulated charges since the last resetting. By allocating reference codes, call costs can be analysed and attributed to the appropriate users. When no call is in progress, the display shows the time of day. (Courtesy of British Telecom)

13.4   Mobile radio telephones

(a) Equipment

Sets for use in vehicles may be purchased or leased from manufacturers and enable users to make and receive telephone calls direct without using an operator's services. Facilities include the storage of frequently used numbers, automatic repeat of the last number called, conference calls and diversion of calls. Hand-held, portable telephones are also available. Charges include connection to the cellular radio system (see below), a quarterly subscription and the cost of calls.

(b) Cellular radio

This system enables the best use to be made of radio frequencies available and reduces congestion on lines. Two competing systems are in use.

Under either system an area is divided into cells, each with its own receiver/transmitter. A car-phone or portable-phone user in a cell dials an outgoing call, which is relayed via a control link to a special computer exchange. This exchange allocates a free radio channel to which the phone user tunes in; it automatically dials the required number into the public telephone network with which it is also linked. This procedure connects the two parties. Incoming calls are received by the computer exchange, which pages all the mobile telephones until the required one responds and the caller is connected. A mobile telephone user moving from one cell to another during a call is automatically passed to a new channel without being aware of the transition. As each cell uses frequencies which are restricted to its own area and cannot be picked up from adjoining cells, the chance of interference on lines is reduced.

13.5 Telex

This British Telecom service enables subscribers to send typed messages instantaneously to other subscribers in the UK or overseas via public switched telex exchanges. Some of these exchanges are now computerized with advanced facilities such as store-and-forward message transmission (see Telex Plus below), short code connection, call redirection, statement of call units used, etc.

(a) Electromechanical and semi-electronic telex terminals

Both parties need a teleprinter with a dial enabling the call connection to be made. The message is keyed-in on a QWERTY-type keyboard and may be transmitted as it is being typed. Accuracy and the speed of transmission are improved if the operator first types out the message with the machine in local mode, i.e., not connected to the telex network; the typed message can be simultaneously punched out in code on paper tape and then played back for checking before transmission at nearly 70 wpm. Paper tape can be reused to send the same message to other destinations. As the telex machine does not have to be manned to receive incoming calls, messages may be received at any time of day or night, making it particularly useful for sending messages to people in different time zones. Messages are printed on a roll of paper. Multi-ply paper enables under-copies to be made of either outgoing or incoming messages. One copy may be filed in a log-book, enabling a record to be kept of the date and time of receipt and dispatch of messages, by whom outgoing messages were sent, and to whom incoming messages were passed. Connections are verified by the recipient's and caller's answer-back codes (identification codes) being automatically printed out before and after the body of the message. Telex numbers and answer-backs are listed in telex directories of inland and international subscribers. Telex messages use only capital letters and the use of punctuation marks is restricted.

(b) Telex Plus

Telex Plus is a British Telecom facility enabling single and multi-address messages to be stored by the computerized telex exchange for onward automatic transmission within UK and overseas at times when lines are less busy. The exchange automatically notifies the user when the message has been transmitted.

(c) Electronic telex terminals

These enable messages to be stored in memory as they are prepared, and transmitted manually or automatically at a preset time. It is easy to prepare correct messages as editing is aided by an LCD or a full display screen. Some models only receive messages. Others like the one illustrated in Figure 13.6 can both receive and send. The preparation of messages is not interrupted by incoming calls, unlike electro-mechanical or semi-electronic telex machines. When making an automatic telex call the equipment automatically checks the received answer-back code to confirm correct connection. These machines are much quieter in operation than conventional telex.

(d) Other ways of sending telex messages

It eases congestion at telex terminals if other equipment not affected by telex conventions and format is used to input messages. This enables members of staff without telex training to prepare messages. The following are examples:

(i) *Interface with electronic telex terminal* Messages can be prepared on word processors, electronic typewriters or microcomputers for transfer

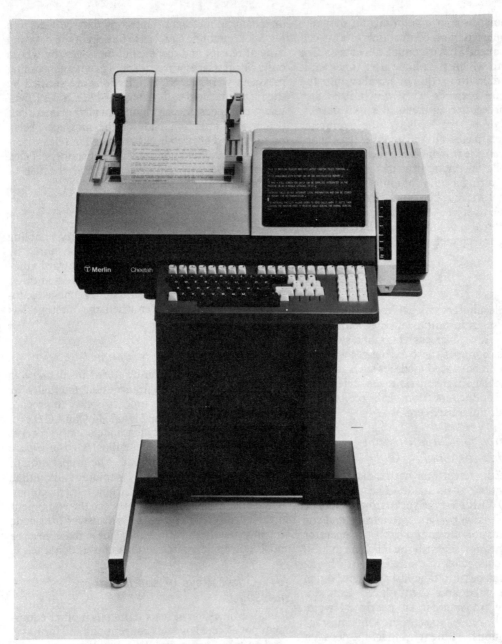

Figure 13.6 Merlin Cheetah teleprinter. Telex messages can be prepared on this machine while a call is being sent or received. Incoming messages are printed sloping to the right, and outgoing to the left. The numbers on the main keyboard are used to call the number required. Commands to the screen and printer are given via the keys on the top bank. The group of keys on the right-hand side control the word processing (editing) functions. The angle and brilliance of the screen are both adjustable. On the extreme right is a floppy disk unit for storage. (Courtesy of Merlin, British Telecom Business Systems)

to an electronic telex terminal for transmission, if an interface is used to link them. The software enables the terminal to reformat the typed message into the form required for transmission.

(ii) *Telex unit*   Another system links a word processor or microcomputer to a telex unit (see Figure 13.7) which transmits messages prepared on these host machines over a telex line. The unit has no keyboard, therefore incoming messages are printed out on a printer linked to the system or on one of the host machines.

(iii) *Telex punch*   A telex punch can be connected to a word processor or microcomputer. When the message has been prepared and edited it is reproduced as punched paper tape, ready for input to an electromechanical telex machine.

(iv) *Telex controller*   (see Figure 13.8) Large systems may use a telex controller which receives messages from display terminals, stores them tem-

porarily on disk, then transmits them either to other telex subscribers, to other terminals, to terminals on private leased telegraphic lines or to subscribers on the public switched telephone network through modems. Outgoing messages are sorted by the controller equipment into priority queues and dispatched accordingly or can be transmitted at a time stipulated by a terminal. If required, terminals can be notified of delivery of an outgoing message. Incoming messages are stored and terminals alerted that messages are awaiting their attention. The controller equipment maintains a daily log of messages sent and received, including a number for each message and the date. This enables any message to be retrieved later for checking. A directory of commonly used addresses and answer-back codes is kept, so that sending terminals need only quote the appropriate name. Standard messages are stored on disk, for retrieval and amendment by terminals as

Figure 13.7   Telex messages may be prepared and edited on the electronic typewriter (foreground), the word processor (left back) and the microcomputer (right back) and sent to the Telex Dispatcher (centre) with which they are linked. The Telex Dispatcher, which is connected to telex lines, sends outgoing messages as soon as it receives the end-of-message signal, or stores them for later dispatch at a preset time. The Dispatcher logs calls handled (incoming and outgoing) on an associated printer (not shown) together with details of failed outgoing calls. (Courtesy of Cescom Electronics Ltd)

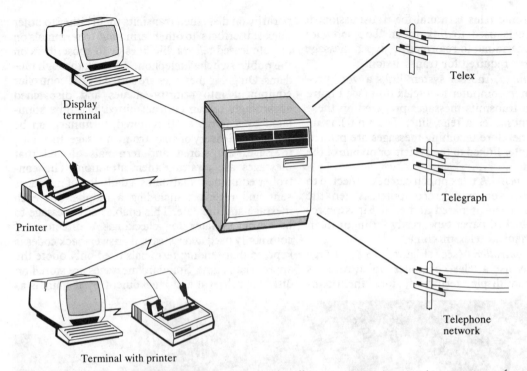

Display terminal

Printer

Terminal with printer

Telex

Telegraph

Telephone network

Figure 13.8   A Ferranti Telex Manager. The controller can transmit outgoing messages from terminals and receive incoming messages to them on a store-and-then-forward principle. The lines in this illustration are used to connect the controller to telex or telegraph lines, the telephone network, or to display terminals or printers. Controllers may be interconnected to meet the requirements of larger installations. (Courtesy of Ferranti Computer Systems Ltd)

required. Access to filed confidential messages can be restricted to certain terminals. The human supervisor of the system needs to decide what action to take if a message cannot be delivered and to which terminals unaddressed incoming messages should go. The supervisor must update directories, inspect message queues and adapt the system in cases of overload or emergency.

(v) *Other electronic systems*   Messages can be sent to telex subscribers by other electronic systems such as electronic mail (see **13.9**), teletex (see **13.11**) and Prestel Link store-and-forward service (see **19.8** (*a*)).

13.6   Private leased circuits

Telephone and telex lines (private telegraph) may be rented from British Telecom for point-to-point communication, e.g., from a head office to a branch

office. As the line is not used for public calls it is always available to the users. Rental is based on distance and type of circuit. No charge is made for the calls.

Links for private digital services are also available (see **13.8**).

13.7   Public switched data transmission services

Information in digital form may be transmitted to and from computers and associated equipment by a number of British Telecom public switched services:

(a)   Datel modem

British Telecom Datel modems enable data to be transmitted rapidly to and from computers, using British Telecom leased circuits or the telephone network, and allow instant access to a computer regardless of distance. The modem converts information passing to and from data terminals into signals suitable for transmission over speech circuits. International services are available to and from many countries overseas.

Datel modems can also be used to link private networks using British Telecom X-Stream services (see **13.8**). Modems can be rented or leased from British Telecom or purchased outright. Charges for use of the exchange line and/or leased line are the same as if the line was used for speech purposes.

(Data in punched paper tape form can be transmitted from a terminal using the telex network (see **13.5**) or over telegraph circuits, which do not require the use of a modem.)

See Figure 13.9 for a Datel modem. Modems are discussed also in **11.11**.

(b) Packet SwitchStream

This service allows users' terminals working at different speeds to communicate with one another, transmitting and receiving simultaneously. Data messages are broken up into individually addressed 'packets' and transmitted over a network of PSS exchanges, located in large towns. Packets enable the network to function economically by carrying the maximum load and may involve data from

several sources being sent together. On receipt, the messages are reassembled in their correct order. Packets are automatically rerouted along different paths to avoid congestion or route failure. Security of information is provided by the system but users can use codes and encryption for added protection if desired. Charges are based on volume of data sent and received and duration of calls. Data networks in many overseas countries can be contacted via PSS, e.g., in Europe, Australasia, the Middle and Far East, North America, the Caribbean and Africa, and the number is increasing. PSS may be used to obtain information stored in databanks and databases (see **8.8**) in Europe and North America on many commercial and scientific subjects; to transfer information from branches to a distant computer; to consult overseas computer bureaux; to make airline and hotel bookings; to send messages to electronic mailboxes (see **13.9**); etc.

(c) InterStream

These are facilities linking users of different networks: One connects inland telex network users to PSS users (see above); another allows Teletex terminals (see **13.11**) on the public switched telephone network to interwork with teletex terminals on PSS; and a third enables interworking between the teletex service and the telex network worldwide.

Figure 13.9 A Datel modem. (Courtesy of Merlin, British Telecom Business Systems)

(d) Integrated Services Digital Network (ISDN)

This is an extension of System X (see **13.2** *(a)*) offering subscribers a network for digital facsimile transmission, teletex, data transmission, and slow scan TV, as well as access to PSS (see above). Subscribers are linked to the network from their own premises via *Integrated Digital Access* (IDA).

13.8   Private digital services (X-Stream)

(a) SatStream

This service enables fast, high quality transmission of speech, data and facsimile to take place as well as videoconferencing across Western Europe, Canada and USA, via satellite links.

(b) MegaStream

This service carries voice or voice and data together from one point to another. It is used by large businesses, for example, to link PABXs, to transfer data between large computer systems and for videoconferencing. The service is being extended to countries overseas.

(c) KiloStream

This is a slower service than MegaStream, and suitable for data links between VDUs, electronic mail terminals, credit verification, slow scan TV, high-speed facsimile transmission, data and voice transmission within the UK and ultimately overseas.

(d) VideoStream

(See **22.8** *(a)*(iii).)

13.9   Electronic mail

In an electronic mail system, each user is allocated a 'mailbox'. This a specified disk file in a central computer's memory on which incoming messages are temporarily held until the recipient has the opportunity to read them. The recipient therefore does not have to be present in order to receive a message. The sender calls up the computer from the telephone at his terminal. The message which he keys in on the terminal's keyboard is translated into binary code by a modem and transmitted over the telephone line.

The modem may be built into the terminal enabling a call to be dialled out or received automatically, or may involve an acoustic coupler into which the telephone handset must be fitted before the number is dialled manually. Messages may be forwarded by the equipment at times specified by the user and identical messages may be sent simultaneously to up to 500 users.

The contents of a mailbox are accessed with a password. The user is notified of the contents of his mailbox. He can *scan* the contents of his mailbox by reading the headings only, or *read* them in full. A number of courses of action are then open to him, e.g., he can instruct the equipment to *delete* the message read, *hold* it in the mailbox for later action, *copy* it on to another disk or *forward* with comments to another user. The sender can receive automatic acknowledgement of receipt of his message if he requires.

Messages are addressed to a person via a code, not to a location. Therefore a user can retrieve waiting messages from any terminal. Some are portable and can be used anywhere where there is a telephone. Terminals may have VDU screens attached, for reading and editing messages; some have an integrated printer which prints out messages sent and received (see Figure 13.10).

Any information stored in electronic telex, facsimile transmission and word processing systems can be sent as electronic mail.

Public electronic mail services, e.g., Telecom Gold enable subscribers with different types of electronic mail terminals to communicate with one another at any time. Every user has a unique password. Charges include a fee for connection to the service's computer plus call charges. Long-distance calls may be made via PSS (see **13.7**) or, if abroad, via IPSS. Users in many countries can be electronically linked by public electronic mail services. Users are charged for space occupied in their mailboxes by incoming messages so a turnover of information is desirable.

Calls to Radiopagers may be made via Telecom Gold. Recipients can be alerted on their pagers that a message has arrived in their mailbox.

In addition to the mail facilities, it is also possible to access telex to 'chat' directly to other users on the system as well as using a Noticeboard bulletin service. Electronic publishing facilities are available.

Figure 13.10 Whisper Writer—an electronic mail terminal. Messages can be prepared and edited before transmission: this reduces the length and therefore the cost of calls when an external bureau service is used such as Telecom Gold. When the machine is switched off the telephone can be used for normal speech. (Courtesy of 3M United Kingdom plc)

13.10 Voice messaging

Voice messaging is a form of electronic mail, in that a message given over the telephone by a caller is stored in the recipient's mailbox until the recipient wishes to retrieve it. Whereas an ordinary telephone answering machine enables a caller to leave a message for the one person he is calling, voice messaging enables him to transmit messages to anyone who has been allocated a mailbox in the system. One call can enable an identical message to be delivered at the same time to multiple mailboxes. The caller does not have to find the recipient in, there is no risk of the message being lost or undelivered, and the system can be used outside office hours.

In one system designed for 'in-house' or company use, the caller quotes the name of the intended recipient, or the mailbox number if known—often the same number as the telephone extension—and records his message. The caller may himself own a mailbox in the system; if so he accesses it via a password (which he can change at will) in order to hear messages left for him in his 'in-tray'. To send messages he transfers to his 'out-tray'·where he has facilities for recording and addressing his message—reviewing and amending it if necessary first. Spoken prompts may guide the user on the necessary routines, if required.

A caller normally uses a multi-frequency telephone in order to access the system, which is allocated an outside line or extension number on the PABX to which it is linked. However, a conventional push-button telephone can be used if a specially supplied pocket tone-generator keypad is fitted over the telephone mouthpiece: this enables the digits to act as operating codes for the system (see Figure 13.11.)

The system is under the control of a supervisor, who can allocate or remove particular facilities, e.g., barring an absent user's mailbox to callers, and monitor the automatic call-logging system for cost allocation and analysis.

RECORD
Press to start recording in the 'IN' and 'OUT' trays.

ADDRESS
Send your message to one or any number of people. Change address for re-direction of message.

PLAY
Press to hear the messages that have been left for you.

SAVE/STOP
Stop playout and save for future reference.

DELETE
You can delete messages you have recorded or ones you have received.

SIGN OFF

FORWARD
Move forward to miss part, or all, of the message you are hearing.

BACK
Rewind to repeat part or all of the message you are playing or recording.

HASH
'IN' and 'OUT' tray access. Also used for system access and addressing.

PAUSE/RESTART
To give time for thinking and then continue the play or recording.

HELP/OPERATOR
Press at ANY TIME for helpful voice prompts from MEMOPHONE or the operator.

ITL Information Technology Limited

Figure 13.11 An instructions reminder card for users of Memophone, an in-house telephone messaging system. A multi-frequency telephone keypad is used to input the commands. Note the star and square signs, not found on a conventional push-button telephone keypad. (Courtesy of Information Technology Ltd)

British Telecom Voicebank is a public bureau telephone messaging service, suitable for brief messages which may be stored for up to 12 hours. Up to 7 messages can be stored at any one time. A subscriber who also carries a British Telecom Radiopaging service pager may be alerted to the receipt of a message in his Voicebank mailbox by a signal from the pager.

13.11   Teletex

This is an international text-communication service based on an internationally agreed standard and uses BT public switched telephone and packet switched data networks.

(a)   System

Any type of terminal from whatever manufacturer that can be fitted with the necessary interface can telecommunicate pages of text from one memory to another. Messages are prepared off-line and stored to be transmitted when required, usually when lines are least busy, and at cheapest rates; also message-passing is very quick (30 times faster than telex, i.e., an A4 page in 10 seconds) and does not occupy the line for long. Incoming messages are stored in the receiving terminal's memory until called to screen by the recipient; if there is no room in memory or the capacity is near its limit the engaged signal is given. Messages do not have to be set out in a special form as for telex, punctuation is used normally, and over 300 characters and symbols are available in upper and lower case. Presentation standard is of typewritten quality. Messages are sent and received automatically so other tasks can be done at the same time from the keyboards of terminals. Engaged numbers are automatically tried again. Procedures or *protocols* laid down for the transmission of text include validation of transmission, i.e., acknowledging receipt of a message by printing out the sender's and recipient's identification numbers, the date and the time. The same message can be sent to several destinations if required. British Telecom publish teletex directories of UK and international teletex users. Teletex terminal identities are registered with British Telecom for entry to the directory.

(b)   Terminals

A variety of terminals exist on the market. Some are designed for use with the telephone network and some with the packet switched data network but both can intercommunicate. The choice depends on the type and volume of work. Electronic typewriters, word processors and text-editing VDUs may be used as terminals and can revert to their original use when not engaged in teletex. A separate telephone line is usually appropriate for teletex, or more than one line if simultaneous receipt and transmission is likely. Users of teletex can send messages to any telex subscriber, so a separate telex terminal may not be necessary. Graphics and signatures as well as text will eventually be transmitted via teletex. British Telecom issue a technical guide to ensure compatibility between different suppliers and terminals.

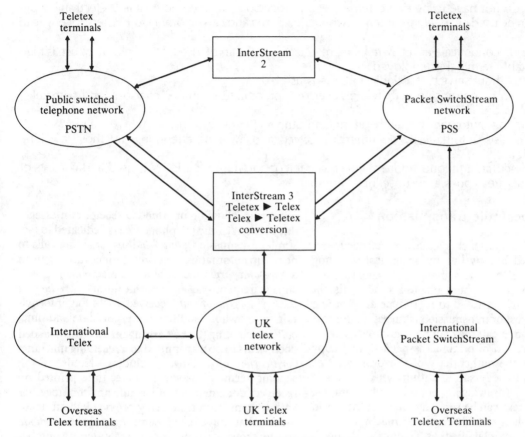

Figure 13.12 Teletex network interworking. (Courtesy of Business Equipment Digest)

In a nutshell: Main features of Teletex

- Because it is an internationally agreed standard all computer-type terminals conforming to it can intercommunicate.
- Communication is from memory to memory.
- Tasks being done at either terminal are not interrupted.
- Outgoing messages can be stored and transmitted when lines are least busy.
- Engaged numbers are automatically redialled.
- Automatically dialled numbers are checked automatically.
- Calls can be made over the public switched telephone network (PSTN) if a modem is used with the terminal. Calls made at off-peak times cost less.
- Failed calls are automatically reported.
- Transmission is at high speed (30 times faster than telex) so call length is cut and costs reduced.
- A4 pages are transmitted, so whole documents are communicated.
- Presentation is of correspondence quality.
- A full character set of letters, symbols and punctuation is available.
- Little operator-training is needed as the system itself guides formatting

- Terminals do not have to be dedicated, so word processors, microcomputers and electronic type-writers can be used (with teletex adaptors where necessary) and can do other work when not engaged on teletex.
- The fast and economical Packet SwitchStream data network can be used if the volume of use is high and a suitable terminal is employed.
- There is a 24-hour service, if a dedicated line is used.
- UK users can communicate with teletex users in appropriate countries overseas, and with telex users worldwide.
- The system logs automatically all incoming and outgoing transmissions.
- The system lists automatically documents received and awaiting attention, and those awaiting transmission.
- A teletex user has a unique 'address' which is a telephone number if PSTN is used and consists of country and area codes and subscriber's number.

13.12   Facsimile transmission

A facsimile transmitter enables an original document to be scanned line by line by an optical scanning system. The electronic signals thus generated are passed down any telephone line to a similar, distant installation and activated to reproduce an identical image. The cost of transmission is therefore the cost of the telephone call plus supplies and overheads.

No preparation of originals is needed, and copy received has the authenticity of the original, e.g., when signed by a person in authority. Any graphic information (drawings, music, photographs, sketches) or text can be sent anywhere in the world where there is a suitable receiving machine.

Machines are classified as Group 1, 2, or 3, according to the technology involved. Technical standards for the three groups have been set by the International Telegraphic and Telephone Consultative Committee, and compatibility between the types and different manufacturers' models is now possible. Group 1 machines have largely been superseded because they are relatively slow and involve many manual operations.

Group 3 machines use a digital process whereby the scanner recognizes the images in each horizontal line as a series of minute black and white blocks. By using compression techniques, plain areas of a sheet and spaces between lines are skipped, reducing transmission time. Information is sent in digital form via a modem over a telephone line. An A4 page can be transmitted in under one minute.

Group 3 machines have a large number of facilities: a *diagnostic panel* displaying coded information about faults in the mechanism; *automatic*

answering, allowing unattended receipt of messages day or night (if the telephone line is dedicated to facsimile transmission); *auto-dialling*, enabling calls to be set up automatically at preset times (arising from a *store-and-forward* capability); *electronic directories* storing frequently used facsimile numbers; *reduction facility*; *logging of calls* received, including information on by whom and to whom sent, date and time; *polling*, enabling (by pre-arrangement) ready-loaded documents to be transmitted to a receiving machine; *verification of message*, including details of the sending terminal's identity, date, time printed on received document—similar information together with transmission time being provided about documents that have been sent; *light-emitting diode display* showing the other machine's identity number and group.

Some machines are *duplex*, i.e., they are transceivers that can send and receive in the course of the same call (see Figure 13.13, page 152). Many have *automatic feed* devices, making batch-loading quicker and making polling possible (see above). The printing of images is usually done by direct thermal method, using heat-sensitive paper, or sometimes by electrostatic process using dry toner (see **9.2**); *resolution adjustment* allows the operator to lower the speed if necessary to ensure clarity of dense originals.

The quality of transmission is affected by interference on the telephone line. Images may be distorted or even omitted. Where data links exist, this does not occur, e.g., when a facsimile machine is linked to a computer which will store messages for transmission to other facsimile machines.

The use of facsimile is rapidly growing, since the

problem of compatability has been solved. Its use is also encouraged by the publication of a facsimile users' directory by British Telecom. Although not yet fully comprehensive, wide publicity is being given to encourage users to submit entries. Copies of the UK directory are free to those who have an entry. Overseas directories are available for sale from British Telecom.

Bureaufax is a facsimile transmission service to over 70 overseas countries for persons or organizations without facsimile machines or whose machines are incompatible. Incoming documents from overseas are transmitted to the recipient's machine, posted or collected. Documents for transmission may be transmitted, posted or handed in at a Bureaufax counter office or, for a slightly higher charge, at a post office which is an Intelpost centre (see Appendix I). They are received on overseas recipients' machines or by arrangements made by the overseas Bureaufax office concerned.

13.13 Radiopaging

(a) Equipment

Radiopaging systems enable staff scattered over an area to be contacted individually. Each person carries a pager or receiver, small enough to be clipped to a pocket, which can be activated by radio signals indicating that he is wanted. On receiving a 'bleeping' (alert) signal on the pocket pager, the carrier goes to the nearest telephone to contact the originator of the call. Some pagers can emit up to 8 different alert tones, indicating for example that the matter is urgent or that the carrier needs to contact his secretary or his home. A flashing light signal is useful in noisy surroundings where a tone may not be heard and in surroundings where it could be intrusive. Some pagers have a liquid crystal display on which numerical codes (representing a branch number, telephone number, etc.) appear when the pager is activated or the numbers may be spoken by a speech synthesizer in computerized systems. Some display letters to form a short message continued in a series of displays if necessary, or a mixture of numbers and letters (see Figure 13.14, page 153). Speech is possible on some equipment: one-way speech enables the paging operator to speak to the carrier; two-way speech enables the carrier to reply. Hearing

the actual message in this way enables the carrier to judge the urgency of a call for himself and makes it unnecessary to go to a telephone.

Pagers controlled by microprocessor automatically store incoming messages in memory as they are displayed and these can be recalled when desired by the carrier. The LCD displays not only a message but also the current situation, e.g., whether the carrier is actually being paged, whether he has selected a tone or silent call signals and whether he has pressed the READ button—if not, a tone alerts him to do so. If required, messages may be temporarily stored on the system's central computer: a special tone is used to alert the carrier that these are being held. Messages may also be stored for longer periods, e.g., during the carrier's absence on holiday for print out and mailing to him if necessary.

Paging calls may be sent by an operator of a manual control unit. Computerized systems allow access also direct from telephone and intercom extensions without involving an operator, and from remote locations either manually by instructions to the control unit operator, or automatically from sensors fitted to alarm and security systems. Calls to the same pager are stored and queued by the system.

(b) British Telecom Radiopaging Service

British Telecom operate a radiopaging service available virtually throughout the UK. Pagers may be rented and the charge is included in the quarterly rental. The carrier of a 'bleep-only' pager is contacted by the caller dialling the pager number (unique to each pager). If the number is valid the caller hears a short prerecorded announcement saying the call has been accepted. Within two minutes the pager 'bleeps'. Where a carrier has a pager that can receive numeric messages the caller may contact the Radiopaging Bureau and quote the paging number and message. Also, messages can be input directly by a telex or datel terminal via a multi-frequency signalling telephone or an ordinary telephone with a hand-held keypad unit. Text messages may also be sent through the Bureau or via telex or datel.

The 'bleep' alert signals on all British Telecom pagers can be linked to Telecom Gold mailboxes (see **13.9**) and Voicebank (see **13.10**) so that the carrier is alerted when a message has been left.

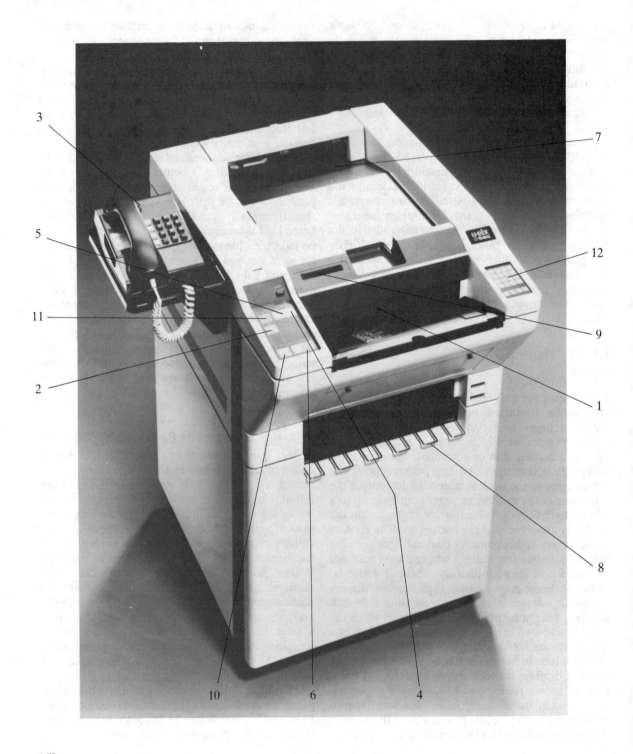

Figure 13.14 A pocket pager which can display alphanumeric messages. Up to four messages can be stored to a maximum of 160 characters. If a message in store remains unread the pager cannot be switched off. Pressing the READ button enables the message to be read and scrolled through a line at a time. To silence the bleeper the SPEAKER button is pressed: the carrier is then alerted visually to a new message when PAGE appears in the display. (Courtesy of Aircall plc)

13.14 Telemessages

Telemessages have replaced the inland telegram system. The sender dials the British Telecom operator and asks for the Telemessage service, then dictates the message over the telephone. Telex subscribers can send a telemessage by dialling the code given in the telex directory. Messages can also be submitted via PSS, electronic mail services like Telecom Gold, Prestel, and senders' own computers.

Messages are transmitted by telemessage computer to Royal Mail sorting offices for postal delivery the next working day. (To qualify for next-day delivery telephone users must send in the message by 2200 hrs on working weekdays and Saturdays and by 1900 hrs on Sundays.)

Telemessages may be sent to the USA and some other overseas countries.

Multiple messages The same text can be sent to additional addresses at a discounted rate.

Multiple Address Processing System This stores senders' mailing lists on computer and dispatches a standard message to addresses at a discounted rate. This is suitable for advertisers sending out mail shots.

Direct Response A sender requesting Direct Response will have a first-class mail prepaid envelope enclosed for delivery with the telemessage to allow a quick reply to be sent without cost to the recipient.

Figure 13.13 The U-Bix IP 585 Facsimile Transceiver (Group 3) machine which is shown opposite can transmit an A4 page in 13 seconds.

Key:
1. Documents to be transmitted are held here for automatic feed (max. 50 sheets).
2. COPY, i.e., telephone line to be used to transmit copy image.
3. Recipient's telephone number is called. When reply tone is heard transmission can start.
4. STANDARD, i.e., for normal definition.
5. FINE, i.e., slower speed for finer definition.
6. START button, to SEND or RECEIVE.
7. Copies received here. Buzzer tells sender and recipient that transmission is complete.
8. Pull-out receiving tray to catch re-emerging original.
9. Alphanumeric display shows recipient's telephone number that has been dialled, number of transmissions, diagnostic code in case of fault, etc.
10. RESET STOP, i.e., enables fresh start after fault.
11. CALL, i.e., telephone line to be used for speech.
12. Controls for maintenance.

(Courtesy of U-Bix (UK) Ltd)

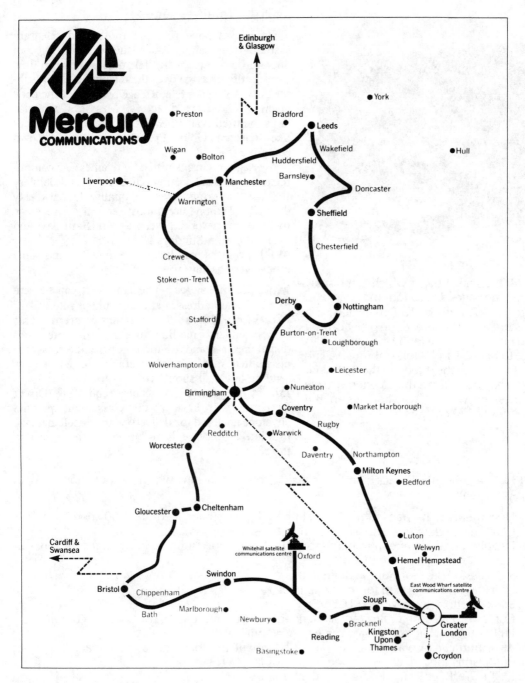

Figure 13.15 The Mercury network. The figure-of-eight loop comprises optical fibre cables laid alongside British Rail Intercity railway lines. Trunk links between Manchester, Birmingham and London and within city areas are made by microwave radio. (Courtesy of Mercury Communications Ltd)

Charges Standard charges are applied for the different services, e.g., for the basic service there is one charge for the first 50 words and a lower charge for the next 50 or part, up to 350 words. Charges may be combined with senders' normal telephone or telex accounts.

13.15 International telegrams

These may be submitted by telephone or telex for transmission from main Telemessage offices to the Telegram Retransmission Centre, a computerized system which forwards them over international routes. Heavy users can rent British Telecom terminals which allow them to input international telegrams direct to the telegram centre.

There is a standing charge for each telegram sent, plus a different rate per word (+ VAT) according to whether the destination is (a) to Europe, North America and North Africa or (b) the rest of the world.

13.16 Mercury Communications Ltd

The government granted a licence to this company in February 1982 to operate as a public telecommunications operator in competition with British Telecom. It uses digital technology, which enables voice, data and video to be transmitted on the same network, to which most terminal devices can be connected. It aims to provide a service in the first instance to big businesses, by linking the main business centres in England (see Figure 13.15). Satellite communication centres give businesses on the network access to international communications via satellite. It is planned to extend the service to Wales and Scotland and to provide spurs from the network in response to local demand in any area.

At present, Mercury is leasing lines to companies for private intra-company communication, including facsimile transmission and videoconferencing. Later it will also provide public switched services, i.e., communication between subscribers via public exchanges, opening the way to smaller businesses and domestic consumers. A compromise between a private leased and a public switched service exists, in that members of one group of users can communicate with members of another group by means of a transatlantic link operated by Mercury Communications Ltd and the Western Union Telegraph Company.

13.17 Did you know?

1. You may be unlucky enough to come across the word 'squawkbox'. This is an American term for 'loudspeaker'.
2. System X digital telephone exchanges are being joined by System Y.
3. Telephone traffic is measured in erlangs, i.e., one hour's use of one line.

13.18 Useful reference books

Dialling code booklets

Europages (lists telephone numbers of many companies in some European countries)

Facsimile Users' Directory
International telephone directories
IDD leaflets
Phone Books
Teletex directories
Telex directories
Yellow Pages

BT International Telephone Guide

Activities

1. (a) Most firms insist that their office staff have a good telephone technique. Why do you think this so important?
   (b) Give a suitable alternative for each of the following expressions which you have heard being used on the telephone in your office.

   (i) Hello (when picking up the receiver). (ii) You'll have to speak up I can't hear you. (iii) Mr Johnson isn't in today, it's his day off. (iv) She's gone to lunch, you'll have to ring back later. (v) What did you say your name was again? (LCCI, SSC)

2. Draw up a check list of information which you would give to a junior making an international telephone call for the first time. (LCCI, PSC)

3. You work for the General Manager of a small company whose staff receive and make a great number of telephone calls. The receptionist/switchboard operator, who handles the present PMBX telephone system, has complained to you that she feels she is neglecting her reception duties as she spends so much of her time operating the switchboard. Write a report to your chief drawing his attention to the problem and suggesting how it might be resolved. (LCCI, PSC)

4. (a) Describe the main features of electronic private branch exchanges, explaining their advantages over more conventional switchboard equipment.   OR

   (b) Describe the main features of TWO of the following, mentioning the type of circumstances in which they are likely to be used:
   (i) Callmakers (ii) Telephone answering systems (iii) Coin/card-operated telephones. (LCCI, PSC)

5. Your company is anxious to reduce the amount it spends on telephone call charges. Suggest a variety of ways in which it might tackle the problem. (LCCI, PSC)

6. The Board of Comlon International plc is anxious to reduce telephone call charges by introducing the following: (a) out of area lines (b) call barring (c) extension group hunting (d) telephone credit cards (e) call logging. Define each term clearly, and then explain how each contributes to reducing call charges (LCCI, PSC)

7. Comlon International plc is considering the possibility of subscribing to the Telex system. (a) What procedure must an operator follow for the reception and transmission of Telex messages? (b) What advantages, if any, does the telex system have over the use of the normal telephone system? (c) Why might the telex system be useful when dealing with overseas customers? (d) What is the

value to the operator of the Telex having a VDU and message editing facilities? (LCCI, SSC)

8. As a secretary in a medium-sized company you have access to both a facsimile machine and a telex machine. Explain the factors you would consider in deciding whether to send a document by either telex or facsimile. (LCCI, PSC)

9. Comlon International plc is considering installing Teletex to replace its current Telex machines. (a) Outline the advantages of Teletex over stand-alone Telex. (b) What implications would the installations have for staff training? (LCCI, PSC)

10. Electronic mail is slowly being introduced into very large companies. Explain what is meant by Electronic Mail and how it operates. (LCCI, PSC)

11. Your office needs to send information frequently to other branches for action today. Describe briefly 4 means of communication, explaining in what context each could be used. (LCCI, PSC)

12. Recently Mr Gibson, Training Manager of Comlon International plc, has experienced difficulties when trying to contact foremen and supervisors of trainees at short notice. Describe 3 methods of communication which may solve this problem, and recommend one for his use. (LCCI, PESD, Sec. Admin.)

Group Activities

13. Why are communications important in an organization? Discuss this in relation to efficiency and good human relations.

14. What do you consider to be the qualifications and qualities an employer should look for when recruiting switchboard operators? After discussing your impressions of switchboard operators at work and any experience members of the group may have had of switchboard operating, draw up a joint list.

14
Financial services

A business exists by buying and selling goods or services. This means that money has to be transferred from company to company. A number of services exist to help business with these transactions.

14.1 Sending payments overseas

(a) Through a bank

(i) *Banker's draft* (see also **14.3** *(b)*)   This is a form of cheque, drawn by the bank on an overseas branch or bank, and payable to a third party. It can be made out for either sterling or foreign currency. The bank will supply the draft for the customer to send to the payee.

(ii) *International money transfer*   The bank will transfer funds from a customer's account to an overseas bank, instructing the latter to pay the customer's creditor in the appropriate currency. Modern telecommunication systems effect the transfer.

(iii) *International money order*   For a small service charge these can be purchased at some banks for amounts up to a specified limit and are dispatched by the customer. They are best used for sending gifts or deposits abroad. They are not suitable when an exact sum is required by the payee because they are negotiated by the banks at the prevailing daily rate of exchange. An IMO may be cashed by the payee or paid into a bank account. Refunds are obtainable in the event of loss.

(b) Through a post office

(i) *Postal orders*   You should consult the *Post Office Guide* for full details of the overseas postal order service (see also Appendix I). With the abolition of exchange control regulations by the government in 1979, it is permissible to make such payments to any country in the world that accepts them, subject to any specific conditions relating to certain countries as set out in the *Post Office Guide*.

(ii) *Reply coupons*   These enable return postage from an overseas country to be prepaid by the sender in the UK. When exchanged overseas at a post office, a coupon (bought at a flat rate in the UK) represents the value of the minimum letter postage payable by surface mail. (See also National Girobank transfer, enabling account holders to make payment to National Girobank and other bank account holders overseas (**14.5**).)

14.2 In a nutshell: Making inland payments through the Post Office

- Registration provides protected delivery by first class mail and, in event of loss, compensation in accordance with the fee paid. Bank notes and coins must be enclosed in special registered envelopes obtained at the post office.
- The delivery of registered (and unregistered) packets may be speeded by the Royal Mail special delivery service to enable delivery the next working day after posting. Packets bearing the Royal Mail special delivery label are picked out from the rest of the mail at the delivery office.
- Postal orders are issued in stated denominations, to an upper limit. A fee is charged for each order, according to its value. No compensation for loss can be demanded, but the Post Office will investigate claims of non-delivery if completed counterfoils are produced within a stated time. Making an order payable to a named person at a named post office offers some protection against misappropriation. Crossed postal orders are payable only through a bank account.

- Cash on delivery is a Post Office service which enables traders to obtain payment up to a specified maximum from customers for solicited goods sent by parcel post or in registered letters and packets. The Post Office delivers the goods and collects the payment, which is then remitted to the trader. A standard fee is payable to the Post Office for each item handled.
- A person without a National Girobank account can use the Transcash service to pay an account holder: the sum required is paid over the post office counter, together with a small fee.

14.3 The High Street banks

The leading High Street banks include most of the London clearing banks. These banks are considered to be Barclays, Midland, Lloyds, NatWest, Trustee Savings Bank, Co-operative Bank and the Royal Bank of Scotland (incorporating Williams & Glyn's). They have branches in most towns and provide services for private individuals and organizations.

(a) Bank accounts

(i) *Opening an account* An applicant must provide some background information, such as occupation and address, a specimen of the signature he intends to use, and the names of up to two referees who can testify to his reliability.

(ii) *Types of account* These include: *Current account*—from this account a cheque book is operated; it earns no interest. *Deposit account*—this earns interest. If money is required at once, seven days' interest may be forfeited, unless notice of intended withdrawal is given. A statement provides a record of transactions. *Joint account*—this may be held by two or more people—e.g., husband and wife, or members of a partnership. *Budget account*—the customer estimates his annual expenditure on expected important items like rates, fuel, insurance premiums, telephone, etc., and divides the total by 12. Each month the resulting amount is transferred from his current account to his budget account, and from this he pays the bills as they arise, using a special cheque book. The banks charge at various rates, in respect of both service and interest. New types of account are being introduced all the time, including interest-bearing current accounts for larger balances and 'cash and save' accounts which carry an automatic borrowing facility.

(iii) *Handling a current account Paying-in* Cash, cheques, etc., paid into an account must be accompanied by a *paying-in slip* or page from a *paying-in book*, part of which is stamped and returned to the account holder as a record of the credit. A *bank giro credit slip* must be used if the cash is paid in at a branch or bank other than the one where the account is held. Bank notes or cheques can also be paid into an account holder's account at *computer-linked terminals* inside or outside some bank premises (see also **14.3** *(c)* (iii)). *Night safes* set into the walls of some banks allow customers, by arrangement with the bank, to deposit cash after banking hours. The cash is enclosed with a paying-in slip or book in a locked pouch, which the customer may reclaim from the bank the following day. Alternatively, the bank will count the money and credit the account.

Drawing cheques By means of a *cheque* the *drawer* (account holder) instructs the bank (the *drawee* bank) to pay the person or organization named (the *payee*) the sum specified. The drawer should record details of the payment for reference on the cheque *counterfoil* or cheque book record sheet provided. The drawer's signature must be in the same form as the original specimen signature submitted. Where a joint account is concerned, the number of signatures required depends on the arrangements made by the holders when opening the account. A limited company's cheques must be signed by the persons authorized by the board of directors to do so; a copy of the relevant resolution is sent to the bank as notification of the arrangement, often contained in a special bank form of mandate.

Bank charges Banks usually issue a tariff of charges for private accounts and negotiate charges with business account holders.

Bank statement This sets out all the transactions which have gone through the account since the previous statement, showing the balance in hand or overdrawn. Statements are issued on a regular basis or as required.

(b) In a nutshell: Terms relating to cheques

Banker's draft   similar to cheque but drawn by bank on own head office or another branch; guarantees to payee the amount specified.

Bearer cheque   amount is payable to bearer of cheque; if crossed, payable only into bearer's account.

Blank cheque   a cheque complete in all respects except the amount, which is left for the payee to complete.

Cheque card   issued to customer by bank to indicate bank's support for customer's cheque (up to £50 in any one transaction) when used, e.g., in paying for goods in shop; drawer signs cheque in presence of payee, who compares signature with specimen on card, endorses cheque with card number.

Crossed cheque   bears parallel lines across face; safer because payment is through bank account.

Dishonoured cheque   cheque which bank refuses to pay; bank sends cheque back to payee in notification, using conventions such as:

orders not to pay ('stopped' cheque);

out-of-date ('stale' cheque);

postdated;

refer to drawer, please re-present (may be honoured by time cheque is next presented);

signature required;

words and figures differ.

General crossing   double parallel lines with nothing added, except possibly '& Co'.

Not negotiable   at payee's risk.

Open cheque   uncrossed cheque; can be endorsed and presented at drawee's bank and cashed, if no suspicious circumstances.

Postdated cheque   bears a date in the future; bank will not process it until that date is reached.

Special crossing   instruction written between crossing, e.g., name of bank to carry out collection, name of account, etc.

Stale cheque   one presented more than 6 months after date on which drawn.

Stopped cheque   one which drawer instructs bank not to pay, e.g., if lost or stolen; drawer telephones details to bank and confirms in writing; duplicate cheque must be sent to payee, provided original one has not been honoured.

(c) Obtaining cash through a bank

(i) *By cheque from own account*   An account holder can withdraw cash from his own account over the bank counter by making a cheque payable to himself or to 'Cash'. A crossed cheque can normally be used for this purpose if presented at the drawer's own branch where he is known. If a cheque is backed by a cheque guarantee card, money (up to £50 in 1985) can be withdrawn from any bank or branch, although a fee may be charged if it is not the drawer's bank.

(ii) *By credit card* (see also **14.3** *(f)* (i))   Presentation of credit cards such as Access and Visa enables cash to be obtained from branches of the parent banks without writing a cheque. Interest is charged on the withdrawal immediately.

(iii) *From automatic teller machines*   At many banks, account-holders who have been issued with cash cards can withdraw up to £100 each day from automatic teller machines. These may be found inside or outside bank premises and enable a central computer to be interrogated concerning the level of the customer's balance before the cash is dispensed. The card is returned directly to the customer. More sophisticated dispensers enable a cheque book or statement of account to be ordered by the customer.

(d) Credit transfer

This system enables payments to be made without any cash physically changing hands: the bank merely adjusts the accounts of the individuals or organizations concerned. The following services fall into this category.

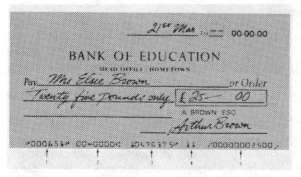

Figure 14.1 Example of a cheque illustrating a completed code line of five sets of E13B characters for magnetic ink character recognition:
1. The cheque number—each cheque has a serial number which is printed on the statement to enable the customer to identify the entry.
2. The bank/branch number—this enables machines called reader/sorters to sort cheques into branch order.
3. The account number—each customer is allocated an individual account number to enable the computer to identify cheques and credits for application to the correct account.
4. The transaction code—used by the banks to identify the type of voucher being processed.
5. The amount—printed by the banks, usually at the branch at which the cheque is paid in (or failing that at the clearing department) from the figures written by the customer at the time of issue. (Courtesy of Bank Education Service)

(i) *Banker's or standing order* The account holder gives the bank a standing instruction to transfer the specified sum regularly to the payee until a given date or until further notice. Typical payments include hire-purchase instalments, mortgage payments, etc.

(ii) *Direct debit* This differs from a standing order in that the *payee* requests the bank to deduct fixed or unspecified sums from the account holder's account. The payee asks the account holder to complete and return a form authorizing direct debits to be made, which is sent to the account holder's bank to authorize direct debit payments. If the amount is not a fixed one, or the interval between payments varies, the payee must tell the account holder in advance the date or amount of the payment. To safeguard the

account holder, only organizations approved by the banks are allowed to operate the system, which must conform strictly to the terms of the instructions signed by the account holder (who may cancel the arrangement at any time by writing to his bank and confirming to the payee notice of cancellation).

Direct debiting is less trouble to the payee's own accounting system than the standing order method, since all sums due by the payee's clients are collected on the proper date and the total of all the direct debits payable is credited to the payee's account in one transaction, instead of in numerous separate ones. Where the amount of a payment changes, direct debiting is less trouble to the debtor than changing a standing order instruction.

(e) Bulk wage/salary payments and traders' credits (blocks)

Instead of making cash or cheque wages payments to its employees, a firm draws a cheque for the combined amount and gives this to the bank, together with instructions to credit the individual accounts of the employees. Employees cannot be paid in this way unless they have given their permission. (Banks also operate payroll services which often provide considerable savings to companies.)

A similar arrangement enables bulk settlement of traders' bills to be carried out.

(f) Sources of credit

(i) *Credit card* The holder can buy goods or services on credit from retailers participating in the scheme, by presenting his card and signing a sales voucher prepared by the retailer. The holder keeps the voucher as a record of the transaction, the retailer retaining copies. (When goods are bought through mail or telephone orders, the customer does not sign a voucher, the firm merely recording the number of his credit card.) The organization issuing the credit card is sent a copy of the voucher by the retailer, pays the bill and sends the card holder a monthly statement listing and totalling the credit transactions. If the total outstanding is settled within a given period, no interest is charged, but interest is added to any remaining borrowing. The individual credit limit set for each card holder must not be exceeded.

(ii) *Bank loan* Loans may be negotiated for varying amounts repayable in regular instalments over a specified period at variable or fixed rates of interest. For example businesses may arrange to borrow money to provide additional working capital or to finance new machinery, etc. Personal loans are at fixed rates of interest and are usually for consumer durable goods, like cars or washing machines. Mortgages are available for house purchase. Bridging loans are made to a purchaser who is waiting for the sale of his house to go through. Income tax relief can usually be claimed on bank loans for house purchase or improvements, or bridging loans (up to £30 000 in 1985).

(iii) *Overdraft* This is similar to a bank loan except the amount of money owed varies and interest is paid only on the outstanding loan. Overdrafts are negotiated in advance with one's bank manager and a limit is agreed. It is then possible to overdraw one's current account to that amount. If an account is overdrawn without the bank's consent then the drawer's cheques will not be honoured. Even a company that is prospering may need to run an overdraft from time to time, sometimes for long periods, to provide working capital.

(g) Other services

(i) *Personal services* These include assistance on such matters as income tax, insurance, management of savings and investments, executorship and trusteeship, and safekeeping of documents and valuables.

(ii) *Financial services for travellers* (see **21.9**)

(iii) *Services for exporters and importers* Services include the supervision of the mechanics of receiving payments for goods delivered abroad, and transferring money to a company overseas in exchange for goods purchased. As more and more British companies export their goods, the banks provide help and assistance on all aspects of foreign trade.

(h) Clearing systems

(i) *Cheque clearing* This system enables the payee's bank to collect payment for the cheque from the drawer's bank. The banks participating are Barclays, Midland, Lloyds, NatWest, the Royal Bank of Scotland, National Girobank, Trustee Savings Bank, the Co-operative Bank, Coutts, and the Bank of England.

Cheques presented at a branch are sorted according to the banks on which they are drawn, and the amounts are listed and totalled. They are then sent on to the bank's clearing department, where the bundles and listings are amalgamated with those from other branches. At the Bankers' Clearing House, the listings are exchanged by the representatives of the participating banks; the cheques are exchanged at the banks' head offices, so that each bank receives the cheques drawn upon it. Back at the clearing departments each bank checks its listings with those of the presenting bank, then sorts the cheques into branch order and sends them to the branches on which they are drawn.

Settlement among the banks is achieved by one bank's indebtedness being balanced against another's, the accounts held by the banks at the Bank of England being adjusted accordingly without any physical transfer of funds.

An interbranch clearing system is operated at banks' own clearing departments for cheques drawn on other branches of the same bank.

(ii) *Credit clearing* Credit vouchers (under credit transfer arrangements such as those for standing orders, direct debiting, traders' credits—see **14.3** (*d*)) are cleared in a similar fashion to cheques.

In addition, a computerized credit clearing system, substituting magnetic tape records for paper vouchers, is operated by BACS (Bankers' Automated Clearing Services Ltd). Details of credits to be transferred are received at the BACS computer centre on magnetic tape from banks, government departments, local authorities, and companies. The entries are then sorted by computer, and details sent to each bank on magnetic tape for adjusting customers' accounts.

(i) Cheque reading and sorting

With the computerized systems now used by the banks, the details represented by the figures encoded at the foot of cheques are interpreted by machine, as explained in Figure 14.1 (see also **11.10**). This enables the cheques to be sorted at high speeds and information on them input into the computer for the updating of customers' accounts and the preparation of balance lists and customers' bank statements.

14.4 Co-operative Bank plc

The Co-operative Bank plc is a wholly owned subsidiary of the Co-operative Wholesale Society. It has been a clearing bank since 1973. It offers services similar to those available from the joint stock (shareholder-owned) clearing banks, including cheque guarantee cards, personal and home improvement loans, deposit and budget accounts. An interest-bearing current account is available on application; interest begins to be calculated on balances of £5 or more (as at 1985). Following the co-operative principle of sharing profits with customers, bank charges are not imposed on customers in credit, but only on debits to overdrawn accounts, interest also being charged on overdrawn balances. The number of branches in existence or planned is only about 78, but for day-to-day business, customers need not depend on these branches, as banking points are maintained at many Co-operative retail stores during normal shopping hours, often including Saturdays. At these points, deposits can be made and cheques cashed on production of a cheque book and Co-operative Bank cheque guarantee card. As well as catering largely for private individuals, the Co-operative Bank serves retail Co-operative societies, business, and other organizations.

14.5 National Girobank

National Girobank offers most of the standard services provided by the clearing banks and has the advantage of using more than 20 000 post offices throughout the UK as its branches, thus offering easy access to cash and convenient hours of business. All customers' account records are held at the National Girobank Centre on Merseyside.

(a) Facilities for personal account holders

(i) *Payments* Customers are supplied with a cheque book of personalized stationery, which includes cheques and transfers. Cheque guarantee cards are available.

Transfer forms are used to pay other Girobank account holders or to make deposits. An account holder may use his own transfer form—on the back of which he can write explanatory details, messages or orders making a separate letter unnecessary—or one supplied by a creditor (most household accounts such as gas, electricity, telephone, rates, water rates, etc., carry a Girobank Transcash form as part of the bill). The form is sent direct to the Girobank where the relevant accounts are debited and credited and the transfer document, together with a statement of account, forwarded to the creditor. Payment may also be made by transfer to account holders in Giro systems in other countries or to customers of any other banking service abroad. The transfer service is free and pre-addressed, postage-paid envelopes are also supplied to customers free of charge for UK payments.

For business customers, bulk transfers—e.g., for payments of wages, salaries or pensions—can be made without separate transfer forms. Instructions for payment can be accepted in list form or on magnetic tape for input to the computer.

Cheques are used to make payments or for withdrawing cash at a post office.

(ii) *Deposits* Cash can be paid into an account at any post office on completion of the deposit/transfer form (made payable to 'Self'). Cheques must be sent by post with the deposit form to National Girobank.

(iii) *Withdrawals* Up to a stipulated limit (£50 in 1985) may be withdrawn every other day using a cheque made payable to 'Self'. Account holders with cheque guarantee cards may cash cheques up to £100 at a nominated post office or up to £50 at any other office (in 1985). Other account holders nominate two post offices for withdrawals when their account is opened. If more than the limit permitted is required the withdrawal may be arranged in advance.

(iv) *Other facilities* Girobank provides a standing order service for regular payments to other account holders. There is no charge for this service or for the direct debit service. Foreign currency and travellers' cheques are also available to anyone. Customers qualifying for the guarantee card can also apply for fixed-term personal loans and bridging loans. A revolving loan known as Flexiplan enables customers to make purchases or pay unpredictable bills up to a limit of £3000.

(v) *Bank charges and statements* There are no bank charges for current account holders. If a payment is made when an account goes into overdraft a small charge is made. Statements of account are supplied, free of charge, every time there is a credit to the account or after 10 debits.

(b) Facilities for business account holders

The *business deposit* service enables retail branches, salesmen and agents to deposit takings at a convenient post office directly into a central Girobank account. Organizations can design their own deposit forms to include relevant information, such as branch or agent reference number.

Rent collection services have been devised to meet the varying needs of local authorities. Many local authorities, for security reasons and for convenience to tenants, have withdrawn rent collection. Instead their tenants pay rent at a local post office.

Wages, salaries and pensions can be paid directly into employees' own Girobank accounts by transfer.

(c) Facilities for non-account holders

Persons or organizations not holding Girobank accounts can make cash payments to account holders by completing a Transcash form at a post office and paying a small fee. In some cases advertisers offer goods for sale and payment can be made by Transcash Freepay—here the payee organization pays this fee. Cheques are sent direct to Girobank for deposit into the account. The Transcash service also enables payments to be made overseas.

14.6 Trustee Savings Bank

Since 1975 the TSB has been a clearing bank. It offers similar services to its customers as other clearing banks, e.g., cheque book accounts, deposit accounts earning interest, standing order and direct debit facilities, and salary credits. Credit facilities include TSB Trustcard (a credit and cheque guarantee card), personal loans repayable with interest in monthly instalments, temporary overdrafts on cheque accounts and secured lending (including bridging advances) negotiated in advance on which interest is payable. There are facilities for home-buying through mortgages. Unit trust investments with life assurance if desired are available at TSB branches through the TSB Trust Co. Ltd, and government and stock exchange securities can be bought and sold. Travellers' cheques and foreign currency are also available.

The TSB in its present form, i.e., as at 1985, consists of regional Trustee Savings Banks, grouped in a federal structure under the TSB Central Board which was set up by Parliament, and directed by the Treasury and other Government departments. It is not certain who owns the TSB, but proposals are now before parliament to change the structure to a public limited company, with resulting full accountability to shareholders and access to new capital as required.

14.7 National Savings Bank

The National Savings Bank (NSB) is part of the Department for National Savings. The Post Office is one of its principal agents.

The NSB is established to encourage savings and investment and, with the exception of a limited standing order service, facilities differ from those offered by clearing banks. Money can be transferred from NSB accounts to National Girobank accounts. The following NSB accounts are available:

(a) Ordinary accounts

Interest is calculated on monthly balances; a higher rate is payable to customers with balances over a stipulated amount maintained for a whole year. Interest is free of income tax up to a limit announced in the annual Finance Act. Deposits and withdrawals can be made at any UK post office which conducts NSB business. Withdrawals on demand are limited to specific sums and one amount per day. In certain circumstances the depositor's bank book is kept for examination. Withdrawals of larger amounts may be made on demand to pay bills without handling cash, e.g., electricity, rates, etc.

(b) Investment accounts

These are designed for long-term savings and attract a much higher rate of interest (which is taxable). One month's notice is required for a withdrawal, obtainable as a warrant, either crossed for payment into a bank account or exchangeable for cash at a post office counter.

14.8 Merchant banks

All the banks mentioned so far have provided services for individuals as well as organizations. Another group—the merchant banks—exist with the primary function of financing trade between companies both at home and abroad and providing services exclusively for company customers. Both groups' activities for companies are diverse, ranging from floating shares for a company to financing the building of roads in remote areas.

14.9   Building societies

A building society exists to finance the construction and purchase of private houses. In so far as they extend loans to individuals over long periods and pay interest to investors, they compete to some degree with the credit and savings facilities offered by banks. The role of building societies is expanding and they are providing a number of new services in the housing and money transmission areas, e.g., cheque facilities. Under proposed new legislation they will be able to offer estate agency, insurance agency and stockbroking services. They will retain Mutual status but in certain situations will have the opportunity to convert to a limited company.

14.10   Accountants

According to the Companies Acts a company must appoint at every general meeting at which accounts are laid before the company an external auditor to hold office until the end of the next such meeting, and the person appointed must hold one of the recognized accounting qualifications. An auditor wishing to resign his appointment later must leave notice to that effect at the company's registered office, together with a statement of circumstances which he feels should be brought to members' or creditors' attention. He has the right to ask for an extraordinary general meeting to be convened to enable him to explain his reasons.

The work of the auditor is to inspect a client's books, checking totals and comparing entries against original documents and vouchers to ensure accuracy. An annual audit of companies' accounts is compulsory under the Companies Acts, but many auditors like to break the work up into two half-yearly audits.

Accountants will sometimes take charge of all the financial records of a client, or they may leave the routine bookkeeping to him and concentrate on presenting an accurate picture of the overall financial position to enable him to make sound plans. They will also advise a client on his plans. Accountants have expert knowledge of taxation. This enables a client, whether an individual or an organization to take maximum advantage of allowances and rebates available and to present his affairs in the most favourable light without breaking the law, i.e., to avoid rather than evade tax.

Dealing with insolvency is a further aspect of accountancy, i.e. the handling of bankruptcies and liquidations. Most firms of accountants specialize in one or more of the above fields.

Companies employ their own internal accountants. As well as keeping the accounts they will prepare financial data to enable the management to run the organization effectively.

14.11   Insurance

Misfortunes of all kinds befall both individuals and organizations, and insurance can provide financial compensation against many of these contingencies, thus freeing the insured persons from the necessity of tying up large capital sums to meet the eventualities.

(a)   Policy

To obtain protection, a person or organization must enter into a contract with an insurance company or society. When this is completed, the insured receives a policy, describing its terms.

(b)   Premium

This is the payment made by the insured each time the contract is renewed—usually annually. The insurance company knows from experience which risks are the greatest and which type of client is most prone to them and so calculates a realistic scale of premiums. From the payments it receives it builds up a fund more than adequate to meet the relatively few claims that do arise.

(c)   Utmost good faith

By their nature, insurance contracts are dependent upon the honesty of both parties in revealing to each other the true facts. This principle, known as *utmost good faith*, is an intrinsic part of every insurance contract; it is a distinctive feature of insurance and is fundamental to it.

(d) Insurable interest

Everyone making an insurance contract must have an insurable interest—i.e., must stand to lose in the event of the particular contingency.

(e) Indemnity

An insured person must have indemnity—i.e., be fully compensated for his loss, without either profiting or losing by the event.

(f) Contribution

The principle of contribution ensures that an insured person cannot make a profit by insuring himself with more than one company against the same risk, since if the event takes place, the loss is shared proportionately by the insurance companies involved.

(g) Looking after insurance arrangements

As a private secretary, it is advisable for you to have a grasp of the general principles outlined above, as you may possibly be involved in your boss's own personal insurance arrangements and the company's business insurance. For either, you must see that policies are kept in a safe place. Premiums must be paid promptly, otherwise protection ceases and the policy is said to 'lapse'—i.e., the contract comes to an end. Usually insurance companies or their agents send out renewal notices to their clients, but there is no legal requirement for them to do so, and it is the policy holder's responsibility to renew the contract. Renewal is a good time to consider whether the amount of cover should be raised—on payment of a higher premium—if circumstances have changed since the initial contract was completed. However, the policy should be altered whenever the adequacy of the cover is in doubt.

(h) Making a claim

You need also to know how to make a claim, if need arises. Details of the mishap, mentioning the policy number, must be sent to the insurance company as soon as possible, in the manner stipulated on the policy. The company will then take steps to deal with the claim and will make all the necessary investigations.

(i) Contingencies covered

A wide range of contingencies may be covered, the most common being mentioned below.

(i) *Business insurance* Business insurance arrangements with which you may be involved may cover types of contingency such as: fire, including damage to building and contents, and resulting loss of income and increased cost of working; accident, including plate glass, bad debts, professional negligence, damage or breakdown of machinery and resulting injuries and production loss, employers' and public liability (see Appendix II); dishonesty, including fidelity guarantee (compensating employer for losses caused through employees' dishonesty), theft, computer fraud; commercial vehicles.

(ii) *Private insurance* Private insurance arrangements your boss may make may include life assurance, personal accident and sickness, motor vehicle, and household (see also **21.8** *(e)*).

(j) Types of insurer

(i) *Limited companies* Insurance firms are usually limited companies, owned by their shareholders, with surplus funds distributed proportionately between shareholders and policy holders.

(ii) *Mutual societies* These are formed by the policy holders, who are the members, claims being met out of their premiums. Profits are shared by all, and losses—unless a society is registered as a company limited by guarantee.

(iii) *Friendly societies* These deal mainly in life assurance, contributions being either gathered by collectors, or taken by members to known collecting points.

(iv) *Underwriters* These are individuals offering insurance, and Lloyd's is their gathering place. To be admitted to Lloyd's they must have a reputation for honesty and the financial resources to meet claims themselves. To spread the risks they undertake to meet, they usually work in groups or syndicates. Members of the public cannot deal direct with underwriters, but do so through Lloyd's brokers (firms of repute recognized by Lloyd's Committee) who negotiate with as many underwriters as is necessary to meet the risk.

14.12 Solicitors

Solicitors are able to advise their clients on the

requirements of the law in their particular spheres—e.g., company law—as well as deal with general matters like the purchase of property, rental agreements, drawing up wills, divorce and matrimonial affairs, winding up estates after death, and lawsuits in respect of, say, injuries, damage, negligence, and unpaid debts. Besides offering informed advice, a solicitor will carry through many transactions, handle court proceedings, and generally represent the interests of his client to the best advantage, acting on his client's instructions. Solicitors are also empowered to witness affidavits and declarations, i.e., documents that can be signed only on oath or in solemn form, such as some statements in court proceedings. Although a solicitor may represent his client in a magistrate's court or county court, or exceptionally in a crown court, he must engage the services of a *barrister*—or 'brief Counsel'—actually to conduct any case in a higher court. As a professional body, solicitors are controlled by the Law Society, which also administers the legal aid scheme to assist litigants on low incomes.

14.13 Consultants

There are consultants in many spheres of business who are able to provide specialist advice, such as:

(a) Organization and method consultants (O & M)

These specialize in studying clients' working methods and the purpose of office procedures in order to recommend quicker and more economical ones. They try to balance the cost of machinery against that of manual labour, and to evaluate the effect of automated systems on staff to produce maximum efficiency. An example of the simplification of procedures might be making one form (with variations) do the work of several existing ones, saving both labour and time. New methods must be well tested and recommended tactfully.

(b) Design consultants

They may advise on the aesthetic aspect of a piece of equipment manufactured by a company, while taking into account its function. Their services may include the designing of letterheads, and packaging and corporate identity schemes, for adoption by their clients.

(c) Office planning consultants

They provide expert guidance on using office space to the best advantage, whether in new or redesigned offices. Their work involves examination of office procedures and communications systems, as these affect the placing of departments within a building.

14.14 Agencies

Unless machinery is used to the full, it is uneconomic. Many smaller organizations especially, cannot spare the money to buy machines that would be in only occasional use or that would need to be operated by trained staff who would not be fully occupied. Others may need extra staff to help out at busy periods or specialized services at specific times. Such organizations might call upon the services of agencies. Sometimes work is sent out to an agency; this has the advantage that it will be done by specialists. It avoids the client having to engage staff especially for busy periods and dismiss them in slack ones. However, arrangements must be made in good time, so that other work handled by the client is not disrupted by possible delays in the completion of the job sent out. This method of getting work done has the disadvantage that, once the job has been handed over to the agency, the client cannot exercise the control over it that it could in its own premises.

There are all kinds of agencies in existence that provide a wide variety of services of assistance to business concerns: recruitment of staff (see **12.1**(*d*)), copying and duplicating, secretarial services, debt collection, catering, market research, direct mail campaigns, advertising and public relations, cash conveyance and security, courier services, floristry, travel (see **21.6**(*c*) (iv)).

14.15 Did you know?

1. EFTPOS (electronic funds transfer at point of sale) is a nationwide system being run experimentally by banks. It should be established by the end of the 'eighties. Customers will not need cash or cheques to

pay for goods bought at shops participating. Instead the customer uses a plastic direct debit card into which the shop assistant punches the price of the goods bought. The customer inserts the card into the computer terminal, keys in his personal identity number, and the computer transfers the amount from his account to the retailer's.

2. LINK is a scheme by which a group of 21 banks and building societies are co-operating to provide a network of 800 automated telling machines throughout the UK, enabling their customers to share the cash withdrawal and other facilities provided. The group includes the Co-operative Bank plc, National Girobank, the Abbey National Building Society and Nationwide Building Society.

3. Charge cards issued, for example, by Diners' Club and American Express offer facilities similar to credit cards. However, no spending limit is imposed on cardholders, who must settle their account in full on receipt of their statements of account.

4. Guaranteed cheques cannot be 'stopped'.

5. Utmost good faith (*uberrimae fidei*) is essential in insurance contracts (see **14.12** (c)), but in contracts of sale in other areas of business, let the buyer beware (*caveat emptor*) is the general rule: although the seller must not actively deceive the buyer about the quality of the goods he is offering, it is up to the buyer to spot for himself any faults or deficiencies in them.

Figure 14.2 (Courtesy of Tony Holland. First published in *Business Systems and Equipment*)

Activities

1. You are often asked to go to the bank to pay in or withdraw money for your firm. Explain how you would

(a) Pay in money received for cash sales
(b) Withdraw a sum of money for salaries. (LCCI, SSC)

2. You are employed by a small firm where wages are still paid weekly in cash and, following a recent incident where an employee of a firm in your area was attacked and robbed of wages money just drawn out of the Bank, you wish to make recommendations to the Manager about an alternative method of paying the wages.

Set out your recommendations in the form of a Memorandum to Mr Jacobson, the Manager, including the advantages to both the Firm and the Employees. (LCCI, SSC)

3. Your immediate superior, Mr Tompkins, the Personnel Manager, has left you the following message and would like a reply as early as possible:

'Miss Evans is moving to a small village and her only way of getting to work in future would seem to be for her to buy a car, as there is no suitable bus service. She is a little worried about going direct to the bank without some knowledge of the ways in which she could possibly borrow money to purchase a car.

167

Please prepare a sheet showing the principles of both a loan and an overdraft so that she can assess which might be best for her.' (PEI, Inter.)

4. (a) Distinguish between Direct Debit and the Standing Order method of payment.

   (b) Which method of payment would you recommend for the following:

   (i) Your annual subscription to a Social Club

   (ii) Payment of your rates which you wish to spread evenly throughout the year

   (iii) A monthly payment to a dependent relative

   (iv) Your subscription to a private hospital insurance plan. (LCCI, SSC)

5. All the following terms refer to cheques. Explain the meaning of ANY FIVE of them.

(a) not negotiable
(b) stale cheque
(c) blank cheque
(d) bearer cheque
(e) postdated cheque
(f) refer to drawer
(g) general crossing
(h) special crossing. (LCCI, SSC)

6. (a) Describe and explain the purpose of a Bank Statement.

(b) Why might you draw up a Bank Reconciliation Statement? Mention 5 types of entry that might be included in it. (LCCI, PSC)

7. Comlon International plc is considering issuing credit cards, to cover travelling and subsistence expenses, to all executives who travel frequently (both in the UK and abroad). (a) Briefly describe how a credit card system works. (b) What are the advantages and disadvantages of such a scheme to the executive and the company? (LCCI, PSC)

8. You are responsible for looking after insurance matters for your employer in your small firm. (a) For what types of risk would the firm be likely to have cover? (b) How would you ensure that suitable premiums are paid at the right time?

9. Describe the services, which businesses can use, offered by three agencies apart from the Post Office and the banks. (LCC, PSC)

10. You have decided to make a regular saving of £10 per month from your salary. Investigate all possible means of depositing this money, and decide which savings scheme would be the most suitable for your particular purposes. (Take care to include commercial banks, building societies, and the National Savings movement in your investigation.)

11. **Group activity** Divide among your group the banks which have branches or outlets in your vicinity, so that each member is responsible for collecting information and leaflets about the services offered. Pool the results of these investigations and discuss the differences which emerge.

15
Taxes and social security

Pay As You Earn enables the government to collect income tax from persons earning wages or salaries (including bonuses, commissions and fees) through their employers. This method keeps down the cost of collection and—since the tax is deducted before the employee receives his pay—ensures prompt and full payment.

15.1 You Pay As You Earn

Your student days are over and you are working with the XYZ Co. Ltd. Soon after the beginning of each tax year you complete a tax return (P1), stating your income for the year just ended and any expenses which may be set against tax, and personal allowances against tax for the coming year.

From this statement of your personal circumstances, the tax office works out what your total allowances are and tells you, on form P2, what your PAYE code is. The form P2 explains how your code has been calculated. The tax office notifies your employer also of your code (on form P6) but does not reveal how your PAYE code is made up.

The PAYE code is simply a number and a letter—e.g., 220L. The number consists of the first 3 digits of the total allowances against tax to which you are entitled. The letter L is usually added to the number if you have been given the single person's allowance or the wife's earned income allowance. A person entitled to the married man's allowance, for example, would usually have the letter H. These letters allow your code to be adjusted quickly if there is a change in the amount of these allowances.

The XYZ Co. Ltd pay you monthly, and each month, following the instructions on form P8, they enter on form P11 (your deductions working sheet—see Figure 15.2) the following particulars in respect of your pay and the tax they deduct from it.

Column 1 The National Insurance contribution due from you (see **15.6**).

Column 2 Your total pay (including any overtime, bonuses, commissions, etc. and any Statutory Sick Pay paid to you) before deducting tax, but after deducting any superannuation contributions which qualify for tax relief.

3 Your total pay so far that year.

4 The amount of free pay—i.e., free of tax—to which you are entitled so far that year, based on your code. To find this, they consult the monthly Table A in the Free Pay Tables supplied by the Inland Revenue. They turn to the table for the appropriate month, look for your code number, and enter the amount printed against it.

5 The total taxable pay so far that year, arrived at by subtracting the total free pay from the total pay.

6 The total tax payable so far that year. Using the Taxable Pay Tables they find the figure corresponding to your total taxable pay to date and enter the amount of total tax due printed alongside.

7 The tax to be deducted that month, arrived at by subtracting the total tax already paid from the total amount due to be paid. (If the total tax already paid exceeded the total amount due, they would make a refund.)

From any query that might arise, they consult the Employer's Guide to PAYE.

169

The income tax year runs from 6 April to the following 5 April, and as soon as possible after it ends, the XYZ Co. Ltd must give you a certificate of pay, tax deducted and National Insurance contributions (P60—see Figure 15.1) during that year. You keep this carefully. You will see why if you read the explanation printed at the bottom of the illustration of the form P60 in Figure 15.1.

After two years you are successful in obtaining a more responsible post, this time with the ABC Co. Ltd. Before you leave, the XYZ Co. Ltd give you parts 2 and 3 of form P45, keeping part 1 themselves, filling it in, and sending it to the tax office. The form P45 shows your code and the amount of your pay and any tax deducted since the previous 6 April. It enables your new employer to take up your tax deductions where your old employer left off.

In the normal way, you would have handed parts 2 and 3 to your new employer, but unfortunately you lose them! As a result, the ABC Co. Ltd do not know on what basis to deduct tax; they have to complete form P46 and send it to the tax office.

While waiting to hear from the tax office the necessary details, such as your code and the amount of tax already deducted by the XYZ Co. Ltd, they start a new deductions working sheet for you and deduct tax in accordance with the code specified for emergency use. The tax office will ask you for information on form P15 to enable them to get you back on your proper code again. You may for a while pay more tax than you should but when the position has been sorted out any excess tax you have paid will be refunded to you.

At the end of the next tax year, and not later than

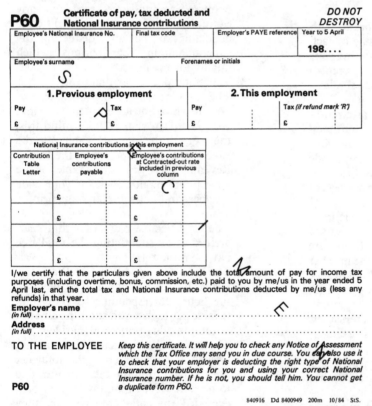

Figure 15.1 Example of P60 (Certificate of pay, tax deducted and National Insurance contributions). This is the third copy of P14: the first two copies are sent to the Collector of Taxes after the end of the tax year. (Crown copyright. Reproduced by permission of the Controller of Her Majesty's Stationery Office)

170

19 April, both the XYZ Co. Ltd and the ABC Co. Ltd must complete an End of Year Return (P14) in respect of your pay, tax, and National Insurance contributions throughout the year. They send two copies of this, together with those for all the other employees, to the Collector of Taxes (one copy being forwarded to the DHSS). The P14s are accompanied by the Employer's Annual Statement, Declaration and Certificate, which sets out totals of pay, tax and NI contributions and SSP in respect of all the employees.

15.2 In a nutshell: PAYE records

P1   Tax return, completed annually by taxpayer and sent to tax office.

P2   Notification of code or amended code, sent to taxpayer by tax office.

P6   Notification to employer of employee's code or amended code, sent by tax office.

P7   Employer's Guide to PAYE.

P8   Instructions to employer on how to complete P11.

P11   Deductions working sheet: an annual pay and tax record maintained by employer in respect of each employee.

P14   End of year return sent by employer to Collector of Taxes, summarizing entries on each employee's P11.

P15   Completed by employee with previous employment but not having a P45.

P35   Annual Statement, Declaration and Certificate. This accompanies the end of year return, and totals pay, tax, National Insurance contributions and Statutory Sick Pay in respect of all employees.

P45   Part 1: Particulars of employee leaving. Part 1 sent to his tax office by old employer, parts 2 and 3 handed by old employer to employee, who passes them on to new employer who keeps part 2 and sends part 3 on to his tax office.

P46   Particulars of new employee for whom no code number was notified to employer.

P60   (copy of P14) Certificate of pay, tax deducted and National Insurance contributions: supplied to employee by employer soon after the tax year ends on 5 April.

15.3 Taxes

(a) Income tax assessment

The amount of income tax an individual must pay depends on (i) the total income he receives, (ii) the deductions he may claim from it (allowances against tax), (iii) the rate of tax applicable to his case.

(i) *Deductions from incomes* These differ according to the individual's personal circumstances and responsibilities—e.g., a single person or a working wife receives less relief than a married man; further deductions may in some circumstances be given for dependants. Other reliefs are allowed on, for example, covenants made for a period of at least four years under which an annual sum is paid to a charitable organization, on mortgage interest and home improvement loans and pension contributions.

(ii) *The rate of tax payable* This depends on the band into which the total income falls and the rates of tax laid down in the annual Finance Act following the Chancellor of the Exchequer's Budget statement in the House of Commons. For example, the tax rate bands for the tax year 1985—86 are:

30 per cent tax on taxable income up to £16 200
40 per cent tax on taxable income from £16 201 to £19 200
45 per cent tax on taxable income from £19 201 to £24 400
50 per cent tax on taxable income from £24 401 to £32 300
55 per cent tax on taxable income from £32 301 to £40 200
60 per cent tax on taxable income over £40 200.

(b) Collection and administration of income tax

Income tax is collected either (i) by deducting it at source, i.e., by the person supplying the income, before it reaches the recipient—for example, in

PAYE and payments of dividends by companies to investors, or (ii) by direct payments by the person to the Inland Revenue—e.g., profits from sole trade or professional businesses and partnerships, and rents. Interest is payable on overdue tax.

Collectors of taxes deal with tax collection, and inspectors with the general administration of the tax laws. Appeals by taxpayers against assessments or decisions are heard by general or special commissioners, if agreement cannot be reached between the taxpayer and the Inspector.

(c) PAYE income tax

Each month the employer sends a bulk cheque to the Collector of Taxes of all the tax that has been collected/deducted from the employees' wages.

At the start of each tax year the same tax codes are applied as for the previous year unless advised by the Inspector of Taxes, who will also supply the necessary tax tables and other documents. An employer can provide his own substitutes for deductions working sheets (and for certificates of pay, tax deducted and National Insurance contributions) if this suits his payroll system better, for example, in computerized systems, as long as these conform to an official specification, but he must keep his pay records for at least three years after the end of the tax year.

(d) Capital gains tax

If individuals or companies dispose of assets for more than they paid for them when they acquired them, they must pay tax on the net capital sum gained above a stated figure. Relief is allowed in some cases, and some types of asset—e.g., tangible, movable property below a certain value, private cars, a sole or principal residence—are exempt.

(e) Corporation tax

This is payable by companies on their profits, including capital gains. The rate is fixed by the Finance Act following the Budget announcement.

(f) Capital transfer tax

This tax applies to gifts made during life and the complete estate at death.

(g) Stamp duty

A tax is paid on certain legal documents, usually transferring ownership. To show that the duty has been paid the documents are stamped.

15.4   National insurance

From the preceding brief description, you will realize that taxes claim a fair proportion of the income of both individuals and businesses. In return, the State provides a wide range of services for the community. The National Insurance scheme also provides services. These are for individuals rather than businesses, but you will see that employers are concerned in the scheme, both in collecting some contributions and in meeting part of the cost. The benefits to which you are entitled through deductions from your salary are therefore partly financed by your employer also.

15.5   State Earnings-Related Pension Scheme (SERPS)

Under the Social Security Pensions Act 1975, an earnings-related pension scheme began in April 1978, bringing improved retirement, widows', and invalidity pensions, building up over a working lifetime. Pensions are in two parts: (a) a basic pension—for the employed and self-employed alike (b) an additional pension—for which the self-employed are not eligible. The scheme is currently under review.

(a) Basic pension

To qualify for this, a retired person must have maintained a minimum contribution record. A married woman who does not qualify for the basic pension in her own right can claim on her husband's contributions but this pension is not payable until the husband retires. The statutory retiring age for men is 65 and for women 60.

(b) Additional pension

This is related to the pay a person earns above a specified lower earnings limit. Only full Class 1 contributions (see **15.6** (a)) count towards it, so the self-employed do not qualify. A person accumulates this

Additional Pension year by year from April 1978 until retirement.

(c) Changing jobs

An employee who changes jobs does not lose the pension rights so far earned, provided he/she is 26 or over and has had at least 5 years' pensionable service under an approved occupational pension scheme. Rights must be preserved by the old employer for payment at normal retirement age. Alternatively, with the member's consent, pension rights may be transferred to a new employer's scheme.

Note For those retiring after the year 2000 there are cash incentives for employers and employees to set up new private pension schemes.

15.6 National Insurance contributions

(a) Classification

National Insurance contributions are classified as follows: Class 1—earnings-related (employees); Class 2—flat rate (self-employed persons); Class 3—voluntary (helping the contributor to qualify for a limited range of benefits, including the basic retirement pension); Class 4—based on profits or gains above a certain level (self-employed persons).

(b) Contributions and collecting procedure

In general, the more a person earns the more he or she contributes. Those earning less than a stated lower earnings limit are not liable for contributions. Class 1 earnings-related contributions are collected along with income tax under the PAYE procedure (see **15.1**). These contributions entitle employees to receive retirement pension, sickness, unemployment and other benefits. The rate of Class 1 contributions depends on whether your company is contracted out or not from the Additional Pension Scheme. Employers can be contracted-out if their occupational pension scheme guarantees a pension at least as good as that provided by the State Additional Pension scheme. The conditions to be met may be found in the Employers' Guide to National Insurance contributions (NP 15) issued by the Department of Health and Social Security.

Employers are responsible for paying the National Insurance contributions due, recovering the employee's share from salary. To calculate contributions, the employer uses contribution tables issued by the DHSS, set out in Volume 1 for not-contracted-out contributions, and Volume 2 for the lower, contracted-out contributions. Each contains weekly and monthly tables for the following categories: A—standard rate contributions; B—a few older married women or widows who are liable to pay contributions at the reduced rate; C—in respect mainly of men over 65 and women over 60 for whom only the employer contributes.

At the beginning of the tax year or when employment starts, the employer selects the appropriate table and enters the table letter in the first space provided at the foot of the employee's P11, entering a new letter on the subsequent line, should a change to another table be necessary during the year (as shown in Figure 15.2). He then finds the total employee's and employer's contribution—the employer's contribution is usually about double the employee's contribution—(column 1a) and the employee's contribution payable (column 1b) by looking up the employee's total pay—or the nearest next smaller figure—in the appropriate table and noting the amounts given alongside. (The employer's contribution is also given in the tables but is not recorded on the P11.)

At the end of the tax year, the employer adds up the appropriate columns and completes the 'Totals' box. At the end of each month, the total joint contributions are sent by the employer with the PAYE tax deductions to the collector of taxes, who passes them to the Department of Health and Social Security.

For queries, the employer can consult the 'Employer's Guide to National Insurance Contributions' leaflet (NP 15).

15.7 National Insurance Benefits

A comprehensive range of benefits is available under the National Insurance scheme, financed to a considerable extent by employers' and employees' contributions. As a general principle two payments cannot be made from public funds for the same purpose at the same time—e.g., a person cannot receive sickness and industrial injury benefit for the same illness.

Some benefits are classified as *National Insurance* benefits (earned through contributions). Others may

Deductions working sheet P11 (New)

National Insurance Contributions				Statutory sick pay	MONTH	WEEK number	Pay in the week or month including statutory sick pay
Total of Employee's and Employer's Contributions payable (1a)	Employee's contributions payable (1b)	Employee's contributions at Contracted-out rate included in Col. 1b (1c)		in the week or month included in col. 2 (1d)			(2)
Bt fwd 876 60	Bt fwd	Bt fwd		Bt fwd	B F from Mth. 7	B F from Wk. 30	Bt fwd
29 22	13 52					31	150
29 22	13 52				6 Nov to 5 Dec	32	156
29 22	13 52					33	150
29 22	13 52					34	150
29 22	13 52				8	35	150
29 22	13 52				6 Dec to 5 Jan	36	150
29 22	13 52					37	150
29 22	13 52					38	150
29 22	13 52				9	39	150
29 22	13 52				6 Jan to 5 Feb	40	150
29 22	13 52					41	150
29 22	13 52					42	150
29 22	13 52				10	43	150
15 70	NIL				6 Feb to 5 Mar	44	150
15 70	NIL					45	150
15 70	NIL					46	150
15 70	NIL				11	47	150
15 70	NIL				6 Mar to 5 April	48	150
15 70	NIL					49	150
15 70	NIL					50	150
15 70	NIL					51	150
15 70	NIL				12	52	150

N.I. Cont'n Table Letter

| A | 1256 46 | 175 76 |
| C | 141 30 | |

STATUTORY SICK PAY TOTAL

N.I. LETTER: Enter letter identifying contribution table used when making first entry on sheet and on any subsequent change of table.

N.I. TOTALS: Enter in columns 1a, 1b and 1c separate contribution TOTALS for each table used.

PAY AND TAX TOTALS:
Previous employments
This employment — Mark net refund "R"

§ Complete this line if pay day falls on 5 April (in leap years 4 & 5 April). See Week 53 instructions in the Employer's Guide to PAYE.

‡ If amended cross out previous code

Employee's Widows & Orphans /Life insurance contributions in this employment £

P11 (New)   *Keep this form for not less than 3 years after the end of the year to which it relates, or longer if directed.*   Printed in the U.K. for H.M.S.O. Dd 8263600 7000M S&K 10/83

Figure 15.2 Example of National Insurance contributions entries on P11 (Deductions working sheet). From weeks 31 to 43 this not-contracted-out employee paid contributions at the standard rate (Table A). In week 44 the employee reached pensionable age and from that point only the employer paid contributions (Table C). (Crown copyright. Reproduced by permission of the Controller of Her Majesty's Stationery Office)

be *means-tested*, or *non-contributory* (available for people in special need whether they have contributed or not).

National Insurance benefits include unemployment benefit, maternity allowances, invalidity benefit, and sickness benefit. Means-tested benefits include supplementary benefit and family income supplement; non-contributory benefits include industrial injury benefit, one-parent benefit, and mobility allowance.

15.8   Statutory Sick Pay

Employers are responsible for paying Statutory Sick Pay to employees for periods of sickness of four consecutive days or more (including Sundays and Bank Holidays) up to a limit of eight weeks in any tax year. Beyond that the employer's own sick pay scheme may provide payment or the employee will transfer to State sickness or other benefit.

SSP paid by an employer is indirectly refunded by the Department of Health and Social Security by the employer deducting SSP payments from the National Insurance contributions sent off monthly to the Collector of Taxes. SSP payments are however shown separately on each P11 (see column 1d of Figure 15.2) so that each employee's National Insurance contributions can be clearly seen, as these affect entitlements to certain State benefits.

For up to three days sickness it is up to the employer whether to issue pay or not as he would bear the cost, but after four consecutive days the employee enters a PIW (period of incapacity for work) and becomes qualified for SSP. The amount due is at one of three levels, dependent on earnings. As it is treated as part of wages or salary it is subject to PAYE income tax and affects the level of National Insurance contributions payable.

An employer may make his own rules about how employees notify him of sickness, and he is entitled to ask for evidence of sickness. He is required by law, on penalty of fines, to keep records of dates of sickness absences of four days or more, and of the Qualifying Days that occur within a period of sickness (i.e., the days on which the employee would have worked, if well). He must also record days within any PIW on which SSP was not paid and why. Records must be accessible to DHSS inspectors.

Employees over minimum state pension age or earning less than the minimum amount required for National Insurance contributions liability or on short-term contracts of under three months are excluded from SSP.

15.9 In a nutshell

When you are ill:

- Notify your employer of sickness as soon as possible during the first Qualifying Day (on which you would normally have worked).
- Follow your employer's rules about *how* he wishes to be notified.
- If you are ill for between four and seven days, including Sundays and Bank Holidays, be prepared to sign a *self-certificate* as evidence of your illness.
- If your illness lasts more than seven days, you may be asked by your employer to obtain a *statement* from your doctor.
- If you wish, you may ask your employer for a written statement explaining his payment or non-payment of SSP.
- You will receive SSP as part of your gross pay, paid by the normal salary arrangements.

15.10 Did you Know?

1. Accident books must be kept for three years from the date of the last entry.

2. An employee injured at work can still bring an action for damages against his employer, who is compulsorily insured against such contingencies under the Employers' Liability (Compulsory Insurance) Act 1969.

3. National Insurance inspectors can visit premises at any time to see that the Acts are complied with, offenders being liable to fines or in some cases imprisonment.

4. P11s must be kept by employers for at least three years after the end of the tax year to which they relate.

5. A successful pilot scheme to computerize PAYE has been running in the West Midlands. It is planned to extend this all over UK by the end of 1987. The computer system will be compatible with one planned by the DHSS linking Social Security offices.

6. You should keep careful record of the National Insurance number allocated to you by the DHSS. Your employer will also need to know this for pay and tax records.

Activities

1. Explain the part played in the PAYE system by the Form P45. (LCCI, SSC)

2. Give details of the information which an employee would receive on his tax position: (a) at the end of the tax year (b) upon leaving the company's employment (c) from the tax office annually. (LCCI, PSC)

3. Using a set of PAYE forms and material

obtained by your tutor from the Inland Revenue, complete the PAYE entries for Weeks 1 to 4 on a P11 for a single girl who has been employed as a junior secretary since leaving college two years ago. Invent necessary details, such as National Insurance number, total pay, etc.

4. A young typist who has just joined your firm does not understand the entry on her payslip relating to National Insurance contributions. Set down briefly what you would say to her. You will need to explain:

(a) on what bases employees' contributions are assessed
(b) the part played by employers in making and collecting contributions
(c) why regular contributions are important to employees, listing *THREE* types of benefit the typist might be most likely to claim at some time.

(Exact figures are *not* required, only a statement of basic principles.) (LCCI, PSC)

5. Explain the following abbreviations and terms:

DHSS; NI; PIW; PAYE; Qualifying Day; P8; SSP; Schedule E; SERPS; Contracted-out.

6. Draft a short explanation of Statutory Sick Pay for inclusion in a leaflet given to new employees during the course of an induction session. Most of these employees are school- and college-leavers.

7. On the P11 used for Activity 3 above, complete the National Insurance contributions in respect of the same employee (contracted out), using tables your tutor can obtain from the Department of Health and Social Security.

8. Salaries in your firm are paid by credit transfer. A new typist is puzzled by her first payslip. (a) Explain the credit transfer procedure for wages. (b) Explain the two main deductions from pay noted on her payslip (LCCI, PSC) (You will need to refer to Chapter 14 to answer part (a).)

9. What information must be obtained in respect of two new employees before accurate deductions can be made from salary? One is a school-leaver; the other has already been employed.

10. Obtain a copy of (a) 'Employer's Guide to PAYE' and (b) 'Employer's Guide to National Insurance Contributions'. List (with a brief explanation) five topics on which each gives guidance.

11. **Group activity** One member should obtain from the local Department of Health and Social Security office one copy of each leaflet available on current National Insurance benefits. Distribute these among the group so that each member can type a brief outline of the payment concerned and the conditions which must be fulfilled. Place the summaries in a folder for reference, together with the leaflets.

PART FIVE

Secretarial skills

16
Dealing with dictation

As a secretary you will be dealing with dictation daily (shorthand or audio) and it is important that you transcribe everything correctly.

16.1   In a nutshell: Hints on taking shorthand dictation and transcription

- Keep your notebook handy.
- Put an elastic band round used pages as an automatic page finder.
- Keep your pen filled, or your pencil sharpened.
- Date each page at the top and bottom.
- Rule a left-hand margin of about 2.5 cm for short corrections and reminders.
- Use asterisks and footnotes for long substitutions or additions.
- Draw a line across the page after each letter.
- Sit quietly during interruptions in dictation.
- Study your notes while waiting, ready for reading back.
- Keep your mind on your work and on the subject-matter of the dictation.
- Leave the room during private telephone calls.
- Take intelligent notes from business calls.
- Do not interrupt dictation to ask questions. At the end of a letter, raise any queries you cannot check yourself.
- Never type nonsense.
- Skim quickly through your notes, then transcribe them in order of dictation, unless otherwise instructed.
- Cross through each letter as you transcribe it.
- Check every letter before you take it out of the typewriter.
- Mark the place you have reached in your notes, if an interruption occurs.
- Date used notebooks and file them for future reference.

16.2   Shorthand systems

There are several systems available, some based on symbols and others on alphabetical forms. The sensible use of any system, once learned, depends upon a sound knowledge of English. Pitman New Era and Gregg shorthand have been used for many years. More recent systems include Pitman 2000, Speedwriting, Teeline and PitmanScript.

16.3   Audiotyping

This involves a typist playing back recorded dictation and simultaneously transcribing it.

(a)   Author's equipment

The author dictates into a microphone of a dictating machine which usually has start, stop, fast-forward and rewind buttons giving remote control of the recording medium. Playback may be through a small loudspeaker or through the microphone. The author can usually check the volume of the recording visually and can adjust the equipment to compensate for poor recording conditions. Some machines have automatic recording control which monitors the voice level during recording. As well as desktop models, small portable versions are available, suitable for staff needing to dictate correspondence or notes away from the office. The latter may work on rechargeable or disposable batteries.

(b)   Recording media

Magnetic recording media are normally used, e.g., cassette tapes or disks. Because these are erasable they may be used over and over again. Permanent recording media are very rarely used. Magnetic media capacity ranges from about 15 minutes dictation per side on mini-cassettes to 90 minutes on standard cassettes (see *(f)* (ii) below for continuous loop machines).

(c)   Transcriber's equipment

To work efficiently a typist should develop the technique of typing and listening at the same time to the succeeding words so that typing is as continuous as possible. To stop the tape in order to catch up with the dictation a foot control is provided. On some models continuous light foot pressure is needed to keep the medium moving and heavier pressure to stop it; pressure on another part will enable selected portions to be played back for rehearing. Hand controls are available, if desired, but using these interrupts the typing. A headphone enables the typist to hear the dictation. The stethoscope type keeps out extraneous sounds more effectively than a single earpiece, though the latter is useful if the typist has to stop frequently to answer telephone calls. Volume, tone and fast forward and rewind controls are provided, and usually a control adjusting the speed of playback.

(d)   Correcting dictation

As magnetic media are normally used in offices, it is possible to correct errors in dictation as they occur by speaking the substituted words over the original ones. It is more difficult to correct in this manner once dictation is complete because the substitution

may encroach on the words following the incorrect ones. Therefore corrections may either be written out on an index slip, or dictated on a separate area of the recording medium, to which the transcriber's attention must be drawn before transcription begins (see *(e)* (iii) below).

(e)   Indexing methods

There are various features on recording and transcribing equipment that enable the contents of recorded media to be indexed and located at the time of use:

(i) *Scales and displays*   A scale on the front of transcribing machines and on some microphones shows the extent of the recording medium. A pointer, or on some machines a flashing cursor, indicates the point currently reached. On the microphone of microprocessor-controlled machines liquid crystal displays indicate the time already used in dictation, allowing the author to deduce the remaining time available. A warning tone indicates the imminent end of the tape.

(ii) *Starting and finishing points*   To display documents satisfactorily the transcriber needs to estimate the space the typing will occupy. This is made easier when the starting and finishing points of individual items are indicated. This can be done by writing down the scale points on a paper index slip handed to the transcriber with the cassette. It may also be done electronically: by pressing buttons on the machine the author can cause visual marks to be made on a calibrated strip on the front of some machines; or the length of each item in minutes and seconds, counted down to zero as transcription proceeds, may be shown in a liquid crystal display. The number in sequence of the item on the tape can also be shown. To help the transcriber prepare for the ensuing item, an automatic pause may be inserted before it begins, followed by a warning tone.

(iii) *Locating instructions*   Similar indications may be made for the points at which special instructions occur on the tape, or where corrections are to be found. By pressing a search key the transcriber can find these places automatically. In some systems, a warning tone at the appropriate point directs the transcriber to switch to the second track of the cassette tape, in order to hear extra material that has to be inserted, or corrections.

(f) Types of installation

(i) *Individual machines* Dictating and transcribing machines can be operated separately and not linked in any system. This may be satisfactory in a small organization, where the typist is easily able to collect the dictation medium from the author and where there is no other typist to share the workload.

(ii) *Tandem systems* These link an author directly with a transcribing machine into which dictation is put via a telephone on the PABX or separately wired network. The typist may have two transcribing units or one machine with two cassettes: in either case, one is used for transcription while the other accepts dictation. Any queries may be resolved by the author and transcriber conferring over the intercom speech link provided.

With one type of tandem system the typist can begin to transcribe a few seconds after the author has begun to dictate onto the same medium. The magnetic tape used is housed in a special container, enabling it to be used as a continuous loop. Safeguards are installed to prevent both transcriber and author from accidentally erasing untranscribed portions of the tape. The number of minutes of recording time to be transcribed are displayed in a small control unit on the typist's desk and are calculated automatically by the tape moving over optical readers.

(iii) *Centralized systems* In these the work is under the control of a supervisor. In *bank* systems authors dictate over internal or PABX telephone networks to communicate with a bank of recording machines placed in a typing centre, authors being automatically switched to free machines. The supervisor's role is important in distributing the recording media to the typists for transcription and in controlling the speed of turnover of the work entering the centre. Authors' instructions are given or queries raised through the supervisor. Monitoring the system by logging the use of the equipment, and ensuring a fair allocation of tasks are other responsibilities of the supervisor.

Computer-assisted centralized systems make the supervisor's work less onerous by providing many automatic features and continuous monitoring of the work. Figure 16.1 illustrates one system, providing facilities for dictation on continuous loop and cassettes. The *transcribers' units* (not shown) display the starting and finishing points of dictated items,

where instructions, corrections and priority items are to be found on the medium. At the end of each task each typist enters a signing-off signal on the transcribing unit. This causes the microcomputer controlling the system to log the time of completion and add the typist's code number to all the other details about the task that have already been stored, namely type of task, the author's telephone extension, the time and length of dictation. All this information appears on the *visual display screen* (centre) and can be printed out on a *printer* linked to the system (not shown) together with resulting analyses of the work done and trends revealed, e.g., total work done by each transcriber, each author and each department, rate of turnover, amount of backlog, the stage reached in the treatment of priority items, etc. In order to link a transcriber to a continuous loop recorder, the supervisor enters the appropriate code on the *system director* console (left). If required, the equipment will automatically route work to the transcribing unit with the fastest turnover. The handset on the system director allows the supervisor to communicate with authors, or with transcribers, who can ask for help with any problems. Dictation may also be recorded on the *cassette recorder* (right). Cassettes may be programmed to be ejected when a certain percentage of the tape has been used, or when a certain number of items have been dictated or after a certain time has elapsed since dictation from the first author finished. This helps to prevent long delays before transcription. Authors hear a warning tone when a cassette is to be changed. Cassettes containing priority items move automatically into a special tray, and signal for prompt attention. The system can accept dictation from any distant telephone onto cassette at any time of day or night if a special unit is installed.

(g) Unattended units

Some types of machine can be left switched on to receive dictation from executives working late, for transcription the following day. Time switches enable the current to be switched off and on again at prearranged times. The maximum capacity can be obtained from media when a blocking device exists: this prevents an executive from hearing or accidentally interfering with dictation already placed on earlier portions of the same medium, but allows him to play back his own.

181

Figure 16.1   A computerized central dictation system. See **16.3** *(f)* (iii) for a description of this equipment. (The partially hidden unit is a disk drive holding disks on which information displayed on the VDU is being stored.) (Courtesy of Dictaphone Company Ltd)

(h)   Outstations

It is possible for a typist working at home to be linked to a dictating machine in an office by way of a public or private exchange line and to post the work transcribed.

(i)   Telephone links

It is possible to link most machines with telephones, so that conversations can be recorded for transcription later, provided British Telecom approval is obtained. With the exception of emergency calls, it is not legally permissible to record telephone conversations unless the parties are explicitly told that this is being done (as in telephone answering machine systems).

(j)   Posting recordings

Recordings may be sent by post as postal packets. Special postal packs can be obtained from the manufacturers for tapes and rigid disks.

16.4   In a nutshell: Tips for dictators

- Introduce yourself.
- Speak clearly.
- Say whether the document is a final copy or draft.
- Indicate the topic of dictation.
- Explain the context of dictated matter, to increase the transcriber's job satisfaction.
- Give instructions before the dictation, e.g., number of copies, initial capitals.

- Indicate how the document is to be indexed for filing , especially if storage is on a word processing system.
- Use a different tone of voice for instructions.
- Indicate where further instructions or corrections are to be found.
- Speak at a fairly even rate.
- Switch off the machine during pauses for thought.
- Specify unusual punctuation.
- Indicate new paragraphs where significant.
- Spell out unusual names or terms.
- Indicate clearly the ends of memos and other documents.
- Explain who is to gather any enclosures and where they are to be found.
- Be willing to accept display in house style format.

16.5   Relative merits of shorthand and audiotyping

(a) With shorthand, the typist has personal contact with the author, who can easily answer queries at the time of dictation. The typist can often learn a good deal about the department's and the organization's work through being with the author.

(b) A shorthand-writer has the advantage of being able to practise the skill at any time, whereas an audiotypist is dependent upon the recorder for hearing the dictation.

(c) Audiotyping has advantages over shorthand-typing in that much time can be saved because the typist does not have to be with the author to receive dictation. Dictation can take place when it suits the author—even after hours or away from the office— and the typist is free to do other work meanwhile, including taking telephone calls to minimize interruptions to the author. However, the lack of personal contact can be a disadvantage in other ways and may reduce the typist's interest in the work. The work itself demands intense concentration: the typist must learn to absorb the sense of what is heard (in order to minimize mishearings and wrong spelling of homophones, and to decide on correct punctuation where this is not supplied by the author); sometimes complicated display must be visualized.

16.6   Typing centres

Some organizations have typing, audio transcription, or secretarial centres, pools, or 'secretariats'. A centre is an advantage to a company in that its main secretarial services are gathered in a specified place or places. An executive merely has to contact the supervisor to enable a suitable shorthand-typist to be sent to him, or to press a button to ensure that what he is about to dictate will be recorded on a dictating machine for transcription by one of the pool. Also, absences of secretarial staff through holidays or sickness cause the least disruption when the extra work can be divided among a number of people.

Supervisors can play an important part in fostering a pleasant working atmosphere among typists, in distributing dictation for transcription, in helping typists with queries and in checking transcriptions before they pass them to the executives for signature. Under a good supervisor, no member of the pool should be idle or overburdened with work, each can ask for advice when she needs it and beginners can gain valuable experience from the variety of work available. On the other hand, pool work can be frustrating, since there is little opportunity for its members to become accustomed to any one executive's methods, to learn to take responsibility or to show much initiative.

A good working environment is especially necessary to the efficiency and well-being of the members of a centre, and many companies realize the importance of quiet rooms, good lighting and up-to-date machines. Carpets and acoustic-tiled ceilings to absorb sound are common. Although messenger services are usually organized for taking completed letters to executives for signature, some companies encourage typists to do this in order to give them some exercise and provide the opportunity for personal contact with authors.

Similar considerations may apply to the organization of word processing centres (see **17.9**).

He's dictating some famous last words!

Figure 16.2   (Courtesy of Tony Holland. First published in *Business Systems and Equipment*)

The existence of centres does not necessarily dispense with the need for some senior executives to have their own personal secretaries, particularly where the work is confidential or demands special knowledge.

16.7   Pleasing appearance of typed letters

Whichever system of taking dictation you use, your letters must be neatly and accurately displayed and correctly addressed. As well as being accurate, a typed letter should look pleasing, so that the reader receives a good impression of the company. The right proportion of white space to typed matter is one of the biggest considerations in artistic display. Paragraphing is therefore important, and the choice of suitable margins to prevent the letter looking cramped or too low on the page. Often, one particular type of layout will be adopted for use throughout an organization. This involves assessing the speed of execution of the various possible styles, and their general effect in conjunction with the printed letter heading (see Figure 16.3).

16.8   Letterheads

Letters addressed to external organizations or persons are invariably typed on headed paper. The

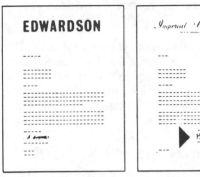
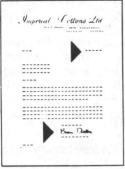
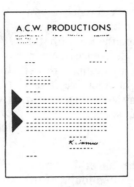

Fully-blocked	Blocked	Semi-blocked
Begin *every* line at the left margin.	Date and complimentary closing as shown.	Date and complimentary closing as shown, with first line of each paragraph indented.

Figure 16.3 Various letter displays.

appearance of this is very important, as it reflects the organization's 'personality' and the image it wishes to present to the public. Many styles of print and design are available, ranging from the restrained and subdued (implying solidity and reliability) to the colourful, eye-catching, and unconventional (suggesting vigour and progressiveness). The same, or slightly adapted, format can be used on all the organization's documents, e.g., memos, invoices, reports, postcards, catalogues, brochures. A simple and appropriate logo or symbol is often incorporated into the design, by which the organization can be quickly recognized—a kind of trade mark. If this is also used on delivery vans, shopfronts, uniforms and on the packaging of the organization's products, it can be a cheap method of advertising. The following features appear on letterheads:

(a) Name

The organization's name is, of course, the most important item, and may be printed in bold capitals. There are many other possible styles: the name might be in italics or another more elaborate type; it might be set to the right-hand side of the sheet rather than centred; colour might be used.

(b) Address

The address must also be very prominent, and should contain full postal details including postcode. Sometimes, addresses of head or branch offices appear in smaller print.

(c) Telephone number and extension, telegraphic address, telex or teletex number, facsimile group and number

(d) Reference numbers

Spaces are sometimes provided for reference numbers, either in the centre of the sheet or at the left- or right-hand margins. 'Our ref.' denotes the organization's own system of reference numbers; 'Your ref.' that used by the correspondent. Reference numbers often contain two sets of initials—the first standing for the author and the second for the typist. If the signature is not legible, this system helps telephone or other queries arising from a letter to be directed to the right person, and also pins responsibility for information given in it firmly on those who sent it. Some reference numbers also have symbols denoting the writer's department—e.g., OM (standing for office manager's department), or A

185

(accounts). Another part of the reference might consist of the name or number of the particular file containing previous correspondence with the person or on the matter involved. Reference numbers help the mailing section to see that incoming correspondence quickly reaches the right executive; it also helps the filing section to put away letters in the right place when they have been dealt with.

(e) Directors' names

To avoid the top part of the sheet becoming overloaded, directors' names are often found at the foot in small print (see **16.13**).

16.9   Features of letters

(a) Reference

Always place your reference on a letter (see **16.8**(*d*)).

(b) Date

Always place today's date on your letter, stating the day, month and year.

(c) Salutation and subscription

These are important. 'Dear Mr/Mrs/Miss/Ms' go with 'Yours sincerely' and the more formal opening 'Dear Sir/Madam' (used when writing to people hitherto unknown) goes with 'Yours faithfully'.

(d) Complimentary close

Often the name of the company appears immediately beneath 'Yours faithfully', etc., indicating that the person who signed the letter is doing so on behalf of that company. You should type the name of the signatory below, just above the designation (or position held). 'Mrs, Miss or Ms' maybe included before the typed name, or after it in brackets.

(e) Enclosures

When you have to enclose material with a letter, type 'enc.' (if it is one enclosure) or 'encs' (if more than one) in the left-hand corner of the letter near the bottom. This reminds you to put them in and helps the addressee to check them on receipt.

16.10   Everyday forms of address

(a) Mr or Esq.

Most organizations nowadays prefer the use of 'Mr' to 'Esq.' when addressing a letter to a man with no other rank or title. 'Esq.' is hardly ever used in English-speaking countries abroad. However, some organizations still prefer it, especially when letters follow a man's name.

(b) When to use 'Messrs'

When writing to two men, address the letter to 'Messrs Jones and Evans' ('Messrs' being the abbreviated version of 'Messieurs' used as the plural of 'Mr'). Partnerships are addressed likewise, unless they have adopted an impersonal name, e.g., The Famous Drug Company, or already possess another title, e.g., Sir Andrew Thorne & Company, which makes the use of 'Messrs' impossibly clumsy.

(c) Writing to a limited company

Some people address a limited company as 'Messrs'. Strictly speaking, this is wrong, as a limited company is regarded in law as one person and so cannot logically be addressed by a plural courtesy title. Instead, write either directly to the company:

Robert Rae & Co. Ltd   (Dear Sirs)

of, if there are no instructions on the headed notepaper to the contrary (see (*d*) below), to a person or official within the company:

Mr W. Williams,
Chief Accountant,
Robert Rae & Co. Ltd   (Dear Sir)

The Chief Accountant,
Robert Rae & Co. Ltd   (Dear Sir)

(d) Attention lines

It is not usually considered polite to address an envelope to, say, 'Mr Brown' without any initials. If there is no previous correspondence to help, try to find out what they are by consulting telephone directories or other reference books, or by telephoning the organization concerned. In the last resort, you can evade the issue by using the words 'For the Attention of Mr Brown' in the inside address and on the envelope:

INSIDE
ADDRESS

> J. C. Jones & Co. Ltd
> 4 High Street
> Amford, etc.
>
> *For the Attention of Mr Brown*
>
> Dear Sirs,

ENVELOPE

> *For the Attention of Mr Brown*
>
> J. C. Jones & Co. Ltd
> 4 High Street
> Amford, etc.

Notice that the salutation must be 'Dear Sirs', since you are addressing the letter to the organization not to Mr Brown.

In some cases, an attention line must be used for another reason. A limited company may stipulate on its headed notepaper that letters should be addressed only to the company itself and not to individual employees. If the writer, nevertheless, wants a particular person to deal with his letter, it will reach that person if an attention line is used.

(e) Writing to women

It used to be the case when writing to a married woman to use her husband's initials, and to a divorced or widowed woman her own initials, after the word 'Mrs' (which is never expanded). These days it is customary to use the woman's own initials in both cases.

Address an unmarried woman as 'Miss'; this is not an abbreviation, and therefore never has a full stop. The plural of 'Miss' is 'Misses'—e.g., 'The Misses Webber'. 'Mesdames' is used when referring to more than one married woman, e.g., 'Mesdames Clinton and Turner'; a letter would begin 'Mesdames' (omitting the word 'Dear' before it).

Some women believe that their married status is a private matter and prefer to be addressed as 'Ms'.

16.11 Special forms of address

Do you know how to address envelopes to a bishop, an admiral, a Privy Councillor? Do you know when a special salutation or complimentary close is necessary in a letter? You can find the correct methods to be used by consulting the standard reference books on the subject.

It is important also to be able to find out the correct forms of address for persons holding hereditary and other titles. When writing to members of the peerage and baronetage, follow this procedure:

(a) Find out to which rank of the peerage your correspondent belongs (e.g., a duke, a marquess, an earl, a viscount or a baron). This can be done by consulting a suitable reference book, such as *Whitaker's Almanack*.

(b) Look up the correct usage in *Titles and Forms of Address or Correct Form*.

Baronets and knights are not peers. They both use 'Sir' before their forenames and surnames, but are differentiated by the presence or absence of letters after their names, e.g.:

- Baronet: Sir James Jackson, Bt (or Bart).
- Knight of the Order of the Bath: Sir Matthew Marfleet, GCB, or Sir Frank Francis, KCB.
- Knight of the Order of St Michael and St George: Sir Brian Biggs, GCMG, or Sir Godfrey Gunner, KCMG.
- Knight of the Royal Victorian Order: Sir Keith King, GCVO; Dame of the Royal Victorian Order: Dame Violet Vernon, GCVO; or Sir Peter Porter, KCVO, and Dame Selina Sampson, KCVO.
- Knight of the Order of the British Empire: Sir Herbert Harris, GBE, and Dame of the Order of the British Empire: Dame Joan Johnson, GBE; or Sir Lionel Lamb, KBE, and Dame Rose Rank, DBE.
- Knight Bachelor: Sir Rupert Raymond.

Knighthoods and other honours awarded by the Queen are announced twice-yearly—in the New Year or Queen's Birthday Honours list, details of which are published in the leading newspapers.

Note. The wife of a baronet or knight is addressed, for example, Lady Lincoln. *The* Lady Lincoln would be the wife of a peer.

Letters after a person's name tell you something about his or her life history, e.g.:

(a) GCMG after someone's name reveals that he has worked for long periods overseas, as this particular honour is reserved for such service.

(b) MC indicates that the holder served as an army officer and showed bravery on the field of battle.

(c) OBE denotes the performance of public service in a wide variety of fields: perhaps work as a civil servant, voluntary services, achievements in the arts, sport, etc.

(d) BA, MA, PhD are examples of academic awards in ascending order, usually revealing a university background. If a person holds two degrees in the same faculty, only the higher is shown.

(e) FCIS reveals the holder to have qualified and had experience as a Company Secretary.

Letters after names fall into several categories: (a) royal orders; (b) military decorations; (c) academic degrees; (d) membership of professional and other associations.

If a person has several sets of letters, you must find out the correct order in which to place them. The following remarks may serve as a rough guide:

(a) VC (Victoria Cross) and GC (George Cross), awarded for conspicuous bravery, precede all royal orders and decorations, and are always quoted in correspondence.

(b) Letters denoting royal orders—i.e., those connected with knighthoods and the Orders of Merit and of Companions of Honour—precede all military decorations (except the VC and GC) and are always quoted in correspondence.

(c) Letters indicating academic degrees (not quoted socially, except for doctorates) follow those in (b) above, and precede those indicating membership of professional and other associations. There appears to be no definite ruling on the order in which to list university degrees where a person holds more than one. Sometimes, they are listed in descending and sometimes ascending order of importance.

(d) Letters such as MP (Member of Parliament) and QC (Queen's Counsel) come last, being offices held, not honours. Others are PC (Privy Councillor), though this is no longer quoted on envelopes, JP (Justice of the Peace) and DL (Deputy Lieutenant), though these are quoted only in official, not social, correspondence.

16.12   Addressing envelopes

(a) Display

Advice on the correct addressing of envelopes, etc., is given in the *Post Office Guide*. The advice covers such points as the position of the address on the envelope, how to obtain the correct full postal address, which parts of the address are to be typed in capitals, when names of counties are not needed, when county names can be abbreviated, the use of postal district letters and numbers, postcodes, etc. Other Post Office publications useful for addressing purposes are: *Postal Addresses and Index to Postcode Directories*, which includes entries for over 20 000 places in the UK, *Post Offices in the United Kingdom*, which gives details of all Post Offices in the UK, and *London Post Offices and Streets*.

(b) Postcodes

These are in operation all over the UK and have been devised to enable sorting to be done electronically. A code consists of two groups of letters and figures—the first indicates the town or district, and the second a street, part of a street, or a large business concern. At the mechanized sorting office, the letter is fed automatically to a coding desk where an operator causes a pattern of phosphorescent dots corresponding to the postcode to be imprinted in two lines on the front of the envelope. These dots are read by the automatic sorting machines, and the letter is automatically sorted: first, to the town or district concerned, then, on arrival at the delivery office, to that area of streets for which a postman is responsible. Copies of directories are available giving the postcodes in each coded area.

(c) Envelope flags

Pocket envelopes can be typed with their flaps either to the left or to the right of the address. Either is satisfactory, but, if your company has a central mailing room, it is important to find out which method they prefer or delay will result in sealing the mail.

16.13   Did you know?

1. EEC regulations stipulate that the registration number and country of registration of a company must be incorporated into its letter heading, also the names of its directors with their nationality (if not British).

2. Stenotyping is a method of machine shorthand. The operator types phonetic syllables almost noiselessly on a continuous roll of paper in a lightweight machine which can be held on the lap if necessary. The typed notes can be transcribed by anyone after a short study of stenotyping theory. This is an especial advantage in law courts or at conferences where notes must be taken continuously but immediate transcription may be needed

16.14   Useful sources of reference

Abbreviations dictionary
Correct Form (Debrett)
English dictionary
Housestyle handbook
London Post Offices and Streets
Post Office Guide
Post Offices in the United Kingdom
*Postal Addresses and Index to Postcode
  Directories*
Postcode directories
Shorthand dictionary
Titles and Forms of Address (Black)
Typewriting dictionary
Whitaker's Almanack

Activities

1. You are secretary to a sales manager. His time is increasingly taken up with interviews throughout the week with existing and potential customers, both in the office and elsewhere. As a result, correspondence accumulates, awaiting his attention, and he has little opportunity to dictate to you or to keep in touch with sales staff. Suggest a variety of measures that might improve this situation. (LCCI, PSC)

2. An audio-typing centre is to be set up in your firm. The office manager has asked you, as secretary, to suggest how the firm could best achieve efficient work and a contented typing staff.

Compile an appropriate list of suggestions with comments on each item. (LCCI, PSC)

3. Your firm has decided to install a multi-bank dictating system and intends to hold courses for all Managers on the art of dictation. Set out a list of points that you feel ought to be covered in such a course. (LCCI, SSC)

4. Your company is installing a central audio-dictation bank system, but you will continue to work as secretary to your immediate employer. In what ways is the new system likely to affect his dictating routines and your own duties? How will you keep informed of all current developments in his correspondence? (LLCI, PSC)

5. Some people are prejudiced against working in typing or secretarial pools. Why is this so? What qualities do you think a supervisor should have to enable pool work to be done efficiently and in a harmonious atmosphere?

6. (You will need to consult *Whitaker's Almanack* and *Titles and Forms of Address*.) Supplying necessary details yourself, type envelopes to the following: The Bishop of Barchester; Stanley Searle, who is a lieutenant-colonel in the army; Dick Whittington, who is the Lord Mayor of London; John Ponsonby, who is a baronet, who holds the DFC, and is a member of the Order of Merit; Harold Sinclair, who is a Queen's Counsel and holds MA and LLD degrees, and is also a Fellow of the Royal Society of Arts; the Regency Co. Ltd (Mr M Petty is to deal with the letter); Philip Lee and Ronald Ware, partners.

7. Consult the *Post Office Guide* for the following: (a) in what position should an address be placed on an envelope? (b) What is a post town and how should it be typed? (c) When is a county name unnecessary? (d) Which are the county names that the Post Office allows to be abbreviated? (e) Where should a postcode be typed on an envelope?

Now type correctly an envelope addressed to yourself.

8. Consult *Postal Addresses and Index to Postcode Directories* for the following: Give five examples of how you could address an envelope to someone living in Newport. In each case, the first two lines will be: Mr J Brown, 112 High Street.

9. **Group activity.** From the business letters received by group members, parents, and friends, make a joint collection of letterheads and compare their different styles.

17
Typewriting and word processing

17.1 How not to copy-type

You are very busy today, and, fearing that you may
not be able to cope with everything that must be
done, you have asked for some help from another
department. They have sent along a junior with very
little experience as a typist. You are doubtful of her
ability, but your boss has no choice but to give her a
letter that must go off today, written in his not easily
legible handwriting. However, she says she can read
it and gets on with her task without apparent difficulty. Figure 17.1 *(a)* shows an extract from the
manuscript.

The junior does a few other jobs and then returns
to her own department. Some minutes later, your
boss emerges from his room with a wry face, and
hands you her letter. 'This is no good at all,' he says.
'You'll have to type it again. Why ever didn't the girl
use the dictionary—and her common sense—and
ask for help? What a lot of everyone's time she would
have saved!'

You can see why your boss is objecting when you
read the junior's version in Figure 17.1 (b).

The Cttee. met on Fri. 17 June & John Russell took the Chair as usual. They decided after all to defer discussion of Item 4 E. This was too disturbing a matter to be handled with so few present — barely more than the quorum, especially as the people affected most were not there

John R... said that on previous Fri 10th June, he had had a letter from Bailey & Son abt. the contract. The tone was rather likewarm. The cttee decided it cd. not let the matter drop altogether & settled on a higher fig.—£ 2000 this time.

Item 6) provoked surprisingly little comment perhaps because Johnson's neighbour was absent! Jane Manning seemed v. relieved.

Figure 17.1(a)   Extract from manuscript.

```
      1   2                        3
   The  Comittee met on Friday, 17  June, and John Russell took the Chair
                    4                                             5   6
as usual. They  decided after all to defer discussion of Item 4 :  This was
      2                                                   6
to  disturbing a matter to be handled with so few present-barely more than
        7   6                             2
the q uom,  especially as the people  effected most were not there.
  8        9                  10                 11    3
     John R.  said that on   previous Friday,   11th  June, he had had a letter
                                                                      7
from Bailey and Son about the contract. The tone was rather likewise.  The
1
 committee decided it  could not let the matter drop all  together and
                                          6
settled on a higher figure-£2000 this time.
      8    5                                          6                         6
        Item  6) provoked surprisingly little comment  perhaps because Johnsons'
                       12                           2
neighbour was absent! Jane  Manning seemed very releived
```

Figure 17.1(b)

17.2   Checklist: Errors in typing from manuscript

Did you spot where the junior went wrong?

1. She was inconsistent in her use of initial capitals.
2. She made spelling errors.
3. She typed the date in different styles.
4. She treated the collective noun 'committee' sometimes as singular and sometimes as plural.
5. She typed the numbered items inconsistently.
6. She made punctuation errors.
7. She did not trouble to investigate unfamiliar words and therefore typed nonsense.
8. She changed from indented to block paragraphing.
9. She did not understand the significance of omission dots.
10. She omitted a word which should obviously have been present.
11. She did not take in the subject matter, otherwise she would have realized one of the dates must be wrong.
12. She could not tell from the writing that June (not Jane) Manning was intended and should have asked.

17.3   Hints on copy-typing

When writing a draft in longhand, your boss is intent on the subject matter and expects you to be able to use your typing skill in presenting the final copy in a clear, neat, and consistent manner. The first essential is to be able to read your boss's handwriting. Familiarity with this and with his or her literary style will help you to type sense rather than nonsense. Read quickly through at least part of the manuscript to get the gist of it and mark up portions that seem obscure. If, on a second reading, they still don't make sense, query them with your boss at the first convenient opportunity. It is much more sensible to do this than to make corrections later, however quickly they may be done on electronic equipment. Where the subject matter is technical and uses jargon or formulae incomprehensible to you, even more care is necessary.

If you know how to spell and punctuate, your boss will be relieved of the irksome and distracting necessity of having to be 100 per cent accurate in these respects.

You may be given *carte blanche* to display manuscripts as you think best. On the other hand, your boss may have definite ideas on this point, in which case follow the general layout indicated.

Observe any corrections your boss makes to the original version. Through your typewriting training you will be acquainted with the standard correction signs; your common sense will help you to interpret any variations on these.

17.4   Checking

Your job is not completed unless you have checked it. Do this with two objectives in mind: to discover and correct your typing errors; and to spot errors in content, arising perhaps from misconstruing words or omitting parts of sentences or paragraphs. Have the original draft by your side for quick comparison. Check especially carefully any master for duplication.

Remember that the more checking you do, the easier it becomes to spot the typing errors. In the end, you hardly have to search them out: they almost protrude from the page.

The onus is on you to read through your work. You may protest that your boss is ultimately responsible and should also check it over before dispatching it. Of course your boss will skim quickly over it, but is not paid to spend time saving the company from the results of your laziness or inefficiency.

Bear in mind, too, that if you can never be trusted to submit accurate work, you will certainly never be trusted with more responsible duties. Aim at being so dependable that the boss can sign a blank sheet of headed paper, and then go off on holiday, confidently leaving you to type in afterwards over the signature a letter which has already been dictated.

17.5   Typing speeches

Clarity is the keynote here. If the speech is to be read verbatim, type it in double or treble spacing, using pica type if possible. Make headings—indicating a new topic or a new development of a theme—as prominent as possible by typing in upper case, in bold type, in red or by underscoring. It may be helpful to pick out any quotations, jokes or other points not essential to the theme of the speech, in case time presses or the audience is unresponsive and your boss wishes to leave them out. Leave room for marginal comments or 'stage directions'. Use parchment or other thick quality paper, which lessens the effect of a trembling hand.

Your boss may need only notes for the speech. For these, use small sheets of paper. Postcards—sometimes called 'confidence cards'—are easy to handle, and can be laid face downwards one at a time on the table after use. Type in double spacing.

17.6   Preparing copy for printing

(a)   Typing display

Work that is to be printed must be typed in an acceptable manner. Wide margins, particularly the left one, and double spacing are required. Footnotes should be typed immediately beneath the line to which they refer and underscored above and below.

(b)   Headings

These must always be consistent and logical, i.e., major ones centred, minor ones either as shoulder headings or marginal headings, or indented and followed on the same line by the succeeding words (run-on headings).

(c)   Importance of accurate copy

The copy should be as correct as possible both in presentation and subject matter. Corrections later will cost you time and money.

(d)   Printing procedure

Before final printing takes place the printer will supply the customer with a set of proofs for checking and approval. He will have marked one set in green ink with any literal errors he has found and will supply a copy for the customer to correct. The customer should correct any printer's errors in red and any additional alterations and instructions in blue/black ink. He should then return the proofs to the printer (keeping a copy for his file) and state whether he would like revised proofs. At this stage he should also confirm the quantity, paper, price, delivery dates, etc.

Proofs may be:

galley proofs	–	rough proofs, printed on poor quality paper, with large margins.
page proofs	—	material is divided into numbered pages, resembling near enough the final product with very few corrections.
dummy proofs	—	sometimes produced for special presentations to show a roughly assembled version of the final book, catalogue or magazine.

(e)   Proof-reading

You must be very thorough when reading proofs; check everything. It may be a good idea to ask a colleague to read the proofs out loud while you check them.

(f)   Proof-correcting

Standard printer's proof correction marks are listed in British Standard 5261, 1976. Each correction sign consists of a mark in the margin and another in the text at the point in question.

17.7   Typewriters

(a)   Manual typewriters

By depressing a key on the keyboard the operator causes the *typebar* bearing the appropriate typeface to strike the paper through the ribbon at the printing point. Space must be left on a desktop for the movement of the carriage, which proceeds from right to left as the keys are struck. The machine is noisy and vibrates because of the impact made by the typebars. Printing is comparatively slow, and a good deal of physical effort is needed from the typist. *Portable* machines are less suitable for regular use than *standard* models.

(b)   Electric typewriters

These may be typebar machines or *single element* ('golfball') machines. With the latter, the characters are embossed round the perimeter of a typing head, which moves across the page. Depression of a key causes the head to rotate to bring the required character against the ribbon. There is less vibration than with manual typewriters because the carriage is fixed but the machine is noisy. The typing heads are interchangeable, to provide different *fonts* (styles) and characters, including foreign language alphabets and scientific symbols. Different *pitches* (number of characters per inch or 2.54 cm) can be supplied: the most common are 12 (*élite*), 10 (*pica*), 15 (*micro*). Proportional spacing is also available on single-element machines and on typebar machines fitted for the purpose. It allows each character to occupy the amount of space its shape demands, e.g., 'm' has a wider allocation than 'i'. Some machines have a *justifying* facility, enabling the right-hand margin to be automatically squared after a first draft has been typed. Other facilities may include: *automatic pressure control* varying the pressure to suit the number of carbon copies required; *half-space keys* enabling omitted letters to be satisfactorily fitted in; *automatic repeat keys*, e.g., turning up, underscore, hyphen, x (delete). The print from electric typewriters is always even and entails much less effort from the typist, as the lightest touch on a key activates it. *Portable* models are also available.

(c)   Electronic typewriters

These have printing heads activated electronically by printed electronic circuit boards. Because they do not work mechanically (unlike manual and electric typewriters) there are few moving parts. Maintenance is simplified, as faults—which may cause the machines to fail—usually lie in the circuit board.

An electronic typewriter is equipped with different kinds of memory:

(i) *Buffer memory* Characters that are keyed in faster than the machine can print out are temporarily stored in buffer memory. This situation occurs at line-ends and means that the operator can continue to type without waiting for the print-head to move to the beginning of the next line. It also occurs when text is input: therefore any character within the last 15 characters or the last line or two (according to the make of machine) can be deleted at the press of a button on the keyboard from memory before it is printed. The characters held in this memory are displayed on a narrow display panel. After a correction has been made within buffer memory, depressing the *relocation* key returns the printing head automatically to the point where typing is to be resumed, but this does not apply to corrections made outside the limits of this correction memory. They are corrected manually, not electronically, e.g., by using a 'lift-off' ribbon which removes the character from the paper, or a 'cover-up' ribbon, which deposits a chalky substance over the error to obliterate it.

(ii) *Working memory* This can store up to a specified number of kbytes of keyed-in text from about 6 to 32 A4 pages, the amount varying according to make of typewriter. Stop codes may be keyed-in at predetermined points to enable the operator to insert variable details. A *phrase memory*, storing short standard phrases, and a *display memory*, storing margins and tabulator stops, for example, for a particular task, also form part of the

Figure 17.2 Electronic typewriter: IBM Thermotronic I. This typewriter uses a heat-sensitive ribbon to produce high-quality dot matrix printing. Electrodes in the print-head generate heat which partially melts the coating of the ribbon, allowing characters to be impressed through it onto the page. To make a correction, heat is applied to a lesser degree to the appropriate characters so that they become tacky and adhere to the ribbon. Interchangeable electronic type fonts act as the print-heads. If two different ones are used at the same time the user may switch from one to the other. Printing is silent and at up to 60 cps. (Courtesy of IBM United Kingdom Ltd)

working memory. A back-up battery supply enables information stored to remain in memory for hours or even days after the electric current has been switched off.

(iii) *Backing stores*   Additional text may be stored on floppy disks, provided the typewriter has a disk drive.

Facilities available vary according to the software used by various manufacturers. They range from basic facilities, e.g., automatic error-correction from buffer memory, choice of pitch, repeat keys, to those with external memories approaching the capability of word processors (see **17.9**). Facilities may include: automatic centring; decimal tabulation; aligning text level with the right-hand margin (e.g., dates); automatic underscore; automatic carriage return; right-hand margin justification; repeat typing for all keys; fast backspace; impression control; automatic paper feed; emboldening; automatic page-end; expanded print; vertical lines and boxes.

Printing usually involves daisy wheel print-head or thermal dot matrix technology (see **11.9**), the heat-transfer dot matrix printing from electronic type fonts.

(d)   Additional features found on electronic typewriters

Besides being used for basic typewriting, electronic typewriters can be interfaced to work with other equipment and devices. For example: they can be linked with *separate disk drives* and thus gain much *greater storage capacity*; with disk drives, a special logic board and keypad (see Figure 17.3), a cathode ray tube display or VDU attached, they can perform *basic word processing functions* for occasional use; if fitted with feed devices for single sheets or continuous stationery, they can be interfaced with microcomputers to act as *printers*; when combined with a telephone and acoustic coupler or modem they can act as *electronic mail terminals* (see Figure 13.10); they can be interfaced with other devices into

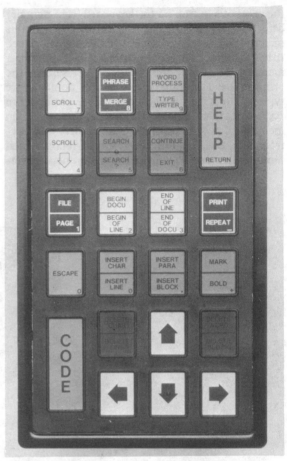

Figure 17.3   A word processing function keypad (used with the Lexoriter word processing 'add-on' system). Each word processing function is controlled by a specific and dedicated control key. (Courtesy of Lion Office Equipment Ltd)

local area networks (see Figure 11.4); interfaces using the *teletex standard* enable them to communicate with one another or with telex subscribers (see **13.11**).

(For *typewriter supplies* see **6.5**.)

17.8   Checklist for typewriter care and maintenance

- Clean typefaces of typebar machines daily for sharp, clear type.
- Dust the inner parts of manual and electric typewriters with long-handled brush.
- If erasing, move carriage of typebar machines so that eraser dust does not clog the typebars in the typebasket.

- Use correctable ribbons on electronic typewriters, since using erasers, correcting fluids and sheets may clog the print-head.
- Renew ribbons regularly.
- Switch off electrically-driven machines before investigating faults and after use at the end of the day.
- Refer major faults to a qualified technician.
- Cover machines when not in use.
- Always use a backing sheet on typebar machines to protect the platen surface.
- If you must lift a typewriter, lock the carriage and support the back of the machine against your body, to reduce strain on back muscles.

Figure 17.4 ICL DRS 8801 Word Processor. The operator is inserting a diskette into one of the two diskette drives in the control unit. The keyboard can be detached from the screen and angled and tilted to suit the operator. The screen can also be swivelled. The daisy wheel printer on the left is fitted with a tractor feed attachment for continuous stationery. This word processor can be used as a stand-alone machine or linked into a network through a telephone line to other word processors for electronic mail; or it may be linked into a local area network where it can share a document storage system with other terminals on the network. (Courtesy of ICL)

17.9 Word Processors

Word processors are very widely used in offices. They have two advantages over conventional typewriters: one is the ability to produce individually printed copies of documents at very high speeds, personalized to the recipient; the other is to enable corrections, reformatting, and insertions to be made easily to edited drafts without the operator having to retype the unaltered portions.

(a) Operation

The operator keys in text on a QWERTY style keyboard. Each keystroke is stored in memory and displayed on the visual display unit screen, which gives a view of the memory. The operator can *scroll* over (move across or up or down) the length and breadth of memory as required, enabling text to be displayed appropriately. Centring is done automatically by the machine. Corrections are very easily made: e.g., a wrong character is deleted and the correct one substituted merely by overtyping; words, sentences and paragraphs can be taken out and inserted elsewhere (*cut and paste*) or fresh material can be substituted. The operator indicates where action is to take place by moving the *cursor* (a moving indicator) to the appropriate point on the screen. The uncorrected parts of the text are automatically adjusted to allow for these changes. The machine automatically arranges line-endings, moving words to the next line as appropriate (*word wraparound*), or can provide a completely justified right-hand margin. If revising the text causes a change in pagination, the machine automatically renumbers the pages in the correct sequence.

The operator must give commands to the machine on what action to take. This may be done via a *menu*

197

(a displayed list of options from which the operator chooses). This is a simple method to learn but rather tedious to operate. An alternative method is via *command sequences* on the keyboard (using the appropriate operating keys in the correct order)—a method more difficult to learn but quicker to operate.

(b)   Facilities available

Additional facilities may be available, depending on the software provided. These include: sorting and arranging information into numerical, alphabetical or chronological order as required by the user; performing calculations enabling figures to be processed with the text; checking spelling (see **18.13**); selecting synonyms; calling up on the screen commonly used phrases merely by depressing an operating key; selecting different styles and sizes of typeface and seeing that results on the screen (i.e., what you see is what you get); locating and correcting the same sequence of letters wherever they appear in a document (*global search and replace*); displaying the whole of a page in miniature, enabling layout to be checked without scrolling; placing footnotes automatically at the bottom of the pages to which they relate.

(c)   Applications

(i) *Standard letters*   The text of a stored standard letter is called on the screen. Before each one is printed out, the operator keys in the variable details applicable to the particular recipient, e.g., name, address, amount of money owed, etc. If appropriate, variable details can be held on a separate disk, and the contents merged by the word processor automatically into the letters as they are printed (*mail merge*). Standard paragraphs (*building blocks*) can be coded for retrieval from store as required and by assembling (*boilerplating*) them a routine letter can be easily composed.

(ii) *Standard documents*   Documents that contain much repetitive material can be prepared and stored, and the variable details added, e.g., specifications, quotations, legal documents.

(iii) *Forms*   The layout of the form is recalled to the screen for the operator to complete as required. This facility reduces the need to keep large stocks of preprinted forms.

(d)   Types of word processor systems

(i) *Stand-alone*   The word processor is operated independently and has its own printer, processor and memory store.

(ii) *Multi-terminal* (or shared resource)   A word processor forms one of a cluster of group of intelligent terminals, i.e., each with its own processing power but all sharing storage devices and printers.

(iii) *Shared logic*   A group of word processors are linked to a master processor which provides shared storage and controls the program. All the terminals depend on the CPU for power.

(iv) *Distributed logic*   All terminals are linked to a CPU but they are all intelligent terminals, capable of functioning if the CPU were to break down.

(v) *Dedicated terminal*   The machine is programmed solely for word processing and is therefore suitable for continuous use. The operating procedures are easier and more direct than with (vi) below.

(vi) *Microcomputer with word processing package*   Word processing is only one of the programs the machine can handle. It is therefore suitable for occasional or shared word processing and has the flexibility to handle other types of work as well, e.g., accounting tasks.

(e)   Alternative methods of input

Because keying-in on a word processor is relatively slow, a backlog of work waiting to be input may occur. The pressure on the word processing operator can be relieved by other typists formatting text on standard typewriters and recording it on floppy disk for automatic input to the word processor, on which only the editing needs to be done. One system enables several typewriters to be linked to a minicomputer, which stores completed pages under code numbers on disks which the word processor accesses for editing. Another method involves fitting typewriters with OCR font (see **11.10**). This enables a typist to type out a first draft on paper which can be scanned by an OCR reader and input directly into the word processor's memory. When the text is recalled to the VDU screen the operator can edit it as required by the author of the document. Time can be saved by the author writing amendments on the paper draft before it is scanned but such amendments will not be read by the scanner, which reacts only to OCR font. If required, the word processor printer can print out a document in OCR font, to act as future input if disk storage capacity is limited.

(f) Operator skills

As operators are dealing with text, they need verbal skills, e.g., wide vocabulary, an understanding of acceptable English, spelling and punctuation. They also need to be able to follow instructions involving codes and symbols. They should enjoy working with a machine so that they are stimulated to make the most of its potentialities. It is essential for them to be conscientious in checking every detail, even though built-in checking devices may be available.

(g) Supervisors' duties

Word processing centre supervisors' skills are similar to those needed by typing and audiotyping centre supervisors (see **16.6**). They must understand the system they are dealing with and have the imagination to initiate new uses. They need to know about the supplies available and to avoid making unwise purchases such as cheap disks resulting in corrupted text and maintenance problems. Working conditions must be their concern, both to promote efficiency and to safeguard operators' health and well-being (see also **24.8** and **5.7**). They must be able to motivate operators to work well as a team. They must help to train newcomers and to explain processes without undue use of jargon. Good relationships with the orginators of work is important so that deadlines can be negotiated and work presented to the operators in a suitable way. They should be able to make informed decisions about which documents should be stored on disk, which should be treated as confidential, and which should be deleted; and able also to devise efficient indexing methods for quick retrieval.

17.10 Phototypesetting

Typesetters are machines by which text is prepared in a form suitable for printing. Earlier methods involved setting up lead type, printing off a copy of the work on paper, and photographing this on film for reproduction by offset lithography (see **9.1**). Computer-assisted systems are now in common use. One consists of a phototypesetter incorporating a microprocessor and backing stores, plus keyboard and visual display unit. The operator prepares the text in the required format on the keyboard, using editing techniques similar to word processors (see above) and calling up the required type sizes and fonts from memory. From this script, film is produced and the image of the text is converted to digital signals. These can be manipulated as desired, e.g., compressed or expanded, enlarged or reduced. They are then scanned by a laser beam which exposes the light sensitive surface of the lithographic plate in the image areas. (See also techniques used in digital copiers, **9.2** (g).) Digitized signals representing graphic images can be processed and included in the text. Other systems use a cathode ray tube rather than a laser beam to 'paint' the image on the plate. Text already stored in computer files can be output in a form recognized by the phototypesetter and used as fresh input. A phototypesetter can be linked to a mainframe or microcomputer, enabling text to be keyed in from a number of terminals.

17.11 Did you know?

1. A specially large and clear type, suitable for typing speeches, is available.

2. The cost of a letter is not only the price of the stationery and the charge for postage: the boss's time, the typist's time, their share of the rent and rates, and of heating, lighting, and ventilation costs all contribute. You waste all this if you are inaccurate and cause the work to be done again.

3. Any employment agency will tell you that an accurate typist is worth her weight in gold.

Activities

1. Read 'How not to copy-type' (**17.1**). The undesirable situation described was not wholly the junior's fault. Where did the firm go wrong?

2. Keep an indexed notebook of the correct versions of words you habitually mis-spell. Type these as they crop up, and compose sentences incorporating them.

3. Your employer has written an article for a professional journal. Describe in detail the various steps to be taken between the original manuscript being handed to you and the final proof as returned to the printer. (LCCI, PSC)

4. What do you consider to be the main areas of responsibility of the Supervisor of a large typing unit and what qualities should she possess in order to do her job effectively? (LCCI, SSC)

5. Once the conventional typewriter keyboard has been mastered and proficiency obtained, it is possible to train a typist to operate a number of modern business machines successfully. Describe 3 such machines, and explain clearly their purpose in office work. (LCCI, PSC)

6. You have been asked to sit on the interviewing panel for a new clerk/typist in the Sales Department (Europe Division) and to devise a skill test to ensure that candidates have sufficient typing ability and can carry out clerical tasks effectively from given instructions. (a) State *briefly* what you would wish to include in the skill test, to last approximately 40 minutes. (b) Devise 4 short questions you would wish to ask *during the interview* to rate a candidate's understanding of the clerical work of the Sales Department. (LCCI, PSC)

7. What advantages do electronic typewriters offer the secretarial worker and employer over manual and electric machines? (LCCI, PSC)

8. (a) By means of a diagram show the main parts of a stand alone [word processing] system. (b) BRIEFLY describe the functions of each of the parts. (LCCI, SSC, WP)

9. Word processors are becoming more common. State eight tasks that can be carried out with a word processor, eight advantages, and one disadvantage. (PEI, Adv.)

10. In a centralized word processing section, the Supervisor is vital to the efficiency of both the system and operators. Describe: (a) the role and duties of the Word Processing Supervisor; (b) the qualities such a person should possess. (LCCI, PSC, IP)

11. Word processors can be set up in several ways, one of which is a *Shared Logic System*. They are capable of many functions including *scrolling, margin justification, decimal alignment* and *merging*. Explain each of the terms underlined. (LCCI, SSC)

12. Productivity in the office is greatly increased by investment in word processing, to automate repetitive manual tasks. Describe how a word processor will be of benefit to a business *as regards time-saving*, in the following areas: (a) Dictation time (b) Drafting time (c) Checking time (d) Revision time (e) Search time. (LCCI, SSC, WP)

Group activities

13. Working in pairs: (a) take five minutes to draft a short letter or memo and hand it to your partner to type (your draft should be legible, but some alterations and deletions will provide good practice for the typist); (b) type the draft she hands you, and check it carefully; (c) sign your own composition, if the typed version is correct. If it is not, your partner must find her errors and retype it.

14. Each member of your group could obtain a brochure of a different make and model of electronic typewriter. Discuss these, then produce a joint report, as to an employer, on which machine you recommend from the viewpoint of versatility, upgradeability, possible networking and servicing arrangements.

18
Composing and compiling

18.1 Composing letters

If you prove to be able and reliable, your boss may hand over routine correspondence to you as you become used to the work. Some of these letters you may sign yourself, but most will probably be prepared for your boss's signature.

(a) Using the right style

When writing letters yourself for your boss's signature try to use his or her style as far as you can, incorporating any habitual phrases and expressions, when suitable, into your letters. Take into account the relationship between your boss and the correspondent and adapt your tone accordingly. Don't be too formal with a close acquaintance or too informal with a stranger. If you are answering a letter, the tone of the original may guide you, as may also the salutation and subscription used.

(b) Compiling letters from notes

Your boss may have drawn your attention to the matters you should include in your letter, and if so you will have already noted these. Otherwise, jot down your main points, but don't waste time by drafting the whole letter. Compose straight on the typewriter all but the trickiest passages. This will help you to think more quickly, and you will not then be so disconcerted when the day arrives for you yourself to dictate to an assistant. In any case, composing letters becomes easier with practice. If you use a word processor you can key in straightaway even the parts that need careful drafting, as amendments are so easy to make.

(c) Paragraphing

Help your correspondent to take in easily what you have to say by starting a new paragraph for each new topic. When answering another letter, it is a good idea to reserve the first paragraph for acknowledging it, quoting its date, and referring briefly to the subject matter (if you have not used a subject heading). Try to avoid the extremes of very long paragraphs in which your reader may lose his way and a series of very short ones, which look scrappy. When you have finished, read through your letter carefully. Imagine that you are the recipient reading it for the first time. You should then yourself be able to detect and put right any ambiguity, abruptness, or repetition.

(d) Using tact

Be especially careful when answering letters of complaint. If the complaint is justified, apologize without grovelling, mention any extenuating circumstances, and assure your correspondent that such an error will not occur again. If, on the other hand, the complaint is unfounded, resist the temptation to crow over your correspondent. For instance, instead of making a customer look foolish because of evidently not having read the instructions supplied with a cooker, say: 'We think you may have mislaid the operating instructions that were originally sent with your cooker. We therefore now enclose a duplicate copy and suggest that you study in particular paragraph 21 that relates to your query.'

It is possible to reprimand someone in a letter in an indirect fashion, and if you can do this you will save much unpleasantness. Say, for instance, 'You will remember that' instead of 'You forgot', or 'As you are aware' instead of 'You should have known'.

(e)   Circular and standard letters

Circular letters need special care. They must be general enough in content to be applicable to each recipient, and must be very clearly worded. The last thing you want after sending out 50 circulars is 50 telephone calls demanding clarification of doubtful points.

For recurring situations, standard letters or paragraphs are useful. You can file and index copies of these, either on paper or on word processor disk for reference when a similar situation occurs. Often you can use almost identical wording in each letter, merely adding or substituting an extra sentence or specific information to suit the particular circumstance.

18.2   Composing memos

Memos are written communications to persons within your own company. Confidential memos are sealed in an envelope. Otherwise memos are usually circulated in a circulation envelope. Memos are used to request or pass on information when a written record is required. They may be signed, initialled, or left unsigned; the office held by the sender is sometimes typed at the end, but otherwise no complimentary close, and no salutation, are used.

(a)   Memo forms

Most organizations use preprinted memo forms, bearing the headings 'MEMO' or 'MEMORANDUM', and 'TO' and 'FROM', which the typist completes by adding the names and/or offices held of the recipient and the sender. She also types the date and usually a subject heading and file reference.

(b)   Tone

Because you are writing to colleagues, you are not concerned so much with 'keeping in' with your correspondent as when writing a letter to someone outside the company; your concern is to put your message across as concisely as possible. You must, however, adopt a tone suitable to the recipient's status.

(c)   Multiple memos

When a memo concerns several people always make sure you take enough copies. The people to receive the memo should be listed at the top. As well as those recipients directly concerned with the memo there may be people who, out of courtesy, should be kept informed. Their names will be listed at the foot of the memo preceded by 'cc' (carbon copy). Sometimes it is undesirable for the person receiving the top copy to know who is receiving a carbon copy, so a blind carbon copy (bcc) is taken. On the carbon copy 'bcc' is typed with the name of the person receiving the copy. If the memo is directed to a special category of persons, e.g., 'All Heads of Departments', there is obviously no need to append a list of recipients.

18.3   Sending out invitations

You can use a type of circular letter for sending out invitations to a business function to a large number of people.

(a)   Duplicated circulars

You may be asked to duplicate an invitation, which you can set out as a form letter: the letter itself will contain details of the event, and the bottom section will form a slip to be cut off, completed as an acceptance or refusal, and return to your office. This saves the recipient having to write a letter.

(b)   Printed circulars

A similar method is to have notices printed and numbered consecutively, one section setting out the invitation and the other acting as a preprinted postcard when detached along a perforation. The serial number also appears on the postcard, and can be of great assistance to you if a signature is illegible, as you can check your invitation list to see to whom that number was allocated. This method saves the recipient even more trouble than the first, as he does not even have to address an envelope.

18.4 In a nutshell: Replying to an invitation

- If the invitation is an informal one, reply in similar form—e.g., by letter or telephone
- If the third person was used in a formal invitation, use it also in your reply.
- If the second person was used, write a letter in reply, using the first person.
- Begin by thanking the sender for the invitation.
- Repeat the original details concerning the nature of the function, the date, time and place.
- Accept or refuse the invitation.
- Where possible, give a reason for declining.
- If you are including the date, type it below your reply.
- No signature is required for replies in the third person.
- Where an invitation is from a husband and wife, reply to the wife only.

Invitation	*Reply*
Mr and Mrs John Davidson request the pleasure of the company of Mr and Mrs Simon Russell at a reception in honour of Mr K. Elmer Kobenski of New York, to be held at the Wyberg Hotel, Notown, on Wednesday, ... 7 for 7.30 p.m. RSVP	Mr and Mrs Simon Russell thank Mr and Mrs John Davidson for their kind invitation to the reception in honour of Mr K. Elmer Kobenski of New York, to be held at the Wyberg Hotel, Notown, on Wednesday, ... They regret very much that they are unable to accept, owing to a long-standing prior engagement. (Today's date)

18.5 Reports

A report should present salient facts clearly so that the person or persons to whom it is directed can take appropriate action. Reports may be:

(a) Spoken

This is the simplest kind, and may consist only of a sentence or two in answer to a question from your boss, like 'How are you this morning?' A written answer would be pointless, as the situation could change so quickly.

(b) Routine

Where information is wanted regularly, a report may be set out in a standard fashion.

(i) *On preprinted forms* To save the compiler trouble, and to ensure that the right kind of information is forthcoming, preprinted documents may be used. You may, for instance, use a telephone message form, designed for a report on a telephone call, or a petty cash voucher, reporting on how a sum of money was spent. Routine reports may be presented in the course of all types of work—e.g., by sales representatives, section heads, staff supervisors.

(ii) *Using a customary layout* For other routine reports for which a preprinted form would be unsuitable, a set layout is nevertheless often used, e.g.: *Annual reports*, presented by chairmen of companies, societies, and clubs, usually follow a set pattern, the format adopted one year being maintained to a greater or lesser degree in subsequent years.

Reports of meetings If you have to compile one of these, you will probably follow a standard layout: the preliminary details, concerning the type, time and place of the meeting and the persons attending it, and the main points following, usually in chronological order of their treatment at the meeting. You should use the past tense, because the discussion has taken place. You should also use the third person, because you are reporting as an onlooker, and not as someone identified with the discussion and decisions taken: you have not yourself presented the facts and made the recommendations, but are merely summarizing the conclusions reached by others.

(c)   Special reports

Because these are compiled to present the facts about a particular isolated event or series of events, there is no set precedent for them, and the form most suitable is therefore adopted. Generally speaking, headings provide the means by which the reader can find his bearings. These may be set out as marginal or shoulder headings. Main sections, subsections, paragraphs, etc., may be made easier to follow by the use of different types of lettering and numbering—

Example of a short, formal report

REPORT OF THE YOUTH DEVELOPMENT COMMITTEE ON THE FOUNDING OF A YOUTH CLUB AT EASTFIELDS, NOTOWN

Terms of reference The Committee was instructed by the Youth Facilities Board at the Meeting on 18 April 19XX to investigate whether a need existed for a youth club at Eastfields and possible steps for its establishment.

Proceedings At a Meeting on 25 April, the Committee compiled a questionnaire, inviting young people to comment on present facilities, to state whether they would welcome and support a youth club in the area and, if so, to indicate what type of activity they would wish to see promoted.

By kind permission of the Headmaster of Eastfields School, the questionnaire was circulated to all pupils between the ages of 14 and 18.

Opinions were also obtained by means of random street interviews and visits to a cross-section of houses in the neighbourhood.

The results were studied at meetings of the Committee held on 2 and 10 June.

Findings (a) Approximately 80 per cent of young people between 14 and 18 considered present facilities inadequate.

(b) 72 per cent of those between 14 and 16, and 55 per cent of those between 16 and 18 would like a club and would join one, if established.

(c) 40 per cent of all age groups hoped that sporting activities could be arranged, and that some coaching could be provided. Among the 14 to 16 age group, outside visits would be particularly popular, and miscellaneous indoor activities (discussions, record sessions, etc.) were favoured by most of those between 16 and 18.

Conclusions The committee considers that a need undoubtedly exists for a youth club and that, provided accommodation could be found, a suitable range of indoor activities would not be difficult to organize. To provide sufficient facilities for the type of sports indicated on questionnaires would be much more difficult and costly.

Recommendations (a) That the board should investigate suitable buildings in the Eastfields area, with a view to the renting of accommodation on weekday evenings.

(b) That the Notown Council be approached to see if there were any possibility of making public sports facilities available to a club at agreed times.

(c) That a public meeting of young residents between 14 and 18 be called meanwhile and a committee formed, if the meeting so desired.

Robert White

Chairman

11 June 19XX

---

e.g., capital and lower case letters, capital and small roman numerals, arabic numbers, etc. In this way it is possible to pick out, say, the main points, while temporarily skipping the subsidiary ones. Where reports of this kind are very long and involved, the compilers often provide a summary of the chief conclusions and recommendations in either an introduction or an appendix. The order of the sections depends on the nature of the situation or occurrence: they may be in chronological order, where the sequence of events is important, or grouped logically, say, according to subject.

Examples of special reports are:

(i) *Reports by special committees* They are usually very formal, because they are generally prepared for the consideration of other committees. For instance, a special committee's report on workers' unrest might be formally laid out under headings dealing with: *when, by whom* and *how* the information was gathered, the investigators' *terms of reference*—i.e., a definition of the prescribed scope and purpose of their investigation—the *facts* they discovered, the *conclusions* they reached on these facts, and the *recommendations* they wish to make to the body to which they are reporting.

Note Do not confuse a report of a *committee* with a report of a *meeting*. The former reports what was *done* perhaps over a period and the latter what was *said* on a particular occasion.

(ii) *Reports by individuals* These may involve similar steps on the part of the compiler as (i) above, but are usually set out in a much less formal style, with less stereotyped headings. They are often written in the first person. Some might be in the form of a letter—e.g., a referee would report in a letter to an employer his assessment of a prospective employee. Others might be an expanded form of memorandum set out, if necessary, under a series of headings. For example, as a secretary, you might be asked by your boss to report on the amount of overtime done by secretaries in your department over a given period and the reasons for it. You would have to sift the information gathered, and decide on a logical presentation of paragraphs. Your choice might lie between listing the overtime in order of occurrence or according to the secretary affected, or according to type of reason. You would give your report a suitable heading, remind your boss in your

opening paragraph of the reason for your writing it, address it clearly, sign it, and date it. It would not be suitable to include a recommendation here, but you would do so if, for example, you were asked to report on two copiers you had seen demonstrated with a view to your boss's purchasing the one you preferred.

18.6 Summarizing

It is useless to try to record the main points in a telephone conversation if you can't understand what the caller says, and your boss will not gain much from your shortened version of an article if you can't make head or tail of the original. Pretending that you *do* understand could be very dangerous in these circumstances. Inability to cope with the telephone call could be due to a bad line, or to panic on your part (cured by practice in using the telephone). Inability to summarize the article might mean that you don't know enough about your boss's or company's work or perhaps that you have a very narrow vocabulary.

How full should your summary be and how important is the style in which you write it? The answer depends on its purpose: brief notes might be enough to bring your boss up to date with events during an absence abroad, but a fairly full version of an article might be called for, written in a more flowing literary style. Distinguish, too, between something compiled for the file and something to be sent outside the firm.

Although your summary must be readily intelligible without the reader having to resort to the original, you should state its source—e.g., the title and author of an article, the name, issue, and date of the periodical in which it appeared. If you are summarizing a series of letters on a topic, give the names of the writer and addressee and the date of each letter.

18.7 Compiling and completing forms

(a) Composition

If you have to compile the form yourself, think carefully what it is for. Sometimes questions can be so arranged that part of the form can be used for another purpose, the unwanted section being masked during duplication. Name, address, and telephone number, for instance, are details needed in many contexts. List the questions in a logical order and express them clearly so that there is no doubt what type of answer is required. It is helpful to type a reference number and the date of compilation at the foot.

(b)   Display

When typing a form, give it a suitable heading, adding the organization's name at the top if it is to go outside the premises. Where lines are needed, type a series of full stops, allocating a suitable number of lines for the details required. Use double spacing to allow enough room for replies. Don't leave excessively wide margins, or you will waste space that might have been more usefully devoted to the details.

(c)   Reproduction

The number and quality of copies needed will, of course, influence the preparation of your master copy. For example, an offset master would provide cheaply large numbers of high-quality copies, whereas a stencil would produce less impressive ones. Consider also how the forms will be completed—e.g., by hand (pencil, ink or ball-point pen) or on the typewriter—so that enough space is left for entries and a suitable quality paper is used.

(d)   Completion

When filling in a form, glance through the questions before inserting it in your typewriter. You will then avoid giving an answer that overlaps that to another question. Align your type just above the dotted lines. If the form was prepared with a view to completion on a typewriter you should be able to line up by means of the variable line spacer, with no need for further adjustment.

18.8   Press releases

Should you be concerned with public relations work you may be called upon to type or compile press or news releases. These are announcements to the press or other media of imminent events—e.g., the opening of new showrooms, the appointment of a new managing director, or the launching of a new product. Because they are regarded as news and not advertisements, no charge is made for their insertion. However, as an editor may receive many demands on the space he has available, he will insert only those that are 'newsworthy' for his particular readership, succinctly and factually written (avoiding any tendency to advertise in glowing terms) and presented in an acceptable way. It is therefore important to approach only those newspapers or periodicals suited to the particular topic and to know their publication dates and deadlines for submitting copy. Stale news is of no interest and will not be printed. Occasionally an embargo is placed on a release prohibiting its publication until a specified date. This ensures the maximum impact.

Acceptable display involves giving a short, factual heading in capitals, perhaps followed by a subtitle in upper and lower case. The body of the release should be typed in double spacing, with wide margins and indented paragraphs (except the first, which may be blocked). If it carries over to another sheet or sheets, repeat the heading at the top right and type 'More follows' or 'More' at the foot of each page, and 'End' at the final point. In general, avoid extensive use of capital letters and underscore. Give the date of issue and, if appropriate, a reference number.

The body of the release should be divided into short paragraphs on clearly discernible topics. If possible, the first paragraph—or sentence—should sum up the essence of the whole announcement, in case the editor has space only for this. As he will cut from the end upwards, make sure that you arrange the paragraphs in descending order of importance. Short sentences also make it easier for him to cut with the least risk of distorting the sense.

Finally, give the name and telephone number of the staff member responsible, so that the editor knows whom to contact for further information or for a photograph of the product (if one has not been sent with the release).

An extract from a news release issued by British Telecom is shown opposite.

PB58   May 1, 1984

WE'RE IN WHEN YOU'RE OUT:
BRITISH TELECOM LAUNCHES VOICEBANK

Essence of
release

British Telecom today (May 1) launched Voicebank, its new telephone message service.

Important topic
mentioned early
in release

Unlike any other telephone message service, Voicebank can also be used with British Telecom's Radiopaging service. The pager 'bleeps' every time Voicebank has a new message.

Short clear
sentences

This new service has been designed for ease-of-operation. When callers wish to leave a message they simply dial a dedicated Voicebank number and speak. The message is automatically stored in the customer's personal electronic mailbox.

Voicebank customers can then later listen to their messages by
– dialling the Voicebank number and sending instructions through a multi-frequency tone keypad, held against the telephone mouthpiece, or by
– dialling a retrieve-only Voicebank telephone number.

By using the keypad, users will be able to sample all their messages, repeat messages they wish to hear again, or delete messages from the mailbox at will.

The keypad also enables customers to change by remote control their greetings or messages in Voicebank from almost any telephone in the world.

Voicebank uses advanced computer software and the latest digital technology to provide an excellent sound quality. There are no clicks or tape hiss normally heard with conventional answering machines.

Up to seven messages, 25 seconds long, can be stored for up to 12 hours.

Expansion of
earlier topic—
may be cut
if required

Voicebank also adds a new dimension for British Telecom Radiopaging customers, who can now be 'bleeped' whenever Voicebank receives a new message for them.

If the message is not retrieved within half an hour the Radiopage provides a second 'bleep' as a reminder. A third and final reminder is given a further half-hour later.

A voice guidance program is built in to the Voicebank service to tell callers when the message store is full, and to help customers when retrieving messages or changing greetings.

Voicebank will be available initially in the London area.

18.9   Articles

Many organizations have house magazines or journals. These are mainly for the benefit of employees but if suitable are sometimes used to promote good public relations with customers. An article treats a subject in more depth than a press release but should always capture the readers' attention at the start. Articles should be written in a lively style, stating the facts illustrated with examples—quoting comments or opinions—and should always end with a conclusion that has impact.

18.10   Jargon

It is important to use vocabulary and style that your reader can understand. If you are both really conversant with a subject there is no harm in using its *jargon*—its own special phraseology, which expresses the exact meaning clearly and concisely to the initiated. You will find some jargon in the news release, above, but it would have been understood by those to whom it was sent.

However, to the uninitiated, jargon is a foreign language. The comment was made in the January

1985 issue of *Business Equipment Digest* that few journalists 'write [about information technology] in a style which the lay person can readily assimilate . . . A prime example . . . can be seen every week in the ever increasing number of newspapers which feature computer pages. Take a recent article in the Daily Mail, for instance. It glibly spoke of ICL's One Per Desk[1] as a machine that is "based around the 68008 microprocessor, offers an expandable 128k of RAM

and is going to enjoy considerable third party software support".' Can *you* translate this?

Some jargon has had to be used in this book, but you will normally find definitions of unfamiliar terms in the sections where they are treated in detail (such as Chapters 11 and 13). There is a glossary in Appendix III to help you when you come across them elsewhere.

18.11   Checklist: Compiling instructions

- Are your instructions in the right order?
- Have you described every step clearly and unambiguously?
- Would a diagram be helpful?
- Have you assumed existing knowledge on the part of readers that they may not in fact possess?
- Have you used any technical terms or jargon unlikely to be generally understood?
- Have you explained why it is important for your instructions to be carried out?
- Have you included the name of someone who can help if further assistance is needed?
- Is the tone you have used likely to produce the right effect? Are you treating your readers as equals or subordinates, adults or children, rational beings or idiots?
- Have you indicated when the instructions are to come into effect and for how long?
- Have you tested them out on a 'guinea pig' before finally issuing them?

18.12   Notices

Notices contain information of concern to a number of people. They should always be displayed in a prominent place with material that is currently being read. The notice should be written clearly and concisely, be positive in approach and always dated and signed. Make sure your notice-board is divided into sections, i.e., social, welfare, etc., so that the reader can find what he requires easily. Urgent notices should stand out—typed in red, coloured arrows on

them, etc. It is important that the board is situated in a good place and that you can place notices on it easily with drawing pins, adhesive, etc. Make sure your notice has a clear heading, the address of the person concerned with the notice, and try to make it 'short and sweet'.

Electronic notice-boards: Electronic mail systems (see **13.9**) may have a notice-board or a bulletin board facility: announcements and general information is held on a regularly updated file available for access by all users.

18.13   Did you know?

1. Some firms reduce the amount of memo-writing to a minimum by using carbon sets of memo forms. With one kind, the top copy, bearing the message on the upper half, is sent with a carbon copy to the addressee (the second carbon in the set is filed). A third carbon copy is kept by the author. The addressee writes his reply on the lower half of the top copy and sends this back, filing the first carbon copy in the set.

2. *Electronic dictionary*: Some word processor or microcomputer programs enable text input to be compared automatically against a stored dictionary. Where an apparent discrepancy occurs, the operator is alerted so that a check can be made on spelling or usage.

1. See Figure 11.5.

3. Electronic dictionaries or glossaries may be compiled automatically by a word processor or microcomputer by analysing previous input and storing those technical terms in most common use. Others may be added by the user as required.

18.14 Useful reference sources

Abbreviations dictionary
The Complete Plain Words (Gowers)
English dictionary
Modern English Usage (Fowler)
Roget's Thesaurus

Activities

1. Draft, and reply to, an invitation to your employer to attend a Centenary Dinner connected with his particular type of business. You may invent the details (LCCI, PSC)

2. Draft a standard paragraph which can be used when writing to remind supporters of a charity that their subscriptions are overdue.

3. You have recently visited an office equipment exhibition. In a memo to the office manager give full details of one piece of equipment which you think your firm should install and give reasons to justify its purchase. (LCCI, PSC)

4. The firm you work for has a total office staff of 20. As it is now experiencing some financial difficulties, you have decided to suggest ways in which economies could be effected in the office. Submit your recommendations in the form of a memo to the office manager, inventing as necessary any details concerning the current organization of the office. (LCCI, PESD)

Figure 18.1 (Courtesy of Tony Holland. First published in *Business Systems and Equipment*)

5. You work for the head of the commerce department in a college. Send memos to three members of staff—Miss Day, Mr Knight and Mr Earl—asking them to represent the department at a meeting of the Secretarial Examinations Board (giving details of time, date, and place). Your boss is asking all the staff to submit any comments to the Board on the revised syllabuses (to be discussed at that meeting) by the end of the month. He suggests that the three representatives meet him to discuss details at 2 p.m. on the first Tuesday of next month. (A copy of the memo is to be sent to the vice-principal.)

6. Your employer has asked you to determine whether or not the office staff would welcome the introduction of canteen facilities. Most of the staff have indicated that they would welcome facilities only if they were of a high standard. Some of the staff would prefer to have luncheon vouchers. Summarize the opinions in a short report to your employer. (LCCI, PESD)

7. Type an application form which candidates for shorthand-typists' posts will complete.

8. Your firm, a large insurance company, has just moved to a different town. The premises are to be opened to the public one Saturday morning, in the interests of good public relations. Write a short press release to be sent to the editors of local newspapers announcing the event.

9. Write an article for your company's house magazine on the work of EITHER the audiotyping centre OR the mailroom.

10. Briefly discuss how effective signs and notices can assist in the smooth running of a 2-day residential conference, to be held in non-purpose-built accommodation. (LCCI, PSC)

11. Your local repertory theatre has offered a reduction in prices to parties of ten or more from your firm. Your employer, Mr James, the Personnel Officer, has asked you to write a notice to be displayed on the staff notice board, explaining the offer, and asking members of staff interested in joining a monthly theatre party to send their names to the Personnel Officer. Design such a notice, including any other details you think necessary. (PEI, Sec. Prac. Inter.)

12. A large amount of the information used in business is collected on forms. What are the basic principles for good form design? (LCCI, PESD)

13. As secretary in a large company which has premises on 2 sites, 10 km apart, you are asked to publish a company newsletter. Suggest items you would include and how you would organise the production and distribution of such a publication. (LCCI, PSC)

Group Activities

14. Type two or three paragraphs extracting the main points from a newspaper article of current interest. A file of weekly summaries, prepared by the members of your group, would provide a useful record of topical events.

15. Your group could compile a quiz on common abbreviations, each person selecting six in a given field (qualifications, decorations, national and international organizations, etc.). You will find examples in various reference books, as well as in dictionaries of abbreviations.

19
Finding facts

If you were to ask a group of secretaries the type of information they were expected to find in the course of a working year their answers would vary enormously. The facts wanted would be determined by the scope of their own, their bosses' and their organizations' work. Your boss will ask you for facts and information. It is very likely that you will not know the answers and have to find them out.

19.1   Information close at hand

First look around you to see if you can find help close at hand, such as:

(a)   A person who might help

Ask a person working near you if they know. This method has advantages in that you can question a person directly and explain your purpose until the answer you get is the exact one you wanted. Also, in effect, the person approached has sifted information for you and proved its accuracy by his or her own experience. The person may be a member of your own organization and this is one reason why you should be familiar with the organization and duties of staff. It is, of course, important to go to a staff member of sufficient seniority, whose judgement and knowledge you can trust and who will have authority to release to you the information you require (provided there are no restrictions on it for security reasons). They may be able to extract information from departmental files or charts or direct you to reports, handbooks, brochures, etc., produced by the company.

(b)   A reference book that might help

A collection of books can yield information far more comprehensive than any one person can hope to have, but you must find the right ones. When you have tracked down a likely book, read the brief description provided on the inside of the front and back covers and the introduction or foreword, to form an idea of its scope and purpose, then glance at the contents pages. To find detailed information on a topic, consult the index usually provided, and turn up the page or pages indicated. The status and qualifications of its author are important, and so is the date of publication. Factual books quickly become out-of-date.

Books found within your own office or company are likely to be:

(i) *Specialized reference books*   Specialized reference books have a definite purpose but their usefulness is not necessarily restricted to their primary purpose—e.g., The *Post Office Guide* has a list of London postal districts, which may save you on occasion from the need to consult a directory. Telephone Directories (PhoneBooks) may lead you to further sources of information concerned with the topic you are pursuing. The classified *Yellow Pages* directories are particularly helpful, especially if you remember to consult the index as a guide to the headings used.

(ii) *General reference books*   Even in the smallest office, you are likely to find the following:

An *English dictionary* for spellings and meanings of words, as well as for other miscellaneous information varying according to the size of the dictionary. The definition of a word may suggest other lines to follow up when tracking down information. An *atlas* with a *gazetteer*: this will help with the spelling of place-names, as well as pinpointing their geographical location. *Local guides* and *street maps, trains and bus timetables* are useful for your boss's movements and your own, as well as helpful to visitors new to the area. Up-to-date *directories* are a guide to the resources and facilities of an area. *Whitaker's Almanack* contains information on a wide range of topics relating both to Britain and countries overseas. Other useful publications of that type are *The Statesman's Year Book* and *Europa Yearbook*.

19.2 In a nutshell: Searching for a book in the public library

- When you want a particular book and you know the author's name, consult the *author catalogue*.
- If you know the name of the book but not the author, the library assistants may be able to trace it for you.
- When you have no particular book in mind on a topic:
  - (a) Look up the subject classification number in the alphabetical *subject index*.
  - (b) Locate the entries bearing that number in the numerical *subject catalogue* to discover what books are available.
- To find the books, select (a) the group of stacks; (b) the particular bookcase; (c) the shelf required, grouped according to the Dewey decimal system.
- The Dewey decimal system is a numerical subject method of filing. It allocates a number to each category of subject:
  - (a) Whole numbers: hundreds (main classification);
    - tens (subdivision of main classification);
    - units (subdivision of secondary classification).
  - (b) Decimal fractions: each number after the point indicates a subdivision of the preceding number category.

19.3 Information farther afield

If your first investigations do not yield the information you want, they may at least lead you on to others.

(a) People and organizations

You may need to telephone a person or organization farther afield, having obtained a likely address from your telephone directory or *Whitaker's Almanack*. The person or organization you want may be in your own local area—e.g., your local authority departments, local offices of government departments, agencies, public facilities (electricity, gas, transport, etc.), local Chamber of Trade and Commerce.

If you know nothing about the staffing arrangements of an organization, ask first for their *press officer* or *public relations officer*. It is the object of public relations staff to present information about the company to the public, with a view to promoting and enhancing its image, rather than specifically to sell its products or services. The information they give is first cleared with the relevant departments of the company to ensure suitability and accuracy. Sometimes public relations work is handed over to an agency with specialized skills in that field. Events of interest to the public are made known to the media by press releases (see **18.8**), feature articles (see **18.9**) or press conferences (see **22.10**).

If there is no PR department, describe your inquiry briefly to the switchboard operator, who should be able to connect you with the most suitable extension. If you need to write, express your request as clearly as possible: sending a stamped, addressed envelope encourages a speedy answer.

Be tactful in asking for information. The majority of people are glad to help, but you have no right to *demand* information. Remember that it may involve the other person in lengthy searches. Also, some organizations reserve specialized and detailed help for members who have paid subscriptions for such services. Some other types of inquiry might lead to answers which would reveal too much about their internal organization or their products. In general, people may resent being asked for information readily available in reference books.

(b) Books and periodicals
If your own organization provides only a limited range of reference books and periodicals, you may need to consult your public library.

19.4 Public library services

(a) Lending facilities
Make yourself familiar with lending facilities at your own public library. Usually, these are available to persons living, working, or in full-time education in the library authority area. In most libraries, the period of original loan can be extended if the book wanted has not been reserved by another reader.

A book that you want that is not on the shelves will be obtained for you (sometimes for a small charge): (i) by withdrawing it from the reserve stock (ii) by obtaining it from other central or branch libraries in the area (iii) (if the book is non-fiction) by applying to the Regional Library Bureau or County Library of the area. If the Regional Bureau is unable to help, it will apply to the British Library (Lending Division) which can obtain it from other libraries, including private and university libraries and even libraries overseas.

(b) Reference facilities
Most libraries of any size have reference rooms, where books can be consulted—but not borrowed—by anyone, not only those accepted as borrowers. You may need to enlist the help of the reference librarian at first until you become familiar with the range of books, because the placing of some volumes in the shelves may depend more on their size than on their classification. Some larger reference libraries have specialized divisions—e.g., Science or Technology, Commerce, etc. A visit may not always be necessary, as certain types of inquiry can easily be handled by telephone or telex.

Make yourself familiar with the books held in your reference library. These will include large sets of encyclopaedias, atlases, yearbooks and even text-books. There will also be back numbers of the journals taken by the library.

19.5 Periodicals
Many public libraries subscribe to a variety of newspapers and periodicals, current numbers of which are put on display. Because of space limitations, back numbers of all cannot be kept by every library, but the library staff will often be able to tell you where to consult those not filed on the premises.

Often, an article in a newspaper or periodical will provide the information you want more readily than a book. Because an article can be published more quickly, a recent one is more likely to be up-to-date. You must, however, know in what publication to look for suitable, well-informed articles. Some newspapers and periodicals have a reputation for informed comment, whereas others, published to meet popular demand, may be sensational and less accurate. Some serve a specialized readership. Most newspaper publishers keep an index of articles, and you can apply to them for copies of back numbers. Libraries often hold indexing and abstracting services to facilitate the finding of articles.

19.6 Guides to current books and periodicals

It is difficult to find the right book or periodical without knowing what exists. Guides, bibliographies (lists of books) and indexes list the choice available.

(a) Books
New books: *British National Bibliography; Whitaker's Cumulative Book List.*
Books in print: *British Books in Print* (Whitaker).
Reference books: *Guide to Reference Material* (Library Association).
Directories: *Current British Directories* (Beckenham, CBD Research Ltd); *Directory of Financial Directories* (Guernsey, Hodgson: compiled by M. J. Campbell).

(b) Periodicals
It is possible to find details of periodicals issued in all parts of the world, and which British libraries take

them, by consulting *British Union Catalogue of Periodicals* (Butterworth). Many periodicals are to be found in the British Library Reference Division, available to persons holding readers' tickets. Many trade journals can be seen (without a ticket) at the British Library (Science Reference Division). *The Writers' and Artists' Year Book* and the *Guide to Current British Journals* list British newspapers and journals and briefly describe their contents. This information is also to be found in *Willing's Press Guide* and *Benn's Press Directory*, which include European periodicals as well. *British Rate and Data* gives similar details plus advertising costs.

19.7   Government publications

The UK government is a major source of published information, mainly through Her Majesty's Stationery Office (HMSO). Government publications are available from Government Bookshops in London and other large cities, official agents throughout the UK, or through booksellers. The following are some of the publications that the government supplies:

(a)   Parliamentary Papers

These are documents necessary in the transaction of Parliamentary business. They include:

(i) *Command Papers* presented to Parliament by Royal Command. They include reports of Royal Commissions and other inquiries, and statements of government policy, e.g., the Report of the Committee on Data Protection, Cmnd 7341. (The prefix Cmnd appears on Command Papers published since 1956; between 1919 and 1956 the prefix was Cmd, and between 1900 and 1918, Cd.)

(ii) *Votes and Proceedings of the House of Commons and Minutes of Proceedings of the House of Lords* concise records of the business transacted each day.

(iii) *House of Commons Papers* largely annual reports from government departments and reports from committees requested by Parliament or stipulated in Acts, e.g., the Expenditure Committee, the Committee on Public Accounts and the Select Committee on Science and Technology.

(iv) *House of Lords Papers and Bills* reports of House of Lords committees, etc.

(v) *House of Commons Bills* documents connected with the passage of Public Bills through Parliament.

(vi) *Parliamentary Debates, Hansard* daily or weekly editions of the verbatim reports of debates in both Houses.

(vii) *Public General Acts* Acts of Parliament resulting from Public Bills.

(viii) *Local and Personal Acts* Acts restricted to particular areas or particular individuals.

(b)   Non-Parliamentary Papers

These deal with many varied topics, from census reports, hints to businessmen, and digests of statistics, to reports on railway and civil aircraft accidents, and a history of the Second World War. The *London Gazette* includes bankruptcy notices, notices under the Companies Acts, Service promotions, and the New Year and other honours lists, changes of name, and the numbers of winning premium bonds.

(c)   Catalogues

In order to acquaint the public with the books and pamphlets available, catalogues are compiled, including (i) daily lists (supplied either daily or in weekly batches) (ii) monthly catalogues (iii) annual catalogues (iv) five-yearly indexes of government publications (v) sectional lists, mainly of non-parliamentary papers, divided into groups according to the government department sponsoring them or sometimes according to subject.

(d)   Central Office of Information

Included in the sectional lists are some COI publications. The COI is the government department which prepares and supplies publicity material on behalf of other government departments.

Some other publications, intended primarily for British Overseas Information Services, are obtainable direct from the COI. They concern Britain and aspects of the British way of life, including industry and science, communications, trade and finance. The Industrial Section arranges publicity for firms taking part in overseas trade exhibitions. Also obtainable from the COI are films and filmstrips, photographs and photoposters.

(e) Government Statistical Service

This consists of the major government departments' statistical divisions, the Business Statistics Office and the Office of Population Censuses and Surveys. Although primarily for government needs, the statistics provided are useful also for business management—e.g., in the fields of marketing, accounts, buying, personnel and management efficiency. Its booklet *Government Statistics: a Brief Guide to Resources* published annually (free) is available from the Central Statistical Office, and contains information on how to find and use government statistics.

(f) Small Firms Information Service

This is a free service provided by the Department of Trade and Industry. Businessmen seeking information on business topics can contact one of a nationwide network of regional enquiry centres and be put in touch with an appropriate source of information. In addition, a counselling service is offered, enabling businessmen to receive advice and guidance from counsellors experienced in their field. The first three sessions are free and after that a small charge is made.

(g) Departmental publications

These are not published by HMSO, but by the government departments which issue them. Included in these are patents, weather reports, explanatory information about Acts of Parliament (e.g., the Consumer Credit Act) and the National Health Service, National Insurance, etc.

(h) International publications

Although not published by HMSO, publications of some international organizations—e.g., the United Nations—are available from Government Bookshops.

19.8 Computer databanks and databases

A great deal of information is now stored within computer systems, and this trend is growing rapidly. Some systems are designed for use only within the company concerned; others provide sources of information for a wider public. Many agencies offer information services, e.g., regularly updated company information, details of products and their manufacturers. Users may pay a subscription for such services, or pay a fee each time they use them. Information accessed may be in several forms—e.g., printout on paper, magnetic media for input into other systems, microforms, visual displays, etc. The following are examples of information systems with which you may well be concerned. (Another, designed for the use of libraries and other organizations, is described in section **19.9** *(a)* below.)

(a) Prestel: British Telecom's Viewdata System

Prestel is a public database retrieval service operated by British Telecom. The data is stored on computers and accessed via telephone lines.

(i) *External information providers* Agencies independent of British Telecom supply the computer-stored information; they are responsible for content and for regular updating. They are charged an annual fee for the provision of information as well as a small storage charge per page. To input information into the system they also need to rent or buy a Prestel editing terminal, though some manufacturers' word processors enable material input to be edited into the format required for Prestel. The extent and range of the information in the databank depend on the willingness of agencies to subscribe, but a wide variety of topics is possible from sports results and household hints to information from tour operators and airline and British Rail timetables. *CitiService* provides consolidated financial information from different sources including the Stock Exchange.

(ii) *Domestic users' equipment* A domestic user of Prestel is able to retrieve information from the databank by calling the computer centre over telephone lines which can be used at other times to make or receive speech calls in the normal way. By using a hand-held keypad the user can, without lifting the telephone handset, call up an index on the television screen, and from this list choose the item required by keying the relevant digit. When that item is displayed the user can then make a further choice, guided by instructions on the screen, until the ultimately required information is located. Direct access to the particular information is also possible, if the required 'page' number is known.

Prestel sets are available or ordinary television sets can be specially adapted for Prestel use.

(iii) *Access via microcomputer* Prestel information can also be accessed using a microcomputer with an interface to a modem, together with special software.

(iv) *Business users' equipment* Business users' screens may be desktop size and attached to keyboards to form terminals. This equipment is obtainable from a number of manufacturers and enables automatic telephoning of the Prestel computer and logging-on to the Prestel service. The *Private Prestel* service enables terminals in a company's branches to gain access to company information held on a central database (see Figure 19.1) thus forming a closed user group to which public access is barred.

(v) *Gateway* This facility allows users access via Prestel (often linked by Packet SwitchStream (see **13.7** (b))) to the databases held on other computers;

for example, of external information providers or a company's own private database (see above). This cuts the user's communication costs, since over 96 percent of the UK telephone population can access Prestel at local rates.

(vi) *Interactive communication* Prestel may be used interactively, allowing a subscriber to use a terminal to send as well as receive information. This enables, for example, *travel information* to be accessed, flight or holiday reservations to be made and confirmation of these reservations received—all via Prestel.

Home banking is also possible. Systems set up by the Nottingham Building Society and the Bank of Scotland enable these bodies' account holders to apply for loans via Prestel, to request information, and to transfer funds in order to pay bills, etc.

Home shopping enables users to access information provided, for example, by mail order companies. They may then complete order forms via response

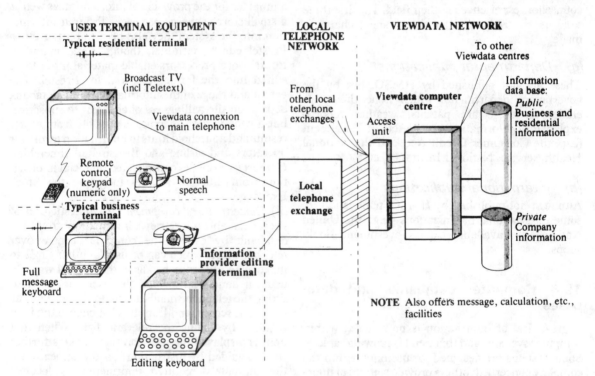

Figure 19.1 A diagrammatic representation of British Telecom's Viewdata system (Prestel) (Courtesy of British Telecom)

216

frames displayed on screen, and quote credit card numbers in order to receive delivery of the goods.

Mailbox is an electronic mail facility (see **13.9**) enabling users to send and receive messages to and from other subscribers. An alphanumeric keypad is needed.

Telexlink enables telex messages to be sent to any Telex subscriber (see Figure 19.2).

(vii) *Charges* The cost of Prestel to the user includes telephone calls to the computer centre included in the ordinary telephone bill. Other charges are set out in a separate Prestel bill, namely: computer-connect time (if connection is made during standard rate period—0800 to 1800 hours Monday to Friday, and 0800 to 1300 hours Saturdays); and a quarterly standing charge (higher for business than for domestic users). In addition, there may sometimes be charges imposed by the external information providers per page of information.

(b) Teletext

This is a television information service broadcasting computer information on topics including news, sport, weather, travel, financial information, puzzles, quizzes and entertainment. The information is broadcast in frames on a continuous loop. The viewer calls indexes onto the screen and by using a keypad on a receiver makes a direct choice of page. Maximum access time is 12½ seconds. The capacity of the service is limited by the loop system of access and by the small number of spare television lines available (most being taken up with conventional programmes).

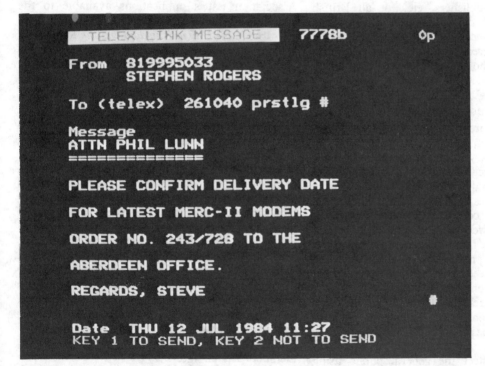

Figure 19.2 Telex Link message. This message has been typed on an ordinary Prestel terminal. By keying 1, the message will be sent through the system to arrive as a normal telex on a telex terminal. A charge per page is made (plus the normal Prestel charges) but only levied on the successful transmission of the telex message. The date and time are inserted automatically when the page is called up on screen. (Courtesy of Prestel, British Telecom)

Teletext services are broadcast by the British Broadcasting Corporation (Ceefax) and by the Independent Broadcasting Authority (Oracle). BBC and IBA correspondents collect the information from news agencies and other sources. The service is free to viewers, who need only a special television set.

19.9   Automated library services

(a)   BLAISE (British Library Automated Information Service)

This service provides database access for the use of libraries and information units in the many organizations subscribing to the system. One database (Blaiselink) is held on a computer in the USA, and contains indexes to publications on medical matters, and in some cases the actual information itself. The other database is in the UK and holds the names, authors, publishers, etc., of all British published material deposited at the Copyright Receipt Office since 1950, including books, periodicals and overseas literature. Many other files are also available, holding references to published material on all subjects.

(b)   Computerized library administration

Some libraries now order books by computer: details of the order are input, then printed out by computer and sent to the library supplier; reminders are sent automatically at specified intervals. Reports on book expenditure, analysed according to subject, can be produced. Catalogues of books held by a library can be printed out by computer. Book issues (book numbers and borrowers' numbers) may be recorded on magnetic tape and input to a computer, which can be programmed to produce overdue notices when loan periods are exceeded. Details of books reserved by readers can be compared by the computer with the details of books returned, signalling to the users when the required books become available. Statistics on book issues can be produced, and periodic checks of books out on loan can be made.

Such systems affect the general public using the libraries. For example, subject or author indexes may be on microfilm, involving the use of microfilm readers, and overdue notices may specify the accession number of a book rather than its title.

19.10   Miscellaneous sources of information

(a)   Special libraries

In London and other parts of the country, libraries exist which specialize in selected topics. You can find information about these by consulting: the Aslib *Library Directory* and also the *Libraries, Museums and Art Galleries Year Book*, both often held by public libraries. In particular, some large towns have Business Libraries, in which are collected a wide range of reference books, periodicals and other sources of information of interest to businessmen. The City Business Library in London is an example.

(b)   The Library Association

Although primarily a professional association for qualified librarians in all fields, the Library Association issues publications available to the general public through booksellers. These include *Libraries in the United Kingdom and the Republic of Ireland* (a complete list of library services and a select list of academic and other library addresses).

(c)   Aslib   (founded in 1924 as the Association of Special Libraries and Information Bureaux)

This specializes in obtaining and making available to its members information on a wide variety of topics. It will, for instance, search out technical and commercial information of all kinds in answer to simple or very complex enquiries; it will locate reports and articles, trace references and search for other bibliographic information; it keeps an index of English translations of articles originally in foreign languages, and maintains a register of translators, with an indication of their qualifications and specialized subjects. It offers training courses for persons engaged in information work, and provides an advisory service for members running information services. A subscription is payable by member organizations, though some publications and sometimes places on training courses are available to non-members at a charge.

(d)   Business Equipment Trade Association

BETA represents over 200 companies, including multinationals and smaller organizations, who manufacture business equipment of all types such as reprographics, word processors, computers, microfilm and general office machines and systems. Members are listed alphabetically and in product groups in a yearbook available on request.

(e) Other sources

Information and publications of all types are available from a multiplicity of organizations—e.g., banks, government departments (in particular the Department of Trade and Industry), Chambers of Commerce, the Confederation of British Industry, the Commission of the European Communities, the Commonwealth Secretariat, newspapers (especially those with business sections, and, in particular, *The Financial Times*). Details about companies can be obtained in the form of microfiche copies of annual reports and accounts from the Companies Register, Cardiff; and continuously updated information from the Industrial Information Service provided for subscribers by Kompass. The British Companies service, from Extel, gives information about companies' directors, subsidiaries and balance sheets, and is available at some libraries.

19.11   Did you know?

1. The Public Record Office houses national and governmental historic records.

2. The British Library, the Cambridge University Library, the Bodleian Library Oxford, the Library of Trinity College Dublin, the National Library of Scotland, and the National Library of Wales have the right to receive without charge a copy of every book published in the United Kingdom.

3. A White Paper is a pamphlet describing government policy on a given topic before legislation is introduced. Blue Books are similar, but have stouter binding. A Green Paper is issued at an earlier stage, so that public reaction to tentative proposals can be taken into account before government policy is decided upon.

4. The classification number allotted to a book is not necessarily a permanent one, as the Dewey decimal system is revised every three years.

5. POLIS is a free Parliamentary information service operated by the House of Commons Library.

19.12   Useful reference books

(a) Encyclopaedias *Britannica, Chambers* (supplements published periodically),

(b) Directories *Advertisers' Annual, Benn's Press Directory, British Exports* (IPC Press Information Service Ltd), *Crockford's Clerical Directory* (of clergy), *Directory of British Importers,* (British Importers' Confederation), *Directory of Directors* (Thos. Skinner Directories), *Guide to Key British Enterprises* (Dun and Bradstreet), *Kelly's Directories,* i.e., of London, or of trades—e.g., *Directory of Merchants, Manufacturers and Shippers, Kemp's Directory, Kompass Company and Product Information, Million Dollar Directory* (US companies), *Product Information* (Kompass), *Retail Directory, Sell's Directory, Stubbs' Buyers' Guide, 1000 Companies* (The Times), *The Times Guide to House of Commons, UK Trade Names, Vacher's Parliamentary Companion, Willing's Press Guide, Who Owns Whom?* (Dun and Bradstreet); also directories of medical practitioners, dentists, schools, etc.

(c) Maps Ordnance Survey maps; *The Oxford Atlas, The Times Atlas of the World.*

(d) Gazetteers *Bartholomew's Gazetteer of the British Isles, Chambers' World Gazetteer and Geographical Dictionary.*

(e) Year books Year books of trades and industries—e.g., *Computer Users' Year Book; Oil and Gas International Year Book, Business Equipment Trade Association Year Book;* of professional associations—e.g. Institute of Chartered Accountants in England and

	Wales: *List of Members;* of countries—e.g., *Statesman's Year Book, Civil Service Year Book, Stock Exchange Official Year Book, Municipal Year Book* and *Public Services Directories, Writers' and Artists' Year Book.*
(f) Literary and language	Dictionaries (English and foreign language); histories of literature; books of quotations; *Who's Who, International Who's Who, Dictionary of National Biography.*
(h) Current events	*Keesing's Contemporary Archives* (loose-leaf, updated), *Annual Register of World Events* (Longman), *Britain: an Official Handbook* (Central Office of Information), *Government Statistics: a Brief Guide to Resources* (annual), *Hansard.*
(i) General	*Whitaker's Almanack, Statesman's Year Book, Europa Year Book.*
(j) Guides to legislation	*Croner's Health and Safety at Work, Croner's Reference Book for Employers.*

Activities

1. If you have not already done so, join your local public library and become a regular borrower. Keep a list of books you read during the current year, trying to widen your interests and knowledge by choosing non-fiction books not concerned with your course.

2. It is your first afternoon as secretary to the office manager (who is out of the office and will not be returning that day). A telephone caller asks for two pieces of information: (a) He wants statistics about recent and current sales of the firm's product in a particular area. Suggest ways in which you might obtain this information and any precautions you might take before passing it on. (b) He wishes to know whether Mr Charles Jones is still on the board of directors. What internal and external sources could you consult to find out? (LCCI, PSC)

3. Your company is considering expanding its range of products and is about to undertake a survey to assess the demand for new products.

Describe the ways in which the necessary information might be obtained for:

(a) likely competitors—who they are, size, up-to-date product information, products manufactured etc.

(b) statistical information on sales trends in the industry. (LCCI, PSC)

4. Many reference books do not contain up-to-the-minute information. What exceptions are there to this statement? What other sources might help you to find up-to-date information? (LCCI, PSC)

5. Computer-based information systems are now available to the public. Compare and contrast two of these, mentioning particularly their business applications. (LCCI, PSC)

6. In what ways is modern technology affecting the form in which sources of information are stored and sought? What advantages and disadvantages do you consider the new systems have when compared with traditional reference books?

7. State, in general terms, how Prestel might be helpful to the office of a business organization. (RSA, DPA)

Group activities

8. Each group member should investigate the contents of three reference books useful to secretaries and businessmen (including as many as possible of those listed in **19.1**), and type a short paragraph of explanation of each. Append to each paragraph five questions which can be answered by detailed reference to the book concerned. These questions can be pooled and circulated among the group to be answered over a given period. The solution (with book titles and page numbers) can be filed separately for checking.

9. Visit your college or local reference library and select a general reference book covering a wide sphere of knowledge. Choose any topic that interests you, and then follow it up, narrowing the line of inquiry by referring to more specialized and detailed reference books. You could chart the 'trails' you have followed over a period, and compare yours with those of other students in your group.

20
Displaying information

20.1 Deciding on a suitable chart

You are a secretary to a firm of nurserymen. Your employer presents you with a set of figures analysing the sales of plants over the past five years. You are asked to display the annual totals of plants sold in the various categories so that an easy comparison can be made. Your boss also wishes to be able to discern clearly trends in popular demand, serving as a guide in allocating future space in the nursery for growing the different types of plants. The matter is to be discussed with one or two individuals, but a wall chart is not required.

There are several types of chart that you could construct, but first of all you type out the figures in a neat, tabular statement as shown in Table 20.1. This will be useful as a file record and can form part of the sales report that your employer is to compile. The figures will be exact, taken, as they are, from actual sales records. However, neither the trend of sales nor a comparison of the numbers of each type of plant would emerge clearly from this presentation.

You therefore consider other methods of display. A pie chart, you decide, is unsuitable because it cannot demonstrate a trend: even if you draw one for each of the five years, your employer will not be able to see quickly the direction sales are taking.

Although the trend of sales of each type of plant can be strikingly portrayed in pictograms, these will not present an accurate enough picture, either. In any case, drawing is not one of your accomplishments. Even if you do succeed in drawing a convincing perennial plant, how much of it will you depict in trying to demonstrate that sales are, say, 100 short of the 1000 represented by a complete plant?

A bar graph may present a solution. By drawing one type, you could represent total annual sales by a block divided into layers varying in depth according to the volume of sales of the different types of plants. This would show clearly the grand total of yearly sales, but it would be less easy to compare at a glance the constituent totals. Another presentation seems more suitable: in this bar graph the difference in height of the separate columns representing the sales of each type of plant will clearly show. Also, their number and the length of time over which the comparison is to be made are sufficiently restricted to provide a chart that can be quickly and easily assimilated. You decide therefore to draw the chart shown in Figure 20.1.

Although your employer could discern the sales trends from the bar graph you decide that a line graph will present a much clearer and more dynamic picture. As the line representing the sales of a particular type of plant rises, falls, or levels out over the base axis divided into yearly sections, your employer will see immediately the direction sales are taking.

Table 20.1   Sales 1982–86

	1982	1983	1984	1985	1986
Perennial plants	4 502	4 100	3 511	3 256	2 120
Shrubs	2 091	2 547	3 100	3 416	3 981
Climbing roses	1 643	1 600	1 310	1 400	1 500
Bush roses	2 517	2 986	3 671	4 248	5 407
TOTAL	10 753	11 233	11 592	12 320	13 008

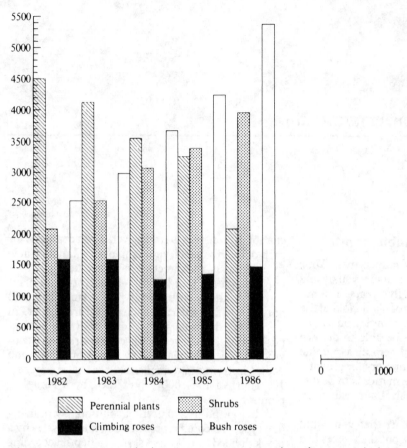

Figure 20.1 Bar graph showing comparative sales of perennial plants, shrubs, and climbing and bush roses for the years 1982–1986.

Your second chart therefore looks like that in Figure 20.2.

These charts are just what your employer wants, and give a clear picture of past sales on which to base future plans.

20.2 Types of chart

(a) Line graphs

These are suitable for depicting fluctuations and trends. Each line on a graph is plotted to extend from left to right over a horizontal axis (often representing the time factor) and at the same time upward or downward against a vertical axis (often representing quantity, volume, income, expenditure, etc.). Thus, the point on the quantity axis reached on one date is joined by a straight line to the point reached on the next significant date. As many trends as it is possible conveniently to depict by means of distinctive lines can be compared on the same *multiline* graph.

(b) Bar graphs

These are useful for comparing statistics over defined periods. Columns or pillars in distinctive markings or colours, arise from each broad division of a horizontal time axis to be measured against a vertical quantity, volume, or amount axis. Graphs using subdivided blocks (see Figure 20.3) are more

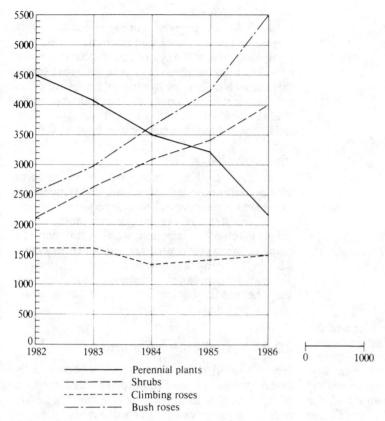

Perennial plants
Shrubs
Climbing roses
Bush roses

Figure 20.2 Line graph depicting trends in sales, 1982–1986.

compact but demand a more extended quantity axis (or smaller scale) since they primarily depict grand totals. If too many items over too long a period are compared in bar graphs the salient points become confused and the visual impact of the graph is diminished.

Bars extended horizontally are often shown in bar charts in relation to a time factor, for example when displaying the progress of work in hand on a visual control board (see **20.3**). *Gantt charts* are a specialized form of bar chart, using two sets of contrasting horizontal bars to show how actual performance measures up against targets set.

(c) Scales and keys
Line graphs and bar graphs and charts are best drawn on squared paper for accurate results, as a set

number of squares can be allocated for each unit along the time and quantity axes. The scale to which they are drawn must be stated. A key may be necessary, explaining the markings and symbols used. Where two or more line graphs or bar charts are drawn for comparison, the same scale must be retained or a distorted impression will result. In particular, the quantity axis should start at 0 on any chart: if not, rising or falling trends may appear to be sharper than they really are. For example, in Figure 20.4 the sales of garden furniture are obviously one-half of those of lawn mowers, whereas in Figure 20.5 they wrongly appear to be only one-quarter.

(d) Pie charts
A broad generalization is given by a pie chart. This enables the proportion of the various segments of the

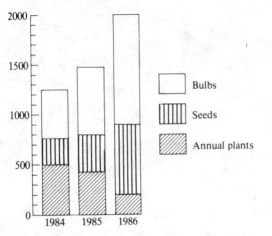

Figure 20.3   Comparative sales of bulbs, seeds, and annual plants in 1984, 1985, and 1986.

circle (or slices of the pie) to each other and to the whole to be quickly grasped. Calculating the correct angle of each segment may involve using a calculator if the figures are complicated. To simplify calculations, approximate figures only are often used, or each segment is regarded as a percentage of the whole, 1 per cent being equal to 3.6° (see Figure 20.6).

(e) Pictograms

In a pictogram a given number or quantity is represented by a symbol, and fractions of it by proportionate parts of the symbol. Multiples are shown by adding to the number of symbols, not by increasing their size. Numbers or quantities represented can only be approximate ones for the overall impression made by a pictogram must be clarity and simplicity, rather than detailed accuracy (see Figure 20.7).

(f) Flowcharts

Flowcharts and diagrams are used in management studies to illustrate by simple lines and symbols the movement of documents between persons or departments, the steps in a procedure, the movement of people involved in performing a task or function, etc. Some of the symbols used are illustrated in Figure 22.1. By studying this type of chart management is able to see where improvements and simplifications may be made. Figure 20.8 illustrates a stores control flowchart.

20.3   Visual control boards

Whereas small charts present information usually for one person or a few people to use—e.g., on sheets of paper, in files, or in portable ring binders, folders or wallets—large charting boards are designed for use by several people simultaneously if necessary.

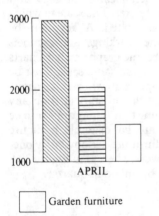

Figure 20.4

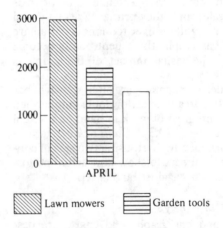

Figure 20.5

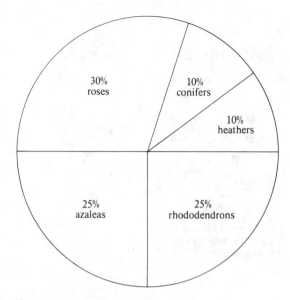

Figure 20.6 Pie chart showing allocation of nursery land under cultivation.

For convenience, these usually consist of detachable sections, and can be mounted in many different ways—on free-standing frames, on walls, stands or panels. Perspex covers offer protection from accidental alteration, and boards can also be covered by lockable blinds when not in use.

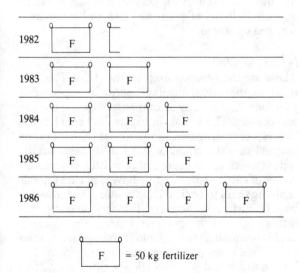

Figure 20.7 Sales of fertilizers, 1982–86.

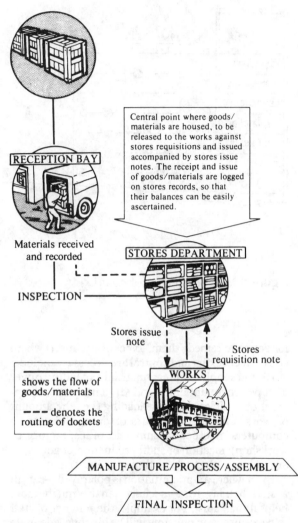

Figure 20.8 Stores control flowchart. (Courtesy of Moore Paragon (UK) Ltd)

(a) Purpose

Most charting boards help their users to exert control over situations and operations by visual summaries of past, present and planned future developments. Thus displays are designed to enable managers to see quickly the current state of affairs, to be able to seize on points where delays in assignments are building up, and to diagnose difficulties so that they can give immediate instructions

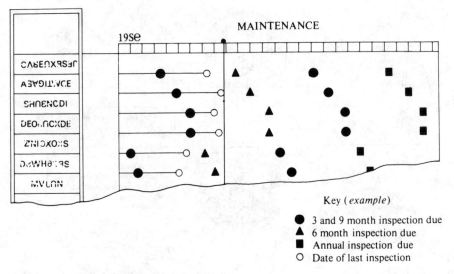

Figure 20.9   Visual control board.

for action to remedy them. Types of situations where constant checking and control are necessary include: stock and supply keeping; financial expenditure over a set period; maintaining and servicing plant, equipment or vehicles; machine loading (i.e., the amount of work, estimated in hours or days, allocated to computers or other machines in office, factory or workshop); location of staff; production of goods; or any other project where timing is important.

Even where a static situation is portrayed—e.g., in a staff holiday rota—a chart can be much more helpful than a list. For example, the number of staff to be away at any one time will be obvious; adequate cover of duties can be assured if distinctive signals are used for different categories of staff; additional leave can be fitted into periods easily seen to be not yet taken up; the reasons for anticipated absences can be shown by using different symbols for holidays, business trips, training courses, etc.

(b)   Axes

Since the time element is so important, most control boards have a time axis; this usually runs from left to right across the top of the chart. As in Figure 20.9 the board is divided into vertical sections or columns for the units of time involved, which may

be months, weeks or days—or occasionally years or hours, according to the type of situation or job charted. The top axis might, of course, indicate other measurements instead—e.g., quantities in stock control charts. The horizontal divisions or channels may represent the parts of the job to be completed, the different machines or personnel concerned in it, or various items of plant or stock to be repaired, serviced or stored.

(c)   Signals

These are the symbols used on the chart. They are fixed to the visual display board, in appropriate positions. Signals can be of many shapes, materials and colours. The signals in Figure 20.9 are circular, square, or triangular, and appear either to be plugged into the board or fixed to it magnetically. Actual words or numbers can be written or typed on pieces of card. Some of these have a plastic top bar enabling them to be fitted into a wire grid across the board's surface. Others are T-shaped and inserted into slots, only the crossbar bearing the essential details remaining visible. Colour coding may be used to indicate types of information (see Figure 20.10). Laminated board surfaces allow written characters to be easily deleted and substituted. Another method

226

uses small discs or wheels, bearing numbers on their narrow edges, which can be rotated to show the desired figures.

(d) Keys

Unless signals actually bear information in the form of letters, words or numbers, a key to their significance must be provided, as the information they denote differs according to the users' needs. Even the use of markers or pins on a wall map indicating the location of a firm's branches, agents, or representatives needs to be explained.

(e) Cursors

In charts, the relationships between work scheduled and the current date must be made immediately obvious. This is often done by means of a cursor or movable vertical bar adjusted daily to coincide with the day's date (see Figure 20.9). Cursors may be transparent or coloured; some are made of woven elastic with clips at either end fastened to the top and bottom of the board. Thus, the current situation can

be clearly seen and jobs either behind or ahead of schedule picked out.

(f) Types of display

Two common types of display are:
(i) *Bar charts* Instead of bars being drawn, they are represented by coloured strips or blocks. The bars may be magnetic or may be slotted into grooves on the display board. Some bars are perforated to hold plugged-in signals, or fitted with blocks to form three-dimensional projections.
(ii) *Line graphs* These can be constructed using boards faced with squares. The lines may be represented by strips of charting tape. Peg boards have perforated surfaces, and a graph may be plotted by inserting into appropriate holes special pegs attached to lengths of elasticated cord.

(g) Space for future planning

As a cursor is moved across a board, the space to its left grows and the space to its right decreases. This means that the space for charting past events grows at the expense of that for future activity. To remedy this many charts are composed of detachable sections: as a section to the left of the cursor becomes freed, it is

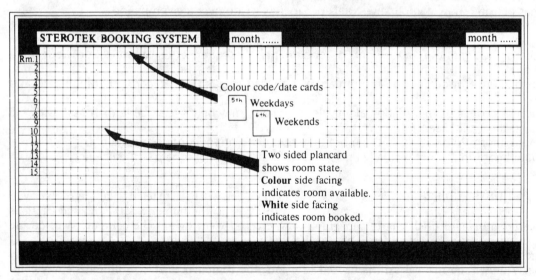

Figure 20.10 Visual control board for hotel room bookings over a two-month period. Colour-coded slotted cards depict either weekdays or weekends (when slotted against the time axis at the top of the chart). Those on the main display depict either booked rooms (white side facing) or vacant rooms (coloured side facing) (Courtesy of Sterotek Systems (Haslemere) Ltd)

removed (the remainder of the board being pushed over to the left) and fitted on the right-hand side. Another type of board is covered with a transparent movable sleeve which bears all the information charted, including scales and signals. This sleeve is rotated each day so that the current date always coincides with the stationary date line marked on the board. Rotating the sleeve also releases more space to the right of the date line, automatically removing used space to the left. Additional space may also be wanted at the bottom of boards, as new jobs are taken on. Again, segments may be added to enlarge the board, or in some charts a complete horizontal strip or channel can be removed when a job is complete, and inserted into the frame lower down. Some fitments enable sections to be slid along tracks in front of the main display. This enables a subsidiary chart to be displayed at the same time, and saves wall space.

(h)   Updating

It is essential that keeping control boards up to date is made as easy as possible. For this reason, some systems have the detailed records (from which the visual summary is taken) filed alongside the chart. Record cards may also be slotted into a card-holder (with their visible edges forming a strip index), to form a panel which can be slid across the chart; a visible card index may be displayed permanently at one side; cards and documents relating to the job charted may be inserted into pockets on the chart itself, only the strip edge being normally visible.

(i)   Standard boards

For routine uses—e.g., timetables and staff holiday rotas—standard charting boards are supplied by manufacturers, but in many cases a special system needs to be devised to suit a company's particular requirements.

20.4   In a nutshell: Effective charting

- The value of charts lies in their striking and compact presentation of statistics in bold outline.
- Every chart should have a heading or title, plus the scale to which it is drawn and a key to markings and symbols used, where appropriate.
- Line graphs most suitably depict fluctuations and trends.
- Bar charts clearly show comparative totals or progress made over a given period.
- Pie charts demonstrate the relationship between parts and the whole.
- Pictograms show broad increases or decreases and are suitable for popular presentations.
- Flowcharts illustrate the movement of documents, a sequence of activities, or steps in a procedure.
- The permanence or otherwise of information displayed affects the choice of charting board and signals.
- Easy access to detailed information alongside the display may be more suitable than portraying full details on the board itself.
- The more informative the chart, the more time and effort are needed to maintain it.
- A control board that is not regularly updated is a hindrance—not a help—to efficiency.

20.5   Computer charts

If suitable programs are used, charts and graphs can be produced using the computer. They have advantages over manual methods in that they are very quickly drawn, no manual skill is needed in their construction, they are accurate, and they are easily updated.

The computer program will construct a suitable graph, piechart, histogram, etc., from the basic infor-mation. You will have to tell it what sort of chart you want, type in the numeric data, and add captions where you want them. The computer will do the rest.

The VDU screen can be thought of as a grid of tiny dots; the computer is able to illuminate any com-bination of dots (and perhaps add colour) to form an image. The amount of detail, or 'resolution', as it is called, depends upon the program, the computer, and the VDU. The program and the type of printer or plotter used determines the resolution of any printed output.

Graphics programs may also make use of a *mouse* (see **11.10** *(c)*), or *light pen*, a pen-like instrument that 'draws' directly on the screen. Alternatively a *graphics pad* can be used. This is a rectangular board the size of a notepad, on which you draw with a stylus. As you move the stylus around the pad, a cor-responding drawing appears on the screen. The computer can make your rough drawing look really professional.

There are many different approaches to using computers for the production of charts, but in all cases the computer removes the need for any drawing skill. (See also **11.12** *(d)*.)

20.6 Did you know?

Pixtels are picture elements which represent the smallest element of any picture on the VDU screen, and determine the resolution obtainable.

Activities

1. Convert the information shown on the bar chart illustrated in Figure 20.3 into a tabular statement.

2. The information in Figure 20.11 could be conveyed equally efficiently by using another type of chart. Decide what that might be, and draw it, giving it a suitable title.

3. Which type of visual aid would you recommend for best expressing local government expenditure on a percentage basis? (PEI, Sec. Prac. Inter.)

4. Design a chart in order to prepare a list of provisional holiday dates for the staff in your department (Manager, Assistant Manager, Chief Clerk, Clerk, Cashier, Secretary, Audio-typist, Junior). The Assistant Manager and the Cashier will be away during the holiday period at different times on a business visit and a course respectively. Describe the points you would bear in mind in order to display the information suitably. Illustrate your answer with a rough sketch. (LCCI, PSC)

5. Describe what you consider to be the most appropriate type of graph/chart to illustrate each of the following and **include a rough sketch** to explain each answer:

(a) the **pattern** of turnover and total costs over a period of five years;

(b) the **apportionment** of the total resources given to each of 3 departments during 1984;

(c) 1983 company profits for inclusion in a public relations booklet to be distributed to school-children. (LCCI, PSC)

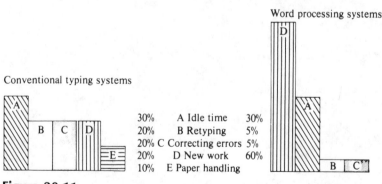

30%	A Idle time	30%
20%	B Retyping	5%
20%	C Correcting errors	5%
20%	D New work	60%
10%	E Paper handling	

Figure 20.11

6. Type a paragraph interpreting in words the meetings procedure set out in the flowchart in Figure 22.1 on page 247. What advantages has the flowchart over the paragraph?

7. You are responsible for organizing bookings for three small conference rooms available for use by all departments of your company and you maintain a visual control board for this purpose. (a) Describe the essential features of such a board. (b) How could you ensure that it was quick and easy to maintain and always up to date? (c) How could you provide for back-up information (e.g., when and by whom requests were submitted) to be available on the spot? (LCCI, PSC)

Group activities

8. Taking statistics from your class register, compile a line graph showing the average weekly attendance of your class as a whole. The chart can be updated weekly, and comparative trends for the three terms shown.

9. Collect examples of charts and graphs from newspapers, dividing your collection into accurate, factual representations and those designed for striking effect rather than attention to detail.

10. Design on paper the form that a visual control board might take, showing the location of classes within your department each week.

21
Travel arrangements

As a secretary you may be expected to make your boss's travel arrangements. This may involve investigating hotels in distant towns and making a suitable booking, ascertaining train times and connections, booking aeroplane seats and perhaps arranging venues for meetings. When your boss leaves the office on a business trip you should have prepared an itinerary, showing travel arrangements, hotel reservations and business meetings as well as all necessary addresses and phone numbers.

21.1 In a nutshell: Typing an itinerary

Set out clearly:

- Day and date.
- Time of train/flight, etc., departure.
- Time of train/flight, etc., arrival.
- Time of checking in (airport).
- Reservation details, e.g., flight/seat number (plane).
- Reservation details, e.g., ticket/coach/carriage/seat/sleeper berth (train).
- Lunch/dinner arrangements where applicable.
- If being met on arrival—where, how and by whom.
- Name, address and telephone number and reservation details of hotel.
- Time, place and purpose of engagements, with names of chief people involved.

For example:

MONDAY (date)	Depart Paddington (seat reservation Coach A Seat 10; refreshment facilities)	1930
	Arrive Bristol Temple Meads Stay overnight at . . . Hotel 18 . . . Street, Bristol Telephone Bristol 00000000; Single room with shower Dinner in hotel on arrival	2104

TUESDAY (date)	James Brown & Co Ltd 25 . . . Road, Bristol Telephone Bristol 11111111; Meeting with James Brown to discuss new contract	0930
	Depart Bristol Temple Meads (lunch on train)	1216
	Arrive Birmingham New Street Met by Philip Harris, our Birmingham representative, who will drive you to the Infotech Exhibition at Birmingham International Conference Centre	1357
	Depart Birmingham International (seat reservation Coach C Seat 12; dinner on train)	1758
	Arrive Euston	1972

21.2   Rail travel

(a)   Facilities available

Fast, InterCity services (with restaurant or refreshment cars) are provided between main centres. Sleeper berths are available on some longer-distance routes. These may be occupied some time before the train leaves, and need not be vacated until a reasonable hour in the morning. Pulman services are available on a few routes, offering meals served to passengers in their seats.

(b)   British Rail timetables

There are two timetables: (i) British Rail Passenger Timetable (including map) published annually, giving schedules for all UK routes and (ii) ABC Rail Guide published monthly but giving only the services to and from London. If relevant, the latter is easier and quicker to read and it does give current fares. The preliminary pages in both publications provide useful ancillary details, e.g., sleeper, rail/drive (car hire) services, Motorail (transporting passengers and their cars), catering facilities on trains and stations, rail/road links with airports, London Underground maps and journey times, etc.

21.3   Air travel

If you are responsible for arranging your boss's flight, book well in advance. On some scheduled flights he may be able to break his journey and still retain the benefit of the through fare, though a stop of more than three days will necessitate his reconfirming his onward or return reservations. Meals are included in the cost of the ticket. Announcements to travellers at airports are preceded by the appropriate flight number, so make sure your boss knows this.

Airline passengers are allowed to take a certain amount of baggage free, but excess baggage can be taken (if there is room in the aircraft) at a charge. It is possible on some airlines to dispatch unaccompanied baggage as cargo at special rates.

At most major airports there are offices for international car-hire companies such as Herz or Budget. Arrangements can be made in advance for a car to be available on arrival.

Although planes cover distances extremely quickly, time can be lost in transit between airports and city centres. Transport between the two points is often provided at a reasonable charge. Rail/air links are sometimes available.

Travel time before or after flights may be cut if 'air taxi' services are used, operating from a large number of smaller airfields not served by the scheduled airlines. The customer can choose his own travelling times, subject to technical considerations such as the speed of the aircraft and the airfields' operating hours. Chartering an air taxi is usually more expensive than a scheduled flight, unless there is a full load and no overnight stops are involved.

Air travel can be physically very tiring and un-settling, especially where drastic changes of time occur. A working day can also be greatly lengthened as a result of time changes; even where a day is shortened it can still be very disturbing to the human system.

21.4 Sea travel

The popularity of ferry travel is increasing due to the ease with which cars with their passengers and luggage, commercial samples, etc., can be transhipped. The main departure ports in the UK handle large numbers of vehicles and passengers every year travelling to the continent of Europe. Bookings can be made via travel agents or through the appropriate shipping companies.

21.5 Road travel

Car journeys may be cheapest for the company if it already provides its executives with company cars. Luggage can easily be carried by car or coach, but driving a car can be very tiring and demanding, especially in congested areas. Road journeys over long distances are slow, compared with air and rail, but a car is generally the most convenient over shorter distances, as no public schedules are involved. Car hire is often a suitable arrangement: your boss can travel by train or fly and then pick up a car at the station or airport for use on arrival.

21.6 Accommodation

(a) Choice of hotel

When choosing a hotel, consider its location in relation to your boss's appointments and the means of transport available. The facilities offered are important. Some hotels offer useful services for business guests—e.g., small conference rooms or secretarial assistance. You must, of course, keep within the budget allowed by your organization.

(b) Confirming bookings

When reserving hotel accommodation for your boss, you may choose to telephone to make the initial inquiry. However, be sure to confirm the booking, by letter or telex, and give a copy of the confirmation to your boss in case it has to be presented on arrival.

Many hotels, especially abroad, will relet rooms if no confirmation is forthcoming. Some will also relet if the booking has not been taken up by a certain time—often about 1830 hours. You can, however, make a 'guaranteed booking' against your boss's late arrival: this means that the room will not be relet but that the hotel will demand payment even if your boss does not take up the booking.

(c) Sources of reference

Your company may have local branches or represen-tatives who can choose a suitable hotel. If not, you could consult:

(i) *AA and RAC Handbooks* The names of hotels appear under the entries for towns listed in the gazetteer, and are classified according to type by from one to five stars. Restaurants and motels (hotels particularly suitable for motorists) are also classified.

(ii) *ABC Railway Guide* This lists recommended hotels throughout Great Britain.

(iii) *Hotel group reservation services* Certain large groups of hotels operate a reservation service for all hotels within the group, including hotels overseas.

(iv) *Agencies* Agencies exist which specialize in hotel bookings. These may charge for services, or may give information free and charge only for a reservation made through them. You can find their names in classified telephone directories.

(v) *British Tourist Authority* This can supply names and addresses, but will not undertake to recommend. Although the service is designed for tourists, information given can be helpful to business-men.

For accommodation overseas:

(vi) *Airlines* Hotel bookings can be made through airlines for stop-overs.

(vii) *Travel agents* will make overseas bookings. They have lists of hotels and 'on-line' booking facilities for many foreign hotel chains. A specialist business travel agency will have detailed knowledge of accommodation and services abroad.

(viii) *Financial Times World Hotel Directory* This lists hotels in the chief commercial centres of 150 countries offering facilities for business travellers. Details are given of numbers and types of rooms available, conference facilities, audio-visual aids, translation and secretarial services, together with brief general information on the countries concerned.

21.7   Booking British Rail tickets

Credit cards, e.g., Barclaycard and Access, and charge cards, e.g., American Express, can be used to buy British Rail tickets from stations or agencies.

(a)   British Rail Direct Account Order
If your company frequently uses rail services and has a direct account with British Rail, you may be able to present a British Rail account order at the booking office. This is an order to British Rail to make out a ticket to the required destination, payment to be made on the company's account later.

(b)   Travel Key Charge Card
This can be used by individuals or companies to pay for British Rail services, e.g., meals on trains, sleepers, car hire. An invoice is sent to the user each month for settlement within seven days. Discounts are allowed on some facilities and incentives offered after certain levels of expenditure are reached.

21.8   Overseas travel documents and formalities

It is wise to keep a record of all travel documents held by your boss, with their dates of issue and renewals, so that all are up to date if needed at short notice.

(a)   Passports
Your boss must have a valid passport for travel to countries outside the EEC. A 10-year passport can be made valid to any country in the world. It may be a standard 30-page passport or a 94-page version, designed for businessmen and others constantly travelling abroad. British Visitors' passports are valid for 12 months only and are not recognized as a passport by many countries.

(i) *Obtaining a passport*   You should obtain an application form from, for example, a Jobcentre, your regional Passport Office, or some banks. This form must be returned to the Passport Office on completion at least three weeks before your boss is likely to need the passport, though a 24-hour emergency service is available. When the form has been completed, it must be countersigned by a British subject of standing (perhaps a bank manager, doctor, a Justice of the Peace, or a clergyman) who has known your boss personally for at least two years. The same person must endorse one of two copies of a photograph, certifying that it is a true likeness. Besides the photographs, you must see that any previous passport is returned with the form for cancellation. British Visitors' passports are obtainable from post offices and Jobcentres.

(ii) *Loss of passport*   See that you and your boss have a record of the passport's number and date and place of issue. If it is lost this must be reported first to the police and then to the nearest British Consular authority.

(iii) *Foreign Office leaflet*   The Foreign Office leaflet entitled *Essential information for holders of UK passports who intend to travel overseas* is obtainable from Passport Offices or post offices.

(b)   Visas
Entry visas and permits (and in some cases exit visas) are required by many countries. Visa requirements are continually changing. Check with either your travel agent or the High Commission or embassy of the country your boss will be visiting about requirements. Sometimes different visas are needed for business trips from those required for holiday visits. Occasionally personal attendance is required before a visa is issued. Always allow plenty of time (months if possible) for these formalities to be completed.

(c)   British Customs requirements
If your boss is likely to bring back articles from abroad, a reminder of the Customs regulations may be useful. You can get detailed information on these from your nearest office of HM Customs and Excise.

(d)   Health precautions
Find out from the overseas country's representative in Britain at least two months before your boss is due to leave, what vaccination precautions he must take. Persons entering or re-entering Britain may sometimes be required to produce cholera vaccination certificates. Precautions against typhoid and para-

typhoid fevers, poliomyelitis, yellow fever, hepatitis and malaria may sometimes be necessary or desirable. You can obtain from your local office of the Department of Health and Social Security a leaflet entitled *Protect your health abroad*, which contains advice on health precautions for most countries.

An arrangement exists which enables a person covered by the British National Insurance scheme to receive medical treatment while visiting another EEC country, on the same terms as its own insured people. To do so, Form E111 must be produced and should be obtained from the Department of Health and Social Security before leaving the UK. There is no charge for treatment in some EEC countries; in others part or the whole of the cost must be borne by the individual. Partial or full reimbursement must be obtained *before* leaving the country concerned. A DHSS leaflet *Medical Costs Abroad* gives information about reduced cost or free medical treatment available.

(e) Insurance

Your boss would be wise to take out an insurance policy covering such contingencies as medical and hospital treatment, loss of money or property, personal accident, death, and—if driving a car—third party insurance and breakdown of vehicle. A Green Card, obtainable from the insurance company, covers the holder while driving in Europe. See that you both have a record of the policy number and the insurance company's name and address for action in an emergency.

(f) Motoring precautions

If your boss is a member of a motoring organization (AA, RAC, etc.) they can help with information about routes and conditions abroad; and also about necessary documents, without which entry may be refused at frontiers.

21.9 Financial services for travellers

As a result of the Government's abolition of Exchange Control Regulations in 1979, there is now no restriction on the amount of cash in sterling that a traveller can take out of the United Kingdom. But note that many foreign countries have very strict regulations about taking currency out of the country. Always check these in advance.

A traveller overseas can obtain money or credit in the ways listed below.

(a) Travellers' cheques

These can be bought from banks or certain travel agents at home in specified denominations of sterling or foreign currency. They are signed by the traveller at the time of purchase. When countersigned and dated in the presence of the paying agent they can be encashed at banks or hotels abroad for their equivalent in the local currency. If lost, the issuing bank should be notified at once.

(b) Foreign currency

This can be supplied in advance from banks at home.

(c) Credit and charge cards

These are accepted in many countries abroad by merchants displaying the agreed sign (see also **14.3** (e) (i) and **14.15**).

(d) Uniform Eurocheque cards

These are special cheques with a Eurocheque guarantee card which are accepted throughout Western Europe to pay bills in hotels, restaurants, shops, etc., as well as to obtain cash from banks.

(e) Open credits

Arrangements can be made in advance for withdrawal of cash up to an agreed limit from a specified branch of a bank, using the traveller's own cheque book.

(f) National Girobank Postcheques

Holders of National Girobank cheque guarantee cards can apply for personalized postcheques which can be encashed in post offices in many countries abroad.

(g) Miscellaneous charges orders

These orders, issued by airlines, can be bought at the same time as the air tickets for use abroad in paying for specific items, such as transportation, excess baggage, car hire, etc. They are particularly useful where additional journeys not definitely provided for in the itinerary have to be made within the country concerned. Orders are made out for specified amounts, any unspent balance being credited on return to the company's account with the airline.

21.10   Local conditions overseas

The success of business trips, especially those taken abroad, can be marred and opportunities lost by lack of advance knowledge of local conditions. Where a company has no local agents or contacts of its own, useful information and assistance can be obtained from other sources:

(a)   Export Services Division of the Department of Trade and Industry

Staff will notify British commercial diplomatic officers at appropriate places abroad of the intended visit. These officers can provide local economic and commercial information and introductions to prospective customers or representatives, and advise on local commercial services—e.g., secretarial and translation facilities available.

(b)   'Hints to Exporters'

This is a series of handbooks issued by the Department of Trade and Industry. Each handbook covers a different country. Information is given on a wide range of matters, including geography, climate, clothing, health, languages, social customs, public holidays, business hours, local time, travel formalities, names and addresses of hotels and restaurants, postal, telephone and telex facilities, economic factors (e.g., banks, industry, imports and exports, import and exchange control regulations), and methods of doing business (e.g., structure of commerce, methods of payment and credit, Chambers of Commerce, etc.). Reading lists are also available that give the names of government and commercial organizations concerned with exporting, overseas publicity for British exporters and useful addresses in the country concerned.

(c)   Local Chambers of Commerce

Facilities offered vary, but larger Chambers of Commerce may arrange group travel and provide technical knowledge and services useful for exporters

and businessmen including the certification of documents. Trade missions and exhibitions overseas may be arranged.

21.11   Services of travel agents

Where a great deal of travelling is done by executives, the services of a travel agency may be used.

Reputable agencies belong to the Association of British Travel Agents. Some specialize in business travel. Besides booking passages and flights, advising on the best routes, assisting with entry formalities and documents and currency and insurance matters, and reserving accommodation, they may also provide useful information about local conditions. For instance, they are notified of the dates of overseas trade fairs, which affect travelling and the ease with which accommodation can be booked. Some may arrange for hire cars to be available on arrival, advise on obtaining secretarial and interpreter services, and even arrange conferences at suitable seasons of the year. No direct charge is usually made, as agencies rely on the commission paid by hotels, shipping and airlines, etc., for their income.

21.12   Travel service departments

Some large companies have travel service departments, which make journey reservations, obtain tickets, arrange car hire, book hotel accommodation, obtain travel documents, and give advice. These departments may also make use of external travel agencies.

In this case, the secretary has an important part to play in acting as a link with the travel department. The secretary should obtain the essential details—when and where the boss is going, for how long, by what method, for what purpose, when and how the boss expects to return, if travelling alone or not, and when the tickets will be required. The travel department will then propose suitable arrangements, with alternatives where necessary, in keeping with the company's policy on travel. For instance, the status of the executive will affect the class of travel and the type of hotel accommodation.

A typical procedure is then for the secretary, having agreed the arrangements with the boss, to submit a formal requisition to the travel department, who will go ahead with firm bookings. It is usual for the secretary to receive a copy of the reservations made, so that an itinerary can be drawn up. The secretary should note the dates when tickets are expected, in case follow-up action is necessary.

The advantages of a travel department to a company are many: executives' and secretaries' time is saved; efficiency is promoted through the specialist staff's accumulated expertise; timetables and reference books can be guaranteed up to date; money is saved on postage and telephone expenses otherwise duplicated throughout the company, and on discounts offered by airlines, etc., on bulk bookings; control is exercised effectively and company rulings more easily observed; new developments in business travel facilities can be followed up; and statistics can be compiled for management.

21.13 The secretary's routine while the boss is away

As your daily routine hinges on your boss's activities his or her absence will naturally affect your work which will now probably fall into several divisions:

(a) Keeping in touch with your boss

This will include typing out reports (from hand-writing or tape or disk) sent back by your boss, sending on any information requested, getting colleagues' opinions or advice for him or her on matters that have unexpectedly cropped up during the trip, helping others to keep in touch with your boss by constant reference to the itinerary and by acting sufficiently in advance to enable any mailed communications to reach him or her promptly if on the move.

(b) Keeping an eye on your boss's office concerns

Some matters will have been anticipated by your boss and he or she will have given you instructions before departure on how to deal with them. Others will arise unexpectedly and will involve you in deciding whether to deal with them yourself (if they

are routine matters) or whether to hand them over to a more senior member of staff (if they are beyond your competence or sphere of responsibility). You should not trouble your boss, unless this is quite unavoidable.

(c) Preparing for your boss's return

To enable your boss to resume control immediately on return, you must provide a clear outline of the most important events during his or her absence and the action you and others have taken on them. To this end, make brief notes *from the very first day*. Urgent matters on which your boss alone can take action should head the list you compile immediately before his or her return, together with notes on unavoidable appointments you have made, though you should try to keep outside engagements to a minimum for a few days. It is a help to assemble the relevant files: your boss can then read up the corres-pondence, take the necessary action and then release the files for filing. Always remember that, however efficient you have been in your boss's absence, you will not be thanked if, on return, your boss is made to appear ignorant of matters on which he or she is expected to be well-informed.

(d) Working for others

You may have less spare time during your boss's absence than other people imagine, but you may quite reasonably be asked to help out sometimes in another department. Make the most of these oppor-tunities to learn about other aspects of the organiza-tion and to observe other people's working methods.

(e) Getting up to date

Use any spare time to advantage in making improvements usually crowded out by the events of an ordinary working day—e.g., making your filing system more effective, bringing address books or telephone number lists up to date, tidying cupboards and cabinets, investigating new methods and equip-ment. You should always be able to find some better way of passing your time than in idle gossip, which can have a demoralizing effect on others and cause them to waste time they can probably ill afford.

21.14   Did you know?

1. Current rates of exchange for foreign currency can be found in the *Financial Times* and certain other leading newspapers.

2. 'Travicom' is a computerized interactive information link between major airlines and chief UK travel agents, giving up-to-date booking and flight schedules and enabling instant confirmation of bookings.

3. A payphone similar to a Trainphone (see **13.2** *(e)* (iii)) is available for outgoing UK calls on some express coaches.

4. For safety's sake you are not allowed when travelling by air to have in your baggage such items as: lighter refills (compressed gases), lighter fuel refills (flammable liquids), petrol lighters, matches, bleaches, instruments containing mercury. However, matches and lighters may be carried on your person.

21.15   Useful reference books

Atlas
AA and *RAC Handbooks*
ABC Air/Rail Guide to Europe
ABC Coach and Bus Guide
ABC Guide to International Travel
ABC Railway Guide (this is a guide only and not
   necessarily wholly accurate)
ABC Shipping Guide
ABC World Airways Guide
British Hotels and Restaurants throughout Great
   Britain and Ireland
British Tourist Authority: *Hotels and Restaurants*
   in Britain
British Rail timetables
Cook's *Continental Rail Guide*
The Financial Times World Hotel Directory
Institute of Directors *Guide to Europe* (gives
   airlines, hotels, local etiquette)
Institute of Travel Managers in Industry and
   Commerce, *Business Travel Newsletter*
   (monthly)
Motorail timetables
Statesman's Year Book (gives economic, political,
   and industrial information about all countries)
Travel Trade Gazette (weekly)
Travel Trade Directory (listing travel agents,
   hotels, etc.)
Whitaker's Almanack (gives brief geographical,
   economic, political, and industrial information
   about all countries)
World Calendar of Holidays (gives public holidays
   and time differences)

Activities

1. An itinerary and an appointment card are both necessary items for an employer who is travelling but there is a distinct difference between them. Show this difference by completing the following sentences: An itinerary is . . . An appointment card is . . . (PEI, Sec. Prac. Inter.)

2. The Sales Manager of your company intends to visit some of the company's largest customers and he requires an itinerary to cover a full week. Explain what an itinerary is, how it could be prepared and what its advantages would be to the Sales Manager and his Secretary. (LCCI, SSC)

3. A travel agent has supplied the itinerary for a journey from India to Canada. Some times are shown as local and some as GMT: what do these initials stand for? (PEI, Sec. Prac. Inter.)

4. Your employer has a number of important business engagements in a town he has not visited before. What action would you take to find and reserve appropriate hotel accommodation for him, and what factors would you consider when assessing its suitability? (LCCI, PSC)

5. Find out as much as you can about current health and currency regulations that a traveller to India would need to know.

6. Your employer is to make a visit overseas. What formalities should be completed, and what steps would you take before his departure to lessen the chances and minimise the consequences of *(a)* illness abroad *(b)* loss of travel documents *(c)* loss of cash *(d)* loss of luggage. (LCCI, PSC)

7. Your employer needs to have cash available

for payments during a business trip abroad. Describe FOUR methods by which this could be provided. (LCCI, PSC)

8. Your employer is contemplating paying a business visit to a country abroad he knows little about. Draw up a checklist of matters you would need to investigate on his behalf, indicating reasons for their inclusion. (LCCI, PSC)

9. Your employer is to make an overseas visit. Describe 4 important formalities (apart from the mode of travel itself) that you must ensure are completed before departure. (LCCI, PSC)

10. Mr R C Maidment, the Managing Director of Comlon International plc, has arranged a trip to the United States Offices in one week's time but is suddenly taken ill. Mrs Forster, Marketing Director, is asked to undertake the trip instead. What arrangements as Mrs Forster's secretary will you make for her? (adapted from LCCI, PESD Sec. Admin.)

11. Your employer attends meetings at irregular intervals in different parts of the country in which he works. Briefly describe: (a) a variety of reminder systems you might use to ensure that the dates in question are kept free; (b) the type of routines you would follow in order to organise his departure for these engagements. (LCCI, PSC)

12. You are secretary to Mr Gibson, Training Manager of Comlon International plc. Mr Gibson will be visiting Training Departments in other firms throughout the country during the week beginning 1 August. What actions will you take before his departure and during his absence to ensure the smooth running of the office? (adapted from LCCI, PESD Sec. Admin.)

13. As personal assistant to the Managing Director of a large company you are required to prepare for his forthcoming visit to the USA. He expects to travel extensively whilst there, visiting a number of industrial companies and making a series of lectures at meetings of business associations.
(a) Outline the arrangements that you will need to make in preparation for his visit.
(b) Indicate the organizational problems that might arise during his absence and suggest how these might be anticipated and/or obviated. (RSA, DPA)

14. While on a business trip to a distant part of the country, your employer will need to discuss an important contract with a foreign visitor over a working lunch. As you cannot yourself inspect the hotel at which your employer will be staying, write a letter to the manager of the hotel explaining the circumstances and outlining the facilities and arrangements you hope he can provide. (LCCI, PSC)

15. **Group activity.** Members of the group (working singly or in pairs, as appropriate) should make investigations in order to compile a short report on travel in one of the Common Market countries that a businessman might find of value— e.g., the distances between the main centres of industry and commerce, best methods of travel, addresses of British government representatives, type of accommodation available, etc. Try to cover all the Common Market countries between you.

PART SIX

The secretary and office diplomacy

22
Meetings and conferences

22.1 Types of meeting

Meetings are a common occurrence in business and other organizations. They enable decisions to be taken, problems to be solved and, if diplomatically conducted, obstacles and difficulties to be removed. As a secretary, you may be concerned with meetings, in that you type the documents connected with them, or attend the proceedings in order to draft a record of the decisions taken.

There are several types of formal meetings:

(a) Annual General Meetings

These provide a means for a company to let its shareholders know how it has used their money and whether it is prospering or not. These meetings are compulsory, according to the Companies Acts, and must be held at intervals of not more than 15 months. They are open to all members, and notice of 21 clear days, i.e., excluding the date of posting and the date of the meeting, must be given. Business transacted includes the declaration of dividends, the election of directors and auditors (absent shareholders being allowed to instruct authorized *proxies* to vote on their behalf on some issues), and the presentation and adoption of the following:

(i) *Annual Report and Accounts* Shareholders receive printed copies of these in advance of the AGM. Together, they present a summary of the company's activities and financial position. The Companies Act 1976 requires that the accounts must comprise a Profit and Loss Account (or Income and Expenditure Account in the case of non-profit-making organizations) and Balance Sheet made up to the accounting reference date, i.e., the end of the financial year. They must be presented to the

Example of a Formal Notice and Agenda of a company Annual General Meeting

THE CHILDREN'S AID SOCIETY LTD

NOTICE IS HEREBY GIVEN that the fifteenth Annual General meeting of the Society will be held at Conway Chambers, Nestall Street, Nobridge, on Tuesday, the seventh day of July 19XX, at three o'clock in the afternoon.

AGENDA

1. Notice convening the meeting.
2. Apologies for absence.
3. Minutes of the Annual General Meeting held on 17 July 19XX.
4. Matters arising from the minutes.
5. Adoption of the Executive Committee's Report for the year ended 31 December 19XX.
6. Adoption of the Statement of Accounts and Balance Sheet for the year ended 31 December 19XX, with the Report of the Auditor thereon.
7. Election of Officers, Executive Committee and Advisory Council Members.
8. Appointment of Auditor
   The following resolution will be moved:

   'THAT Mr J. Green, FCA, of 18 High Road, Nobridge, be and is hereby appointed Auditor for the ensuing year at a nominal fee of £XX.'
9. Any Other Business of an Ordinary Meeting.
   DATED this fifteenth day of June 19XX.

BY ORDER OF THE EXECUTIVE
COMMITTEE
E. E. Youngman
Secretary

shareholders within seven months of that date and accompanied by the directors' and auditors' reports. They must also be presented in one of the approved styles as laid down in the Companies Act 1981. (For an explanation of accounting terms see **10.3**.)

(ii) *Chairman's Review*   The chairman will present the Annual Report to the shareholders in an introductory speech. This review will often consist of extracts from the Annual Report, and may include reference to profits, dividends, taxation, justification of the board's policy, and a brief summary of developments and future plans.

The Annual General Meetings of social organizations, clubs, etc., are run on similar lines. Their object also is to review past activities and to make future plans public, and to enable members to elect officers and committees for the coming year.

(b)   Extraordinary General Meetings

These are also open to all members. They are not held at regular intervals, but only when needed, in order to transact the special business (and no other) for which they are convened.

(c)   Committee meetings

These are attended only by those elected to serve on them, and are held, usually at regular intervals, as often as is necessary—e.g., weekly, monthly, or quarterly. Committees may be of several types:

(i) *Executive committee*   This is elected by the members of an organization and has definite powers delegated to it in the running of the concern. The board of directors of a limited company is a type of executive committee.

(ii) *Subcommittee*   This is a committee set up by a parent committee to study and discuss certain matters; the subcommittee has no power to take action without approval from the parent committee, to which it must regularly report back.

(iii) *Standing committee*   This is one permanently established to deal with recurrent matters like finance, social activities, etc.

(iv) *Ad hoc (or special) committee*   This is set up for one purpose only—e.g., to arrange a conference, and is disbanded when its business is completed.

(v) *Statutory committee*   In some cases—e.g., local government—committees may be statutory, i.e., required by Act of Parliament to be established.

(vi) *Advisory committee*   This has no power to take decisions but only to make recommendations for action by another body.

22.2   Checklist of preparations for a meeting

Make sure that you:

- Arrange the required number of chairs round the table.
- Have name cards ready, if appropriate.
- Open the minute book ready for the chairman's signature.
- Place spare copies of the circulated agenda and minutes on the table.
- Provide a small supply of scribbling paper and pencils.
- Prepare the attendance register for circulation.
- See that ventilation, lighting and heating are adequate.
- Set out a water carafe, glasses, and ashtrays.
- Gather any files and documents needed for the meeting.
- Type out the chairman's agenda.
- Take a shorthand notebook and pen.
- Place a 'Meeting in Progress' sign outside the door.
- Sit where you can easily hear the proceedings.

22.3 Terms and documents used in the conduct of meetings

Certain terms and documents are commonly used in the conduct of meetings. Their acceptance and use enable the persons concerned to concentrate on the matters for which the meeting has been called, to reduce time lost in disputes that might otherwise arise over procedure, and to present the necessary information in a concise and readily understood manner.

In order to set the following terms and documents into some sort of context, they have been arranged to follow the order of events at a meeting. You will find an alphabetical glossary of meetings terms in **22.13**.

(a) Convening the meeting

The *notice of meeting* describes the type of meeting that is to be held (AGM, committee meeting, etc.) and states clearly the time, date and place concerned. It is sent by the secretary in advance of the meeting to everyone entitled to attend (or, occasionally, it is displayed in a prominent place instead), the length of notice needed being stated in the organization's rules. In practice, the notice often appears on the same sheet as the *agenda* (see examples of notices of meetings on pages 243 and 246; on page 252 the notice is in memo form, suitable for less formal meetings). The agenda sets out the items to be dealt with, in the order in which they are to be discussed. Only with the consent of the members should the chairman change that order. The more clearly items on the agenda are worded, the more thinking the members can do before the meeting, and the easier it is for the chairman to conduct discussion on lines that will produce a decision (see examples on pages 246, and 252). The *chairman's agenda* (see page 246) is an expanded version of the ordinary members' agenda. It leaves room at the right-hand side for the chairman's own notes and contains the more detailed information necessary to enable him to lead the discussion sensibly.

(b) Preliminaries at the meeting

Before any meeting begins, the chairman should check to see that a *quorum* is present, i.e., the minimum number of members laid down in the organization's rules to make the proceedings valid.

Members present must sign their names in an *attendance register*, which provides proof of their attendance. Usually, the committee secretary reads out the names of members not present who have sent *apologies for absence*.

(c) Consideration of the minutes of the previous meeting

Before any new business is discussed, the record of the previous meeting's proceedings must be considered. Sometimes, this is read aloud by the committee secretary, but if copies have been circulated in advance to the members, the chairman usually asks the committee's permission to *take the minutes as read*. If the members agree that the record is an accurate one, the *minutes are adopted*, and the chairman signs and dates the copy in the minute book. If any change in wording is considered necessary, the chairman writes in the alteration in his own hand and initials it. The members are then given an opportunity to raise any *matters arising from the minutes*.

(d) Stages in reaching a decision

A suggestion put before a Committee goes through several stages before it can become a decision:

(i) The proposal is stated as a *motion* (usually in writing before the meeting so that it can be included on the agenda) with the name of the person suggesting it (the *proposer*) and of the person supporting it (the *seconder*).

(ii) The chairman reads out the motion and the members discuss it. Strictly speaking, each member should speak only once on the matter, though the proposer may speak twice, as he is allowed the *right of reply* to points raised during the discussion. However, this formal procedure may not always be observed.

(iii) The chairman *puts the question*—i.e., he presents the proposal to the committee for their vote. It may be that a member other than the chairman wishes to bring discussion to a close, and he may move that the *question be now put*. If the committee agree, the vote is taken: if they do not, discussion can continue. By passing a motion to *proceed with the next business* a committee can postpone reaching a decision at that meeting. A matter is sometimes left *in abeyance*—i.e., deferred until a later meeting—if,

Example of notice of meeting and chairman's agenda (the bracketed items are additions which appear on the chairman's agenda only)

The 20th Meeting of the South-Eastern Branch Committee of the Association of Architects will be held at 1430 hrs on Wednesday 10 October 19XX at 14 Chesgrave Square, Notown.

[CHAIRMAN'S] AGENDA   [Notes]

1. APOLOGIES FOR ABSENCE [Mr A. Lister, Mr H. Marshall, Mr S. Oliver]
2. MINUTES OF MEETING HELD ON 8 July 19XX
3. MATTERS ARISING FROM THE MINUTES
4. ANNUAL NATIONAL CONFERENCE
   (*a*) To consider draft programme [Copies available at meeting. Comments must reach HQ by 1 November]
   (*b*) To receive suggestions for Saturday morning lecture [SE Branch's turn to arrange this. Perhaps F. Christopher on Local Authority Housing Estates, or someone conversant with European developments?]
5. APPLICATIONS FOR MEMBERSHIP [From R. Watts, G. Williams, W. Bremner. Details on file]
6. FORTHCOMING EXHIBITION ON SCHOOL ARCHITECTURE [Press publicity stimulating. Ask for representative to attend: 20 November at Hobbs Hall]
7. ANY OTHER BUSINESS [Mr Wren's visit to Germany in January—offer to undertake commissions]
8. DATE OF NEXT MEETING [7 January 19XX]

---

for example, the committee lacks sufficient information on it. If a report is being considered from another committee and further facts are needed, the matter is *referred back* to them. A document that is *laid on the table* has been considered, but the committee decide to take no action on it.

(iv) The committee vote.

(v) The motion, if passed, becomes a *resolution*, i.e., a decision, and its wording is recorded exactly in the minutes.

(e)   Amending a motion

If a member wishes to change the wording of a motion he can move an amendment—i.e., propose that some words in it be altered or taken out, or others added in an *addendum*. Several amendments may be moved, if necessary. If the amendment is seconded and accepted by the chairman as relevant it is voted upon. If it is carried it is incorporated into the original motion; this then becomes the *substantive motion* and is voted upon. (Should the substantive motion be defeated, the original motion cannot then be put to the vote.) If the amendment is not carried, the motion as it originally stood, is voted upon.

(f)   Rider

This is a statement or recommendation added, with the consent of the meeting, to a motion or to a resolu-

---

ABC COMPANY PLC

FORM OF PROXY

FULL NAME ....
BLOCK CAPITALS PLEASE

ADDRESS ....

ANNUAL GENERAL MEETING

I/We the undersigned being (a) holders(s) of Ordinary shares of ABC Company PLC hereby

appoint MR. A. FRIEND, or failing him, MR. E. MANN, or failing him, MR. F. OTHER,

all of whom are directors of the Company, or ....

of .... as my/our proxy to vote

for me/us and on my/our behalf at the Annual General Meeting of the Company to be held on

Wednesday 30th June 19__ and at any adjournment thereof.

Please indicate with an 'X' in the appropriate box how you wish your proxy to vote.

RESOLUTION	1	2	3	4	5
FOR					
AGAINST					

The resolutions are numbered as in the Notice of Meeting.

Signature ....   *Date* ....

Figure 22.1 Meetings procedure flowchart showing how to deal with motions and amendments.

tion after it has been passed. It may comment upon the motion or resolution—e.g., point out that the decision taken in the resolution is not to be regarded as a precedent.

(g) Voting

A motion is passed if the greater number of committee members agrees to it; how big that *majority* must be is decided by the organization's rules—e.g., a *simple majority* (more votes cast for the motion than against it) may be enough, or perhaps a majority of two-thirds or three-quarters of the votes cast is required. Sometimes a motion is passed *unanimously*—i.e., all the members vote in favour of it, or it may be passed *nem. con.* (*nemine contradicente*) or *nem. dis.* (*nemine dissentiente*), meaning that nobody opposed it, though some members *abstained*—i.e., refrained from voting. In some organizations, the chairman has in addition to his ordinary vote a *casting vote* which he can use when votes for and against an issue are equal. Provision for this will usually be stated in the organization's rules. Often a committee will vote by *show of hands*—i.e., when the chairman says 'Those in favour of the motion', each person voting for it raises his hand; 'Those against' and the same procedure follows with those opposing it. Sometimes a *poll* or written vote may be demanded, listing those for and against the motion. This enables account to be taken of the number of votes each person holds (where appropriate) and may allow for postal votes from absentees. A *ballot* enables votes to be cast without revealing the voters' names; voting slips may be put into a ballot box or collected by *tellers* appointed to count votes. *Card* voting is used typically at large conferences where delegates represent varying numbers of members: each delegate's vote is weighted according to the colour of his voting card. In some organizations a member can nominate a *proxy*—another person, not necessarily a member of the organization—to vote on his behalf, either in accordance with specific instructions or left to use his own discretion. A proxy form, usually sent out with the notice of meeting, must first be completed and returned to the organization a stipulated time before the meeting by the member who expects to be absent (see Figure 22.2).

(h) Closing items

After all the specific items listed on the agenda have been discussed, miscellaneous matters may be raised under *Any other business*. Such matters, however, should not be controversial; if they are, they should be excluded and deferred as a separate item to a subsequent meeting, because all members eligible to attend should be given the opportunity to be present to express their views. Matters that ought to have members' detailed consideration before a meeting are also unsuitable. Occasionally, instead of 'Any other business' the term 'Other competent business' is used, and this is more descriptive of the situation. The *date of the next meeting* is the last item. This may be only a formal reminder, if meetings are regularly held at predetermined intervals. If all the business of a meeting is not concluded within a reasonable time (or if there are not enough members present to form a quorum, or discussion has to be postponed), the committee can agree to *adjourn* and meet again on an arranged date. It is possible to limit discussion on particular items by passing a motion of *closure*. If a meeting is not held on an agreed date, but put off until a later one, it is *postponed*.

(i) The chairman

When members speak, they should address all their remarks to the chairman in charge of the meeting thus: 'Mr (or Madam) Chairman.' In large meetings, members should stand up to *address the chair*, but this is not necessary in small ones. It may happen that a committee disagree strongly with the chairman's actions or conduct of a meeting. If they pass a *vote of no confidence in the chair*, he or she must give up the chairmanship in favour of the deputy, the *vice-chairman*, or someone else nominated by the committee.

(j) Composition of committee

On request to the members at a general meeting or to a parent committee, a committee may be given

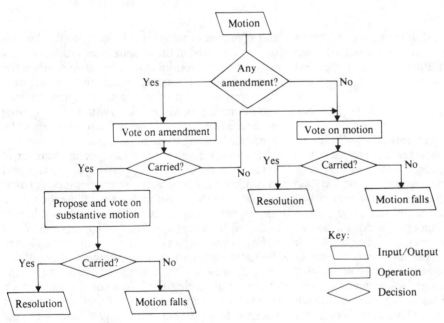

Figure 22.2 A typical proxy form.

Example of minutes

The 20th Meeting of the South-Eastern Branch Committee of the Association of Architects was held at 1430 hrs on Wednesday 10 October 19XX at 14 Chesgrave Square, Notown.

PRESENT:
        Mr C. Driver (Chairman)
        Mr J. Hopkins
        Mr R. James
        Mr H. Lambert
        Mr B. Munro
        Mr M. Napier
        Mr R. Seymour
        Mr E. Wilson
        Mr J. Clarke (Secretary)

1. Apologies for absence	Apologies for absence were received from Mr A. Lister, Mr H. Marshall, and Mr S. Oliver.
2. Previous meeting's minutes	The minutes of the meeting held on 8 July 19XX, having been circulated in advance, were taken as read. They were confirmed and signed as a correct record.
3. Matters arising	There were none.
4. Annual national conference	Copies of the draft programme were circulated, and studied by members.
(*a*) Draft programme	It was agreed that headquarters be notified of branch approval, with the suggestion that dinner should be put back from 1900 to 1930 hrs to suit possible late arrivals on the Friday evening and that delegates be allowed more time for individual activities on the Saturday afternoon.
(*b*) Saturday morning lecture	The chairman reminded members that arrangements for the Saturday morning lecture were the responsibility of the branch, and invited suggestions for speakers.
	After discussion, it was agreed that Mr F. Christopher of the Design Scheme be invited to speak on Local Authority Housing Estate Architecture; if he was unable to accept, Mr W. Amor, national adviser on high density developments, was to be approached.
5. Applications for membership	The chairman asked members to consider applications for membership of the Branch.
	It was RESOLVED that Mr R. Watts, Mr G. Williams, and Mr W. Bremner be admitted to membership of the branch.
6. Forthcoming exhibition on school architecture	The committee noted recent press notices concerning the exhibition to be held on 20 November.
	Mr R. Seymour was asked to attend as the committee's representative and to report back at the next meeting.
7. Any other business	The chairman reported that Mr J. Wren, a branch member, had written to say he was visiting Germany in January and was willing to undertake small commissions on behalf of branch members.
	The secretary was asked to thank Mr Wren, and it was agreed that details of his offer be circulated in the November newsletter.
8. Date of next meeting	It was agreed that the next meeting be held on Wednesday 7 January 19XX at 1430 hrs at 14 Chesgrave Square, Notown.

                                      Chairman
                                  7 January 19XX

powers of co-option—i.e., to ask additional persons up to a stated limit to serve on the committee. Such persons are often experts on a particular matter; not being elected, they have no vote and serve only until the next AGM. *Ex officio* members have votes and serve by virtue of an office they already hold, e.g., a president may be allowed to attend all committee meetings within his organization. Persons said to be *in attendance* are present in a non-voting capacity—e.g., to perform a job, such as taking the minutes.

(k)   Committee procedures and powers

The rules governing the conduct of meetings (among many other matters) are set out in a company's *Articles of Association*, a club's *constitution*, or a local authority's *standing orders* (see also Chapter 2). Occasionally, a member may raise a *point of order*, that is, he queries the correctness of the procedure; perhaps he may question whether a particular matter is within the committee's *terms of reference* or limits of their powers, or whether voting is being carried out in the manner specified in the constitution. In general, committees that can take action on their own without reference back to any other body have *delegated powers*, and those that are enabled to make only recommendations have *advisory powers*.

(l)   Minutes

The *minutes* of a meeting should contain essential details only. The time, date, and place of the meeting, and the names (or in the case of very large general meetings, the number) of those present must be recorded. The practice varies: sometimes the names of those present only are given; in other cases, all those eligible to be present are listed and an asterisk or other symbol typed against the names of those who actually attended. Items should be noted under headings (either shoulder or marginal), so that they can be quickly picked out, and the problem or question under discussion clearly set out. A summary of the points made at the meeting, including suggestions that were not accepted, may be required as well as the actual decisions reached. Such details form the content of *minutes of narration*—i.e., they record events leading up to the decisions. *Minutes of resolution* set out the actual wording of the decision reached—often set out on a separate line and numbered, for ease of reference (You will see

Extract from formal, brief minutes

981. *Minutes*
     The chairman signed the minutes of 8 July 19XX as a correct record.

982. *Treasurer's report*
     The committee received a report by the treasurer (see Appendix C).
         RESOLVED that the report be approved.

983. *Purchase of calculating machine*
     The secretary submitted a report from the accountant, containing details of calculating machines which had been available for trial.
         RESOLVED that an AZ calculating machine be purchased at an estimated cost of £XX.

examples of minutes on pages 249, and 250.) Some minutes include an *action column* on the right-hand side, recording the names of the persons who it was agreed should take action on the decisions reached.

As the record has to be clearly understood by members not present at the meeting and may have to be consulted on occasion even many years later, each minute must be not only brief, but clear. In order to understand it, it should not be necessary to refer to any other minute or to any other meeting.

(m)   Minute book

A *minute book* is the official legal record of a committee's proceedings. A loose-leaf book is convenient for typing, but, to avoid the possibility of any unauthorized person removing or tampering with the pages, it should be locked away and each page signed by the chairman. A bound book involves writing minutes in by hand or pasting in typed pages. Items can be *indexed* alphabetically on index pages at the front or back of a book and the page numbers or resolution numbers recorded each time the topic is discussed. This enables the history of the discussion of any one topic to be traced.

(n)   Reports

A *report* of a meeting may be less formal than true minutes and may contain more detail—e.g., mentioning speakers by name. Headings are helpful, as in any report on whatever subject. A *verbatim report* is a word-for-word report and not often required in business.

22.4 Chairman's duties

Unless acting in an *ex officio* capacity, the chairman is elected or nominated by the committee. His or her business is to take charge of the conduct of its meetings. For this reason, the chairman must be someone determined enough to ensure that a decision is reached within a certain time. This may mean curtailing speeches from over-talkative members to enable quieter ones to have their say, while maintaining a harmonious atmosphere. When discussion on a subject has ended (and, when appropriate, from time to time during discussion) the chairman should sum up the conclusions reached, so that a clear decision can be recorded. When guiding the discussion, he or she must bear in mind the scope of the question to be considered, and must also take into account the limits of the committee's powers, so that no aspect is omitted making it necessary to reopen discussion at a later date. Especially where meetings are infrequent, a chairman is usually given the power to act on the committee's behalf between meetings. He or she must therefore be thoroughly conversant with the organization's affairs and be readily available to the secretary and other executives for consultation and guidance at such times.

22.5 Committee secretary's duties

The committee secretary is responsible for arranging committee meetings and seeing that their decisions are carried out. Usually this is a paid official and when not is often referred to as the honorary secretary. He or she has no power to make important decisions without the committee, but acts as a result of their decisions, in their name. However, in effect, the committee secretary has a good deal of unofficial power: being well acquainted with the daily running of the organization, the committee secretary has a practical knowledge which he or she can use to influence the committee's decisions. The committee secretary may be relied on heavily by the committee for advice; and being responsible for drawing up the agenda for meetings (in consultation with the chairman) is able to select which matters should receive their attention.

22.6 Minute secretary's duties

(a) Before a meeting
(See 'In a nutshell', **22.2**.)

(b) During a meeting
The most nerve-racking part of the minute secretary's duties is, of course, the actual task of note-taking. The best preparation for it is familiarity with the business involved, so that the proceedings are understood, an awareness of the detail required for the record (obtained by studying previous minutes), and getting to know the names and faces of the committee members so that speakers are easily identifiable. After that, a clear, cool head and skill in shorthand-writing are the best aids.

However, the fact that you can take down the spoken word quickly and easily in shorthand can make your job *more* difficult, if you do not resist the temptation to write too much. Limit your notes to the essential points, sifting the important from the trivial or irrelevant *at the time of hearing*. If you do not, you will face a most laborious task when compiling the minutes. This is one reason why recording machines are of little help—unless a verbatim report is wanted—as they record everything, instead of selecting and discriminating as a good minute secretary should.

You should also be prepared to meet any small crisis that may occur—e.g., fetching documents needed suddenly, or altering room arrangements. You may also be asked to serve tea before the meeting commences (see **22.11** *(a)* (ii)).

(c) After a meeting
(i) Clear the table and restore the books and documents to their proper places.

(ii) Type out your draft of the minutes at the first opportunity. Not only is it easier to do this when your memory can help you, but also the committee secretary will want to have as soon as possible a complete record of the proceedings so that he or she can set about taking necessary action on decisions reached.

(iii) It is customary to let the chairman see the draft of the minutes so that he or she can make any comments before the fair copy is prepared. Keep these amended drafts, in case of queries, until the minutes have been adopted at the next meeting.

(iv) Type the minutes in their final form (often for duplication).

(v) Reserve one copy for the minute book.

(vi) You may find it helpful to place a copy of the minutes on a special file to avoid constant reference to the minute book.

(vii) Keep the duplicated copies of the minutes in a safe place until you are ready to send them out with the agenda for the next meeting. If meetings are held infrequently, however, or if committee members are due to take action on decisions recorded, the minutes are usually sent in advance of the next agenda.

(viii) Make your own note of any matter which you know has had to be deferred, and add to this any other information which will help the committee

---

Example of a notice, agenda and extract from the minutes of a company's Staff Association sports committee

MEMORANDUM

TO: Members of the sports committee
FROM: Welfare officer

SUBJECT: Sports committee meeting
Your are reminded that the next meeting of the sports committee will take place on Wednesday 27 February 19XX at 1700 hrs, in the small meetings room. If you are unable to attend, please let me know.

AGENDA

1. Apologies for absence
2. Minutes of previous meeting
3. Matters arising
4. Cricket fixtures list
5. Tennis fixtures list
6. Practice rotas
7. Need for more staff involvement
8. Any other business
9. Date of next meeting

J. Jones
20 February 19XX

Minutes (extract)

4. Cricket fixtures list
This was approved, and Mr Hall was thanked for his work in arranging the details. The dates of matches would be included in the next issue of the house magazine.

5. Tennis fixtures list
Mr Evans reported that this was not yet complete. It was agreed, on Mr Pearce's suggestion, that the dates of matches so far arranged should be displayed on staff notice-boards, as some players were anxious to have as many details as possible before fixing their annual leave.

6. Practice rotas
The chairman recalled that there had been some dissatisfaction among players with the practice arrangements made last year. Miss Wilson proposed, and it was agreed, that each representative should sound out his or her department to assess the demand before any rota was drawn up. She said it was frustrating for keen tennis players to have practice times restricted, when courts allocated to some departments were standing idle. Mr Evans thought the time had come to abolish the departmental rota system, and it was agreed to discuss this at the next meeting.

secretary to compile the agenda for the next meeting. This information may crop up at any time and may arise from correspondence, telephone calls, or events and discussions inside or outside the company. Following up one meeting will often merge into preparing for the next, and you must always have that next meeting in mind. Write reminders of this kind in your desk diary on the memoranda pages, or under the date on which the next agenda will be prepared.

(ix) Avoid discussing the events of the meeting with anyone not concerned with them—e.g., other members of staff. It is always best to be discreet in this matter, and silence on your part is essential when the meeting is obviously a confidential one.

22.7 Informal meetings

This chapter has dealt primarily with meetings of a formal nature, since these are the ones for which a knowledge of accepted procedures may be useful for you, as a secretary working in business. You may, however, be called upon at work to attend or help arrange other meetings, at which the proceedings are more relaxed and the more formal terms and documents dispensed with. For example, a small group of staff may be called together for an informal discussion. The participants may be assembled by the convenor's secretary sending a memo or telephoning those concerned, at the same time indicating the purpose of the discussion. There may be no formal agenda, apart from a few notes written by the convenor for his own guidance. Perhaps the convenor's own room is used for the meeting, so no preparation is necessary beyond bringing in a few extra chairs. No formal minutes may be prepared: if any written record is needed a brief memo compiled by the convenor and circulated to those who took part may be enough.

22.8 Remote conference facilities

It is possible to hold conferences by telephone or television connection, without the parties having to meet face to face. This saves travelling and overnight accommodation expenses.

(a) Videoconferencing

(i) *Confravision* This British Telecom Service enables small groups of people many miles apart, in separate television studios, to hold a conference. Places served are Aberdeen, Belfast, Birmingham, Bristol, Glasgow, Ipswich, London and Manchester. Two or three studios can be linked at any one time for a Confravision call, which must last for at least 30 minutes and must be booked at least two hours in advance. Calls can be extended in multiples of 15 minutes provided that notice is given 20 minutes before the call was due to end. Charges vary according to the length of the call, the number of studios involved and the distance between them. As proceedings can be controlled by the users without the assistance of British Telecom, staff conferences can be held in complete privacy. Pictures of documents, charts, etc., needing to be discussed can be transmitted by means of a display camera provided. Up to nine people can take part in any one studio, though further numbers can be accommodated as onlookers in studio reception areas.

(ii) *International Videoconferencing* Special terminals may be rented with this public British Telecom service and include a camera, monitor screen, microphone and loudspeaker, together with a *codec* (digitized converter) which encodes the information transmitted (image, speech, text or data) into digital pulses. Picture signals are compressed during encoding and only the changes in picture content from one frame to the next are transmitted. This reduces the transmission capacity needed and therefore the cost. The service links private customer premises, as well as some Confravision studios, with Canada, the USA, Germany and other countries in Europe. The minimum length of a call is 30 minutes. All calls are on contract, with regular users qualifying for a lower tariff. Customers with their own terminals only pay the international portion of the tariff; Confravision users pay a charge for the use of a studio and codec in addition.

(iii) *VideoStream* This is a British Telecom private videoconferencing service providing colour pictures and sound plus auxiliary data channels over a digital circuit. Terminals may be purchased or rented (see Figure 22.3).

(b) Audioconferencing

(i) *BT Conference Calls service* The telephone

Figure 22.3   A videoconference between staff at the NatWest Bank computer centre in Aldgate, London (pictured here) and Kegworth, Leicestershire, using VideoStream, the British Telecom private videoconferencing service. The terminal with the visual display screen showing the Kegworth staff incorporates a camera and loudspeaker. The participants control proceedings via the keypad (centre). The telephone is provided in case participants wish to telephone their own offices. A codec (not shown) is encoding the images and speech into digital pulses which are transmitting down the telephone network. (Courtesy of British Telecom Visual Services)

numbers of participants are supplied to the BT operator who makes the connections at the pre-arranged time. Each participant is charged a facility fee, plus a set fee per person per minute. A similar service is available for overseas conference calls.

(ii) *Digital call-connect conference calls facility*
Conference calls usually involving up to four extensions (including a participant on an external line, if required) is an automatic facility available on digital call-connect systems.

(iii) *Telephone conferencing equipment* Equipment can be installed in a user's premises, linked to the public or private telephone line, enabling up to 10 individual users of ordinary telephones to dial in to an audioconference. Other equipment enables groups of people to confer over the telephone using ordinary telephones. Systems also exist that use a specially installed telephone line linking two groups of people: each participant has a microphone to enable his voice to be picked up over the circuit. Loudspeakers situated at the distant point relay the conversation. With some systems it is the strongest voice at any one time that is picked up for transmission. Where reference to documents is needed, facsimile transmission may be used. Another system uses two ordinary telephone lines: microphones and loudspeakers at each end pick up and transmit speech evenly from around the conference table.

(iv) *Chairman's technique* The chairman needs to be very firm when conducting a telephone conference, and must ensure that everyone who wishes to has the chance to speak. This may sometimes involve asking each individual for an opinion. Participants should identify themselves when speaking. The chairman should discourage long periods of speech in favour of frequent summaries and questioning. He should also check periodically to make sure that no participant has unexpectedly left the meeting and that nobody not entitled to attend has joined the conference.

22.9 Arranging a conference

Although long and elaborate conferences are often handed over to professional organizers, it may be that you become involved in minor conference planning, perhaps as secretary to an organizing team or committee. The following notes set out some of the considerations to be borne in mind.

(a) Planning stages
Divide the work of organizing into stages to be completed by set dates, working backwards from the conference date.

(b) Venue
This will be affected by the date chosen (e.g., avoid a seaside resort in the height of the holiday season), by the type of social activities planned (e.g., visits to local places of interest, expeditions for delegates' wives, etc.), by the conference facilities available for the number of delegates expected, by the distance which delegates will have to travel. Make a preliminary, exploratory visit if necessary.

(c) Conference facilities
Consider the size of the hall and/or smaller rooms, seating accommodation, lighting, heating and ventilation, facilities for meals and light refreshments, cloakroom facilities, office and communication facilities.

(d) Chairman and speakers
Approach these in good time to allow for finding substitutes if necessary, so that as full details as possible can be included in the invitations to attract delegates. Arrange platform furnishings and decorations, votes of thanks to speakers, bouquets, etc.

(e) Audio/visual aids
Check on microphones, overhead projectors and spare bulbs, film projectors (and operators), tape recorders and the provision of electric plugs and sockets, making sure that an adequate power supply is available without overloading the system.

(f) Overnight accommodation
Decide whether delegates will be based at the conference venue itself or in nearby hotels, or asked to make their own bookings from a list of suitable hotels provided. Ensure that both single and double rooms are available to suit either single delegates or those accompanied by husband/wife.

(g) Invitations and programmes
When sending out invitations, give full details of location and provisional programme arrangements, including to whom and by what date replies must be received and how remittances for fees/deposits are to be made out. A tear-off slip or separate form can be provided for delegates to complete and return and this can be used to supply reference information about delegates' requirements. Final programmes can be sent out to delegates later or handed to them with other conference literature on arrival.

(h)   Luncheons/dinners

Decide whether these are to be formal or informal, buffet or 'sit down' meals. If applicable, make a seating plan. Consider choice of menus, wines, etc., and whether speeches and toasts are desirable.

(i)   Registration and reception arrangements

Pointers and notices should be on display to guide visitors to the conference room. Alternatively, instructions can be handed out at reception, or staff delegated to act as guides. Decide how delegates are to be received and identified—e.g., delegates may collect badges or personalized folders of conference documents, sign registers, etc. Make special arrangements for reception of speakers and distinguished guests. At short, one-session conferences guests may be asked to sign attendance sheets at the door, or these may be circulated for signature once everyone is seated. Where guests hand in cards at the door these can provide a useful record later of those attending.

(j)   Press arrangements

Notify the press, if the conference is of general interest. Arrange for a suitable person to greet reporters and provide them with agreed information. Make sure that they are seated where they can observe the proceedings.

(k)   Follow-up arrangements

Arrange settlements of accounts, letters of thanks to chairman and speakers, action arising from decisions taken or opinions expressed by delegates, distribution of records of proceedings. Suggest a committee meeting soon after the conference to tie up loose ends and to review the degree of success of the arrangements made.

22.10   Press conferences

These are usually short (lasting for about half an hour) as journalists' time is limited; they are called when a press release is insufficient or inappropriate for publicizing a particular event. Invitations should give enough information to encourage the press to attend, without divulging too much in advance. The object of the conference is to enable the press to give the event or product publicity. Therefore speeches must be brief and to the point, to allow time for questions and for informal conversation. Photographs may be on display for orders to be taken if desired, and 'press kits' available, containing information about the company and its products. Refreshments are usually buffet-type rather than set meals, to enable press to circulate. Invitation lists should be regularly updated for accuracy and suitable coverage, and where possible addressed to a specific person rather than impersonally to 'The Editor'.

22.11   Entertaining

You may sometimes be required to make arrangements to help your boss entertain company visitors at meetings or on more extended visits and this may involve arranging catering and organizing programmes of events.

(a)   Serving tea or coffee

(i) *To individuals*   If you are expected to serve your boss and a visitor with coffee or tea, organize matters so that you need to stay in the room for only a brief while, in case your presence interrupts confidential discussion. If possible, place your tray on a side table and pour out the tea there. Coffee can be prepared in advance, leaving only milk to be added if white coffee is preferred. Make a note of regular visitors' preferences—e.g., white/black coffee, strong/weak tea, sugar/no sugar. Always serve the visitor first.

(ii) *To meetings*   If you should have to serve tea to a meeting, a side table is even more helpful. Serve in the following order: chairman, other officers, then committee members, serving ladies first. Serve from the right-hand side of each person, so that you can place the cups in a convenient position, with handles of cup and spoon facing the right. Be careful not to fill the cups too full in case your hand shakes. Sugar can be placed in bowls down the table, along with plates of biscuits or cakes. If the meeting is a large one, try to find someone else to help you. This is very necessary should you also be the minute secretary.

(b)   Arranging business lunches

Sometimes your company will have a suite where executives can entertain business guests to lunch more cheaply than at outside establishments. Early booking is necessary, as accommodation will be limited. If this is not possible, try to establish a connection with a local restaurant so that your boss can expect 'regular customer' treatment. If it is to be a working lunch, see that a menu of easily consumed dishes is available, with the minimum of waiter service in case the discussion is confidential. Take into account not only your boss's preferences in regard to the meal but also the type of fare the guest may expect, depending, for example, on the guest's status, purpose of visit, degree of acquaintance with your boss, etc. A table in a quiet position, away from gangways and kitchen entrances, is preferable if a private room is not available. Check whether the meal can be paid for by cash, cheque, credit card, or on the firm's account, if applicable. It may be possible to have a regular arrangement with a restaurant, if your boss's visits are frequent, on the understanding that the table, if not wanted, is released for public use by a prearranged time.

(c) Arranging programmes for visitors

If you have to plan a programme for a day or longer for business visitors there will be several aspects to look after:

(i) *Boss's requirements*   Make sure you have a clear picture of what your boss envisages for the visitors and how far you can go in the arrangements without referring back to him or her. Obviously, before finalizing details you should present a draft programme for approval.

(ii) *Other staff involved*   If other managers will be involved, contact their secretaries first to find out at which part of the day they expect to be free or, if no actual date has been fixed, which day would be most convenient. Electronic diary systems (see **23.4** (f)) would be helpful here. When arrangements are complete, notify them of the final programme and confirm details of their part of the proceedings.

(iii) *Timing*   Do not plan too tight a schedule, remembering that introductions and social conversation all take time. Also, an overseas delegation may have already had several consecutive days filled with engagements. Naturally they will not want to waste time, but rushing from one place to another blurs their impressions and leaves no opportunity for informal discussion. Allow time for moving from one place to another. If possible arrange the most tiring part of the programme for the early part of the day.

(iv) *Transport*   If visitors are travelling by plane or rail they will need to be picked up from the airport or station, perhaps by coach or company cars. Make sure that the drivers and visitors know how they can recognize each other. If your company has premises on separate sites transport between appointments may have to be arranged.

(v) *Preparatory information*   It will help visitors to receive in advance of the visit as many details as possible about the company, its products and the discussions to be held. You may have to co-ordinate the compilation, production and dispatch of these. Set early deadlines for receiving the information from the different departments in case of last-minute hitches. Visitors to whom English is a foreign language will particularly welcome the opportunity to study this information in advance. In some cases you may have to arrange for a translation from an appropriate member of staff or an agency before the material is prepared for dispatch. An interpreter on the premises at the time of the visit might be necessary as well.

(vi) *Follow-up arrangements*   Particularly where visitors are making a round of visits to different establishments you need to reinforce the impression your company has made on them. Make sure you gather together any follow-up letters from the departments concerned to send on to them as soon as possible afterwards. It may be appropriate to include small business gifts bearing the company's logo.

(vii) *Entertainment*   On a longer visit there may be time for the visitors to attend an evening concert or show. Contact a theatre booking agency to find out what is available. It may be that your company regularly holds a few seats at a convenient theatre until an agreed date, and you may be able to take advantage of this.

(viii) *Accommodation*   The organizers of a delegation's main itinerary will probably book the hotel accommodation needed for the whole of the visitor's stay in this country but for briefer visits or those at short notice you may need to book accommodation for them. Guidelines as to type of accommodation and price may well be on file, together with names of recommended hotels. Otherwise, suitable reference books (see **21.6** (c)) and agencies can help.

22.12   Did you know?

1. The chairman of a large meeting may use a *gavel* (hammer) and *block* (on which to strike the hammer) when calling for order.

2. An electronic 'whiteboard' on the market allows A4 paper copies to be made of notes written on it, using facsimile techniques—a useful aid at meetings and training sessions.

3. A *representative* attends a meeting or conference in order to speak on behalf of those he represents, and to report back to them. Often he may be expected to use his own discretion—whereas a *delegate* has a more defined role because he is *instructed* to put forward certain views or take certain action on their behalf.

4. British Telecom offer advice on the conduct of formal meetings held by telephone to users of its audioconference equipment.

22.13   In a nutshell: Glossary of meetings terms

Abstain   to refrain from voting.

'Actions'   to receive reports by persons who were instructed at the previous meeting to take certain action.

'Actions' column   displays the names of persons who are to carry out agreed action.

Addendum   an addition to a motion.

Address the chair   to direct all remarks to the chairman.

Adopt   to accept.

Agenda   a list of items to be discussed at a meeting.

Amendment   an alteration to a motion.

Any other business   the opportunity at the conclusion of a meeting to raise items not specified on the agenda.

Apologies for absence   the reading of the names of members who have indicated that they cannot attend the meeting.

Articles of Association   the rules governing the conduct of a company.

Ballot   a secret written vote.

Card vote   a vote indicated by displaying a card signifying numbers of votes for or against a motion.

Casting vote   a second vote exercised by a chairman to resolve a deadlock.

Chairman's agenda   an elaborated version of the agenda for the chairman's use.

Closure   to end discussion on an item.

Constitution   the rules governing the running of an organization.

Convene   to call a meeting.

Co-opt   to invite someone to serve on a committee for a limited period, usually on account of specialized knowledge.

Ex officio   by virtue of an office—the right to attend a meeting because of another office held.

In abeyance   a matter is left until it can be dealt with on a later occasion.

In attendance   a person not elected but present at a meeting, usually in a professional capacity.

Lay on the table   a matter is presented to a meeting but no action is taken on it.

Matters arising from the minutes   Matters recorded in the previous meeting's minutes that need to be reported on before the main business of the meeting can start.

Minutes   a brief record of the proceedings of a meeting.

Minute book   the official record containing the signed minutes of a committee.

Minute of narration   a minute giving explanatory details.

Minute of resolution   a minute setting out a resolution verbatim.

Motion   a proposal for discussion and vote.

Nem. con. (*nemine contradicente*)   no one opposes the motion (but not everyone has voted).

Nem. dis. (*nemine dissentiente*)   no one dissenting (same as above).

Notice of meeting   the announcement of the place, date and time on which a meeting is to be held.

Point of order   a matter raised at a meeting in connection with the conduct of the proceedings.

Poll   a written vote.

Proceed with next business   to conclude discussion on one item and move on to the next.

Proposer   the person who puts forward a motion.

Proxy   a person nominated in accordance with an organization's rules by an absent member to act for him at a meeting.

Proxy vote   a vote indicated in advance on an authorized form by a person unable to be present, instructing another to vote on his behalf.

Put the question   to bring a matter under discussion to a vote.

Quorum   the minimum number of persons present at a meeting to make the proceedings valid.

Refer back   to send a matter back to the person or committee that originated it for further comment or information.

Resolution   a formal decision arising from a vote.

Rider   an addition to a resolution in the form of a comment.

Right of reply   the right of a proposer of a motion to speak again at the end of the discussion in order to answer objections that have been raised.

Seconder   the person who officially backs up the motion put forward by the proposer.

Show of hands   raising hands to indicate a vote for or against a motion.

Simple majority   the greater number (no percentage specified) of persons for or against a motion.

Substantive motion   a new motion incorporating an agreed amendment to the original motion.

Standing orders   rules for the conduct of meetings of public bodies.

Table   to present an item for discussion not indicated on the agenda.

Terms of reference   defined limits of discussion or powers of a committee.

Unanimous   all present are of one mind and vote the same way.

Verbatim   word for word.

Vice-chairman   person appointed to act when the chairman is absent.

Vote of no confidence   a vote passed by members at a meeting that they are not prepared to accept the chairman's ruling.

Working party   a group formed to work out the practical details of a matter and to report on its feasibility to the main committee.

Activities

1. (a) Select **4** of the following terms and explain their meaning:

   quorum;   ad hoc committee;

   rider;   ex officio member;

   nem con;   amendment.

   (b) Once a meeting has taken place, list the tasks which must be completed by the secretary before the next meeting. (LCCI, PSC)

2. (a) Prepare a **list** of points to enable a junior secretary to take and transcribe Minutes of a Committee Meeting effectively.

   (b) Express the following item in minuted form:

   Matters arising—16/84—Mr Jones said "I should like to report that after further discussion with the interviewing panel it was decided to appoint Mr Frankland as Safety Officer." (LLCI, PSC)

3. In connection with meetings procedure, what might be done in the following circumstances? Answer FIVE only.

(a) The Chairman fails to arrive
(b) There is no quorum
(c) An inaccuracy is found in the minutes of the preceding meeting
(d) A dispute arises about procedure
(e) There is an equal number of votes for and against a motion
(f) The meeting overruns its allotted time. (LCCI, PSC)

4. In connection with meetings (a) What is meant by (i) nem. con. (ii) a teller (iii) a proxy (iv) a casting vote (v) a simple majority? (b) Describe three methods of voting, explaining when each is likely to be used. (LCCI, PSC)

5. A multi-establishment industrial company has a joint consultative committee comprising elected representatives of the employees and appointed representatives of management.

(a) What organizational arrangements and action by management might be necessary in anticipation of one of the regular two-monthly meetings of the committee?
(b) Explain the detailed procedures in which you might be involved as secretary to the committee prior to, during, and after such a meeting. (RSA, DPA)

6. Your employer is responsible for organizing a large number of committee meetings, attended by different groups of people. Describe methods you would use to ensure that all the right people receive the right documents at the right time. (LCCI, PSC)

7. You are secretary to the Company's Social Club. Expand the following notes on the Agenda for presentation as Minutes. (LCCI, PSC)

Meeting of the EVERGREEN LAWN TENNIS CLUB to be held on 23 November 1984 at 2030 hours.

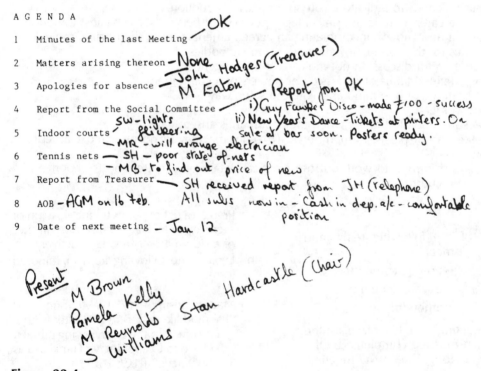

```
A G E N D A

1   Minutes of the last Meeting — OK

2   Matters arising thereon — None   Hodges (Treasurer)

3   Apologies for absence — John
                            M Eaton      — Report from PK

4   Report from the Social Committee —  i) Guy Fawkes Disco – made £100 – success
                sw-lights               ii) New Year's Dance – Tickets at printers. On
5   Indoor courts — flickering             sale at bar soon. Posters ready.
            — MR – will arrange electrician
6   Tennis nets — SH – poor state of nets
            — MB – to find out price of new
7   Report from Treasurer — SH received report from JH (telephone)
8   AOB — AGM on 16 Feb.   All subs  now in – Cash in dep. a/c – comfortable
                                               position
9   Date of next meeting — Jan 12
```

Present   M Brown
          Pamela Kelly   Stan Hardcastle (Chair)
          M Reynolds
          S Williams

Figure 22.4

8. Every formal meeting must have a chairman to ensure that it is conducted in a proper manner. List sixteen actions you would expect a chairman to take at a meeting to achieve this. (PEI, Sec. Prac. Adv.)

9. (a) Make notes to enable a junior secretary to prepare and type an agenda for a meeting.
   (b) In what ways does a Chairman's agenda differ from the above? (LCCI, PSC)

10. Part of your duties as a secretary involve organising committee meetings.

(a) Describe how you would prepare the Minute Book for meetings, and how you would look after and maintain it as a source of reference when required.
(b) Some newly-elected members are to attend the next meeting, including 2 or 3 from other organizations. What special arrangements would you make before their first meeting? (LCCI, PSC)

11. The Marketing Division of Comlon International plc has a monthly meeting. The next meeting coincides with your annual summer holiday, and Miss Stevens, who is secretary to Miss Jones, the Advertising Manager, will be present at the meeting and has been asked to draw up the draft Agenda and make the arrangements for the Meeting. Write a checklist for Miss Stevens' use. (Adapted from LCCI, PESD, Sec. Admin.)

12. (You are secretary to Mr Colin Gibson, Training Manager of Comlon International plc.) The commercial trainees will be given a series of lectures on meetings procedure. Prepare a hand-out on the duties of a secretary before and during a meeting. (Adapted from LCCI, PESD, Sec. Admin.)

13. Prior to attending a meeting of your firm's Social Committee you are asked to act as Minute Secretary. What do you think the work will entail and what information will you require to enable you to carry out the job? (LCCI, SSC)

14. The Sales Director of a manufacturing company is expecting an overseas customer and his wife to visit your factory premises. He has asked you to plan an itinerary for one day. Local accommodation is arranged but they have little knowledge of the English language. Prepare the itinerary from mid-morning. How would you deal with the language problem? (LCCI, PSC)

15. You are secretary to Mr Colin Gibson, Training Manager of Comlon International plc. Mr Gibson has decided that all trainees and apprentices will begin their training with Comlon International plc on Thursday 1 September 198– and that their first day should consist of an introductory session, followed by a tour of the works and offices. You are asked to organise the first part of the day from the welcome by the Managing Director until after lunch when the guided tours will begin.

Mr Gibson has indicated that he would like the programme to include a brief history of the firm, a description of its activities, proposed developments, and any other topic you may think appropriate or of interest to young trainees.

Prepare a checklist for organising the morning session and lunch, indicating when action would be initiated, and enclose copies of all relevant correspondence sent by you prior to 1 September, and include a draft of the programme for the day. (LCCI, PESD, Sec. Admin.)

16. What alternatives are there to holding a meeting face-to-face? Discuss the advantages and disadvantages of these remote conference facilities.

17. A Senior Manager of your medium-sized private company is retiring after 20 years' service. You are asked to arrange an informal buffet lunch for him and his wife. Prepare a timetable to ensure that the arrangements are carried out in a logical order for a successful farewell presentation. (LCCI, PSC)

18. You work for a large nation-wide charitable organization. What factors would you consider when suggesting a suitable date and venue for a one-day conference of branch delegates that your employer is to organize? The chair is to be taken by the president, a well-known public figure. The agenda, to be sent out in advance, will include suggestions from branches for a new fund-raising campaign. Detailed financial statements and reports will be needed from each branch for duplication at head office before the conference. (LCCI, PSC)

19. A new chairman has been appointed to head your medium-sized company and a press conference is to be held to introduce him to

members of the press and, through them, the public. As Personal Assistant to the press officer it is largely your responsibility to make the conference arrangements. Draw up a work schedule listing action to be taken before, during and after the conference, which will be held in the boardroom suite where all company meetings take place. (LCCI, PESD)

Group activities

20. If possible attend a meeting of your local authority council or one of its committee meetings that are open to the public, and observe the meetings procedure followed. You may be able to attend as a group. If not, hold a discussion on the different meetings attended by the members.

21. With the co-operation of your tutor, select seven members of your class to hold a meeting of your school or college students' council, appointing one as chairman. Items to be discussed could include: Need for improved facilities in students' canteen; Rag Day (a) suggestions for charities to be supported (b) preliminary arrangements for students' evening concert; proposal for second-hand textbooks stall during the first week of next session. Type out a notice of meeting and an agenda, adding any other appropriate items you consider necessary. Prepare also a chairman's agenda. Those not taking part in the meeting should write either minutes or a report of the meeting. (If a recording is available, committee members can also take the minutes after play-back.)

23
Planning and priorities, reception, and reminders

23.1 In the office: Receiving visitors— a mix-up in appointments

'Mr Green of JKL Co. has arrived. He has an appointment with Mr Grey at 10.30,' the receptionist tells you on the internal telephone.

Mr Green? You don't recollect anything about such an appointment. In fact, you thought Mr Black, a very important client, was due then. To give yourself time to sort the matter out, you say 'Thank you. Would you please ask him to take a seat? I'll be along to see him.'

Hastily you look in your own diary. There is no mention of Mr Green at all—only Mr Black. You can't check with your boss, Mr Grey, as he does not wish to be disturbed, but in any case you compared his diary entries with yours only an hour ago, so you are sure he has nothing down about Mr Green.

You must take action quickly, and get Mr Green removed from reception before Mr Black arrives and announces *his* appointment for the identical time. Neither will have a high opinion of your company's efficiency if that happens!

Fortunately, Mr Black has not arrived, so you are able to escort Mr Green safely to your room, relieve him of his coat and settle him down with a newspaper. You must find out the purpose of his visit so you say casually, 'Oh, Mr Green, you want to see Mr Grey in connection with . . . ?' and pause hopefully. A little surprised, Mr Green answers, 'My trip to South America next month.'

'Oh, yes, of course,' you reply. 'I shan't keep you a moment.'

Mr Grey is now free in readiness for Mr Black and is horrified by what you tell him. He remembers that he made the appointment with Mr Green when they met recently outside the office but quite forgot to transfer it to his office diary. As Mr Black is announced, he just has time to say, 'Ask White to see him—about South American agents—and I'll come along as soon as I'm free.'

With a pleasant smile and a 'Good morning' to Mr Black, you retreat into the corridor and hurry along to explain the situation to Mr White, who, fortunately, is free and says he will join Mr Green in a few minutes.

This means that you must make some excuse to Mr Green, whose appointment is already five minutes overdue. 'Mr Grey is so sorry to keep you waiting, Mr Green', you say. 'Something unforeseen has occurred (true enough!), but he hopes to be with you shortly. Meanwhile, he's asked our Mr White to talk to you, as he has all the information about South American agents.'

Mr Green looks at his watch, frowns and replies rather brusquely, 'Ah, I see. I hope he'll be along soon, as I've another appointment at 11.45.' However, he calms down a little when you offer him a cup of coffee, and is actually smiling by the time Mr White appears!

You heave a sigh of relief. You have saved your boss's face without resorting to a lie, and the awkward situation is resolved.

23.2 The daily routine

Although no two days ever follow the same pattern, it is important to try to follow a daily routine. This ensures that essential, regular activities are not forgotten, even if they have to be postponed on occasion.

Punctual arrival in the mornings helps. You can

then get yourself tidied up and organized before your boss arrives. A late start can sometimes ruin a whole day—especially if it is the morning when the chairman telephones with a message and you are not there! See that your boss's room is in order and the desk tidy. Open his or her diary at the correct page, or put out a typed list of the day's appointments. Then get out your own working materials, prepare your typewriter, and organize your desk for action. If you are responsible for opening the mail, this should be done before the boss arrives. It is also a good time to clear up filing and to look out files and documents that will be needed later.

At the end of the day, tidy your own desk, to avoid an accumulation of papers and to make sure that no important job is outstanding. When you leave, see that no papers are left out that might fall to the floor and be swept away by the cleaners.

23.3 Managing the time available

Many activities enter into a typical day, and each has its own place and importance. You must learn to switch quickly from one to another, regarding interruptions not as annoyances, but merely as changes of activity.

The way in which you manage your time is, of course, affected by how well organized your boss is. If he or she is disorganized you must accept the challenge and try to improve matters—a real test of your tact and diplomacy. If inefficiency in your office spills over to affect service departments and other staff, it is essential for you to take action. Encourage your boss to reserve certain periods of the day for giving dictation, discussing staff queries, planning immediate and future activities, etc. A more organized day may incidentally involve more delegation of work to you, giving greater job satisfaction. Suggested reforms stand a better chance of adoption by your boss if you can make them appear to have emanated from him (or her)!

In spite of all this, if one type of work is regularly completed only at another job's expense, something is wrong. Perhaps you are being asked to do too much. If you think so, point it out to your superior. Perhaps more automation is the answer, or a rethink of your job description. But take care that it is not your own inefficiency or inability to plan and establish priorities that is at fault.

There are some activities that occur in the course of most secretaries' working day:

23.4 Using appointments systems

(a) Diaries

Your boss will have his or her own business diary, containing details of engagements. As you may not always have access to this make a habit of copying the entries into your own.

Your own diary will contain details of your own activities as well: jobs you have in mind (like ordering supplies, sending out notices of meetings, making telephone calls, etc.); planning for future events—e.g., possible items for inclusion on an agenda or notes on the various stages of a bigger project, such as arranging a conference or overhauling a filing system. At the close of the day always check through the diaries to make sure that nothing is overlooked, and transfer any outstanding entries to the next appropriate day. At the same time, preview the next day's entries to see if any advance action needs to be taken.

(b) Appointment sheets

These are typed lists of a day's appointments and are less bulky to carry than a diary, when the boss's appointments are away from the office.

(c) Itinerary

This is a detailed, specialized list of engagements and arrangements and is used when the boss is undertaking a journey (see **21.1**).

(d) Year planner

This is a type of visual display, outlining the main events of a calendar year. Different types of engagements or jobs to be undertaken can be represented by distinctive types of symbol adhering to the surface. A planner gives a useful superficial view of activities but detailed information is not possible. Five-year planners are also available.

(e) Visual control boards (see also **20.3**)

In some organizations these are maintained to show the movements of key personnel for the benefit of senior management. They depict the location of staff rather than detailed information about their engagements.

(f)   Electronic diaries

Details of appointments are keyed in for computer storage and are recalled to the visual display screen when required. Recall may be under whatever heading is required, e.g., name, date, time, type of appointment, etc. These systems are also useful when a suitable time for an appointment needs to be arranged between a number of people. The computer checks and compares entries in all the diaries and displays a list of dates and times when all are free. A message notifying everyone concerned may be sent instantaneously by electronic mail (see Figure 23.1).

23.5   In a nutshell: Handling appointments

- Note in your own diary all your boss's appointments for handy reference and to avoid double bookings.
- Check that all new appointments are entered in both.
- As soon as possible, obtain your boss's confirmation of appointments you have made. Experience will teach you what type of person your boss is usually willing to see.
- If in doubt, make a provisional appointment only, especially if an engagement extends into after-office hours or involves his or her spouse.
- Obtain the caller's telephone number, in case of later queries. Confirm in writing any appointment made verbally.
- Notify receptionist of expected visitors.
- Delete cancelled appointments immediately.
- If your boss has caused the cancellation offer the other party another date and time, if appropriate.
- Check with the calendar both the date of the month and the day of the week of an appointment.
- Keep a note of your boss's regular activities, outside and inside the office, to avoid making appointments at these times.
- Allow your boss time to travel from one engagement to another when making several appointments for the same day.

23.6   Keeping reminder systems

Your boss should be able to depend upon you for a reminder of matters which have to be dealt with. The simpler the reminder system the better, otherwise you will generate more work than the problem is worth. Sometimes, merely applying the principles of efficient filing and indexing is sufficient—e.g., keeping documents in obvious places where they catch your attention, maintaining files for separate jobs complete with instructions on procedures to follow at specified times, using colour in filing and card index systems to draw attention to different categories of documents and types of jobs. However, the following methods are some of those commonly used:

(a)   Diary notes

A note in a diary may be sufficient, but if too many small details are written there, important appointments may be difficult to disentangle.

(b)   Card index tickler system

Reserving a card index for brief memos or notes about future action is helpful. You will need 12 guide cards, each labelled with the name of a month, and 31 index cards numbered consecutively. File each memo as it arises behind a guide card, so that all notes regarding action to be taken in any one month are grouped together. Then at the beginning of the current month, take your memos for that month and sort them into order of date of desired action, slipping each behind its appropriate index card.

(c)   Cabinet drawer tickler system

This is a similar system, but using folders in a filing cabinet drawer. Slip into the folders duplicate

Figure 23.1 Executel, an intelligent loudspeaking telephone with diary, directory and reminder facilities for external and internal calls. Diary entries covering a 20-year period may be keyed in and stored, with instant recall to screen of any day's entries. An alarm may be programmed to sound as a reminder of meetings or appointments. The machine automatically compiles a monthly planner from all the diary entries. Automatic dialling is provided to any of 250 entries in a stored telephone directory. These entries can be cross-indexed into convenient groupings, e.g., types of business or internal departments. Automatic dialling without reference to the directory is provided to any person listed in the directory whose name also appears on a diary page or on a notepad page for informal jottings. Arithmetic can be done on the inbuilt calculator, which can also store up to seven different numbers that are repeatedly used, e.g., discount rates. Changeable information personal to the user is stored on a special cassette which can be taken out and used at another terminal if convenient. The telephone offers abbreviated dialling and automatic redialling of an engaged number that has just been called. A handset is provided for confidential calls.

The telephone may be linked to a secretarial unit which can be used as an intercom. It also enables a secretary to access and maintain directory and diary entries. Calls to the main unit can be intercepted by the secretary and switched through if required.

Both units can also be used as electronic mail terminals, and and as viewdata terminals enabling telex messages to be sent via Prestel line (see **19.8** *(a)*). Courtesy of STC Telecommunications Ltd) carbon copies of letters and memos, as well as rough notes of your own composition.

(d) File reservation notebook

Keep a notebook of files to be withdrawn for action. Write the file names or numbers in a notebook indexed according to date and cross the items off as they are dealt with. By means of a similar register, clerks operating a central filing system can reserve files for executives wanting these on specified dates.

(e) Pending files and trays

If correspondence cannot be dealt with at once because further information is first awaited, it can be placed in a pending (waiting) tray, with a note attached to explain its presence. A pending file serves a similar purpose. In either case, the contents must be regularly reviewed in case it proves necessary to chase up the information required. This type of correspondence should not be allowed to build up, otherwise time is wasted sorting through it and others may be inconvenienced by the delay in completing the matters in hand.

(f) Electronic reminders

Reminders for the day stored in advance in computer memory may be recalled to the VDU screen, along with any general notices still held in your boss's electronic mailbox (see **13.9**).

23.7 Reception arrangements

(a) Large organizations

In a large organization, reception of visitors may be a full-time occupation. A register of callers is usually kept, with a note of the person to whom each is referred. This is useful for providing statistics of work handled and for any executive who wishes to check up later on some detail; it also helps a new receptionist to learn to whom to send callers, since the record should be amended if a caller is subsequently redirected. Sometimes a card index is maintained which can be consulted for details of callers who have paid visits to the firm before. The receptionist also keeps an appointments register: this records the names of expected visitors, the arranged time of their arrival and the executive awaiting them. It is usually the responsibility of the

executive's secretary to let the receptionist have these details in advance. When an unexpected visitor arrives the receptionist may consult the secretary in the first place to discuss what action to take.

In many cases, there are special waiting rooms or open-plan areas where visitors can wait in comfort, and where newspapers, periodicals, and literature concerning the organization's work are provided.

Messengers may be on duty to conduct callers to executives or executives' secretaries may sometimes do this. For security reasons, it is usually inadvisable to leave visitors unescorted (see **24.4***(b)*(i) for entry passes and other security arrangements affecting reception).

Receptionists can sometimes fit in other jobs, such as routine typewriting that is not urgent or confidential and does not need continuous concentration. Working a busy telephone switchboard at the same time is often not practicable, as either the telephone caller or the personal caller is likely to be kept waiting. A good internal communication system (e.g., internal telephones, pocket pagers, etc.—see **13.3** *(d)* and **13.13**) is essential to enable a receptionist to contact an executive or his secretary quickly, with, of course, a list of departments, specifying extension and room numbers of executive and secretarial staff. Stored electronic directories enable updated lists of staff, together with extension and room numbers, names of deputies, etc., to be stored on computer and recalled to screen as required. Annotations may be keyed in against names as applicable e.g., 'on holiday', 'at conference', etc. Where a flexible working hours system is operated, receptionists particularly need to be kept in touch with staff's hours of attendance, either through secretaries, the personnel department or time recorder indicator panels (see **12.11** *(c)*).

(b) Small organizations

In a small organization you may have to combine secretarial and reception duties. You must create a favourable impression of your organization in visitors' minds, make them feel welcome and direct them to the right person and place. It is not difficult to deal with callers with definite appointments with particular people, but unexpected visitors can pose problems. You must find out tactfully why they have come and what status they hold, so that you do not involve a senior member of staff in a routine enquiry or a junior in a matter requiring some authority.

(c) Your boss's visitors

Even a secretary not otherwise engaged in reception duties must make her boss's visitors welcome. If a caller has to wait in your room, see that he is seated in a comfortable and convenient position. Unless you know him quite well, it is wise not to get engaged in prolonged conversation, as he may be trying to 'pump' you for information; anyway, this would prevent you from getting other work done. Anticipate expected visitors by checking your boss's diary, by reminding him or her about them and by getting out relevant papers and files. No one with an appointment should have to wait, but if the caller arrives very late and finds your boss has embarked on some other task, a delay is not unreasonable.

(d) Shielding your boss

You must try to compromise between letting anyone see your boss who asks to do so, and being such a dragon that even visitors he would have liked to see can't get past you. If you consider that seeing a certain caller will probably waste your boss's time, suggest instead a more appropriate member of staff, or say you think your boss's time is already fully reserved and perhaps a telephone conversation another time would be more suitable, or propose that the caller writes in to enable your boss to consider the matter. If all this is to no avail, explain the situation to your boss (in person rather than on the internal telephone). If he or she agrees reluctantly to see the caller, you can explain to the latter that your boss happens to have a few minutes free before his next appointment—as a hint to keep the proceedings short. It is also possible to 'rescue' your boss, perhaps by taking in a note or telephoning at a prearranged time, to give the caller an impression that another visitor is waiting. For the sake of good public

relations, it may sometimes be unwise to antagonize a caller who may have travelled at some expense and inconvenience to see your boss, foolish though he may have been not to make an appointment. These cases especially you should refer to your boss as the final arbiter.

Note In dissuading a caller, avoid telling a direct lie. Apart from the moral issue involved, you would succeed only in humiliating your boss, your company and yourself if your deceit were discovered.

(e) Dealing with salesmen

You should be especially cautious when dealing with unknown travelling salesmen. Unless your boss's work is in their field, he or she probably won't want to be troubled, and you yourself must take care not to commit your organization in any way to buying new products without asking someone else in authority. (You must, of course, recognize your organization's regular suppliers.) Particularly avoid signing any unfamiliar documents. If appropriate, take the salesman's card and make a note of the goods he has to offer that might prove useful. Be as courteous to a salesman as to any other visitor: he is only doing the job he is paid to do.

(f) Dealing with the press

Refer journalists and press reporters to a senior member of the staff. Many companies have public relations officers or press officers who can quickly provide them with accurate information in the required form. Should your company be 'in the news' for any reason, be extremely careful in case some unguarded comment of yours is misconstrued or taken out of context. It is best to say as little as possible on such occasions. A journalist primed with the right information about your company can prove most helpful in promoting its public image, so do not necessarily regard him as an enemy to be fended off at all costs.

23.8 Did you know?

1. In *Whitaker's Almanack,* you can consult a perpetual calendar, enabling you to find out on what day of the week any date (AD) falls.

2. The chief difficulty with reminder systems is remembering to use them.

Activities

1. You are employed as Secretary to the Personnel Manager. A number of embarrassing moments have occurred recently due to your employer, yourself and the receptionist making appointments for employees to see your employer resulting in two, and somtimes three, people arriving at the office at the same time.

Explain how you might tackle this problem in order to avoid the likelihood of it happening again. (LCCI, SSC)

2. You are a minuting secretary at a Committee Meeting arranged by your employer, scheduled to end at 1200 today. Because important business is still outstanding, it is agreed at 1215 that the meeting be adjourned at 1230, to resume at 1430 for 1 hour. A Sub-committee (including your employer) appointed during the morning session is to meet over a working lunch and report back at the afternoon session, which the Personnel Manager or deputy is to be asked to attend. You do not have to minute the Sub-committee meeting but you must prepare a summary of the morning discussion, for circulation to the full Committee after lunch. Describe the action you would take between 1215 and 1430. (LCCI, PSC)

3. As secretary to a busy executive, what steps would you take in your daily routine that would lessen the inconvenience caused to your employer and the colleagues who would be dealing with your work if you were unexpectedly absent from the office for a few days? (LCCI, PSC)

4. It is 9 a.m. and the following jobs have to be done before your employer, Mr Brown, sets off this evening on a business trip. He expects to be out of the office from 9.45 a.m. until about 2.30 p.m. but hopes to look in for a quarter of an hour at 12 noon

Finish typing draft report for Mr Brown to vet before urgent circulation to staff concerned.
Take dictation arising from today's post—letter expected from Smith will need urgent reply.
Obtain files from central filing relating to Mr Brown's appointments.
Book table for lunch for three, for 12.30 p.m., and let John Evans and Derek Jones (ABC Co.) know time and place.
Get statistics from sales department ready for 10 a.m. appointment.

Ring back Joan Smith (NB—they work flexible working hours).
Type final itinerary for Mr Brown.
Mr Brown to draw out cash from bank for trip.

(a) Comment on the factors you would need to consider when arranging these jobs in order of priority.

(b) Suggest measures that might have been taken which could have relieved the pressure (LCCI, PSC)

5. You often need to stay late to complete your work. What questions would you ask yourself to find out why? (LCCI, PSC)

6. Write a handout for secretaries emphasising the points that must be kept in mind when making appointments for their employers. (LCCI, PESD, Sec. Admin.)

7. Your predecessor kept a diary, which is really only suitable for appointments, and you eventually find a folder crammed full of items, scraps of paper, etc., which seems to be the reminder folder which was used. (a) How will you rectify these oversights? (b) What form of reminder would you suggest in order that these disasters do not occur again? (PEI, Sec. Prac. Inter.)

8. How should the Receptionist and the Secretary to a Middle Manager work together regarding the making of appointments and the reception of people to see the Manager with and without appointments? (LCCI, SSC)

9. Your employer, the Office Manager, has asked you to suggest items of furniture and equipment that you think will be necessary for a new central reception area. Present a suitable list, with reasons for your choice. Include in it the type of reference material and records you think would be helpful. (LCCI, PSC)

10. Rule up a diary page and make entries for your executive for the following engagements for Wednesday of next week: (a) morning visit with property agent to view building for possible new branch shop—travel by car—10 miles from office (b) appointment before lunch with Personnel Manager to discuss interviews for position of Manager-Manageress of proposed new branch; (c) immediately after lunch, meeting of all branch managers to consider and compare past three months' trading (d) visit to local further education college to give talk to possible trainee staff. Use

appropriate times, inserting other essential details as you think necessary. (PEI, Sec. Prac. Inter.)

11. What are the main qualities that an employer might look for in a Telephonist/ Receptionist?

Explain why you feel that each quality is important. (LCCI, SSC)

12. As a secretary to the Sales Manager, who is responsible for 8 representatives, you are required to carry out all shorthand and typing duties within the department. State and briefly explain your order of priority of work to be dealt with, bearing in mind that you are often requested to help with the Manager's correspondence concerning a local charity. *Your answer should relate to the Department.* (LCCI, PSC)

Group activities

Discuss the following situations in your group:

13. The reception of visitors is an important part of a secretary's duties. State how you would deal with the following situations: (a) An important client, who has an appointment, arrives on time, but you realize that your employer has not yet arrived back from a business lunch with another client. (b) A persistent salesman calls without an appointment. You know your employer has no time to see him, but you realize your firm will need to do business with him in the fairly near future. (c) An irate lady arrives and demands to see your employer regarding a complaint. He is, however, attending a meeting which you expect to last at least another hour. (LCCI, JSC)

14. (a) You work for the office manager of a large firm. A visitor arrives unexpectedly in your office, asking to see your employer, whom he says he knows personally. The office manager is engaged and you cannot contact him for another 20 minutes. The visitor seems to want to engage you in conversation, and you discover he is a reporter from the local press who wants to write an article about the firm. What would you do? (b) A visitor without an appointment has been conducted to your office from reception and has been given the impression that he could see your employer immediately. Reception have not passed on to you any details about him. How would you deal with this visitor? (LCCI, PSC)

15. Your employer, a busy sales manager, has outside engagements for most of today, though he has a gap between appointments in the early afternoon. He will be calling in at the office for a few minutes at about 10 a.m. and again just before it closes at 5 p.m. The following matters will need his attention (a) accumulated correspondence (b) telephone messages from potential customers (c) a telephone message from a sales representative who needs his advice before 3 o'clock (d) a request from one of the office staff who urgently needs to see him on what may be a very time-consuming matter.

What will you do to see that the short time your employer spends in the office today is used to the best effect? (LCCI, PSC)

24
The human factor

24.1 Human error

However carefully the organization, documentation and office services of a company are planned, and however well prepared and qualified the staff may be to carry out their duties, things may sometimes still go wrong as a result of human error. Errors of judgement may be made by the owners when formulating policy; the managers may under- or over-estimate resources or deal ineptly with staff, creating poor relationships; executives may misinterpret policy and take wrong decisions in their daily work; staff maintaining office services may make mistakes when completing documents, keying into computer systems from source documents, ordering supplies, passing on information, preparing documents for duplication, dealing with the mail, and filing. There is plenty of scope for error, too, where figures and charts are concerned, and in dealing with outside agencies. Machines—which, after all, are made and operated by human beings—may break down. The secretary also is just as susceptible to error. The causes are numerous, but lack of knowledge, inexperience, carelessness, and haste are among the most common.

24.2 Human weakness

Besides human error, there is human weakness, where someone yields to temptations of various kinds or even sets out deliberately to cause trouble, perhaps by exploiting the weaknesses of others.

24.3 Safeguards

As neither error nor weakness can be eliminated, both have to be allowed for. Safeguards include:

(a) Delegation of authority
A system of delegation of authority under which staff know what work they are expected to perform and to whom and for whom they are responsible, helps to create concern for results.

(b) Supervision
Adequate supervision, e.g., in typing and secretarial pools, within departments and on the factory floor, helps to reduce error and waste (see **24.7** below) and encourages efficiency.

(c) Checking
(i) By the person doing the job after completion—e.g., a secretary will check a letter she has typed.
(ii) By a second person or supervisor—e.g., the secretary's boss will check the letter before he signs it.
(iii) By a device on a machine which causes a person to check, e.g., a warning signal given by an electronic franking machine when a high rate of postage has been set.
(iv) By a procedure built into a system, e.g., the verification of the identities of the sender and receiver of a telex message.
(v) By a computer program being tested out in a sample run, or test data to which the answer is already known being used to test the integrity of a new system.

(d) Insurance
Insurance policies can be taken out to cover accident, theft, etc. (see **14.11**).

(e) Efficient staff selection
Improved selection techniques make it more likely

271

that the most suitable applicant for the post is chosen.

(f)   Efficient communication

Trouble can be averted or reduced if care is taken to communicate accurately (e.g., by giving clear and unambiguous messages and instructions) and promptly (e.g., by the management circulating authoritative information to prevent facts being distorted by ill-informed rumour).

(g)   Security precautions (see **24.4**)

24.4   Security of property and information

What is of value and confidential to a company may not always be obvious to more junior members of staff. Sales figures, ideas about future products, extracts from the accounts could be important to a competitor. As a secretary you may be privy to personal details of staff that they would not like to become common knowledge. Property and information need to be protected from theft, tampering, and unauthorized use. As such risks may come from outside or within an organization appropriate measures to combat them need to be wide-ranging.

(a)   General precautions

As a secretary you should be aware particularly of the following security aspects:

(i) *Need for discretion*   If you are concerned in any way with confidential matters—e.g., staffing, policy discussions, and decisions—resist the temptation to talk about these to colleagues, some of whom may try to 'pump' you for information. In your own office a confidential conversation may carry farther than you imagine. Be even more careful with outside callers. Casual 'shop talk' with a colleague on public transport may prove of great interest to another traveller.

(ii) *Discouraging thefts*   Handbags, wallets, and purses should not be left where they may tempt potential thieves: not all thefts are premeditated.

Keep cash and other valuables locked away—and don't leave the keys close at hand where an intruder could easily find them.

(iii) *Keys*   Duplicates of desk keys may be easily obtainable, as they are often repeated by the manufacturers. The safest locks are those with registered keys, which can only be replaced upon authorization by the original holder. Combination locks used on safes offer a high degree of protection.

In some organizations, keys are kept and issued centrally, and returned by the users on leaving the premises. An index needs to be kept: colour coding used in this and on the key tabs can be helpful in indicating the department, location, grade or function of the members of staff concerned. Duplicate keys can be held for emergency use.

(iv) *Secret and highly confidential information*   It is wise to keep a register of all highly confidential documents and those regarded as 'classified' (secret) under the Official Secrets Act, recording by whom each copy is held at any one time. Keep the number of copies to the minimum, and make and distribute extra copies only when authorized to do so by one of the holders. Number each copy and indicate its place in the total set—e.g., 4 of 5 refers to the fourth copy in a set of five. You should use recorded delivery when sending a copy by post.

At a meeting it is wise to distribute confidential documents in numbered folders and to note to whom each is issued. On collection, check the contents. If documents do not need to be studied at length they can be displayed on an overhead projector screen and thus do not need to be distributed.

Use a shredder (see Figure 24.2) to destroy confidential documents—torn-up pieces of paper or carbon or a discarded carbon ribbon in a wastepaper basket can be reassembled and read. Special shredders are obtainable for destroying microfilm.

To protect information displayed on wall charts from scrutiny by callers, the axes can be left unmarked, and annotated strips prepared which can be held alongside the charts when required. Avoid leaving confidential documents lying on your desk when temporarily leaving the room. Take anything confidential out of your typewriter, or turn the paper up or down so that important passages are hidden. Similarly, scroll text out of sight if you are word processing.

"The acoustic screens are perfectly positioned – I can hear everything that's going on!"

Figure 24.1 (Courtesy of Tony Holland. First published in *Business Systems and Equipment*)

Insert confidential letters into their envelopes rather than leaving this to be done by mailroom staff.

(v) *Incoming mail* Incoming mail containing remittances must be kept secure from theft. Precautions include providing staff supervision and keeping adequate records. Threats to office security may also arise in the shape of postal bombs. If you are opening mail, examine letters and packets with care if any unusual feature causes you to be suspicious—e.g., undue weight for the size packet, lopsided appearance, greasy marks or small holes in the packing, an unusual smell, very heavily gummed envelope flaps, or protruding wires. Leave such packets severely alone, and tell your firm's security officer or the police. Some firms use metal detectors, which emit a noise when in contact with metal. Screening devices are also obtainable which X-ray suspect packages and can be operated by remote control.

(b) Organizational precautions

Some security arrangements affect a firm's organization and procedures:

(i) *Reception* On arrival, visitors may be issued with identity discs which they hand in on departure. They may be asked to deposit any bags or cases in the

Figure 24.2 An office shredder. (Courtesy of OBM)

reception area. If possible they are not left unescorted. Staff may carry passes authorizing them to enter sensitive areas. Many companies issue employees with laminated identity cards, incorporating a photograph of the holder.

(ii) *Telephone bomb threats* A switchboard operator may be required to follow a prearranged drill on receipt of a telephoned bomb threat, passing on the warning immediately to a designated person in authority. She must keep calm and if possible engage the caller in conversation in case she can pick up some clues to his or her identity which may help the police. Meanwhile, a search of the premises should be conducted and staff evacuated.

(iii) *Protection of premises* Precautions may include

high fences to make unauthorized entry more difficult, and guard dogs and watchmen patrols during non-business hours. Burglar alarms may be installed to help to detect intruders, and devices such as closed circuit television and hidden cameras and microphones linked to the company's security office or an agency security centre. Some areas may be protected by electronic locks which can only be released by authorized staff pressing certain combinations of push-buttons on door panels or by inserting pre-punched cards.

(iv) *Machinery* Security arrangements are desirable with some machines. For example franking machines may be locked to prevent unauthorized use at the end of the day, and the date changed in advance. Two keys, held by two different people, may be needed to operate cheque signers. The use of copiers may be restricted by making it necessary to insert a key counter which activates the machine and records the number of copies taken. Outgoing telephone calls can be restricted by dial-locks on some instruments or barring devices on switchboards affecting certain extensions. Incoming telex messages can be protected from view if wound automatically on to a spool beneath a locked cover.

(v) *Wages and cash* Where wages are not paid by cheque or credit transfer (see **14.3** *(d)*) large sums of money may have to be collected from the bank. This can be undertaken by security agencies specially equipped for the work. Staff collecting or delivering cash, even if the amount is small (which would not be known to a potential thief) would do well to vary times and routes, facing oncoming traffic if on foot, to avoid being trailed by a car. Special security cases are available which emit a shrill noise or smoke or dye when violently snatched. Wages routines are usually under careful supervision and staff's duties rotated to reduce the risk of fraud from within.

(vi) *Documents* Some documents representing value to the company need special precautions before being dispatched. For example, counter-signatures authorizing orders and requisitions are common, invoices and statements of account must be passed for payment by a person in authority, entries in remittances books must be countersigned, and outgoing cheques require more than one signature.

24.5   Security within computer systems

Security is becoming more difficult to achieve because so many organizations and individuals have access to computers and are conversant with the techniques used to preserve security. As well as the possibility of unauthorized disclosure of information there is a risk of corrupting financial transactions, since funds are regularly transferred by electronic messages. Security can be promoted by:

(a)   Passwords

A user is allocated a password to allow access to the system. In large systems the password is used to select a route through the filing system of the computer, so that the user is limited as to which files he can have access to and how he can use them. For instance, he may be able only to interrogate the files, whereas a senior member of a company may be allowed to change their contents. A company's financial files, for example, may be accessible only to senior personnel such as directors, the company secretary, or senior accountant.

Computer filing systems usually incorporate directories, which give the addresses of the files available in the backing stores and list the people permitted to use them and the manner of their use. The user of a file can lay down rules on the way in which his own files may be used and by whom, and can change these rules as necessary. A computer can be programmed to log the use of all files, giving the identity of the user of each and the date, and this record can be printed out as required.

(b)   Encryption

Security may be at risk when data is transmitted on public networks. Encryption devices or *scramblers* can be used, which scramble the signals leaving the telephone before they enter the modem and unscramble them after leaving the modem at the other end.

(c)   Security programs

Security programs are available but these are slow to run and use valuable space in primary memory.

They check to see who has been accessing each file.

(d) Non-erasable storage

Non-erasable storage media such as optical disks can be an advantage because unauthorized addition or deletion is not possible, e.g., the addition of fictitious names to a payroll, or insertion of instructions into a program causing payment to be made to fictitious suppliers, and then deletion of evidence of the fraudulent transaction.

24.6   In a nutshell: Data Protection Act 1984

- The Act protects personal data about living, identifiable individuals.
- The data must be held on automatically processed systems.
- Data Subjects are the individuals about whom data is held.
- Data Users are persons and organizations who control the use and contents of such data.
- Data Users and computer bureaux must register with the Data Protection Registrar. They must describe in their register entries the data held, why it is held, where they obtained it and to whom they will disclose it.
- Data Users must comply with eight internationally agreed principles of data protection, i.e., data must be:

  obtained fairly and lawfully;
  held only for the purpose specified in the register entry;
  disclosed only as set out in the register entry unless otherwise required to do so by law or for
      national security or to prevent injury or damage to health;
  adequate, relevant and not excessive for the purpose;
  accurate and up to date;
  kept no longer than necessary;
  made available to Data Subjects on request;
  properly protected against loss or disclosure.

- Data Subjects have the right of access to data, except in certain cases, and are entitled to have it corrected or erased.
- Data Subjects are entitled to compensation if they suffer damage from inadequately protected or inaccurate data.
- Certain data is exempt from the Act if, for example, it is:

  on mailing lists of names and addresses;
  held for national security purposes;
  held only for payroll and accounting purposes;
  held for preparing text of documents, e.g., on a word processor.

- The Date Protection Registrar has power to investigate complaints, and can issue: an enforcement notice requiring compliance by a User breaching the principles; a transfer prohibition notice preventing the User transferring information abroad, if doing so might lead to a breach of the Principles; a deregistration notice preventing User from processing personal data automatically. Appeals against notices may be made to the Data Protection Tribunal. Courts enforce legislation where an offence has been committed, and if compensation is involved. They can issue Court Orders to Users.

24.7   Waste

Waste can occur in several forms—e.g., waste of time (through procrastination, slow working, inefficient methods), waste of effort (through cumbersome equipment, badly-worded instructions), waste of materials (through thoughtlessness, lack of skill resulting in repeated attempts at a job, misappropriation, poor choice of materials). Wasteful habits can be discouraged by better supervision, stricter control over timing and output and the issue of supplies and stock, and by drawing employees' attention to the cumulative effects of waste.

24.8   Need for motivation

In addition to error and malpractice, the efficiency of an organization can be seriously reduced by staff discontent. This may result from poor working conditions (which the Factories Acts, the Health and Safety at Work Act and the Offices, Shops and Railway Premises Act are designed to improve), or from serious strife between employers and employees which has brought about labour relations legislation (see Appendix II). Sometimes it may be the fault of managers and organizers in tending to treat subordinate staff more like machines than people.

In some ways, machines and people *are* alike: they may both cease to function if given unsuitable jobs or too much or too intensive work; they both need inspection and an occasional overhaul; they may both have to be retired from service and replaced. In other ways, they are quite unlike: a machine is designed for repetitive work, but a person tends to like variety and change; if it has no defects a machine always co-operates, but a person may become awkward and rebellious; a machine's performance is constant, but a person's may vary according to mood and circumstance; a machine needs no reward for past services or inducement to future ones, but a person needs to be recognized and encouraged, to feel satisfied by the work itself and the rewards received for performing it; unless it is modified, a machine cannot improve on its output, but a person may achieve very little or reach great heights. People have feelings. They will do their work much more happily if they can see the purpose of it, and if their

superiors can present them with a worthwhile goal, not for themselves alone but for the whole organization.

24.9   Unexpected situations

Although you obviously can't prepare totally for the unexpected event you can cope with it more easily if, for example:

> you are well organized, so that you can find anything needed in a hurry;
> your work is up to date, so that a crisis won't bring other crises in its wake;
> you know where your boss is supposed to be at any one time, in case you need advice or need to contact others who should be with him or her;
> you are aware of departmental and company organization (executives and their deputies) in case you need to contact someone outside your own section.

Your company will have devised its own ways of meeting emergencies by, for example:

> training staff in first-aid;
> installing back-up generators in case of power failure;
> devising firefighting routines, etc.

For your part, ensure that crises don't occur because of lack of foresight or because of procrastination in tackling tedious or distasteful tasks.

24.10   Relationships between individuals

An organization is made up of individuals, and in the last resort it is the relationship between those individuals that contributes most towards their happiness in their work. These internal relationships are not the only ones that matter: staff must also communicate with the general public, and it is the manner in which such dealings are handled that does much to enhance or diminish the organization's image. Coping with human relationships is really the business of living, but there are some particularly important to you, the secretary, in your job:

(a) Relations with the public

When face to face with a customer or client, your expression, your dress, and your general demeanour colour much of what you say and influence the other person. When speaking on the telephone, inflection and tone of voice are all-important, and when writing a letter it is choice of words and neatness of display that count. On such occasions you are an unofficial public relations officer for your company—and for your boss, whom you are directly representing. Your courtesy, efficiency, and willingness to help reflect on them. Especially when dealing with a complaint, use your discretion and tact. It may not always be diplomatic to reveal all the circumstances which led to an error on the company's part. For instance, it will certainly not help public relations if you try to justify your own or your boss's actions by throwing blame on to another department or member of staff.

(b) Relations with the boss

This is the crucial relationship, for you must be able to work together in harmony. You may both be admirably equipped for your jobs, but if your personalities clash, you would be better apart.

It is your place to work with your boss in the service of your organization. Your boss is your superior in the firm's hierarchy and you must do as he or she asks. If for some reason you are not prepared to do this and cannot respect your boss as a person, you should resign or ask to be transferred to another department. It would be wrong to stay on and not give your complete loyalty.

Your relationship is based on co-operation, which breaks down if either party defaults. Is either of you hampering the other's work or making life less pleasant than it could be?

If you have to work for two people, friction can result if a regular pattern is not worked out for the division of your time. Becoming a buffer between them is undesirable. You must be seen by both to use efficient systems—e.g., separate appointment diaries, shorthand notebooks, filing equipment, etc.; to be discreet in dealing with the confidential work of each; to be equally obliging to both; and to note their individual preferences.

(c) Relations with juniors

In many ways, you should treat junior colleagues as you would like your boss to treat you. If you pass a job over to a junior, explain clearly what is to be done, and let him or her have the satisfaction of completing it and the credit for doing it. This will encourage him or her to work thoroughly and improve skills. If you have to reprimand a junior, do it tactfully, without humiliating. Suggest action rather than demand it. Try to ensure that your own standards are high, but don't be ashamed to admit to an occasional error.

(d) Relations with servicing staff

Staff of servicing departments—e.g., the filing section, the copying room, must work to meet the requirements of many people, and they may not necessarily be able to meet yours immediately. You must certainly not be impatient or irritable with them if the fault is yours for not allowing for possible delays when planning the work.

(e) Relations with colleagues in general

Your colleagues will be a mixed bag—of different ages, backgrounds and temperaments. You may be drawn instinctively to some, but others you may not find so congenial. Make up your mind to be polite to the latter, but to avoid possible conflict don't have more to do with them than you can help. Avoid time-wasting gossip. If you have grievances, resist airing them to the whole office, or you may unsettle other hitherto contented people and become obsessed with what may be only minor contentions. Instead, tell your boss and get them sorted out—but don't let it appear that you are asking for preferential treatment: if others suspect you of trying to curry favour or of manipulating people or events for your own ends, you will become much disliked. Don't treat older or younger people as a race apart. They are all human beings with similar needs, hopes and fears to yours. Always treat others as you would like to be treated yourself.

24.11   In a nutshell: Some test questions on the boss–secretary relationship

The boss

- Does he (or she) treat you as an intelligent person with some initiative?
- Does he organize his work efficiently and hand jobs over to you in time for you to complete them without staying late?
- Does he take it out on you for no apparent reason?
- Does he let you take over a job and see it through, or must he have a finger in the pie throughout?
- Do you suspect that he blames you behind your back for mistakes he himself has made?
- Do you learn through others information he should have given you?
- Does he give you credit where credit is due?
- Is he considerate?

The secretary

- Do you arrive late and keep him or her waiting?
- Do you take advantage of his absences by leaving early or taking an extended lunch hour when you should be 'holding the fort'?
- Do you wear a long face when something is amiss in your private life?
- Are you secretly pleased if there is a muddle when you are away, showing that he can't manage without you?
- Do you denigrate him to others?
- Are you interested in your work or only in your pay packet?
- Do you stay late, without being asked, when there is urgent work to finish?
- Do you do tasks not listed in your job description when you know it will help out your boss?

Activities

1. Accuracy and attention to detail are essential in secretarial work. Mention some areas in your daily routine where accuracy is particularly important and how you would achieve it. (LCCI, PSC)

2. As a secretary, suggest how you could keep costs down and reduce waste.

3. Discuss the factors which motivate people to work hard. (LCCI, PESD)

4. You are responsible for the smooth running of the entire office. If the supervisor of the typing pool approaches you regarding the unpunctuality of one of the copy-typists, what series of steps would you take? Present your answer in a logical sequence. (PEI, Sec. Prac. Adv.)

5. Most days there appears to be someone, but not always the same person, who is up to 20 minutes late in your company. Give your suggestions as to how staff could be encouraged to be more punctual and how their time of arrival could be monitored. (LCCI, PSC)

6. At your end-of-year performance appraisal your manager has pointed out the following weaknesses. What steps would you take to remedy these?

(a) bad time-keeping
(b) nervousness in dealing with telephone enquiries
(c) difficulty in completing assignments on time
(d) inability to use the office junior's services to the best advantage. (LCCI, PSC)

7. You have recently been involved in preparing a confidential report. A junior member of staff has told you of information contained in that report which was only to be seen by the Directors of the company and yourself. What would you do and how would you prevent this happening again? (LCCI, PSC)

8. You are secretary to the senior partner of your firm. His duties include the recruitment of new staff, in consultation with other partners or senior staff concerned with particular appointments. A new audio-typist tells you she is disturbed to realize how much her fellow-typists in the 'pool' appear to

know already about her personal background. Suggest how this information might inadvertently have been disclosed and how the situation could be avoided in the future. (LCCI, PSC)

9. The organization you work for handles top secret information which could be of use to unscrupulous competitors. Naturally, businessmen from other companies must visit your offices but what arrangements could be made to minimize the security risk presented by visitors? (LCCI, PSD)

10. In what respect is there a possible need for confidentiality and security of information within the business organization? (RSA, DPA)

11. Suggest measures which might be taken in a firm to improve security in wages systems. (LCCI, PSC)

12. Because your boss is a poor dictator, the typists in the audiotyping centre waste much time and effort when transcribing his work. The supervisor hopes that you, his personal secretary, may be able to suggest tactfully to him some ways in which he might improve his methods, as he makes constant amendments, gives muddled instructions and frequently pauses for long periods in the course of a letter. How would you approach your boss and what would you tell him? (Refer, as necessary, to **16.** for your answer.)

13. What qualities are needed on the part of both employer and secretary to make an ideal working relationship? (LCCI, PSC)

14. Ten car parking spaces hitherto allocated to some of the staff are to be reserved for visitors in future and substitute spaces in a less convenient area will be offered to the staff. Discuss possible ways of notifying the staff displaced (e.g., memo, notice, etc.) and say which you think would be most suitable. (LCCI, PSC)

15. You are secretary to Mr Colin Gibson, Training Manager of Comlon International plc. One morning Mr Gibson, who is normally punctual, fails to arrive at the office when expected. How will you deal with this situation? (LCCI, PESD, Sec. Admin.)

16. **Group activity**   Discuss the following situation: Your employer is concerned about friction caused by two typists in your office who do not get on well together. One is a widow in her fifties, rather staid and set in her ways, and not in tune with the modern generation. She shows little initiative (though she has had varied office experience) but is very accurate and reliable. The other is a girl of 18, willing but careless, of lively personality and leading an apparently dazzling social life. You are the third person in the room, and the senior in rank. What attitude will you adopt and what means will you devise to bring more harmony into the office?

Appendix I: Summary of the principal Post Office services

The following is a brief summary of the principal available Post Office services, but there may be other services provided in certain areas on which information can be obtained locally. An example is Nightrider, a next-day parcels delivery service available in the Greater London area. The Post Office is also willing to discuss the provision of 'tailor-made' services for a business where a need exists and to negotiate contracts accordingly.

The information contained in this Appendix is up to date (1985), but you should check details in the current *Post Office Guide*.

1. Inland

First class service—delivery by next weekday after posting. Second class service—delivery by third weekday after posting.

(a) Letter post—first class

Advice of delivery: Available for registered and recorded delivery items. Extra fee, higher if service requested after posting.

Airway letters: By arrangement with British Airways letters taken to certain airport offices and sent by first available air service to destination, to be called for, or postal delivery. No valuables accepted. Postage, plus fee to British Airways.

Business reply service: Sender prints prepaid reply postcards or envelopes to design approved by Post Office, pays postage plus small fee on each reply received from clients; annual licence fee; deposit payable equal to one month's estimated charges. Replies delivered 1st class, daily on second delivery. *Priority service:* As above but delivery by first delivery in return for higher fee per item; discount available on the higher fee for high volume of replies.

Cash on delivery: See under *(c) Parcels* but packets and letters must be registered.

Discounts on first class letters: For minimum of 5000 letters (one-off) or fewer, if use is consistent. Must be pre-sorted by postcode or post towns; items identical in shape; posted between stipulated times, etc.

Recorded delivery: For items of no monetary value; nominal flat-rate compensation; sender has certificate of posting, Post Office proof of delivery. Postage plus fee.

Registration: For money and valuables; secure packing necessary; sender has certificate of posting, Post Office has proof of delivery. Compensation for loss or damage. Postage, plus fee on scale according to amount of compensation allowed for.

Royal Mail Special Delivery: Envelopes picked out from mail at delivery office for hand delivery if too late for ordinary delivery. Can include registered or recorded delivery packets. Postage plus fee. Sender has certificate of posting. Fee automatically refunded if item not delivered next day, if posted by latest recommended time of posting.

(b) Letter post—second class

Bulk rebate postings: Rebate between 15–30 per cent of postage payable according to number of packets posted at one time; to qualify, packets must be identical in shape and size, bundled and sorted as required by Post Office. At least 24 hours' notice must be given.

Business reply service: Available as for first class service ((a) above) but replies sent second class. *Priority service* as (a) above.

Discounts on second class letters: For minimum of 5000 letters (one-off) or fewer if use is consistent. Must be pre-sorted by postcode or post towns; items identical in shape; posted between stipulated times, etc. By contract.

Freepost: Similar to BRS but clients use own stationery, quoting advertiser's address containing word FREEPOST. *Priority service* (as for BRS Priority service).

Recorded delivery: Available as for first class service.

(c) Parcels

National rate
Area rates (for parcels to be delivered within same county or group of counties as sender).

Cash on delivery: Amounts to be collected for goods delivered is specified by sender, collected by postman on delivery of goods and remitted to sender by Girobank cheque. Postage plus fee. Special address label. For ordinary parcels, Compensation Fee parcels (see below) or Datapost packages (see below).

Compensation fee: Postage plus fee on scale for compensation allowed for; sender has certificate of posting. No special marking required; no special treatment in transit.

Contract services: For 1000+ parcels per annum by contract. Discount available. Simplified payment procedures.

Postage forward: Similar to BRS (letters) above but recipient uses printed label to return parcel without paying postage.

(d) Miscellaneous

Admail: Provides advertiser with local address for replies posted as a result of TV, press, radio or direct mail advertisements, and redirection if required to distant address.

Consequential loss insurance: Available through Post Office on registered items. Extra charge. Sender writes amount of cover required on Cover Note. Claims must be made on form 'Enquiry about a missing or damaged letter or parcel'.

Datapost—Overnight: Nationwide courier service for goods or documents. Next-day delivery guaranteed; if not, fee refunded. Items collected or handed in at Datapost post office. Discounts available for large users.

Datapost—Sameday: Fee payable on collection of goods and documents by courier, or by account for regular users (who may earn discount). Items delivered same day. Money back if not delivered same day. Travels separately from ordinary mail. High value goods not accepted.

Deposit accounts: For regular, large users; advance payment of estimated week's/month's postage, adjusted at end of period as necessary.

Electronic Post: Customer provides text of letters, etc., on computer tape; information transmitted electronically to one of six regional EP offices where text is printed, enveloped (plus enclosures if required), then posted for first class delivery. Customer's own letterheads and signatures can be used. Personalized insertions into text possible. *Standard service:* negotiated in advance for specified date; *Priority service* for urgent mailings. Processing done in secure conditions.

Franked mail: Machine obtainable from private manufacturers, prints stamp impressions; payments in advance necessary for postage credit; machine meters units used; control cards to post office each week; value cards can be purchased to reset certain makes of machine; or remote meter resetting via computer (see **7.4** *(b)* (iii)). Franked mail must be batched, faced up and handed in to post office or collected by mail van.

Franked by Post Office: Post Office will frank mail 'Paid' if advance arrangement made and posted at specified post office. Cash paid at time of posting or by deposit account. For 120+ postal packets or 20+ parcels.

Free collections: Of 1000+ letters; or 100+ parcels, or regular collections of 20 parcels.

Household delivery: Post Office will deliver unaddressed items to every address in a specified area from postman's round or specific postcode sector. Notice required. Carried out within two weeks of starting date.

Incentive growth discount: If inland letter postage amounts to more than specified sum each year discount may be given if 3 percent growth in real terms year by year. Up to 20 percent discount for real growth of 10 percent plus.

Intelpost: High speed facsimile service between Intelpost centres in UK. A4 documents. Hand in at centres or collected by messenger (extra fee). Recipient can collect copies (telephone advice of document awaiting can be arranged) or messenger delivery if within specified delivery area. Account holders can transmit from own facsimile machine to Intelpost centre for collection, messenger delivery or post; or via Intelpost centre direct to recipient's facsimile machine if compatible and if Post Office is informed of facsimile machine number.

Late Posting facility: On payment of extra fee in stamps, packets that would miss last collections from post offices can be posted in special boxes at London rail termini and other stations and transferred to mail trains' sorting compartments, enabling next-day delivery.

Poste restante: Letters and parcels addressed to a person at a post office; marked *poste restante* or *to be called for.* For convenience of travellers in an area; service may not be used in same town for more than three months. Proof of identity must be produced by addressee.

Printed postage impressions: (PPI)   Sender prints or stamps *postage paid* on envelopes, parcels, etc., and pays cash at time of posting at specified post office, or by account. Single postings of not less than 5000 letters, 1000 packets or 100 parcels. By prior arrangement.

Private box: Box at delivery office rented by addressee who collects own mail; annual charge.

Redirection by Post Office: Undertaken for periods of 1, 3 or 12 months provided official application made; fee payable.

Selectapost: Post Office delivers mail presorted into specified departments; for large organizations; fee by arrangement.

(e) Newspapers

Must be newspapers in course of distribution by publishers, printers, or agents and registered at Post Office; sent first class at second class rate if marked *Newspaper Post* and posted by the publishers in an agreed manner. Otherwise, normal rates apply.

2. Overseas

Air mail—Fast delivery; higher charge based on weight and zone of destination.

Surface mail—Slower delivery; lower charge based on weight and zone of destination.

(a) Letter post

This is the speediest service for items up to 2 kg.

To Europe: All-up (normal surface rates only payable and no air mail label required).

To outside Europe: Surface mail. Air mail labels or mark AIR MAIL. Aerogrammes: flat rates, no enclosures.

Express: Mark EXPRESS; red Express label; postage plus fee; normal post but fast delivery from delivery office; not available to all countries.

(b) Small packets

The cheapest service for goods up to 1 kg (or 500 g to some countries) and faster than parcels; wrapping must allow inspection; mark SMALL PACKET; can include samples; customs declaration.

(c) Parcels

Parcels can be sent to most countries; rates vary according to destination; limits on weight and size; customs declarations; International FDD (Franc de Droits) service (available to some countries) enables sender to prepay addressee's customs charges to reduce delay; certificate of posting.

Cash on delivery: Collection, on delivery, of trade charge specified by sender and remitted to sender by International Giro; not available to all countries. May be insured.

Express: See under *Letter Post* (above).

(d) Printed papers

Cheap rates available: ordinary rate for commercial items, e.g., circulars; and Printed Papers Reduced Rate for registered newspapers and books; wrapping must allow inspection; mark *Printed Papers/Printed Papers Reduced Rate*, as appropriate.

Bulk printed paper postings:

Direct agents bag: Surface mail; bulk postings to single addressee in another country; must be prepared in a specified manner.

Bulk air mail: To Europe; charges according to destination and size of consignment; sender must sort, bundle and bag postings on own premises before collection by Post Office.

Accelerated surface post: To some destinations outside Europe; surface transmission in UK and country of receipt, by air between countries; charge basis as for bulk air mail (see above). Contract service. Sender must sort, bundle and bag postings on own premises before collection by Post Office. Between air and surface mail in speed and price.

(e) Miscellaneous

Customs regulations: Necessary to consult *Post Office Guide* as customs declaration (green label/declaration form/despatch note) required varies from country to country. Some countries require commercial invoice plus certificate of origin (see **4.2**).

Insurance: Proof of posting; advice of delivery (if required); high degree of extra security during postal transmission; higher amount of cover beyond limits of registration service available for loss or damage; letters or parcels but not to all countries.

Intelpost: High speed facsimile service between Intelpost centres and 19 overseas countries. A4 documents. Hand in at centres or collected (extra fee). On arrival, copies called for (telephone message to say document has arrived can be arranged at some international offices) or messenger delivery if within delivery area.

International Datapost: Fast, reliable courier delivery service to 53 overseas countries—number continually increasing; business documents to all, and to some countries merchandise as well. Door to door prescheduled services available—or if *Datapost on demand* service used over-the-counter service to most countries on Datapost network.

International reply coupons: Exchangeable by addressee at post offices abroad for cost of surface mail reply to UK; flat rate; available to all countries.

Prohibitions: Items not allowed to be sent by mail listed in *Post Office Guide*—i.e., general prohibitions and those specified by individual countries.

Registration: Standard indemnity for loss, also for damage in service with some countries; for all postal packets except parcels and bulk printed papers; proof of posting; advice of delivery (if required); some extra security during postal transmission.

Swiftair: Normal postage plus fee plus label at top left-hand corner. All letters to Europe and airmail letters and printed papers to countries outside Europe eligible, including registered and insured items. Accelerated treatment within UK and in country of destination, i.e., express delivery. Certificate of posting available. Customs documents may be necessary.

3. Remittance services

(a) Inland

Postal order: Available in specified values and in specified steps plus postage stamps for intermediate values; fill in name of addressee and post office where payable, or cross for payment through bank account; fee payable on each order.

National Girobank: See **14.5**.

(b) Overseas

Overseas postal order: May be sent only to countries that accept them; maximum limit on each order.

International Girobank: See **14.5**.

Appendix II: Summary of legislation affecting the office

1. Consumer Protection

(a) Sale of Goods Act 1979
(b) Trade Descriptions Act 1968
(c) Unsolicited Goods and Services Act 1971
(d) Fair Trading Act 1973
(e) Consumer Credit Act 1974
(f) Unfair Contract Terms Act 1977

2. Employment Legislation

(a) Employers' Liability (Compulsory Insurance) Act 1969
(b) Equal Pay Act 1970
(c) Employment Agencies Act 1973
(d) Rehabilitation of Offenders Act 1974
(e) Trade Union and Labour Relations Acts 1974 and 1976
(f) Sex Discrimination Act 1975
(g) Race Relations Act 1976

1. Consumer Protection

(a) Sale of Goods Act 1979

The Sale of Goods Act 1979 provides that where a seller sells goods in the course of a business there are implied conditions that the seller has the right to sell the goods, that the goods are of merchantable quality (except as regards defects specifically drawn to the buyer's attention before the contract is made or which he ought reasonably to have noticed when he examined the goods), that the goods are fit for the purpose for which they were bought (except where the buyer does not rely or where it is unreasonable for him to rely on the skill and judgement of the seller), and that the goods correspond with any description given. This applies as much to goods bought in a sale as to any others. Similar terms are implied for goods acquired under hire-purchase and other credit arrangements. The Supply of Goods and Services Act 1982 further implies similar terms for goods acquired under a contract where goods and services are contracted for together, e.g., car repair. Further, the services given must be of reasonable standard at a reasonable price and within a reasonable period of time unless otherwise agreed.

(The Unfair Contract Terms Act 1977—see below—provides that in consumer transactions the seller may not exclude or restrict liability for breach of these implied terms.)

(b)   Trade Descriptions Act 1968

This prohibits the use of false or misleading trade descriptions (whether in advertisements, labelling or in oral representations) in relation to the supply of goods or services in the course of trade. The term 'trade description' in relation to goods includes information as to quantity, size, composition, method and place and date of manufacture, manufacturer, and fitness for purpose. The Act also prohibits the use of any indication that the price is less than that price at which the goods are actually being offered or any false indication that the price is less than the price at which goods of the same description have previously been offered.

Persons selling goods bearing a false description are guilty of an offence, even if they did not themselves apply that description, and the penalty for an offence may be a fine and/or imprisonment. Local authority trading standards departments are responsible for enforcing the Act. Officers are empowered to make test purchases, to enter premises, and to inspect and seize goods or documents.

(c)   Unsolicited Goods and Services Act 1971

In the past, some consumers were forced to pay for goods for which they had made no request, but which were sent through the post or otherwise delivered at their homes. With the passing of the Unsolicited Goods and Services Act, if goods are sent to a consumer even though he has not ordered them and if six months have elapsed without the sender reclaiming the goods, the recipient has the right to treat them as a gift. If demands for payment are made by the sender, he can be fined up to £200, or up to £400 if he threatens to take legal proceedings.

In other cases, firms were charged for entries in directories, even though they had not requested the entry to be made. The same Act stipulates that no one is liable to pay for a directory entry unless he has (i) signed an order for its insertion, on his own stationery bearing his name and address, or (ii) signed a note (a copy of which must have been supplied to him before signing for retention) agreeing to the charge. Such a note must identify the directory and give the name and address of the compiler, the proposed date of publication, the price, the minimum number of copies to be put on sale (or made available, in the case of a free publication), and details of the entry to be inserted. The compiler is liable to a fine of an unlimited amount if he demands payment when these conditions have not been fulfilled.

The Act was amended in 1975 to enable the Secretary of State to make regulations about the content and form of notes of agreement, invoices, and similar documents relating to directory entries.

(d)   Fair Trading Act 1973

The Act establishes a Director General of Fair Trading and a Consumer Protection Advisory Committee appointed by the Secretary of State. The functions of the Director General include: (i) recommending to the Secretary of State that orders should be made in relation to trade practices which mislead consumers, subject them to undue pressure or cause the terms on which consumers enter into contracts to be inequitable; these recommendations are scrutinized by the Consumer Protection Advisory Committee; (ii) obtaining an assurance from any trader that he will cease a persistent course of conduct which is unfair to consumers in that it consists of contravention of the criminal law or of breaches of civil obligations; and the taking of proceedings against a trader who refuses to make such an assurance or has failed to observe it; (iii) publication of information and advice for consumers.

Local authority trading standards departments are responsible for enforcing orders made under the Act in relation to trade practices. Officers have powers to make test purchases, enter premises, and examine goods and documents.

The Director General also has powers relating to monopolies and mergers. Where he suspects there to be a monopoly situation in relation to the supply of goods or services, he can request certain information from any person who supplies or is supplied with goods or services of the description in question. Where he believes that a monopoly situation exists or may exist the Director General can refer the matter to the Monopolies Commission for investigation. He must also keep himself informed of actual and proposed mergers.

(e)   Consumer Credit Act 1974

The following is a summary of the Act's provisions. The Act rationalizes the law governing the provision of credit and hire to individuals—i.e., both ordinary and trade consumers but not limited companies—and is concerned with transactions where the total credit is for not more than £5000—and, in case of hire of goods, where the agreement may last for more than three months. It does not cover normal trade credit. The Director General of Fair Trading is, in general, responsible for its supervision and enforcement.

The Act defines different types of credit agreement between creditors and debtors. It gives powers to the Secretary of State to make regulations ensuring that the true cost to the debtor of the credit provided is made clear—e.g., in credit advertisement, quotations and legal agreements—thereby enabling the consumer to compare the cost of different credit facilities available. The APR rate must be shown on any hire-purchase material.

Businesses dealing in consumer credit (e.g., consumer credit businesses, consumer hire businesses, credit brokers, debt counsellors and collectors, and credit reference agencies) must be licensed and the register of licensed businesses kept by the Director General must be available for public inspection.

Credit businesses are not permitted to canvass for customers off their premises—i.e., they must not call on people in their homes or in the street to offer loans, for example. The Act prohibits the issuing of unsolicited credit tokens—e.g., credit cards,unless in renewal of ones already supplied.

Agreements between debtors and creditors must be clear and legible and embody all the terms of the agreement, including the credit charge. A copy of the agreement must be given to the customer. In some cases—e.g., the mortgage of land—debtors must be given opportunity to study without harassment by the creditor a copy of the agreement seven days before it is presented for signature, and must be told of this right. A 'cooling-off' period is also allowed during which a debtor can cancel a credit agreement already signed, provided that there has been personal contact between customer and salesman.

Where securities are given in an agreement, these must be in writing and copies kept by the parties. Receipts must be given for articles taken in pawn and the pawn is redeemable at any time within six months after it was taken.

If an agreement is broken, a court may issue an enforcement order reducing the sum payable by the debtor in compensation or discharging him from it altogether; or it may issue a time order allowing the debtor to pay what he owes in instalments. Where a customer breaks an agreement, a trader must first serve a default notice on him, explaining the defaults and allowing the customer at least seven days to put them right. Where the terms of an agreement are found to be extortionate, the court can reopen the agreement and adjust the terms—e.g., by ordering the creditor to repay unreasonable interest charges.

A consumer applicant for credit is entitled to ask for and receive from the creditor he has approached the name of any credit reference agency from which the creditor obtained information about him. On request, the agency must then give him a copy of his file and have this amended if the information is incorrect.

Where a credit broker arranges a mortgage or some other loan for a client, he cannot charge more than £1 in fees if the client does not sign an agreement with the source of credit within six months.

The Act is enforceable by the trading standards departments of local authorities, who have powers to inspect records. Penalties for infringement are fines or imprisonment or both.

(f) Unfair Contract Terms Act 1977

In addition to the provisions of the 1977 Act mentioned in relation to the Sale of Goods Act 1979, the Act makes provision relating to terms of contracts for the supply of goods or services by a business. It provides that terms of such contracts which purport to exclude or restrict the liability of the business for death or personal injury due to negligence are void. The same applies to notices purporting to have a similar effect. The Act provides that contract terms and notices which exclude or restrict a business's liability for other loss or damage caused by negligence are binding only if they are found to be reasonable.

Where a business contracts with a consumer, any contract term excluding or restricting the liability of the business for breach of contract is binding only if it is reasonable. The same is true of terms which would enable the business to render a performance substantially different from that which was reasonably expected of it or to render no performance at all, or which would require the consumer to idemnify the business in respect of liability incurred by the business for breach of contract or for negligence. In all these cases it is for the business to show that the term is reasonable.

The Act also makes provision relating to the terms of contracts made between businesses.

2. Employment Legislation

(a) Employers' Liability (Compulsory Insurance) Act 1969

Under this Act, which came into force on 1 January 1972, most employers are required to take out approved insurance policies with authorized insurers against liability for bodily injury or disease sustained by their employees while employed in Great Britain. Employers must be insured for at least £2 million for claims arising out of any one incident.

Almost anyone who works under a contract of service (whether implied or expressed, whether in writing or not) is regarded as an employee under the Act. However, visitors from overseas employed in Britain for fewer than 14 consecutive days are excluded, and also employees closely related to their employer. Employers exempted include nationalized industries, and local and police authorities.

Insurers must issue a certificate of insurance to every employer within 30 days of his entering upon or renewing an insurance contract. The employer must display the certificate where it can easily be read by his employees, and continue to display it throughout the period of the contract.

To ensure that the provisions of the Act are being carried out, certain inspectors in the Health and Safety Executive are authorized to visit employers' premises to check certificates and insurance policies, or employers may be required to send certificates or copies to the Health and Safety Executive for verification. Employers who default are liable to fines. A fine may be imposed for each day on which an employer is not insured in accordance with the Act.

(b) Equal Pay Act 1970 (as amended by the Employment Protection Act 1975 and the Sex Discrimination Act 1975)

The Act establishes the right of an individual woman to equal treatment with a man in respect of pay and other terms of her contract of employment, when she is employed on the same or broadly similar work to that of the man, or work which though different has been given an equal value under job evaluation, unless the employer can show that any variation in their treatment is genuinely due to a material difference (other than the difference of sex) between her case and his—e.g., differences in qualifications, length of service, etc.

All individual workers are affected by the Act, irrespective of length of service, number of hours worked, or size of firm.

Complaints are heard by industrial tribunals, if the Advisory, Conciliation and Arbitration Service set up by the Employment Protection Act 1975 has not been able to bring about a settlement through conciliation. The Act also provides for the Central Arbitration Committee to remove discrimination from collective agreements and employers' pay structures.

(c)   Employment Agencies Act 1973 (as amended by the Employment Protection Act 1975)

The Act aims to secure the registration and proper conduct of employment agencies and businesses throughout Great Britain, in order to protect the interests of job seekers and employers who use their services. (An employment business employs its own workers whom it hires out to work under the control of others, whereas an agency aims to provide staff for others to employ.)

All employment agencies or businesses—whether profit- or non-profit-making—must hold and display a current licence from the Secretary of State for Employment, except where services are provided by university appointments boards, local authorities, trade unions, charitable organizations, or for particular categories of people—such as seamen, qualified nurses, ex-prisoners, etc. Fees must not be charged to workers for finding them jobs (unless they are performers, entertainers, or fashion or photographic models). Neither the fees charged to employers nor the rates employment businesses pay their workers are regulated by the Act.

Employment agencies and businesses must get adequate information from employers and clients to select suitable workers for a vacancy. They must not offer workers any financial benefit to induce them to use their services nor must they approach a worker they have already placed in employment and for whom they have received a fee from the employer, in order to arrange employment with another employer. They must ensure that young people under 18 have received vocational guidance from local authority careers officers before introducing them to an employer; they must obtain written consent from the parent or guardian if the young person wishes to work abroad, and ensure that suitable accommodation is arranged abroad at a suitable price. Any worker recruited for a post abroad must be given before departure a written statement giving details of the employment; the overseas employer must similarly be given details of the worker.

Employment agencies and businesses must keep detailed records for inspection by officers of the Department of Employment. Inspectors have powers to enter and inspect premises and records. Fines are payable on summary conviction for offences under the Act.

(d)   Rehabilitation of Offenders Act 1974

The Act provides that if persons convicted of certain offences are not convicted again during a period stipulated according to the nature and duration of the sentence the conviction becomes spent and cannot give proper grounds for dismissal from employment nor for prejudicial treatment while employed. Certain occupations and professions are excluded from its terms, e.g., those dealing with specially vulnerable sections of society, e.g., teachers, doctors; those involved with administration of justice, e.g., police or prison officers; those whose jobs have a national security element, e.g., civil servants; and senior employees of certain financial institutions.

(e)   Trade Union and Labour Relations Acts 1974 and 1976 (as amended by the Employment Protection Act 1975, Employment Protection (Consolidation) Act 1978, Employment Acts 1980 and 1982, Trade Union Act 1984)

Provisions in these Acts include:

(i) *Trade Unions and the law*   Trade unions and employers' associations are required to keep proper accounts, audited by qualified auditors, and must be listed by the certification officer appointed under the Employment Protection Act 1975. Employers' associations may register with the Registrar of Companies as corporate bodies, but a trade union cannot do so. Nevertheless, trade unions and employers' associations have the power, like companies, to make contracts and to sue or be sued. However, trade unions and trade union officials have certain immunities, i.e., they are in general protected by law against being sued for activities in contemplation and furtherance of a trade dispute. A trade dispute is defined as a dispute between an employer and workers, connected with such matters as terms and conditions of employment and physical conditions of work. A trade union or official is only immune from being sued for civil wrongs (torts) such as inducing others to break contracts of employment through strikes, if the wrongs were done in furtherance of a trade dispute; also the strike must be supported by members in a secret ballot and must not involve secondary action by others not in dispute with their own employers. No trade union or union members can be sued effectively for peaceful picketing at or near their own place of work.

A government agency called the Advisory, Conciliation and Arbitration Service (ACAS) exists to attempt to settle disputes between unions and employers.

Trade unions have the right to be consulted over redundancies, and to be given certain information from management for collective bargaining for negotiating purposes provided that disclosure does not cause substantial damage to the employer's business.

(ii) *Individual employee rights:*

Redundancy payments provisions cover nearly all employees except those over normal retiring age or who work less than 16 hours per week. Payment is made as a non-taxable lump sum, the amount depending on the employee's age, length of service with the one employer (to a maximum of 20 years) and salary (up to a specified ceiling, reviewed annually)—i.e., half a week's normal pay is given for every year after age 18 up to 22; one week's pay for every year after age 22 up to 41; and one and a half weeks' normal pay for every year after age 41 to 65 (60 for women). The employer must give the employee a written statement, at or before the time of payment, explaining how the amount is arrived at.

To qualify for payment, an employee must have given 104 weeks' continuous service normally to the one employer (including any time taken under the contract of employment for holidays or sickness) and must have been dismissed for redundancy. An employee who has been on short-time working or laid off for several weeks for reasons other than strikes or lock-outs may also be entitled to a redundancy payment. An employee may have been made redundant because his own job ceased or because fewer employees of his particular kind were wanted, for whatever reason. Other reasons for dismissal do not count; neither does service given before the age of 18.

If an employee gives in his notice before he receives notice from his employer, he forfeits payment. However, he can still receive payment if he has started to work out his notice but wishes to leave before the end of it and his employer agrees to this. If he accepts (or refuses unreasonably) another suitable job on the same terms from the same employer, he is not entitled to payment; where he accepts an offer from the same employer of a job on different terms or in a different place, the employee is allowed a trial period of four weeks (or longer if retraining is necessary) to decide whether the job is suitable. If he decides it is not and terminates the new contract, he is regarded as redundant.

If an employee thinks he is entitled to a redundancy payment but does not get one soon after dismissal, he must send a written claim (advisedly by recorded delivery) to his employer, or submit an application to an industrial tribunal, within six months of the end of his employment, otherwise the employer normally ceases to have any obligation to pay.

For every redundancy payment made to an employee under the provisions of the Acts the employer can claim a rebate from the Redundancy Fund, which is financed by an allocation from NI contributions paid by employers and employees but if he gives insufficient notice of his claim his rebate may be reduced. He can set his share of the redundancy payment and his contributions to the Fund against tax as business expenses. If an employer cannot make the required redundancy payment to an employee because of insolvency or financial difficulty, the employee may be able to obtain payment from the Redundancy Fund (which would recover the employer's contribution later). Similar arrangements within certain specified limits, may be made where an employee is owed holiday pay, arrears of pay, or pay in lieu of notice by an employer who is formally insolvent.

Contracts of employment provisions cover employees of all ages who work 16 hours or more a week (8 hours a week where an employee has worked for the same employer for at least five years).

A contract of employment exists as soon as the employee proves acceptance of its terms and conditions by starting work. The terms are then enforceable in the civil courts. It can be an oral contract for there is no legal obligation for an employer to give a written contract of employment (unless the employee is an apprentice).

An employee who has worked for his employer for any continuous length of time over four weeks needs to give a statutory minimum period of notice of one week. The employer, however, must give a period of notice calculated according to the length of continuous service the employee has given him— i.e., at least 1 week for 4 weeks' service or more (unless the contract of employment was for a fixed term of 4 weeks or less); at least 2 weeks for 2 years or more; and one additional week for each further year up to a maximum of 12 weeks for 12 years' service or more. If a contract of employment provides for longer periods of notice than the minimum in the Act, then the longer period applies.

Neither an employee nor an employer is prevented by the Act from waiving his right to notice or from accepting payment in lieu of notice. Neither employer nor employee is obliged to give any notice if the behaviour of the other party justifies terminating the contract without it: whether dismissal without notice is justified is a matter for a court of law. If an employee is not able to work part of his notice because he is sick, injured, or on holiday, or because the employer has no work for him to do, the Act guarantees him minimum pay—e.g. his normal wages if these are at a fixed weekly rate.

An employer must give every employee, within 13 weeks of starting work, a written statement of particulars of the main terms of employment—i.e., job title, pay, hours, holidays and holiday pay, sick leave and sick pay, pensions and pension schemes, and notice.

If changes occur in the terms of employment, the employer must issue a further written statement, setting out the change to the employee within a month of the change. If the employee is not given a personal copy, one must be readily accessible to him. In a written statement an employer can, if he wishes, refer an employee for some or all of the information to other reasonably accessible documents guaranteed to be regularly brought up to date. No written statement of terms is necessary if an employee has been given a written contract of employment which includes all the matters required to be covered in it by the Act, but any such contract must be kept up to date.

An employee who is dissatisfied because he considers that his employer has given him an inaccurate or insufficient statement, or no statement at all, can refer the matter to an industrial tribunal, which will determine what particulars should have been supplied. Redress for loss resulting from an employer's failure to observe the terms of contract is only available, however, by means of a lawsuit in an ordinary court.

The Acts give the rules for computing continuity of employment, upon which most of the individual rights of employees depend. The hours worked must normally be at least 16 hours a week, but 8 or more hours is sufficient if the employee has worked for the same employer for at least 5 years. Continuity of service is not normally broken by absences for holidays, sickness, pregnancy—as long as the contract of employment continues. Sometimes it is not even broken by a change of employer—e.g., in cases of takeovers, mergers, changes in partnerships, etc.

General protection for employees provisions include the following:

Pay is guaranteed subject to certain conditions for up to five days in any three-month period to employees laid off or on short-time working because no work has been provided by the employer.

Pay is guaranteed for up to 26 weeks for employees suspended for statutory medical reasons—e.g., over-exposure to radiation.

Provided she meets certain conditions, a pregnant employee is entitled to receive maternity pay from her employer for the first six weeks of statutory maternity absence, and in most cases to return to her job (or a suitable alternative job) or to receive redundancy pay.

Employees are entitled to a remedy from an industrial tribunal if their employer dismisses or selects them for redundancy as a result of their belonging to a trade union, or takes other actions designed to prevent or deter them from belonging to a trade union. Remedies from industrial tribunals are available also to employees as a result of similar action taken against them because they do *not* belong to a trade union. In a *closed shop*, certain employees are required by agreement between the employer and a trade union to belong to a trade union, but every closed shop must have had the approval of a given majority of the employees concerned in a secret ballot held within the previous five years. If a ballot has not been held, then employees dismissed or otherwise discriminated against because they are not trade union members are entitled to a remedy from an industrial tribunal.

Employees are entitled to reasonable time off in working hours for certain trade union duties as union officials, for trade union activities, for duties as a safety representative, for some public duties as Justice of the Peace or local authority members, or for seeking work or training when made redundant, or to receive antenatal care.

Every employee is entitled to a detailed, itemized statement setting out gross pay, variable and fixed deductions and net pay, or to one which summarizes fixed deductions, provided these have been explained in an annual statement.

Dismissed employees with not less than six months' service with an employer must be given a written statement of the reasons for their dismissal within 14 days if they ask for one.

Most employees have the right not to be unfairly dismissed and, if they feel that their dismissal is unfair, the right to complain to an industrial tribunal within three months of date of termination. However, some employees cannot complain of unfair dismissal, e.g., if they work full-time but have not been continuously employed for two years, or if they work under a fixed term contract for one year or more and have agreed in writing to waive their rights to unfair dismissal at the end of their employment.

In determining whether a dismissal is fair or unfair, industrial tribunals look to see whether the employer had a 'fair' reason for dismissing the employee and whether he acted 'reasonably' when carrying out the dismissal. Fair reasons for dismissal include: misconduct, incapability (e.g., lack of skill, aptitude or qualifications), redundancy, cases where if the employer continued to employ the employee the employer would be breaking the law; or some other substantial reason. Automatically unfair reasons for dismissal include: unfair selection for redundancy, dismissal for reasons relating to pregnancy, dismissal on the grounds of race or sex (and dismissals for membership/non-membership of trade unions given above).

Employees found to have been unfairly dismissed must either be reinstated (i.e., given their original job back), re-engaged (i.e., given a different job) or compensated financially by their employer.

(f)   Sex Discrimination Act 1975

The Act makes sex discrimination unlawful in employment, training and related matters, in education, and in the provision of housing and goods, facilities, and services to the public. In the employment field, discrimination against married people is also made unlawful.

The Act, which applies to discrimination against both men and women, defines two kinds of sex discrimination: *direct*—where, for example, treatment of a woman is or would be less favourable than that of a man on account of her sex; or *indirect*—where the treatment may be equal in the formal sense, but the requirements or conditions are more likely to be fulfilled, for example, by men because a considerably smaller proportion of women than men can comply. The Act is contravened unless such requirements can be justified. Discrimination against married persons in the employment field *only* is also defined; i.e., *direct,* where a married person is or would be treated less favourably than an unmarried person of the same sex would be, and *indirect,* where a requirement is applied equally to both married and unmarried people but in practice excludes more married than unmarried people. To be lawful, such a requirement must be justified. The Act also describes as discrimination victimization of a person because he or she has, for example, taken action under the Act (or under the Equal Pay Act.). When making comparisons the relevant circumstances of the woman or man complaining of discrimination must be the same or not materially different from the man or woman with whom the comparison is being made—e.g., a woman who claims she has been discriminated against by being refused a loan must compare her treatment with that of a man of comparable standing. Comparisons in cases of direct and indirect discrimination against married persons must be between persons of the same sex.

In the employment field, it is unlawful for an employer to discriminate when arranging who should be offered a job, or in the terms on which a job is offered; by refusing to consider an application for employment or by rejecting an applicant. It is also unlawful to discriminate when affording opportunities for promotion, transfer, training, and other facilities and benefits, and when dismissing employees. The Act does not apply to employment for the purposes of private households, or in small firms with five or fewer employees, or when a person's sex is a *genuine occupational qualification* for a job. An employer can claim a genuine occupational qualification for a particular job, for example, where a man (or woman) is needed for reasons of physiology, e.g., as an actor or model (but physical strength or stamina cannot be used as a g.o.q.), where considerations of decency or privacy require the job to be done by a man (or woman), where the job is in a single sex institution, or where the job needs to be done by a man because of legislation regulating women's employment—e.g., night work in factories. Discriminatory advertisements are unlawful. Where one-sex terms are used, an advertisement must make clear that no discrimination is intended; this can be done by saying, for example, 'waiter or waitress', 'open to both men and women'. If an exception applies, however, it is not unlawful to specify men or women only.

(g)   Race Relations Act 1976

The provisions of this Act are similar to those in the Sex Discrimination Act. It makes unlawful discrimination on racial grounds (i.e., on grounds of colour, race, nationality (including citizenship) or ethnic or national origins in employment, training and related matters, education, housing, and the provisions of goods, facilities, and services). Discrimination can be *direct*—where a person is treated less favourably on racial grounds—or *indirect*—where an unjustifiable requirement or condition is applied equally to people of any racial group but operates in a disproportionately disadvantageous way upon persons of a particular racial group. It also includes the victimization of someone who has, for example, been concerned with proceedings under the Act and segregating a person from another on racial grounds.

In general, the Act covers discrimination by employers in matters concerning the recruitment of employees and the treatment of existing employees. There are certain exceptions—for example, employment in private households and some specified jobs where being of a particular racial group is a genuine occupational qualification.

Complaints about discrimination in the employment field are dealt with by industrial tribunals. Complaints in other areas are dealt with by designated county courts (in Scotland, sheriff courts). The Commission for Racial Equality was established by the Act to help enforce the legislation, work towards the elimination of discrimination, to promote equality of opportunity and good relations between people of different racial groups and to keep under review the working of the Act. It can conduct formal investigations for any purposes connected with the carrying out of its duties and may issue non-discrimination notices requiring the people on whom they are served not to contravene specified provisions of the Act.

A Code of Practice was issued in 1984 to help eliminate discrimination and promote equal opportunity in employment.

Appendix III: Glossary of computing and information processing terms

Access time The length of time it takes a computer to obtain information from *primary memory* or from a storage device.

Applications software Programs written to perform tasks for the users (compare *operating system*).

Backup disk A copy of a *disk* made as a precaution in case the disk currently in use should become damaged or defective.

Backing store A data storage medium other than *primary memory*.

Bar code A printed code, consisting of stripes of various thicknesses, that can be read into a computer with a pen-shaped reader.

Batch processing A method of information processing in which work is saved up for a set period (perhaps a day) and then processed by the computer in one run (compare *real time*).

Baud rate The rate at which the computer can transmit information to or receive it from another device; approximately the number of *bits* per second.

Binary Arithmetic to base two. All computers use the binary numbering system internally for processing, but translate the results into *denary* for human beings to read.

Bit A contraction of Binary digIT—a single binary digit, either 0 or 1.

Boot Computer staff talk about 'booting the system' when they mean starting it up. It comes from an allusion to lifting oneself up by the bootstraps because early computers couldn't read in a program until there was a program already in place to tell them to read a program in!

Byte Eight *bits*, the smallest item of information used by most computers and the smallest *binary number* used to represent a *character*. The word is a contraction of 'by eight'.

Central processing unit (CPU) The computer itself, without any of the *peripherals*.

Character A single letter of the alphabet, digit, or symbol.

Chip A tiny piece of silicon containing complex electronic circuits. Used inside all computers.

Continuous stationery Computer paper. Made in a continuous length with the join between sheets perforated. Sprocket holes along the edges engage a *tractor feed*. May or may not be printed with letterheads, etc.

Corrupt   Said of a computer file or program that has become error-ridden.

CPU   See central processing unit.

Crash   When a computer system fails catastrophically it is said to have 'crashed'. Also 'head crash', used by computer staff to describe a certain type of serious failure in a hard *disk* system.

Cursor   A flashing symbol on the *monitor* screen, to show where something is expected to happen.

Daisy wheel printer   A *printer* with a mechanism similar to that of an electronic typewriter. The results are indistinguishable from those produced on a typewriter.

Denary   Normal base ten arithmetic. Used by human beings. Computers have to translate from *binary* so that people can understand what they are saying.

Disk   Random access storage device, using a metal or plastic disk coated in magnetic oxide. Note that the American spelling is standard.

Disk drive   A machine that enables the computer to *read disks* or *write* on them. Even small computers usually have at least two, so that you can make *backup disks*.

Electronic dictionary   A feature of some word processor software, that checks your spelling and queries any words it doesn't recognize.

Electronic mail   A system whereby messages, either spoken or printed, can be sent from one *work-station* to another. The receiving station can store the message if the intended recipient is not there.

Facsimile   An exact copy. Facsimile machines can transmit reasonably good copies over long distances using networks.

File locking   The process by which a computer in a *network* prevents other users looking at a file on which it is currently working.

Formatting   Preparing a *disk* for use. The computer must check the disk and record various pieces of information on it before the disk can be used for data storage.

Friction feed   Paper feed in a *printer*, similar to that of a typewriter.

Function keys   Extra keys on a computer keyboard. What they do depends on the program.

Graphics   Pictures; any printed computer output except letters and numbers. In business the graphics tend to be graphs.

Icon   A symbol on the *monitor* that represents a function. For example, you might make a calculation by moving the cursor over a picture of a calculator.

Ink-jet printer   A *printer* that works by directing ink droplets onto the paper. Good quality print, fast, silent, expensive and requires more maintenance than most printers.

Input device   Anything that feeds information into an information processing system—a *keyboard, modem, bar-code* reader, etc.

Joystick   A control stick that can be moved in any direction. Usually made to control a *cursor* on the *monitor*. Often has a 'fire' button in the centre of the stick, to initiate some action by the computer. Derived from the slang expression for a light aircraft control column, which looks similar.

Keyboard   Most popular *input* device for information processing.

Line printer   High-speed *printer*. Usually very fast, but large and noisy.

Local area network   A *network* within an office or building.

Mailmerge   Software in which a standard letter is merged with information from files to produce a large number of apparently personal ('personalized') letters.

Mainframe computer   The most powerful class of computer. Needs an air-conditioned room to itself.

Matrix printer   A *printer* using a matrix print-head. Faster than a *daisy wheel printer* and capable of graphics, but average to poor print quality.

Memory   See *primary memory*.

Menu   A list of options, presented on the *monitor*, that enable the user to select the one required.

Merge   To mix together two or more items of text or files.

Microcomputer   The cheapest class of computer, having the main part of its electronics (the processor) on a single silicon *chip*. Microcomputers can be self-contained or networked. The whole thing will fit on a desktop.

Microdisk   Small *disk* (3½-inch standard) used in microcomputer systems.

Microwriter   Small hand-held word processor, with an unusual keyboard that is operated with one hand.

Minicomputer   A class of computers that is a step down from the *mainframe*. Usually in a room on its own, serving several terminals.

Modem   A device that lets computers send information down telephone lines. The name is from MOdulator/DEModulator.

Monitor   A screen like that of a TV, but giving sharper pictures. Used in computer systems to display information for the user. The picture may be in monochrome (often green) or full colour.

Mouse   An improvement on the *joystick*. Move the mouse around your desktop and the cursor on the screen moves the same way.

Network   Computers and other devices linked together in such a way that they can share information and communicate with each other.

OCR   See *optical character recognition*.

On-line processing   See *real time*.

Operating system   The software used by the computer to control the system (compare *applications software*).

Optical character recognition (OCR)   The reading of printed text by a computer. Rather expensive, but works reliably for clean typewritten or printed material.

Output device   Anything controlled directly by the computer and used to provide information or action. For example, *printers, terminals, plotters, modems*.

Password   A secret word or number that is typed into the computer at the appropriate time to allow the user access to information that is restricted.

Peripheral   Any machine connected to the computer and part of the system. For example, all the *input* and *output* devices.

Plotter   A form of *printer* that is specially designed for the production of high-quality graphics. May use more than one colour.

Primary memory   The electronic memory in which the computer stores the program and the data on which it is currently working. The primary memory is *volatile*.

Printer Any machine for producing printed output from the computer (see *daisy wheel, ink-jet, line, matrix*).

Program The detailed set of instructions written by the *programmer* to tell the computer what to do and how to do it. Note that the American spelling is standard.

Programmer Someone who writes *programs*.

Punched card A form of data storage in which information is stored in the form of holes punched in cards. Bulky, expensive, and becoming obsolete.

Ram Random Access Memory. See *primary memory*.

Random access memory (RAM) See *primary memory*.

Read The process by which the computer takes in information from a *backing store* or *input* device. See *write*.

Real time Happening now, as opposed to later. Real-time processing involves the computer dealing with information immediately it is fed in. Compare *batch processing*.

Sheet feed A machine for feeding individual sheets of paper into a *printer*, one after another.

Software See *program*.

Source document A written document from which information is input into the computer system.

Systems analyst A person who looks at the requirements of a business then specifies the computer, *peripherals*, and *software* that will be needed.

Systems software See *operating system*.

Terminal A *monitor* and a *keyboard* (and sometimes a *printer*) connected to a *network* or directly to a *mainframe* or *minicomputer* serving more than one user.

Thermal printer A *printer* that works by blackening heat-sensitive paper. Fast, quiet, moderate quality print, requires special paper.

Time-sharing If several companies want to use a *mainframe computer* but can't afford one, they can share it. A powerful computer allocates its own time according to the demands of the users. For the user, there simply seems to be a slight reduction in speed when the computer is busy.

Touch screen A *monitor* fitted with a system that tells the computer which part of the screen you are touching. Used for selection of options, etc., where a *keyboard* is undesirable.

Tractor feed Part of a *printer* (or an attachment) that enables *continuous stationery* to be used.

VDU Visual display unit. See *monitor*.

Visual display unit (VDU) See *monitor*.

Volatile Information that evaporates when the power is cut off. For example, the contents of *primary memory*.

Wide area network A *network* that extends outside a single building. May be countrywide or international.

Winchester disk A *disk* in which a single high-capacity disk is permanently sealed inside its own disk drive.

Window In some systems the *monitor* can show you more than one thing at a time. A rectangular space appears on the screen, with the new information displayed in it. When you have finished with the new information, the original display returns. The effect looks like a window opening in the original display, showing you something else 'behind' it.

Workstation   A *terminal* or computer connected to a *network*, at which someone sits and works.

Write   Record information on a *disk* or in *primary memory. See read.*

Index

Page numbers printed in bold type refer to
Did you know? items.

Absence:
  of boss, secretary's routine during, 237
  secretary's 175
Accident book, **175**
Accidents, industrial:
  Employers' Liability (Compulsory Insurance)
     Act 1969, 175, 288
  Offices, Shops and Railway Premises Act 1963, 40
Accommodation on business trips, 233–234
Accountants, 164
Accounting, 97–99
  financial 97–98
    terms, 97–98
  machines and devices, 99–101
  management, 98–99
Address, forms of:
  everyday, 186
    attention lines, 186–187
    for limited companies, 186
    use of Messrs, 186
    for women, 187
  special, 187–188
Adressing systems, 63
Advertisements:
  box numbers, 119
  choice of newspapers, 119
  discriminatory, 293
  for jobs, 118–119
    classified, 118–119
    display, 119
    timing, 119
Agencies, 166
  employment, 119
    Employment Agencies Act 1973, 289
  travel, 236
Annual General Meetings, 243–244
  annual report and accounts, 243
  annual return, 15
Anthropometrics, **43**
Application forms, 119—120

Applying for a post, 125–128
Appointments:
  diaries, 264–265
  making, 264–265
  sheet, 264
  year planner, 264
Articles of association, 15
  conduct of meetings laid down by, 243–244
  Memorandum and, 15
Articles, press, 207
Aslib, 218
Audiotyping:
  advantages and disadvantages of, 183
  correcting dictation, 180
  dictating media, 180
  author's equipment, 179–180
  indexing methods, 180
  posting recordings, 182
  dictation techniques, 182–183
  types of installation, 181–182
  typist's equipment, 180
  unattended units, 181
Auditors:
  external, 164
  internal, 102
Automated tellers, 159, **167**

Balance sheets, 98
Bank accounts:
  charges, 158
  current account, handling a, 158
  opening an account, 158
  statements, 158
  types of, 152–153, 158
Banking services:
  credit transfer, 159–160
    banker's/standing order, 155, 160
    bulk traders' credits, 155, 160
    bulk wage payments, 160
    direct debiting, 160
  for exporters/importers, 161
  personal services, 161
  for travellers, 235, 237

Banks:
  clearing, 156
  cheque, 161
  credit, 161
  Co-operative Bank, 161
  High Street, 158
  merchant, 163–164
  National Girobank, 162-163, 235
  National Savings Bank, 163
  Trustee Savings Bank, 163
Bibliographies, 213–214
Binding machines, 52
Blue books, 219
Bookkeeping, 97–98
  double-entry, 97
British Approvals Board for
  Telecommunications, 139
British Rail:
  facilities, 232
  parcels, 64–65
  tickets, 234
  timetables, 232
British Standards (*see* Standards, British)
Building societies, 164
Bursters, 53
  imprinter-bursters, 53
Business Equipment Trade Association, 218–219
Business names, **18**

Calculators, 99–100
Calendar, perpetual, 268
Capital gains tax, 172
Capital transfer tax, 172
Carbon paper, 51
  double-sided, 100
  one-time, 50
  spot, 50
Carbonless paper, 50, 100
Cash, methods of obtaining through a bank:
  from automatic tellers, 159, **167**
  by credit card, 159
  from own account, 159
Caveat emptor, **167**
Ceefax, 218
Cellular radio, 140–141
Central Office of Information, 214
Centralization, 3–4
  audio-typing, 181
  filing, 82
  office services, 3
  travel, 236–237
  typing and transcription, 183
Charge cards, **167**, 234, 235

Chairman:
  of committee, 248
  audio-conferencing techniques, 255, **258**
  gavel and block, **258**
  company, 14
    chairman's review, 244
Charts, 221–229
  axes, 226
  comparing different types of, 221–222
  by computer, 115, 228–229
  cursors, 227
  effective, 228
  keys, 223, 227
  organization, 20–21
  scales, 223
  signals, 226–227
  types of:
    bar graphs, 222–224
    flow, 224–225, 247
    line graphs, 222–223
    pictograms, 224
    pie, 223–225
  visual control boards, 224–228, 264
Checking:
  in computer systems, 271
  devices and systems, 271
  for transposition of figures, **104**
  typing, 193, 271
Cheque writers and signers, 99, 101
Cheques:
  clearing, 161
  sorting, 161
  stopping, 159, **167**
  terms relating to, 158–159
CIF, **30**
Circulars, 202
  composing, 202
  sending, 202
Civil Service grades, 22–23
Clerical function, 3
Coin and note counters, 101
Collating, 60-61
  collators, 62
Committees:
  composition of, 248–250
  chairman, 248, 251
  minute secretary, 251–252
  procedures and powers, 250
  secretary, 251
  types of, 244
Companies Acts, 14–15, **18**, 164
Companies, types of:
  limited by guarantee, **18**

Companies, types of: (*continued*)
  private limited, 14
  public limited, 14
Company ownership and management, 14
  board of directors, 14
  chairman, 14
  company secretary, 14, 21
  managing director, 14
  shareholders, 14, 15–16
Company terms, 15-16
  annual report and accounts, 15, 243–244
  annual return, 15
  companies registry, 15
  company seal, 15
  debentures, 16
  dividends, 15–16
  incorporation, 15
  insider dealings, **18**
  memorandum and articles of association, 15
  prospectus, 15
  registrar of companies, 15
  stocks and shares, 15
  trading certificate, 15
Computer systems, 106–116
  backing store, 107, 109–110
    disks, 107, 109–110
    floppy disks, 109
    hard disks, 108
    microdisks, 110
    Winchester disks, 110
    tapes, 110
  byte, 107, **117**
  central processing unit, 107
    RAM, 107
  databanks, 78, 215–218
    Prestel, 215-217
  Teletex, 217–218
  input devices, 111–112
    bar-code reader, 111
    joystick, 111
    keyboard, 107, 111
    MICR, 111
    Microwriter, 111–112
    Mouse, 111
    OCR, 111
    touch screen, 111
  menus, 109
  networks, 112–113
  office organization, effects on, 116
  output devices:
    COM, 81
    daisy wheel printers, 110
    ink-jet printers, 111

    laser printers, 109
    line printers, 108
    matrix printers, 110–111
    thermal printers, 111
    visual display unit, 107
  peripherals, 110–111
  programming, 106
    languages, 106
  programs, 106
    operating key functions, **117**
    operating system, 107–108
  security, 274–5
    encryption, 274
    passwords, 109, 274
  software, 113–115
    file handling, 114
    graphics, 115, 228–229
    spreadsheets, 100, 115
  systems analysis, 106
  terminals, 108–109
  turnkey, **117**
  types of:
    mainframe, 106–107, 108–109
    microcomputers, 106–108
    minicomputers, 106–107, 112–113
Computing terms, 294–298
Conferences:
  arranging, 255–256
  delegates to, **258**
  facilities for remote, 253–255
    audioconferencing, 253–255
    conference calls, 253–254
    videoconferencing, 253
  press, 256
  representatives, to, **258**
Consultants, 166
  design, 166
  office planning, 166
  organization and method, 166
Contingencies, preparing for, 276
Continuous stationery:
  computers, for, 50
  envelopes, 50
  equipment, 52–53
  forms, 50
  labels, 62
  sets, 50
Conveyor systems, 29–30
Co-operative movement, 16
  Co-operative Bank, 161
  Co-operative Union, 16
  Co-operative Wholesale Society, 16
  retail Co-operative societies, 16

Co-operative movement (*continued*)
  worker Co-operatives, 16
Copiers, 89–92
  clamshell design, **93**
  colour, 91–92
  costs, 86
  digital, 91–92
  management systems, 91
  microchip facilities on, 90–91
Copying processes, 86, 89–92
  diazo, 90
  direct electrostatic, 90
  plain paper, 89–90
    xerographic, 90
  thermal, 90–91
  transfer, electrostatic, 89–90
Copyright, 92–93
Copy-typing, 191–193
  errors in, 191–192
  hints on, 192–193
Corporation tax, 172
Credit, 97, 159–161
  clearing systems, 161
  control, 101–102
  sources of, 160–161
    bank loan, 160–161
    credit card, 160, 235
    overdraft, 161
Credit sale, **23**
Crimpers, 51, 52
Curriculum vitae, 127
Customs requirements:
  customs declaration (exporting), 25
  overseas letter packets and parcels, 65
  travel abroad, 234

Daily routine, secretary's, 263–264
Data Protection Act, 1984, 275
Data transmission services, public, switched:
  Datel modem, 144–145
  Inter Stream, 145
  ISDN, 146
  Packet Switch Stream, 145
Data transmission services, private, digital:
  Kilo Stream, 146
  Mega Stream, 146
  Sat Stream, 146
  Video Stream, 253
Databases, 78, 215–218
Decollators, 53
Delegation, 21, 271
Departmental organization:
  in central government, 22–23
  in large businesses, 20
  in local authorities, 22
  in small businesses, 21–22
Dewey decimal system, 212, 219
Diary office, 264
  electronic, 265
Dictation, taking:
  for audiotyping, 180
  shorthand notes, 179
Dictionaries, electronic, **208–209**
Directors:
  board of, 14
  names on letterheads, 186, 189
Discounts, 28, **30**
Doctor's statement, **175**
Documents:
  for external communication, 25–27
  internal, 28–29
  terms used on, 30
  for travel overseas, 234–235
  and VAT, 27–28
  for wages, 102–103
Documents, standard:
  advice note, 28
  bill of exchange, 25
  bill of lading, 25
  catalogue, 25, 27
  certificate of origin, 25
  consignment note, 25
  contents note, 28
  credit note, 25, 28
  customs declaration, 25
  debit note, 25, 28
  delivery note, 28
  estimate, 25
  goods received note, 28–29
  indent, 27
  inquiry, 25
  invoice, 26–27
    proforma, 26
    sets, 28
    tax, 26–28
  letter of credit, 26
  overdue account letters, 102
  price list, 26
  purchase order, 26
    set, 29
  quotation, 26–27
  receipt, 26–27, 28
  receipt note, 28
  remittance advice, 27
  requisition, 28, 47
  sales order, 27
  service agreement, 27
  statement, 27

Documents, standard (*continued*)
   stores issue note, 28
   warehouse order, 28
   works order, 28–29
Duplicating, 86–89, 93
   costs, 86
   ink stencil, 86–87
     electronic stencil, 87
     electronic stencil cutter, 87
     thermal stencil, 87
   offset litho, 87–89
   spirit **93**

EFTPOS, **166–167**
E & OE, **30**
Employers' Liability (Compulsory Insurance) Act 1969, 288
Employment Agencies Act 1973, 289
Employment, terms of 121, 291
Enclosures:
   incoming mail, 56
   indicated on outgoing letters, 186
Entertaining, 256–257
   business lunches, 256–257
   programmes for visitors, 257
Envelope display, 188
   postcodes, 188
Envelope preparation:
   addressing machines, 63
   addressing systems, 63
   chain feeding, 61–62
   continuous labels, 62
   envelope flaps, 189
   reducing envelope addressing, 64
Envelopes:
   aperture, 49
   banker, 49
   internal, 49
   International sizes, 49–50
     compatability with International paper sizes, 49
   pocket, 49
   polythene, 49
   POP range, 49
   printed paper, 49
   reusable containers, 64
   for wages, 103
   window, 49, 64
Equal Pay Act 1970, 288–289
Erlang, 155
Error, safeguards against, 271–272
European Economic Community directives, **18**
Exchange rates, **238**
Extraordinary general meetings, 244

Facsimile transmission, 150–153
Fair Trading Act 1973, 286–287
Feed devices:
   dual feed, 100
   friction feed, 111
   sheet feed, 111
   tractor feed, 111
Filing:
   centralized systems, 82
   computer databanks, 78
   computer file handling systems, 114
   cross-referencing, 77
   departmental systems, 67, 82
   file reservation system, 267
   general principles, 68
   lateral, 69
   microfilm, 78–82
   out markers, 67
   releasing for, 68
   retention periods, 69
     bills, **84**
     for income tax, **84**
   safety precautions, 67
   sifting and discarding, 68–69
   transfer systems, 69
Filing equipment:
   automated systems, 71–73
   box files, 70–71
   cabinets, 69
   card indexes, 69–70
   closed circuit television, 72
   collapsible, 69
   compressor plates, 70
   cupboards, 69, 71
   folders, 69
   movable, 71
   rotary units, 69
   suspended, 70
   tiered, 71
Filing, special purpose systems:
   for computer media, 82–84
   for ledger cards, 82
   for microforms, 83
   for photographs, 83
   for plans, 83
   for transparencies, 83–84
Financial services for travellers, 235–236
Fire precautions, 40–41
   in filing equipment, 70
   Fire Precautions Act 1971, 41
Flexible working hours, 123–124
Floppy disks, 82, 84, 109–110
FOB, **30**
Folding machines, 62

Forms:
  application, 119–120
  compiling, 205–206
  completing, 206
  reproducing, 206
Franking machines, 59–61
Furnishings and furniture (*see* Office planning)

Glossaries, electronic, 209
Glossary of Information Processing Terms, 294–298
Government publications, 214–215
Government Statistical Service, 215
Green papers, **219**
Guillotines, 52

Headings, best use of, 193, 204–205
Health and Safety at Work Act 1974, 41–42
Health in the office, 40–43
Health precautions abroad, 234–235
Hire Purchase agreements, 23
Human relations, 276–278
  secretary and boss, 277–278
  secretary and colleagues, 277
  secretary and juniors, 277
  secretary and public, 277
  secretary and servicing staff, 277

Illness of employee, procedure to follow, 175, **175**
Income expenditure account, 98
Income tax:
  assessment, 171
  collection and administration, 171–172
  PAYE, 169–171, 172
Indexing:
  classification systems, 76–77
    alphabetical, 76
    alpha-numerical, 77
    chronological, 77
    geographical, 77
    numerical, 76
    subject, 77
    terminal digit, 77
  coding and signalling devices, 75–76
  colour, coding 76
  feature cards, 74–75
    edge-punched, 74–75
    optical coincidence, 75
  free standing systems, 74
  guide cards, 75
  signals, 75
  strip indexes, 74
  visible systems, 73–74
Induction procedures, 121
Information, sources of, 211–220
  books, (*see* Reference books)

computer databanks, 78, 215–218
  on conditions overseas, 236
  government publications, 214–215
  on hotels, 233
  people and organizations, 211–213
  periodicals, 213
    guides to, 213–214
Information processing, 115
Information processing terms, 294–298
Inserters, 63
Instructions, compiling, 208
Insurance, 164–165, 271
  overseas travel, 235
    for travellers to EEC countries, 235
Interviews:
  attending, 128–129
  conducting, 120
Invitations:
  to conferences, 255
  sending out, 202
  replying to, 203
Itineraries, 231–232

Jargon, 207–208
Job descriptions, 118
Job evaluation, 122
Job specifications, 118
Joggers, 62

Laminating, 52, 90
Leaving, staff:
  redundancies, 122
    legislation, 290
  resignations, 122
  retirements, 122
Ledger, 97
  cards, 97
    filing of, 82
Legislation affecting office, summary of, 285–293
Letter openers, 57–58
Letterheads, 186
  company registration number, **189**
  design of, 184–185
  directors' names, 186, **189**
  features of, 185–186
Letters:
  composing, 201–202
    circular and standard letters, 202
    from dictated notes, 201
    paragraphing, 201
    style, 201
    tact, 201
  costs, **199**
  layout, 185–186

Letters: (*continued*)
  presentation of, 184, 185–186
Libraries:
  automated services, 218
  computerized administration in, 218
  public, 212–213
    finding books in, 212
    lending facilities, 213
    periodicals in, 213
    reference facilities, 213
  special, 218
  with statutory right to United Kingdom
      publications, **219**
Library Association, 218
Lunches, arranging business, 256–257

Machines:
  choice factors, 33
  compatability, 34
  purchasing/leasing/renting, 33
  security precautions, 274
  suppliers, 34
  updating, 34
Mail:
  circulars, 60–63
  incoming, 54–58
    equipment, 57–58
    large organizations, 57–58
    small organizations, 56
  outgoing, 58–60
    equipment, 59–60, 63
    large organizations, 59–60
    postage book, 59
    small organizations, 58–59
  security precautions, 273
Mailing room organization, 57–60, 62
Mailing scales, 59, 61
Manifold bill boards, 100–101
Manpower Services Commission, 5
Mechanization in office function, 4
Meetings, 243–255
  action following, 251
  closing items, 248
  informal, 253
  preparing for, 244
  terms, 245–251, 258–259
  types of, 243–244
  voting, 247–248
Meetings documents, 245–251
  agenda, 243, 245–246, 252
    chairman's, 245–246
  attendance records, 245, 256
  minutes, 245, 249–252
    action column in, 250

  adoption of, 245
  content and display, 250
  drafting, 251–253
  motions, 245–247
  resolutions, 246, 250
  minute book, 250
    indexing of, 250
  notice of meeting, 243, 245, 252
  reports, 250–251
Memos:
  composing, 202
  forms, 202
  multiple, 202
Mercury network, 154–155
Message sheets, **54**
Metric measurements, 54
Microfilm systems, 78–82
  advantages, 81–82
  cameras, 80–81
  certificate of authenticity, **84**
  computer-aided, 81
  filing, 83
  indexing and retrieval, 80–81
  legal evidence, used in, **84**
  microforms, 78–80
    aperture cards, 80
    COM, 81
    fiche, 79–80
    jackets, 80
    roll film, 78–80
  printout, 80–81
  processors, 80
  readers, 80

National Insurance, 172–174
  benefits, 173–174
  state earnings-related pension scheme, 172–173
  contributions, 173–174
  inspectors, **175**
  number, **175**
  reciprocal arrangements with EEC countries, 235
Networks, 112–113
Noise:
  in open-plan offices, 33
  safety hazard, 43
  white noise, 43
Note and coin counters, 101
Notices, compiling, 208
Notice-boards, 208
  electronic, 208

Office design:
  cellular, 32
  open-plan, 32–33
Office function (*see* Clerical function)

Office furnishings, 35
Office furniture, 36
Office planning, 34–39
  air-conditioning, 36–37
  cable management, 35
  chairs, 36, 38–39
  décor, 35
  furniture, 36
  heating, 36–37
  lighting, 36
  planning techniques, 38–39
  ventilation, 36–37
  workstations, 34–35
Office services:
  automated, 4
  centralized, 3–4
  departmental, 3
  manual, 4
Office supplies, 47–52
Offices, Shops and Railway Premises Act 1963, 40
Oracle, 218
Organization charts, 20–21
Overseas, local conditions:
  sources of information on, 236

Paging systems, 151–152
  BT radiopaging service, 151
Paper, 48, 50, **53**
  International sizes, 48
  qualities, 48
Parcels services, 64–65
  British Rail, 64
  customs requirements, 65
  Post Office, 64
  private carriers, 65
  shipping and forwarding agents, 65
Parliamentary Information Service, **219**
Partnerships, 13
  limited, 13
Passports, 234
PAYE, 169–171
  codes, 169
  documents and records, 169–171
  deductions working sheets, 169–171
  procedure, 169–171
    computerization, **175**
Payments:
  inlands, 157–158
  overseas, 157
Pension scheme, state earnings-related, 168
Perforators, 51, 60
Periodicals, 213
  guides to, 213–214

Petty cash, 95–98
  VAT in, 28, 95–96
Phototypesetting, 199
Pixels, **229**
Post Office services, 280–284
  bulk collections, **65**
  compensation, **65**
  postal, 280–284
  remittances, 157–158, 284
Postage book, 59, 88
Postage meters, 59–61
Postcodes, **65**
Press releases, 206–207
Prestel, 215–217
Printing, preparing copy for, 193–194
Profit and loss account, 98
Proofs, 193–194
  correcting, 194
    British Standard 5261, 194
  dummy, 194
  galley, 194
  page, 194
  reading, 194
Public authorities:
  central government, 17–18
  local government, 17
Public corporations, 16–17
Public Lending Right Act 1979, **93**
Public Record Office, **219**
Public relations:
  officers, 212, 268
  press articles, 207
  press conferences, 256
  press releases, 206–207
  and the secretary, 277
Punched cards, 111
  edge punched, 74–75
Punched paper tape, telex, 141
  telex punch, 143

Race Relations Act 1976, 293
Radiopaging, 151, 153
Reception of visitors, 263, 267–268
  in large organization, 267
  press, 268
  salesmen, 268
  security precautions, 267
  shielding the boss, 268
  in small organization, 267–268
References, 128, **129**
Reference books:
  for correspondence, 189
  general, 209, 211–212

Reference books: (*continued*)
    guides to, 213–214
    lists of, 219–220
    postal, 65
    specialized, 211
    telecommunication, 155
    travel, 238
Reference, sources of, 211–220
Refreshments, serving:
    to individuals, 256
    to meetings, 256
Rehabilitation of Offenders Act 1974, 289
Reminder systems, 265–267, **268**
Remittances:
    in incoming mail, 56
        registered mail book, 56
        remittances book, 56
    inland Post Office services, 157–158
    overseas, 157
        through bank, 157
        through Post Office, 157
Reports, 203–205
    routine, 203
    special, 204–205
        by committees, 205
        by individuals, 205
Reprography, 86–93
Resolution, stages in reaching a, 245–247
Responsibility, chain of, 4
Retention of documents:
    accident books, **175**
    P11, **175**
    P60, **170**

Safety in the office, 39–43
    checklist, 42–43
    in filing equipment, 67
    Health and Safety at Work Act 1974, 41–42
    legislation, 40–42
    noise, 43
    Offices, Shops and Railway Premises Act 1963, 40
Sale of Goods Act 1893, 285–286
Secretarial work:
    grades of, 4, **8–9**
    openings in, 5–6
    prospects in, 7–8
    qualifications for, 6–7
    training for, 5
Secretaries:
    within departments, place of, 20
    duties of, 1, 41
        daily routine, 263–264
    personal qualities in, 8

Secretaries, Institute of Qualified Private, 8
Security, 272–275
    bomb threats, 273
    of information, 272–273
    with cheque signers, 101
    with cheque writers, 101
    computer systems, 274–275
    incoming mail, 273
    lockable containers, 70
        night safes, 158
        safes, 70
    machinery, 274
    of premises, 274
    reception, 273
    register of documents, 272
    registration of money and valuables, 157, 280
    shredders, 272–273
    in wages systems, 160, 274
Sex Discrimination Act 1975, 292–293
Shorthand:
    machine, **189**
    notebooks, organization of, 179
    systems, 179, **189**
Shortlists, 120
Shredders, 52, 58, 272–273
Signals:
    on charts, 226–227
    in filing systems, 75–76
Small Firms Information Service, 215
Sole traders, 13
Solicitors, 165–166
Sorting devices, 58, 60
Speeches, typing, 193, **199**
Squawkbox, 155
Staff:
    assessment, 120–122
    induction, 121
    leaving, 122
    management, 21
    motivation, 276
    organization, 21–23
        charts, 21
        in central government, 22–23
        in large businesses, 20–21
        in local authorities, 22
        in small businesses, 21
    records, 122–123
    recruitment, 118–121
    welfare, 122
Stamp duty, 172
Standards, British:
    BEAB mark, **43**
    for envelopes, 50

Standards, British: (*continued*)
  Institution, **43**
  Kitemark, **43**
  for proof marks, 194
Standards, International, **53**
Staplers, 52
Statutory Sick Pay, 174–175
Stenotyping, **189**
Stock:
  controlling and ordering, 47–48
    British Standards guide, **54**
  miscellaneous items, 51
  record cards, 47–48
  stocktaking, 48
Summarizing, 205
Supervision, 271
Supervisors, 199
Switchboard operators, facilities for, 137–138
System X, 134

Tape printers, 52
Tax covenants, 171
Tax tables, 169, 171
Taxes, 171–172
Telegrams, international, 155
Telemessages, 153
Telephone circuits, private leased, 144
Telephone equipment, 136–141
  advanced telephones, 114, 137, 266
  answering machines, 140
  autodiallers, 139
  call-connect in-house systems:
    facilities, 137
    PABX, 137
    PMBX, 137
  cordless telephones, 136
  internal telephone systems, 139
  key systems, 139
  with keypads, 136
  logging systems, 140
  loudspeaking telephones, 136–137
  meters, 139–140
  multi-frequency telephones, 136, 148
  radio telephones, 141
Telephone service, public switched, 134–136
  digital exchanges, 134
  direct dialling, 134
  directories, 133–134
  Mercury Communications Ltd, 154–155
  payphones, 135–136, **238**
  standard telephone services, 134–135
  Star telephone services, 135
  telephone credit cards, 135
  Trainphones, 136

Telephone technique, 133–134
Teletex, 148–150
Teletext information services, 217–218
Telex, 141–144
  electro-mechanical, 141
  electronic terminals, 141
  other equipment for message preparation, 141–144
  Prestel link, 217
Teleprinter circuits, private leased, 144
Testimonials, 128
Tickets, booking, 234
  British Rail, 234
    BR direct account order, 234
    Travel key charge card, 234
Time, management of, 264
Trade Descriptions Act 1968, 286
Trade Union and Labour Relations Acts 1974 and 1976, 289–292
Trade union membership, 124–125
Training:
  adult training schemes, 5
  for audio dictation, 182–183
  in-service, 121–122
  secretarial, 5
  Youth Training Scheme, 5
Trainphone, **238**
Travel arrangements, 231–238
  accommodation, 233–234
  air, 232–233
  baggage prohibitions, **238**
  computerized information link, **238**
  rail, 232
  road, 233
  sea, 233
Travel documents and formalities, overseas, 234–235
Travel service departments, 236–237
Travellers, financial services for, 235–236
Tying machines, 63
Typewriters, 194–196
  care and maintenance of, 196–197
  electric, 194
  electronic, 194
    additional features, 196
    buffer memory, 194–195
    corrections, 194–195
    facilities, 196
    working memory, 195–196
  manual, 194
  pitch, 194
  proportional spacing, 194
  single element, 194
  supplies for, 51–52
    cleaning, 51
    correcting, 51–52

Typewriters, (*continued*)
    print-heads, 51
    ribbons, 52, **54**
    typebar, 194
Typewriting:
    accuracy in, value of, **199**
    audio, 179-183
    centres, 183-184
    copy typing, 191-193

Unfair Contract Terms Act 1977, 288
Unsolicited Goods and Services Act 1971, 286

Vacancy, finding a, 128
Vaccination, 234-235
Value added tax, 27
    in business documents, 27-28
Visas, 234
Visual control boards, 224-228, 264-265
Voice messaging, 147-148
Voting, 247-248

Wages:
    by cheque, **104**

computerized systems, 103-104
    documents, 102-103
    envelopes, 103
    security arrangements for, 274
Waste, 276
Welfare, staff, 122
White noise, **43**
White Papers, 219
Whiteboards, electronic, **258**
Word processors, 112, 114, 197-199
    alternative input methods, 198-199
    applications, 198
    facilities, 198
    operation, 197-198
    operator skills, 199
    supervisors' duties, 199
    supplies, 51-52
    software, 114
    types of system, 198
Working conditions:
    in different types of organization, 5-6
    dissatisfaction with, 276
    flexible working hours, 123-124
    large v small organizations, 23
    Offices, Shops and Railway Premises Act 1963, 40